# CIVIL WAR II

## CHOOSING SIDES

EARTH'S HEROES PREVENTED A CATACLYSMIC EVENT THANKS TO A NEW INHUMAN NAMED ULYSSES WHO SEEMS TO BE ABLE TO PREDICT THE FUTURE. BUT IRON MAN WARNED AGAINST USING HIS POWERS AGAIN, BELIEVING THAT THE FUTURE HAS TO BE ALLOWED TO TAKE ITS COURSE.

CAPTAIN MARVEL DISAGREED, ARGUING THAT SAVING LIVES WAS WORTH THE RISK.

AS TENSIONS RISE, EACH HERO WILL HAVE TO MAKE A CHOICE: PROTECT THE FUTURE OR CHANGE THE FUTURE?

### WRITERS

DECLAN SHALVEY, BRANDON EASTON, CHAD BOWERS, CHRIS SIMS, JEREMY WHITLEY, BRANDON THOMAS, MING DOYLE, DEREK LANDY, CHUCK BROWN, JOHN ALLISON, CHIP ZDARSKY, ENRIQUE CARRION, CHELSEA CAIN & CHRISTINA STRAIN

### ARTISTS

DECLAN SHALVEY, PAUL DAVIDSON, LEONARDO ROMERO, MARGUERITE SAUVAGE, MARCO RUDY, STEPHEN BYRNE, FILIPE ANDRADE, CHRIS VISIONS, ROSI KÄMPE, RAMÓN PÉREZ, ANNAPAOLA MARTELLO, ALISON SAMPSON & SANA TAKEDA

### COLOR ARTISTS

JORDIE BELLAIRE, ANDREW CROSSLEY, MIROSLAV MRVA, MARGUERITE SAUVAGE, MARCO RUDY, STEPHEN BYRNE, MEGAN WILSON, RAMÓN PÉREZ, NOLAN WOODARD & SANA TAKEDA

### LETTERER

VC's CLAYTON COWLES

### EDITORS

WIL MOSS & CHRIS ROBINSON

COLLECTION EDITOR
JENNIFER GRÜNWALD

ASSOCIATE MANAGING EDITOR
KATERI WOODY

ASSOCIATE EDITOR
SARAH BRUNSTAD

EDITOR, SPECIAL PROJECTS
MARK D. BEAZLEY

VP PRODUCTION & SPECIAL PROJECTS
JEFF YOUNGQUIST

SVP PRINT, SALES & MARKETING
DAVID GABRIEL

BOOK DESIGNER
JAY BOWEN

EDITOR IN CHIEF
AXEL ALONSO

CHIEF CREATIVE OFFICER
JOE QUESADA

PUBLISHER
DAN BUCKLEY

EXECUTIVE PRODUCER
ALAN FINE

CIVIL WAR II: CHOOSING SIDES. Contains material originally published in magazine form as CIVIL WAR II: CHOOSING SIDES #1-6. First printing 2016. ISBN# 978-1-302-90251-3. Published by MARVEL WORLDWIDE, INC., a subsidiary of MARVEL ENTERTAINMENT, LLC. OFFICE OF PUBLICATION: 135 West 50th Street, New York, NY 10020. Copyright © 2016 MARVEL No similarity between any of the names, characters, persons, and/or institutions in this magazine with those of any living or dead person or institution is intended, and any such similarity which may exist is purely coincidental. **Printed in Canada.** ALAN FINE, President, Marvel Entertainment; DAN BUCKLEY, President, TV, Publishing & Brand Management; JOE QUESADA, Chief Creative Officer; TOM BREVOORT, SVP of Publishing; DAVID BOGART, SVP of Business Affairs & Operations, Publishing & Partnership; C.B. CEBULSKI, VP of Brand Management & Development, Asia; DAVID GABRIEL, SVP of Sales & Marketing, Publishing; JEFF YOUNGQUIST, VP of Production & Special Projects; DAN CARR, Executive Director of Publishing Technology; ALEX MORALES, Director of Publishing Operations; SUSAN CRESPI, Production Manager; STAN LEE, Chairman Emeritus. For information regarding advertising in Marvel Comics or on Marvel.com, please contact Vit DeBellis, Integrated Sales Manager, at vdebellis@marvel.com. For Marvel subscription inquiries, please call 888-511-5480. **Manufactured between 9/16/2016 and 10/24/2016 by SOLISCO PRINTERS, SCOTT, QC, CANADA.**

10 9 8 7 6 5 4 3 2 1

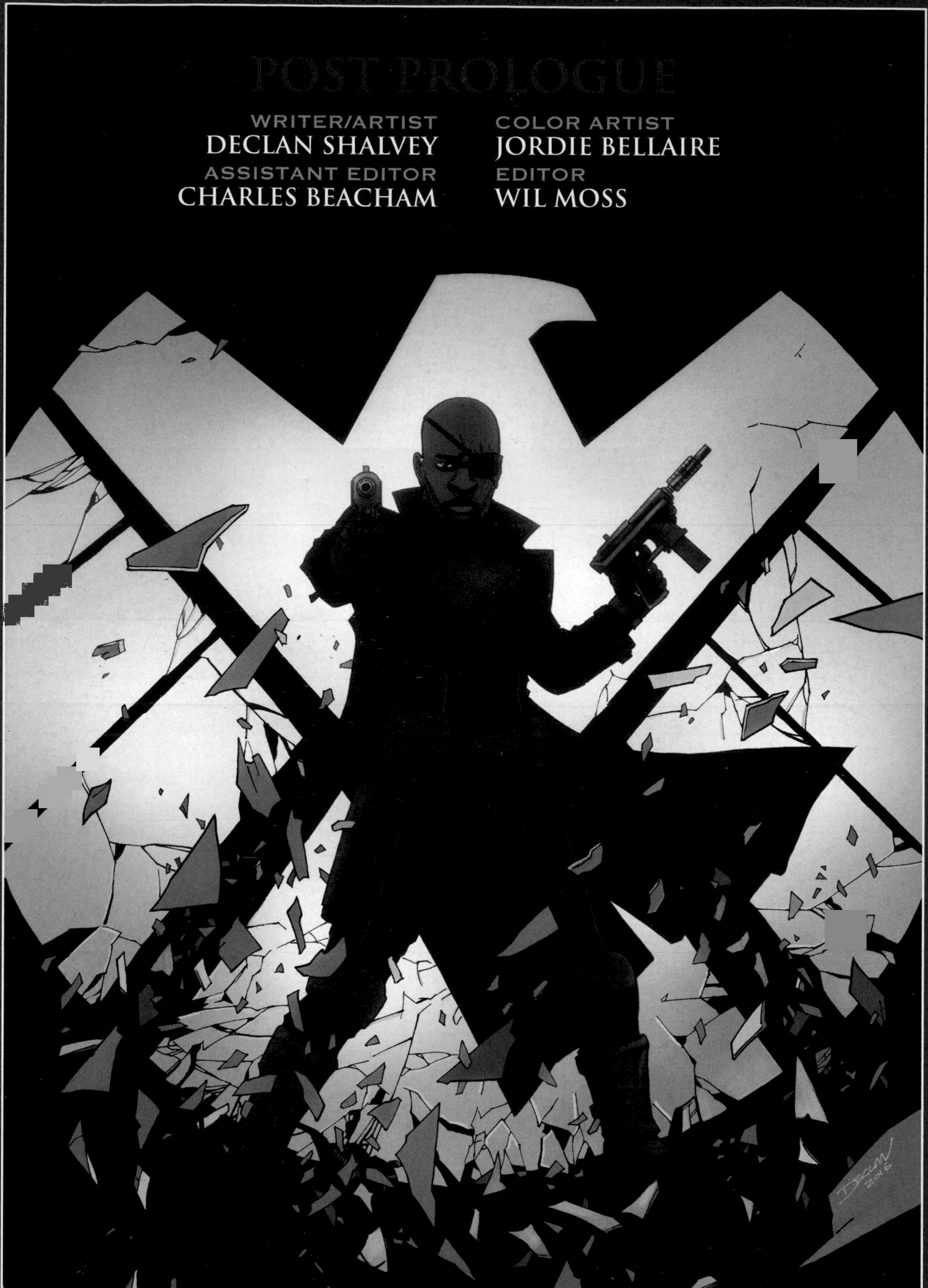
POST PROLOGUE
WRITER/ARTIST
DECLAN SHALVEY
COLOR ARTIST
JORDIE BELLAIRE
ASSISTANT EDITOR
CHARLES BEACHAM
EDITOR
WIL MOSS
DECLAN 2016

#1 VARIANT BY DECLAN SHALVEY

# S.H.I.E.L.D. HELICARRIER.
1,800 M. OVER ARIZONA. 15:32 HRS.

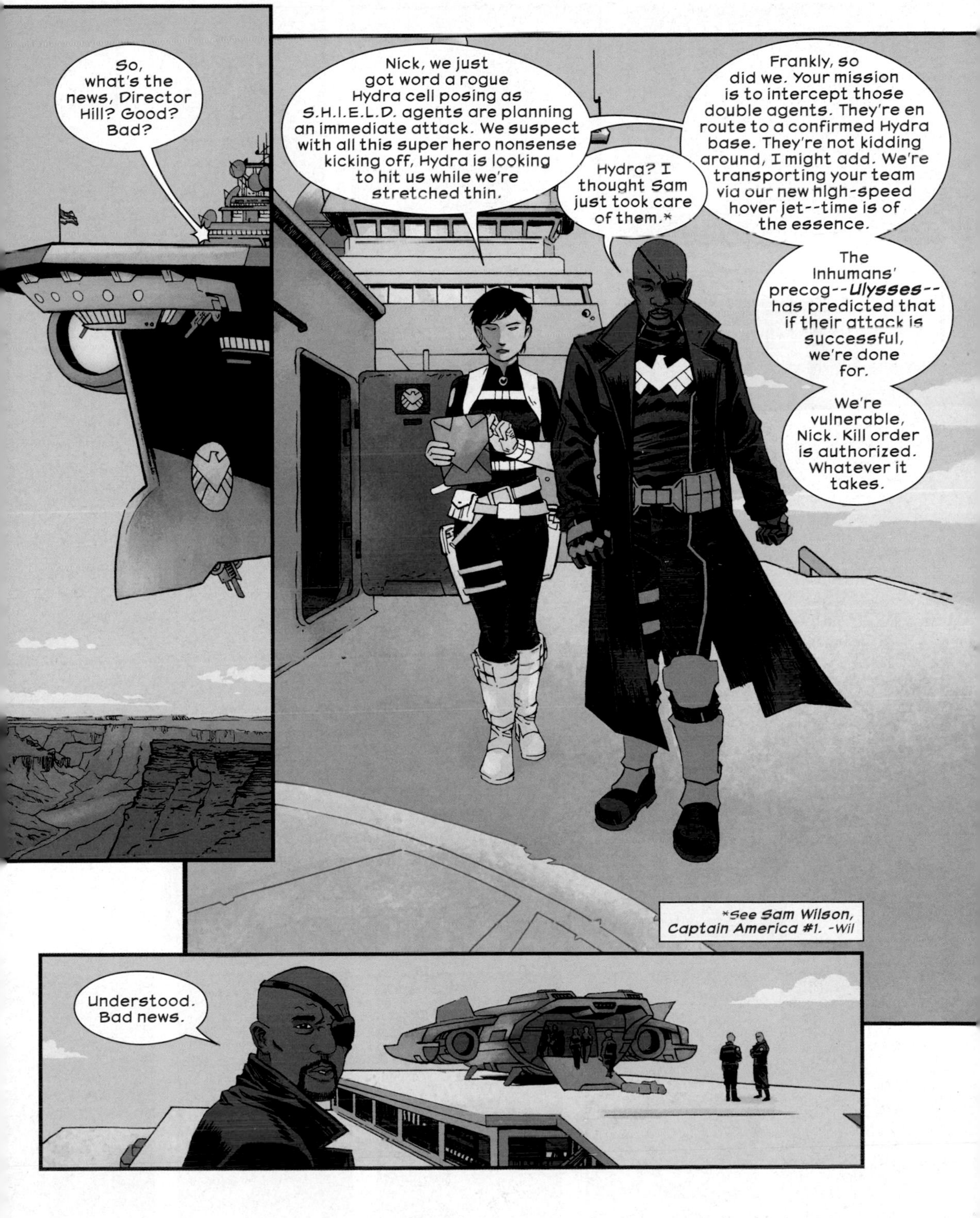

So, what's the news, Director Hill? Good? Bad?
Nick, we just got word a rogue Hydra cell posing as S.H.I.E.L.D. agents are planning an immediate attack. We suspect with all this super hero nonsense kicking off, Hydra is looking to hit us while we're stretched thin.
Hydra? I thought Sam just took care of them.*
Frankly, so did we. Your mission is to intercept those double agents. They're en route to a confirmed Hydra base. They're not kidding around, I might add. We're transporting your team via our new high-speed hover jet--time is of the essence.
The Inhumans' precog--*Ulysses*--has predicted that if their attack is successful, we're done for.
We're vulnerable, Nick. Kill order is authorized. Whatever it takes.
*See Sam Wilson, Captain America #1. -Wil
Understood. Bad news.

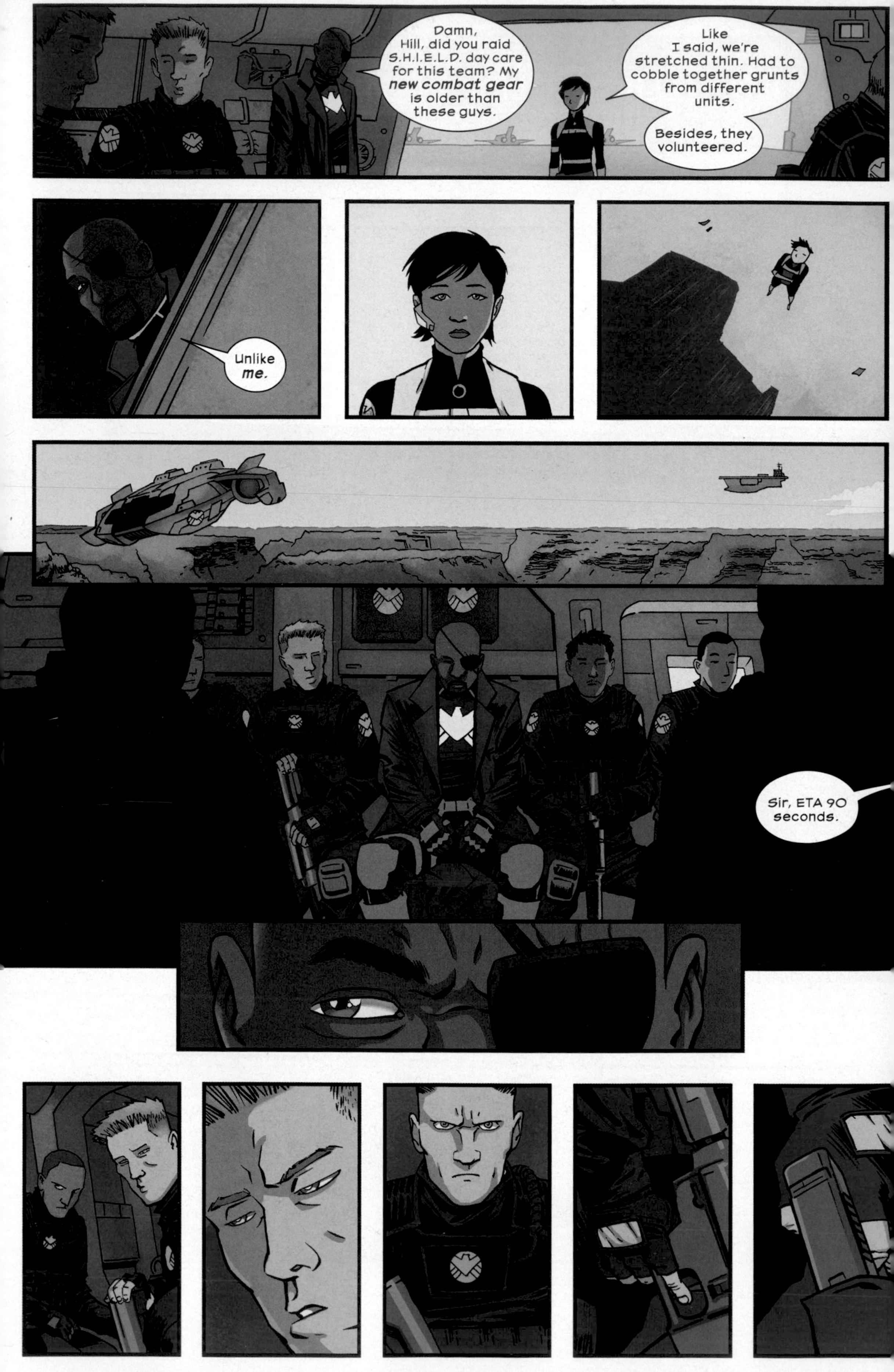
Damn, Hill, did you raid S.H.I.E.L.D. day care for this team? My *new combat gear* is older than these guys.
Like I said, we're stretched thin. Had to cobble together grunts from different units.
Besides, they volunteered.
Unlike *me.*
Sir, ETA 90 seconds.

**unh!**

**S.H.I.E.L.D. MUST LIVE!**

**FURY MUST DIE!**

**S.H.I.E.L.D. MUST LIVE!**

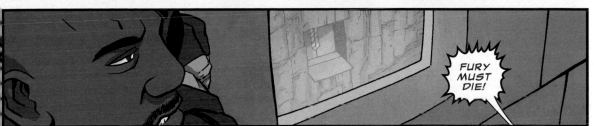

**FURY MUST DIE!**

This is my stop, fellas...

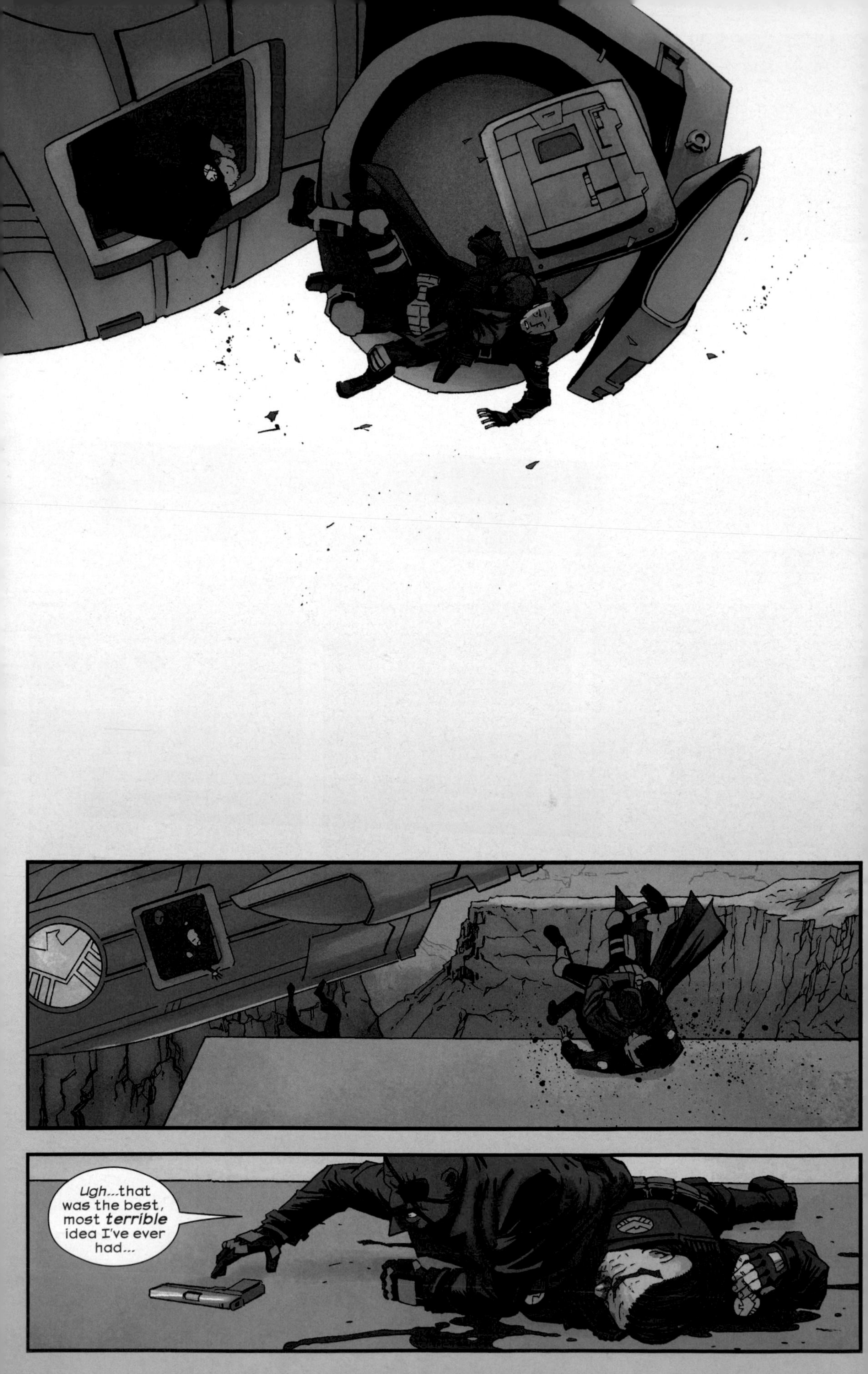
Ugh...that was the best, most terrible idea I've ever had...

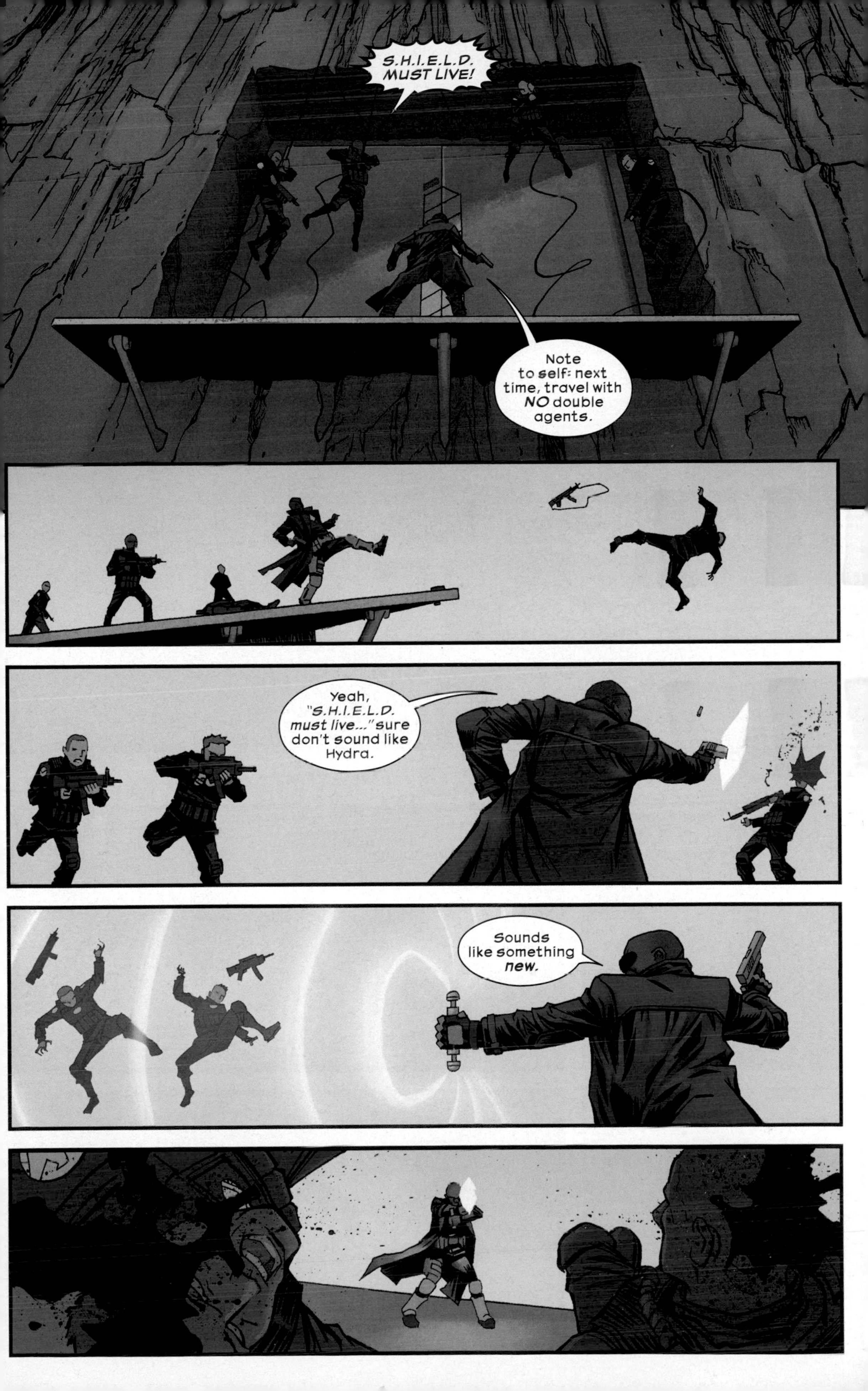
S.H.I.E.L.D. MUST LIVE!
Note to self: next time, travel with NO double agents.
Yeah, "S.H.I.E.L.D. must live..." sure don't sound like Hydra.
Sounds like something new.

The prophecy is clear. Nick Fury is essential to the future of S.H.I.E.L.D.

Yeah? Funny way of showing it.

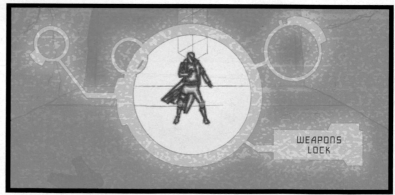

WEAPONS LOCK

FIRE!

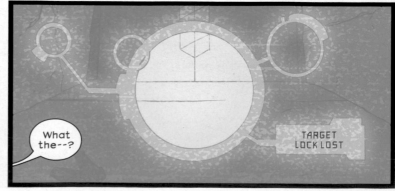

What the--?

TARGET LOCK LOST

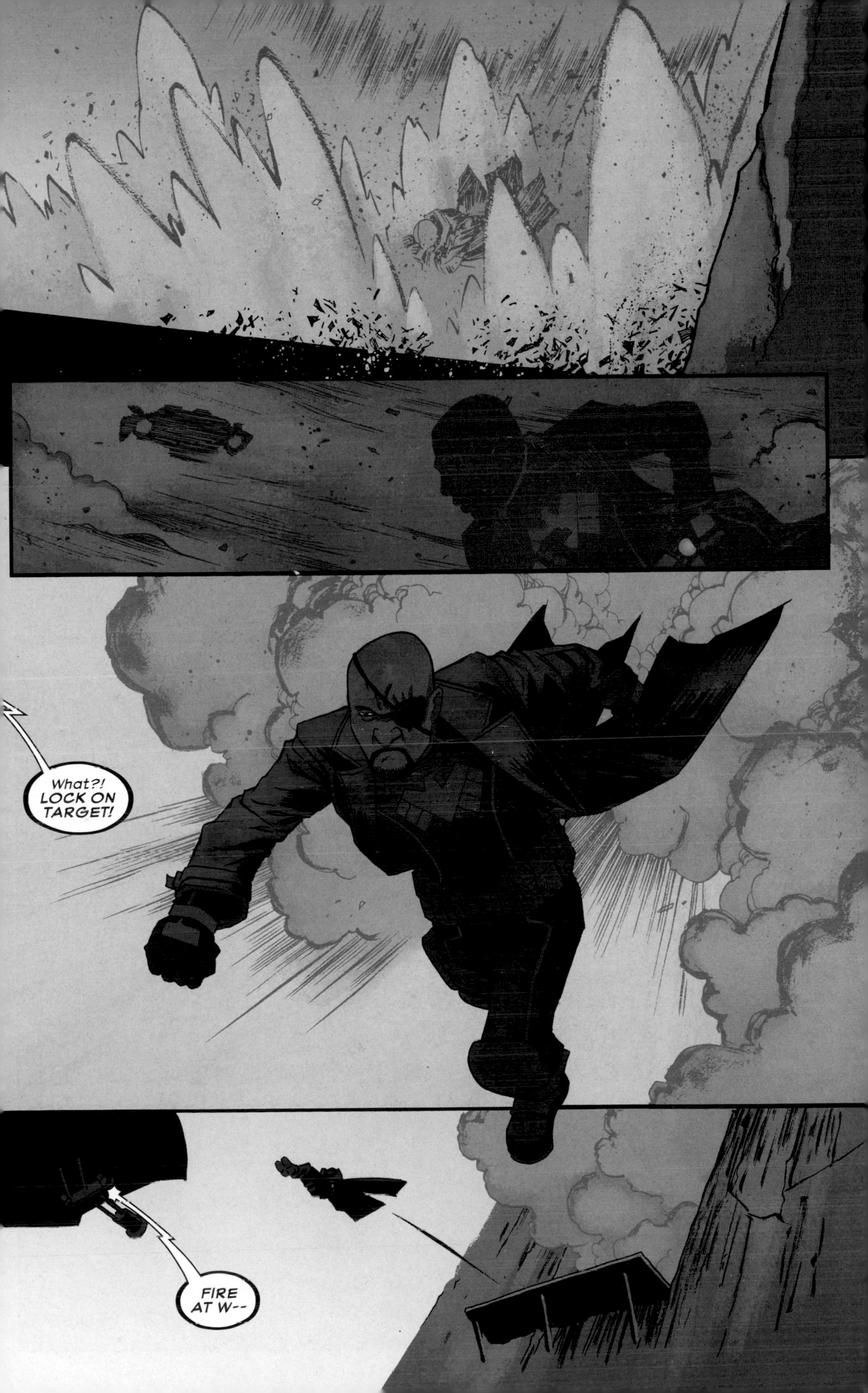
What?! LOCK ON TARGET!
FIRE AT W--

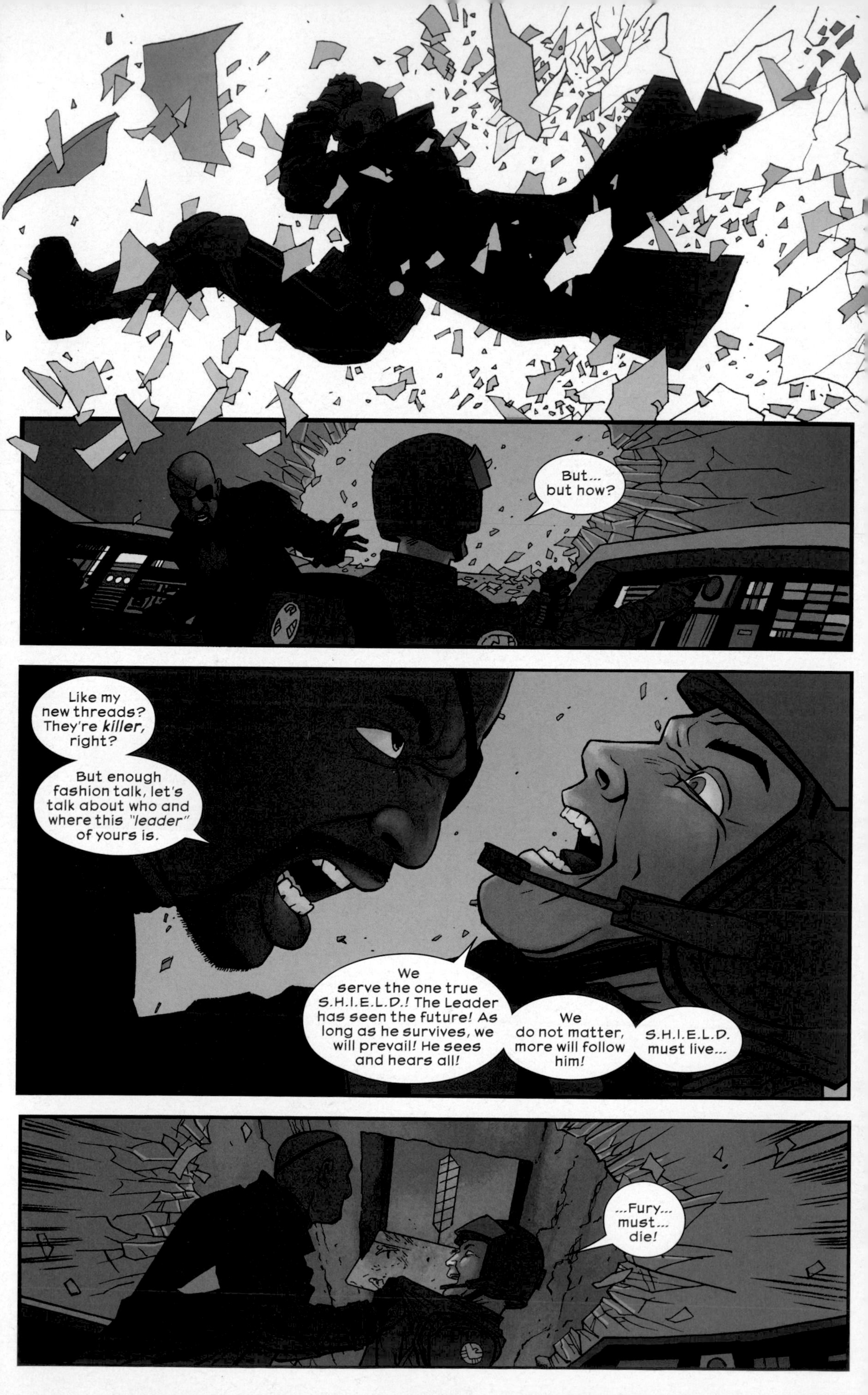
But... but how?
Like my new threads? They're *killer*, right?
But enough fashion talk, let's talk about who and where this *"leader"* of yours is.
We serve the one true S.H.I.E.L.D.! The Leader has seen the future! As long as he survives, we will prevail! He sees and hears all!
We do not matter, more will follow him!
S.H.I.E.L.D. must live...
...Fury... must... die!

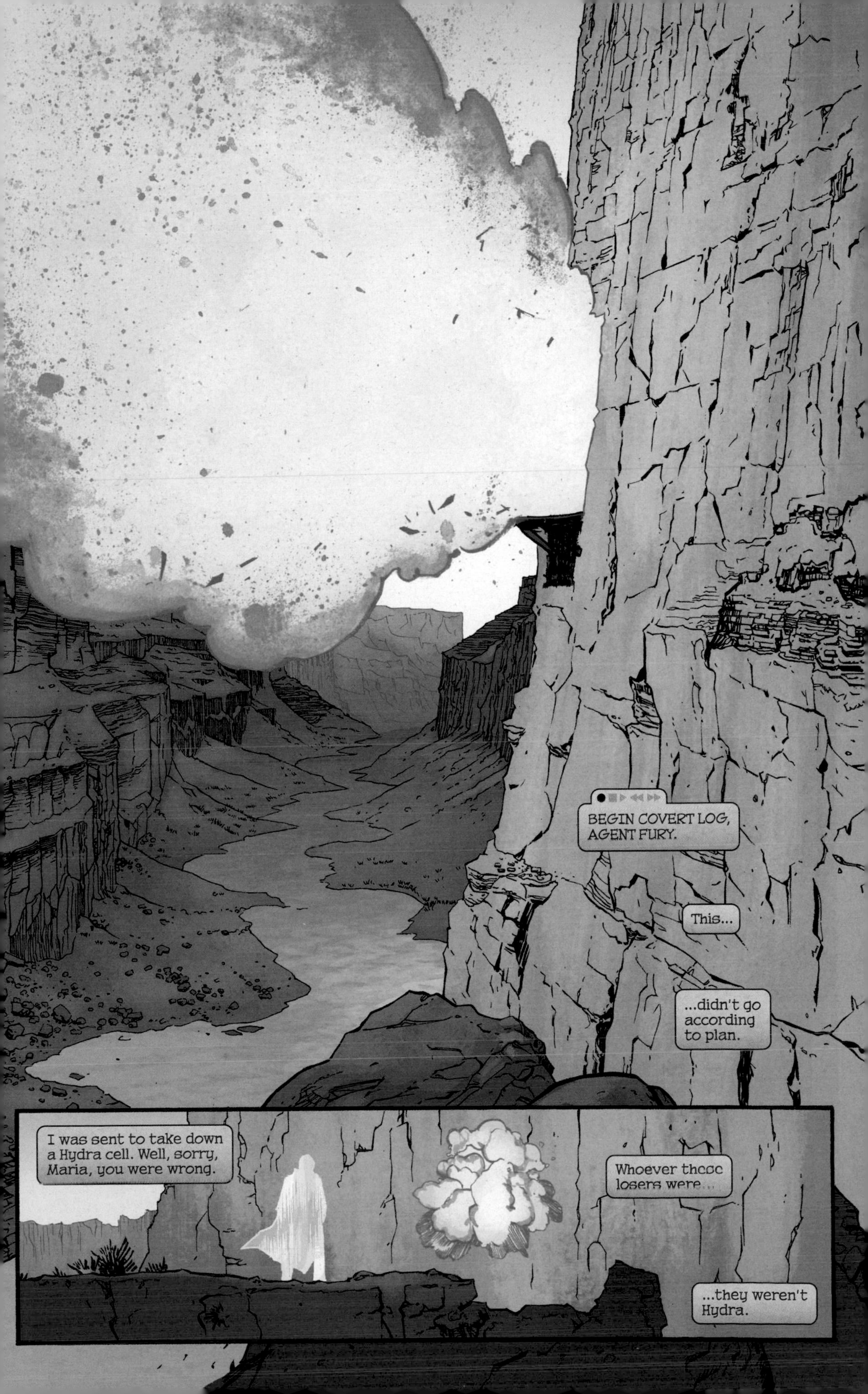
BEGIN COVERT LOG, AGENT FURY.
This...
...didn't go according to plan.
I was sent to take down a Hydra cell. Well, sorry, Maria, you were wrong.
Whoever these losers were...
...they weren't Hydra.

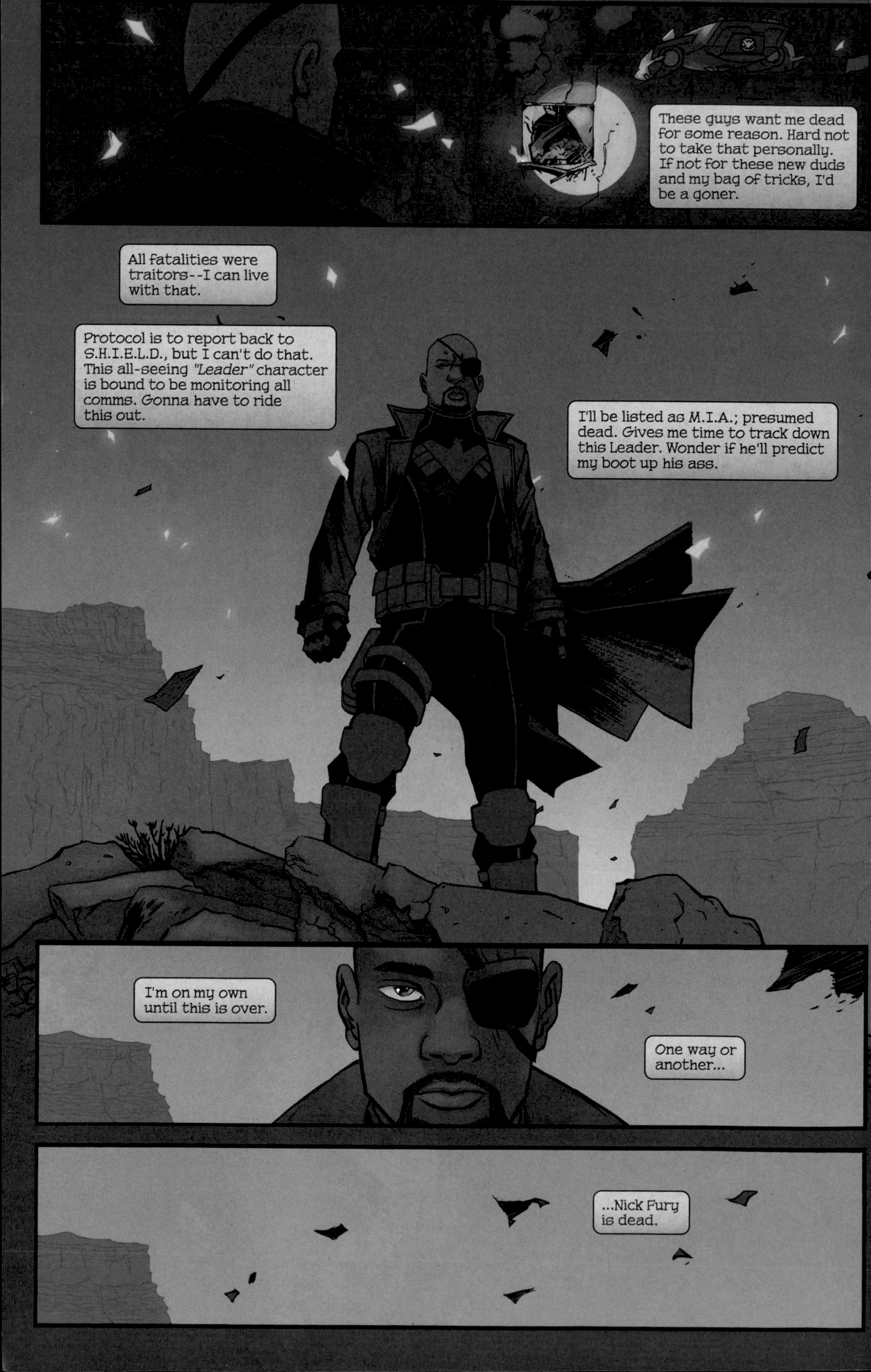
These guys want me dead for some reason. Hard not to take that personally. If not for these new duds and my bag of tricks, I'd be a goner.
All fatalities were traitors--I can live with that.
Protocol is to report back to S.H.I.E.L.D., but I can't do that. This all-seeing "Leader" character is bound to be monitoring all comms. Gonna have to ride this out.
I'll be listed as M.I.A.; presumed dead. Gives me time to track down this Leader. Wonder if he'll predict my boot up his ass.
I'm on my own until this is over.
One way or another...
...Nick Fury is dead.

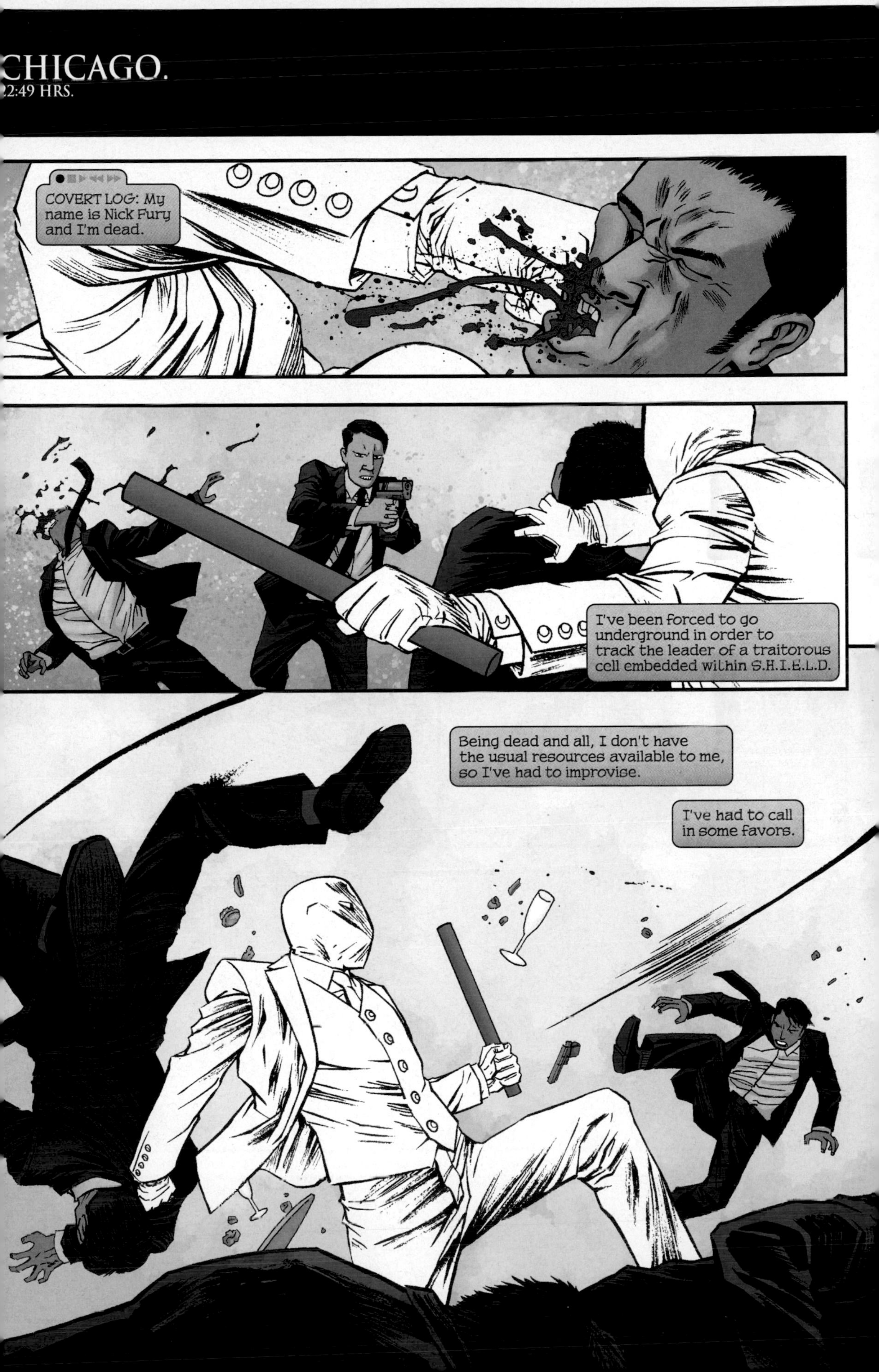
CHICAGO.
2:49 HRS.
COVERT LOG: My name is Nick Fury and I'm dead.
I've been forced to go underground in order to track the leader of a traitorous cell embedded within S.H.I.E.L.D.
Being dead and all, I don't have the usual resources available to me, so I've had to improvise.
I've had to call in some favors.

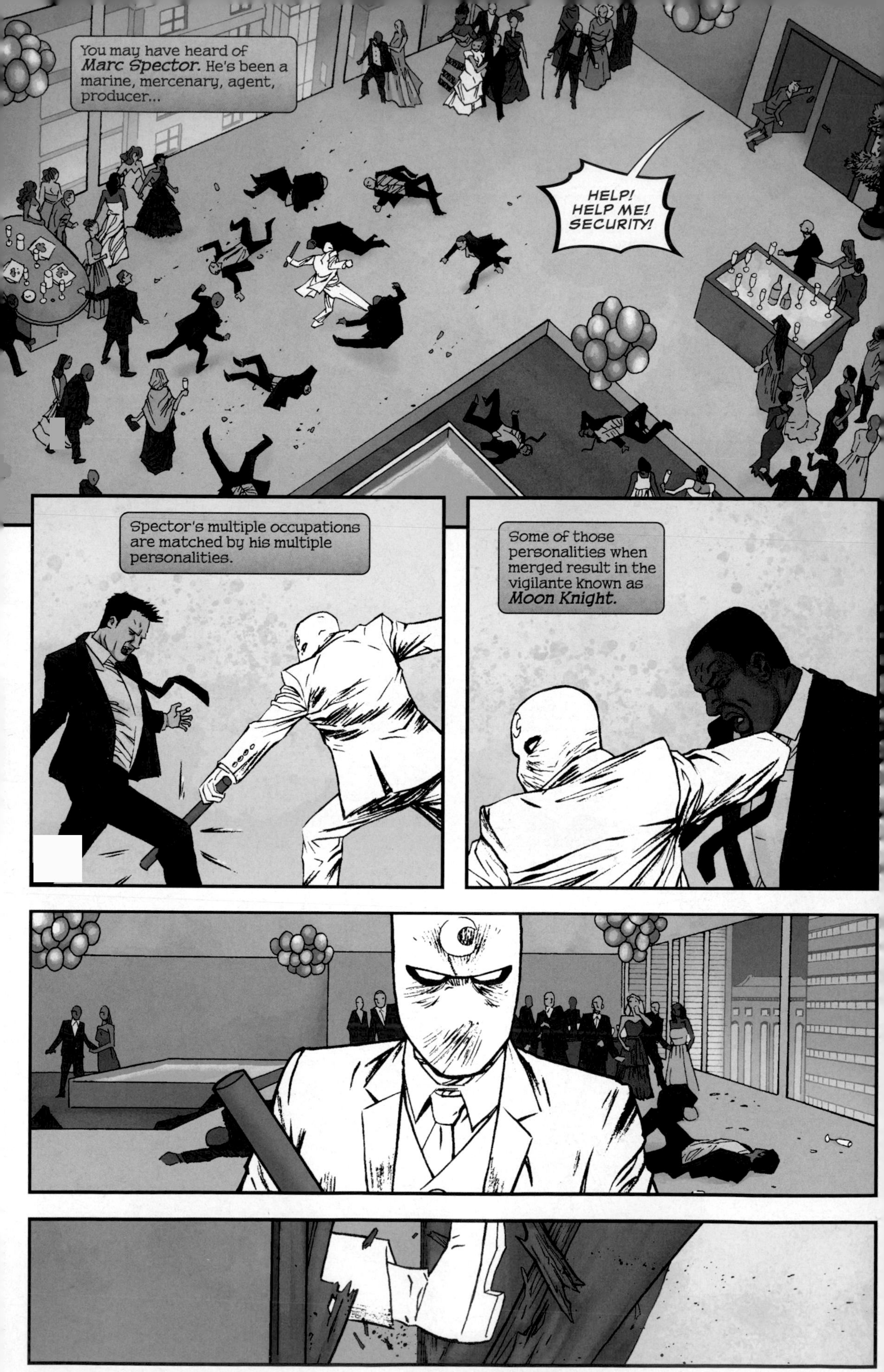
You may have heard of Marc Spector. He's been a marine, mercenary, agent, producer...
HELP! HELP ME! SECURITY!
Spector's multiple occupations are matched by his multiple personalities.
Some of those personalities when merged result in the vigilante known as Moon Knight.

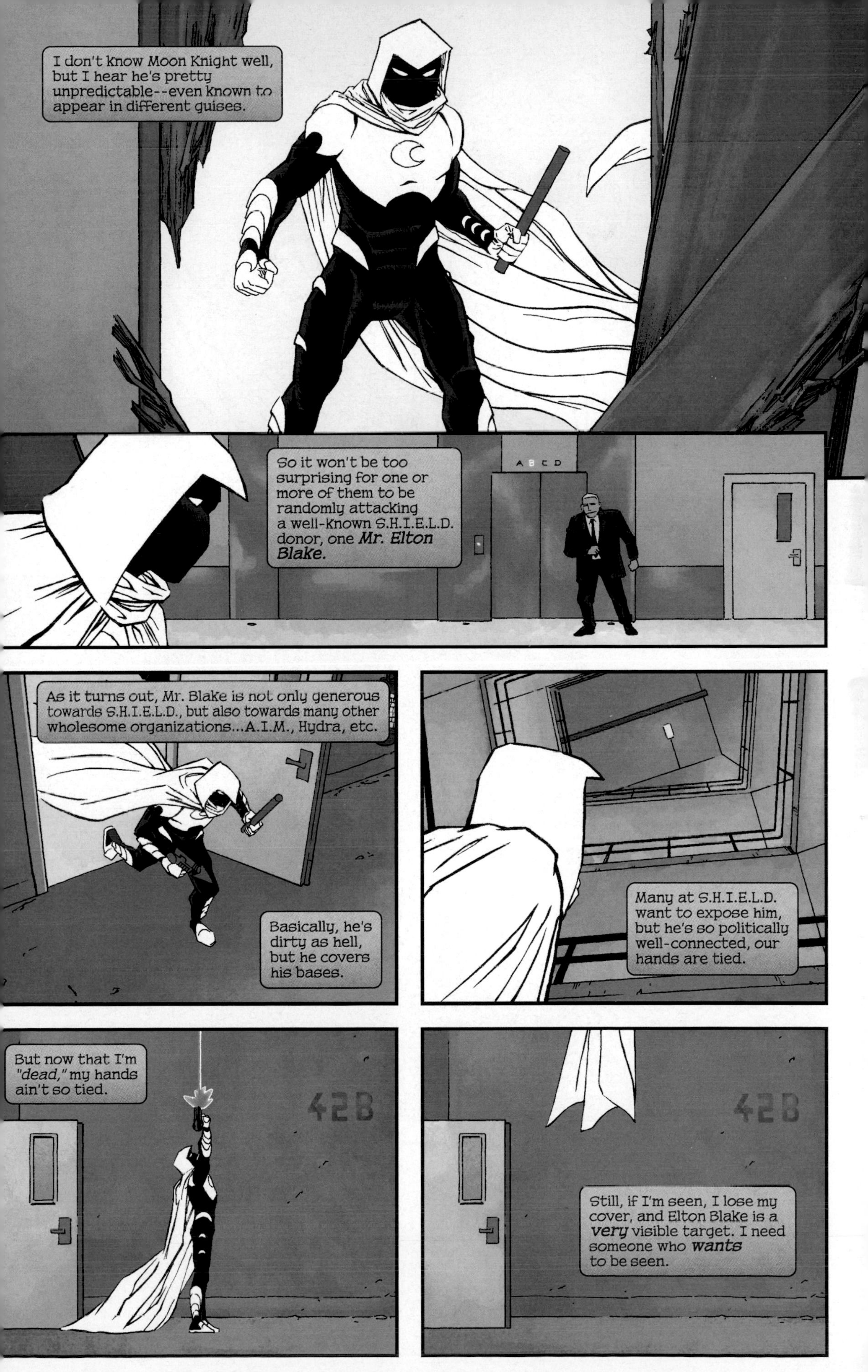
I don't know Moon Knight well, but I hear he's pretty unpredictable--even known to appear in different guises.
So it won't be too surprising for one or more of them to be randomly attacking a well-known S.H.I.E.L.D. donor, one *Mr. Elton Blake.*
A B C D
As it turns out, Mr. Blake is not only generous towards S.H.I.E.L.D., but also towards many other wholesome organizations...A.I.M., Hydra, etc.
Basically, he's dirty as hell, but he covers his bases.
Many at S.H.I.E.L.D. want to expose him, but he's so politically well-connected, our hands are tied.
But now that I'm "*dead,*" my hands ain't so tied.
42B
42B
Still, if I'm seen, I lose my cover, and Elton Blake is a ***very*** visible target. I need someone who ***wants*** to be seen.

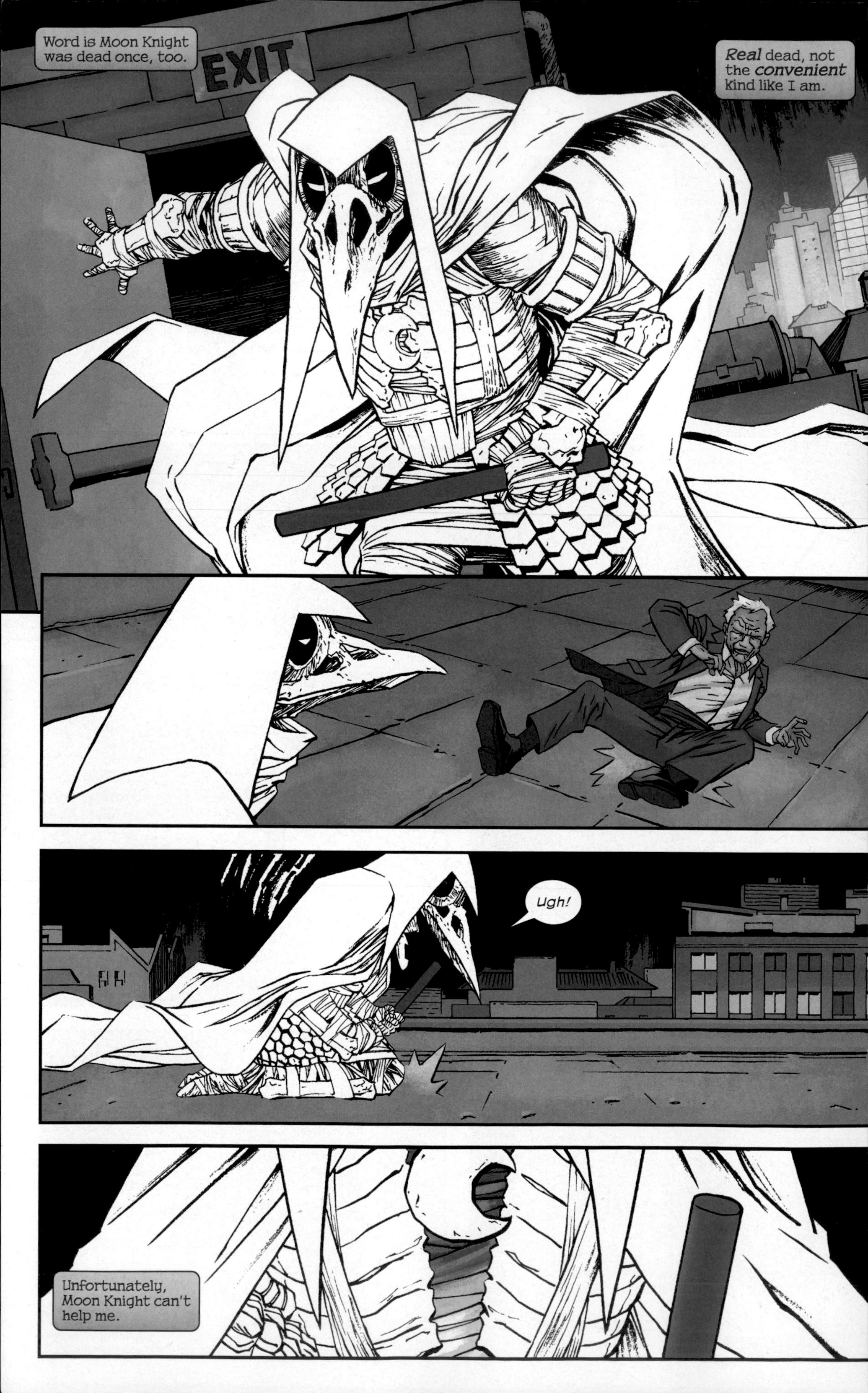
Word is Moon Knight was dead once, too.
EXIT
Real dead, not the convenient kind like I am.
Ugh!
Unfortunately, Moon Knight can't help me.

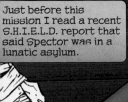

Just before this mission I read a recent S.H.I.E.L.D. report that said Spector was in a lunatic asylum.

Which makes Moon Knight the perfect cover since it also gives Spector the perfect alibi.

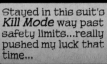

Stayed in this suit's *Kill Mode* way past safety limits...really pushed my luck that time...

...so damn *lucky*...

Ha, good, it's just you.

Being honest, that's not the terrified response I was looking for.

Are you kidding me?! Moon Knight is a *lunatic*, who knows what he would have done to me? But you, I know exactly how dangerous *you* are, Fury.

Though I'd heard you recently died.

Yeah, heard the same myself.

Thankfully this holo-projector means I didn't have to debunk that rumor in order to get to you. You're a hard man to reach, Mr. Blake.

All this subterfuge to protect S.H.I.E.L.D...? I don't *want* S.H.I.E.L.D. harmed, Fury. It's *you* who will be its downfall-- you just don't see it yet.

Uh-huh.

Cut the bull, Blake. We know you're dirty, just could never prove it. But now I have hard info.

Those double agents I took out all had one thing in common: they were receiving payments from stocks in one of your companies...stocks that they didn't buy. You're funding them. Why?

He has shown us the way. You have to die.

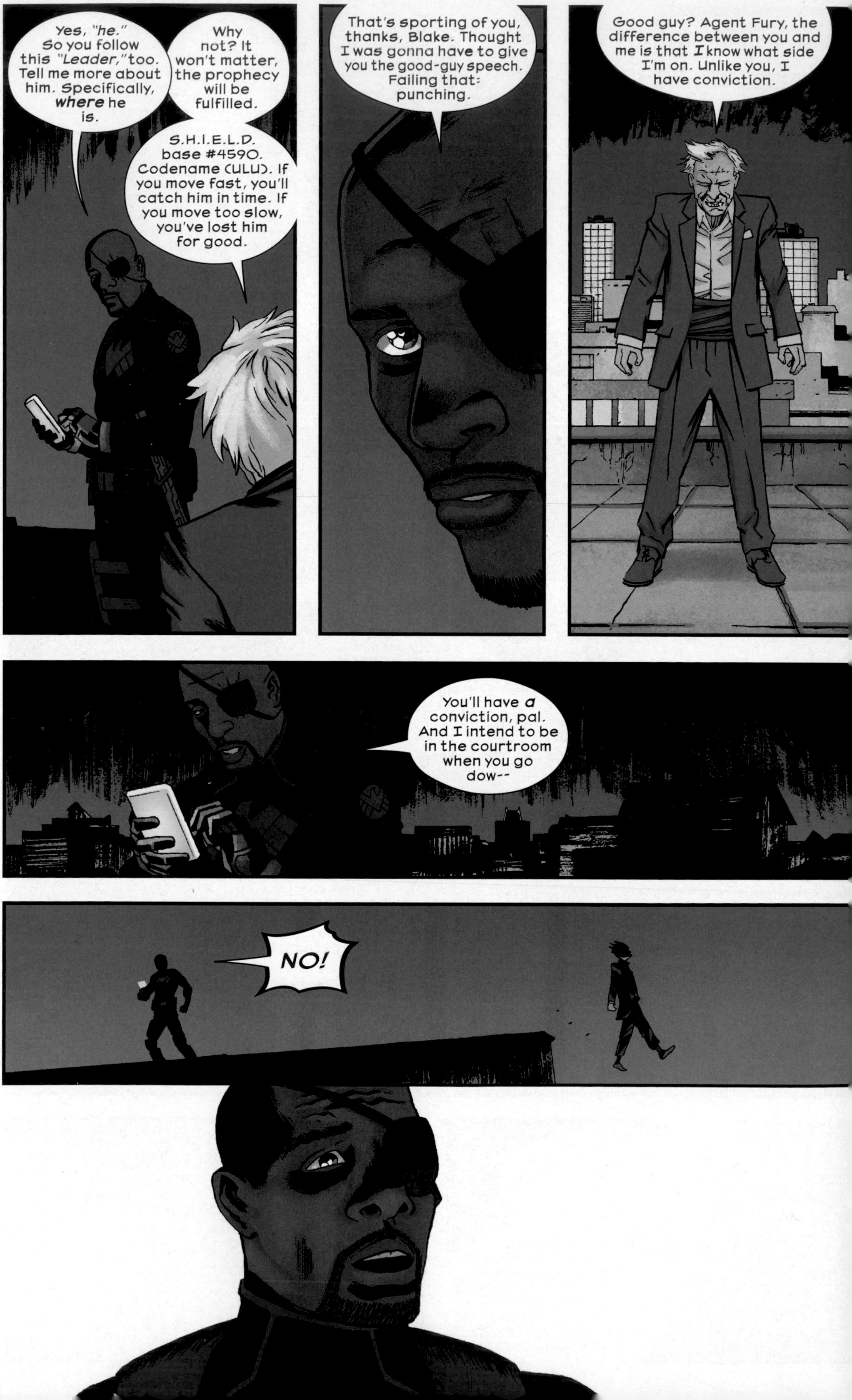
Yes, "he." So you follow this "Leader," too. Tell me more about him. Specifically, where he is.
Why not? It won't matter, the prophecy will be fulfilled.
S.H.I.E.L.D. base #4590. Codename (ULU). If you move fast, you'll catch him in time. If you move too slow, you've lost him for good.
That's sporting of you, thanks, Blake. Thought I was gonna have to give you the good-guy speech. Failing that: punching.
Good guy? Agent Fury, the difference between you and me is that I know what side I'm on. Unlike you, I have conviction.
You'll have a conviction, pal. And I intend to be in the courtroom when you go dow--
NO!

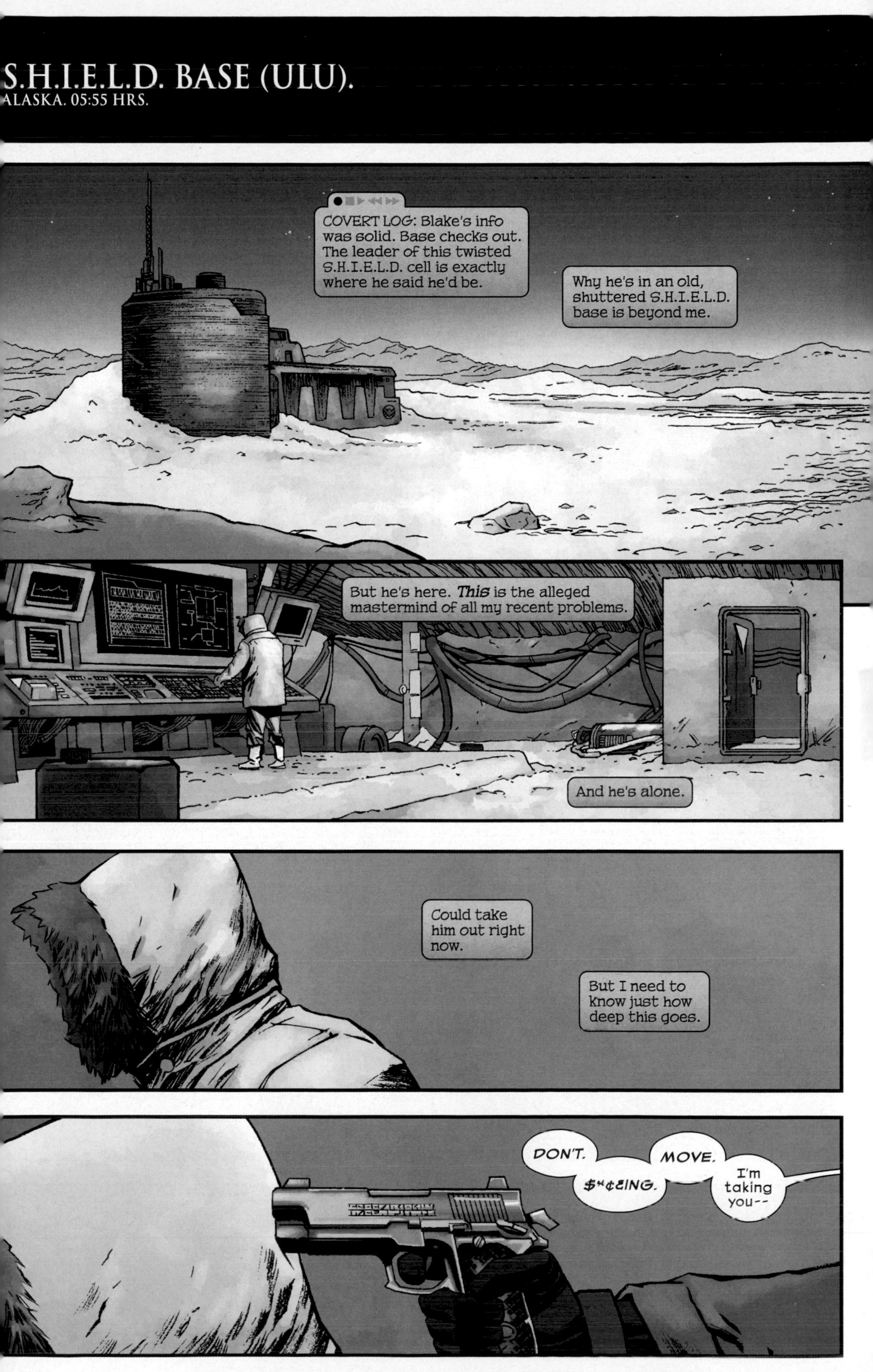
S.H.I.E.L.D. BASE (ULU).
ALASKA. 05:55 HRS.
COVERT LOG: Blake's info was solid. Base checks out. The leader of this twisted S.H.I.E.L.D. cell is exactly where he said he'd be.
Why he's in an old, shuttered S.H.I.E.L.D. base is beyond me.
But he's here. *This* is the alleged mastermind of all my recent problems.
And he's alone.
Could take him out right now.
But I need to know just how deep this goes.
DON'T.
$*¢&ING.
MOVE.
I'm taking you--

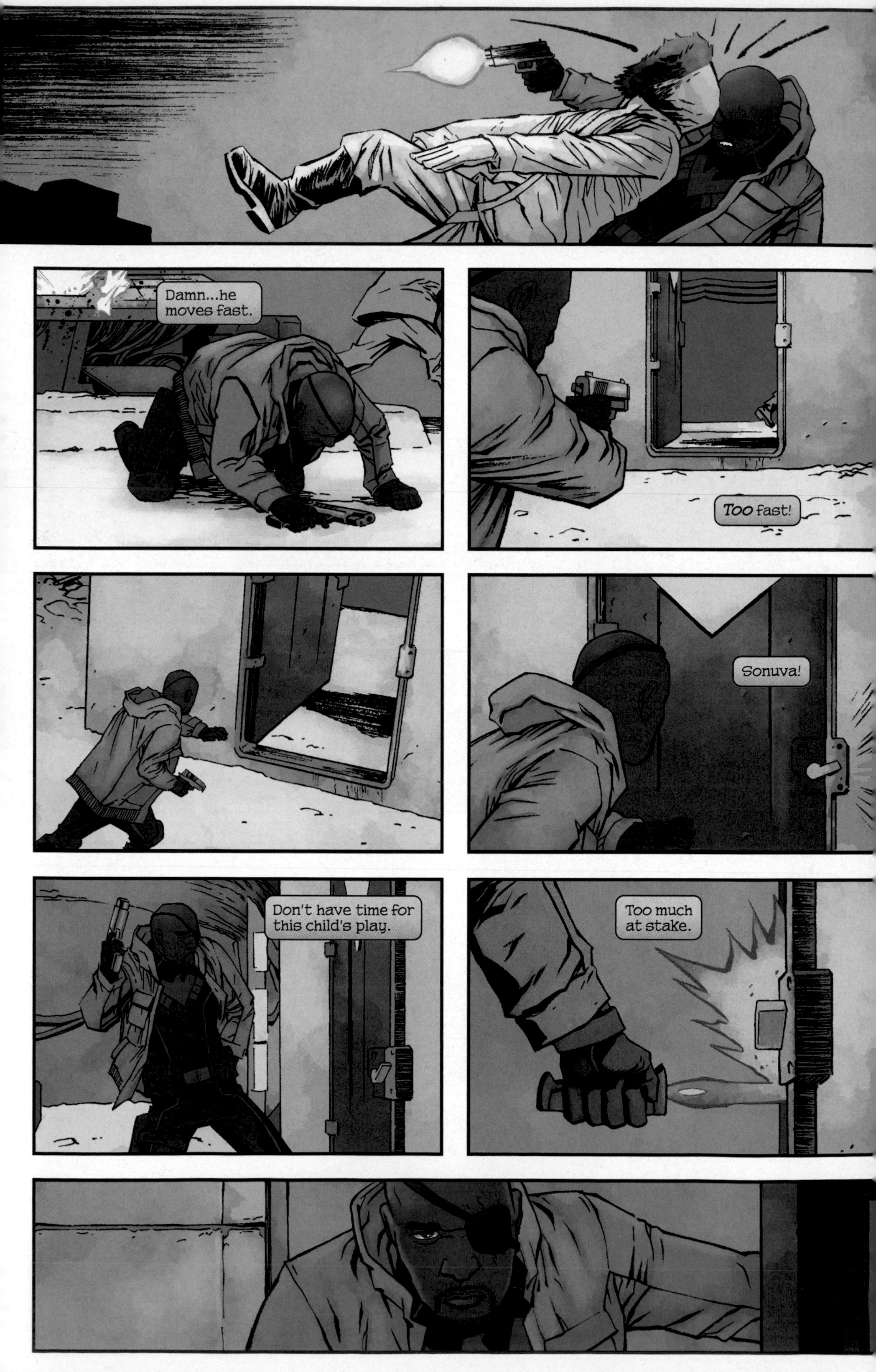
Damn...he moves fast.
Too fast!
Sonuva!
Don't have time for this child's play.
Too much at stake.

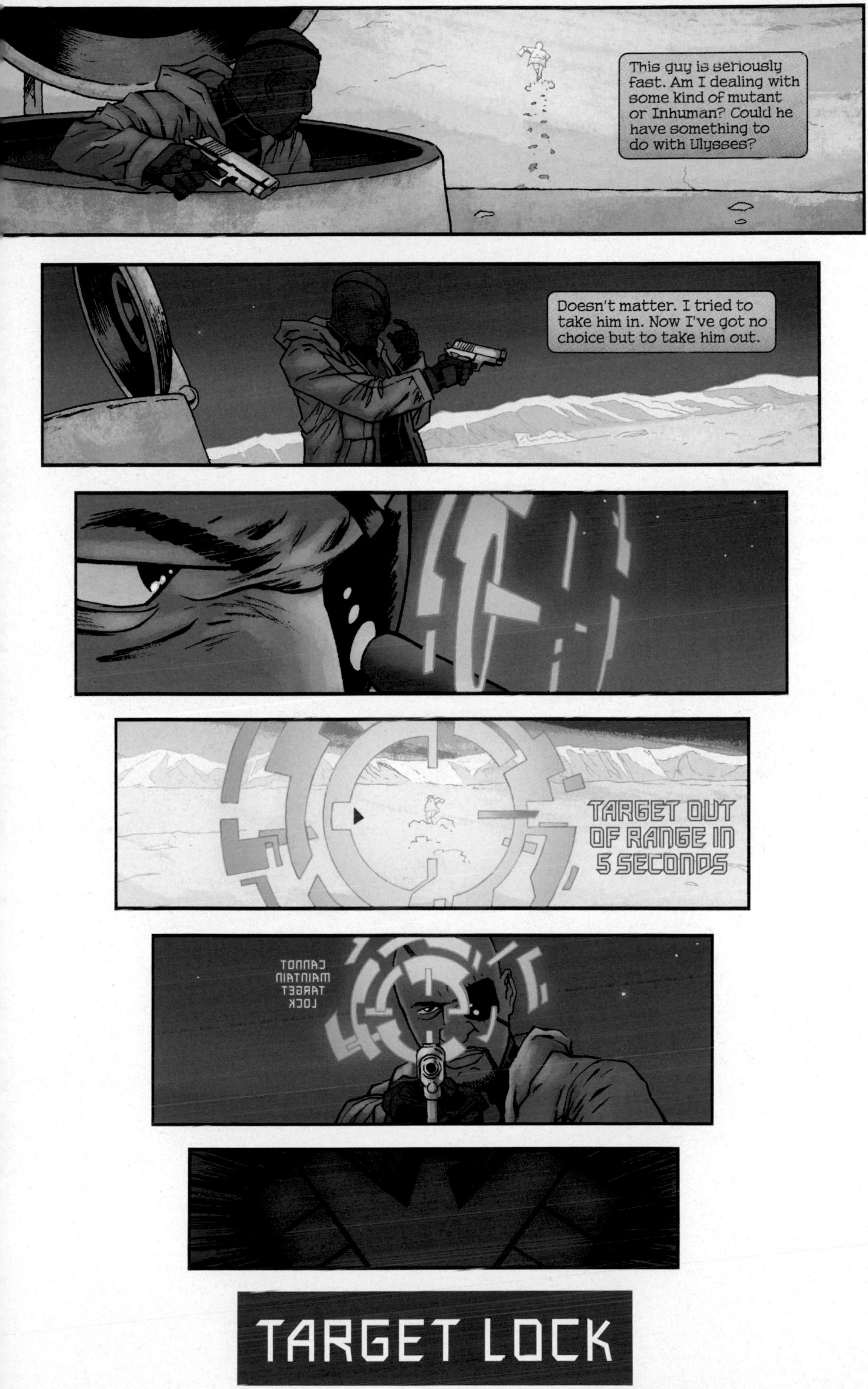
This guy is seriously fast. Am I dealing with some kind of mutant or Inhuman? Could he have something to do with Ulysses?
Doesn't matter. I tried to take him in. Now I've got no choice but to take him out.
TARGET OUT OF RANGE IN 5 SECONDS
CANNOT MAINTAIN TARGET LOCK
TARGET LOCK

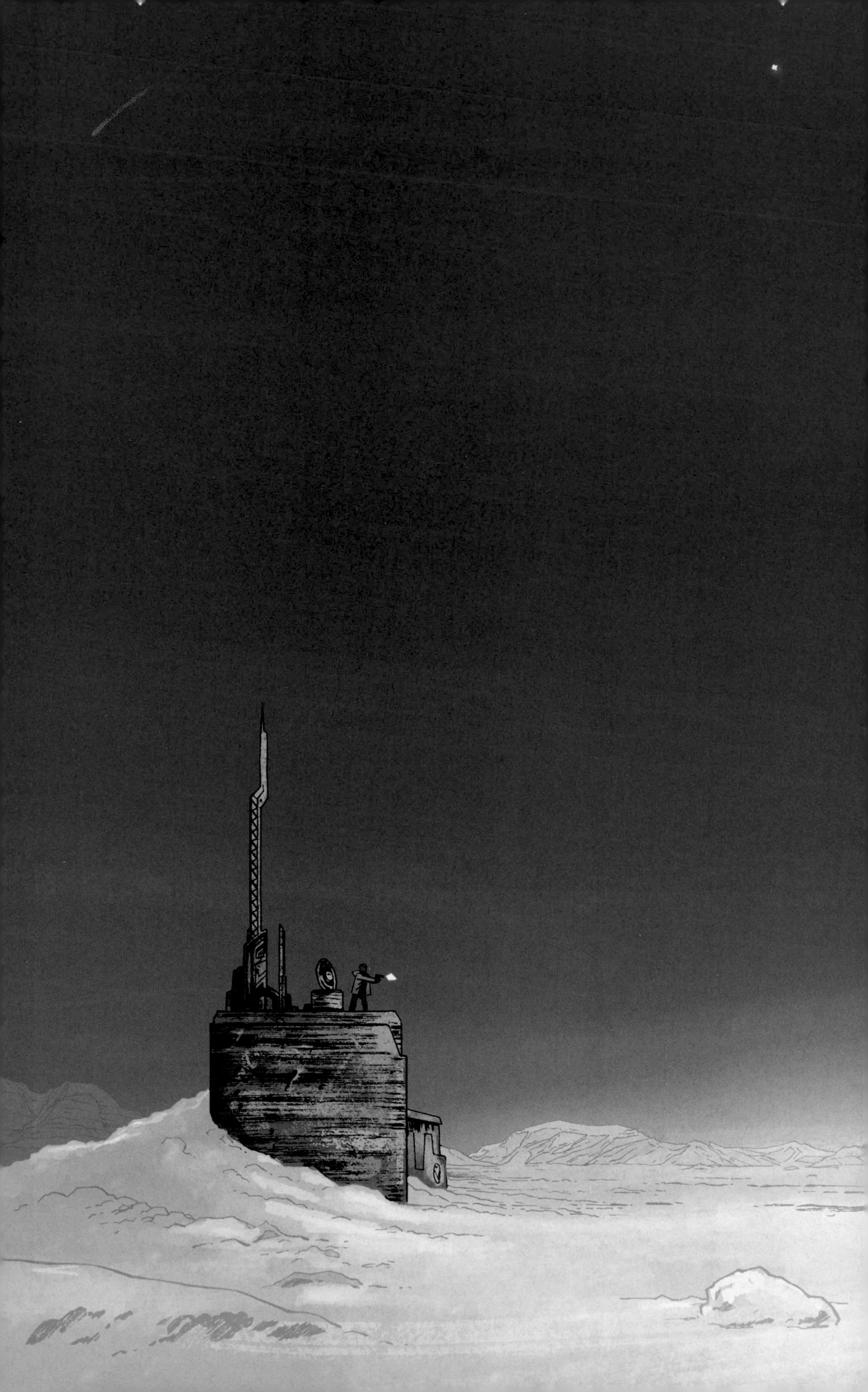

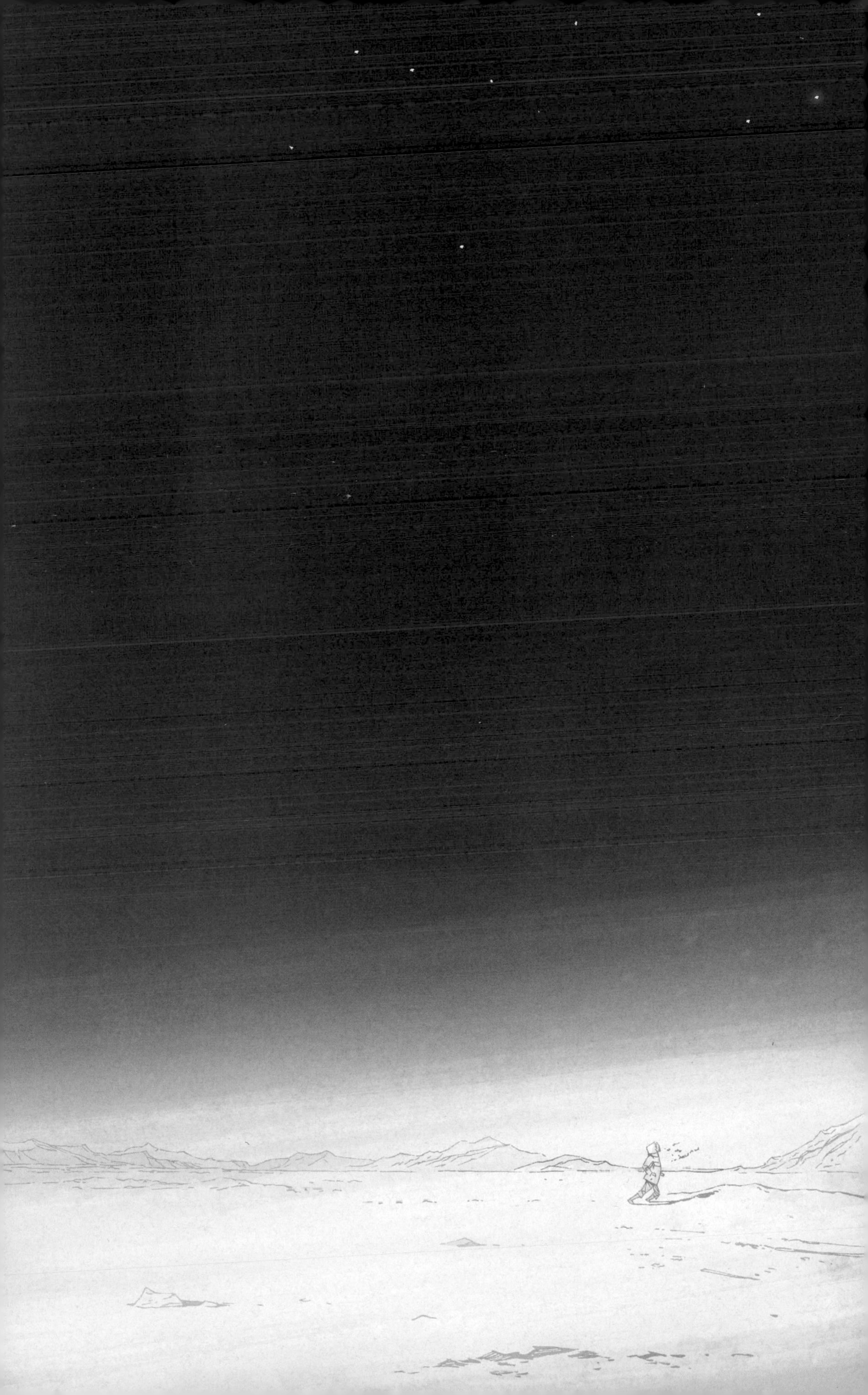

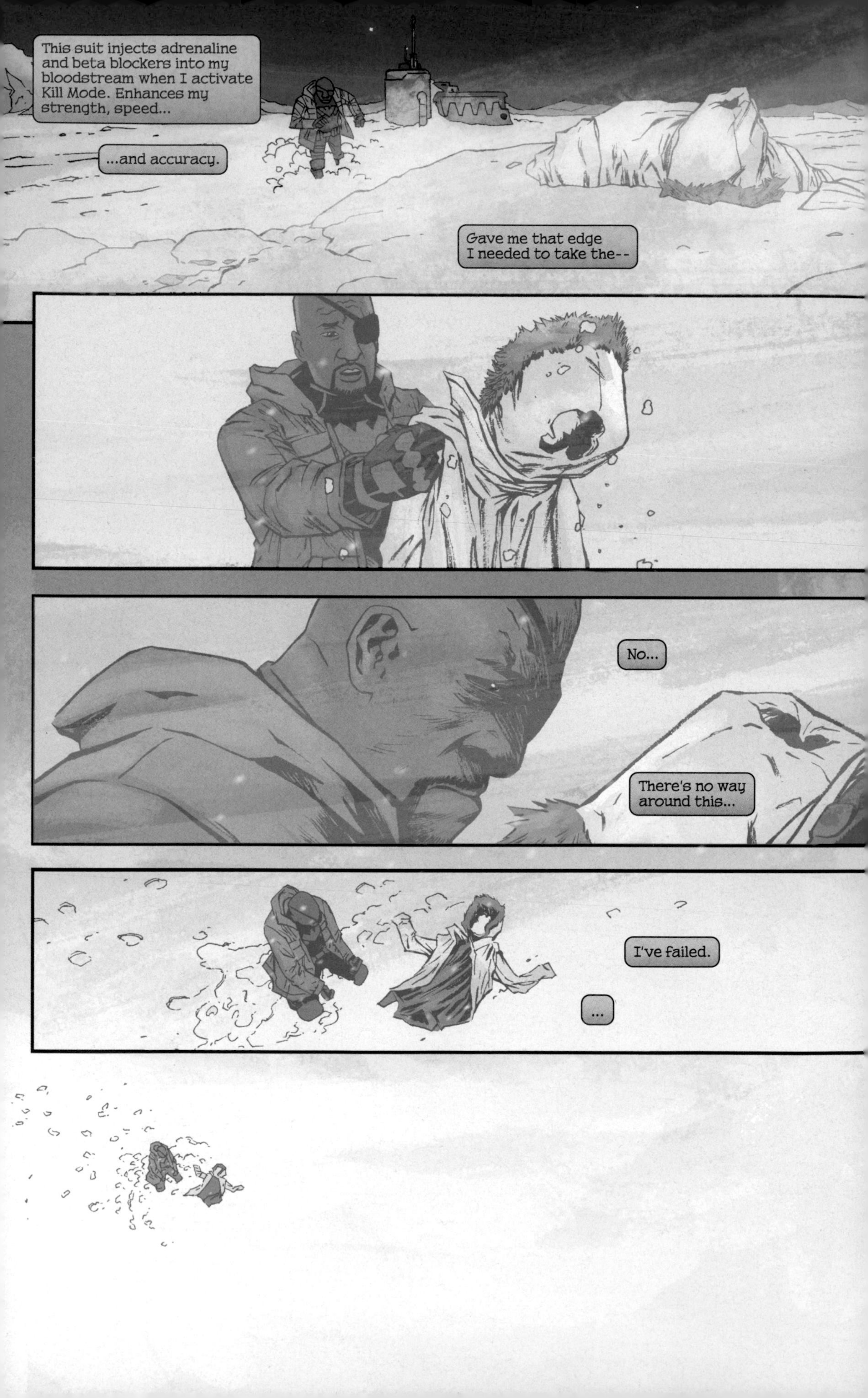

This suit injects adrenaline and beta blockers into my bloodstream when I activate Kill Mode. Enhances my strength, speed...
...and accuracy.
Gave me that edge I needed to take the--
No...
There's no way around this...
I've failed.
...

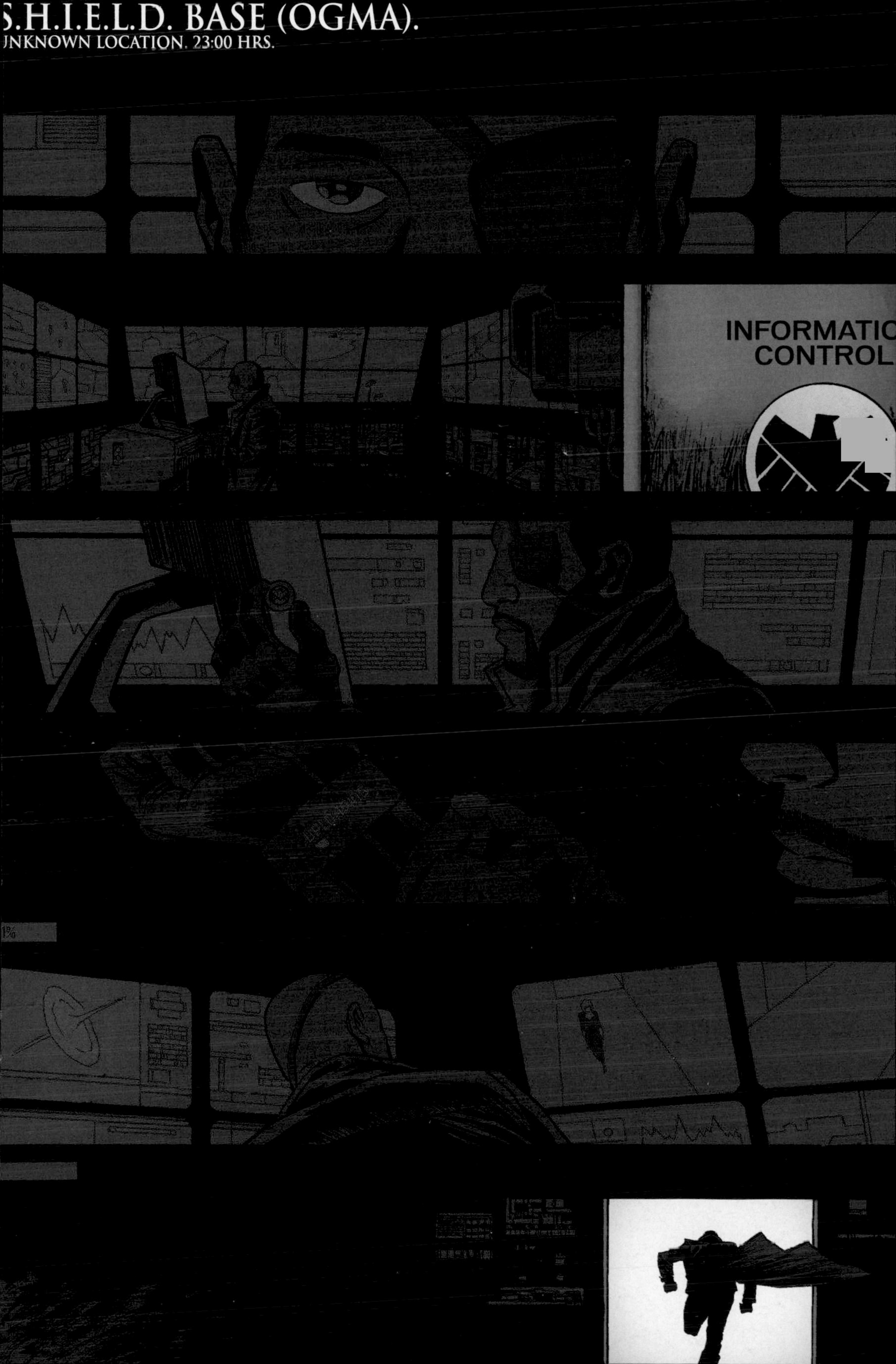
S.H.I.E.L.D. BASE (OGMA).
UNKNOWN LOCATION. 23:00 HRS.
INFORMATIC
CONTROL

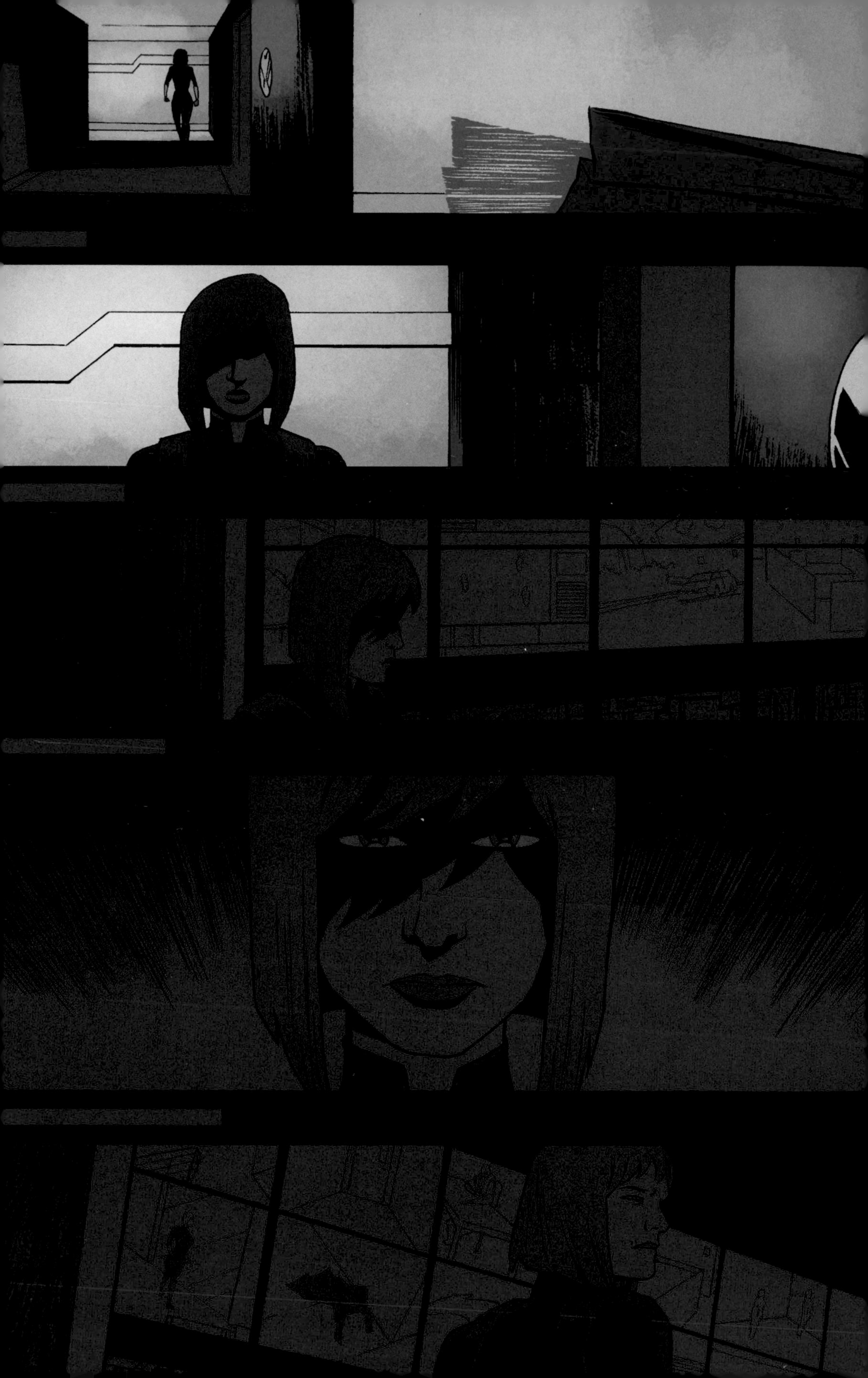

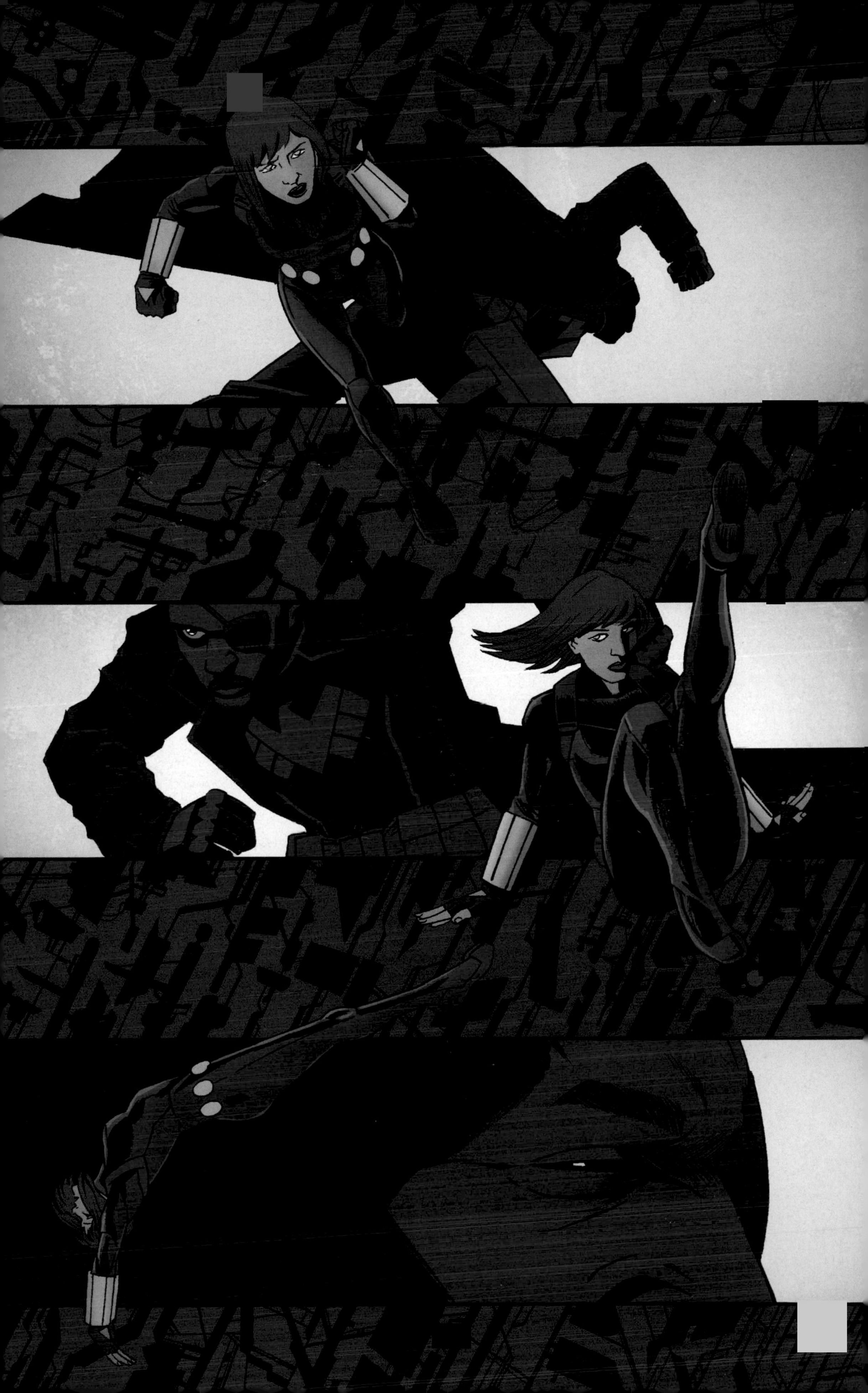

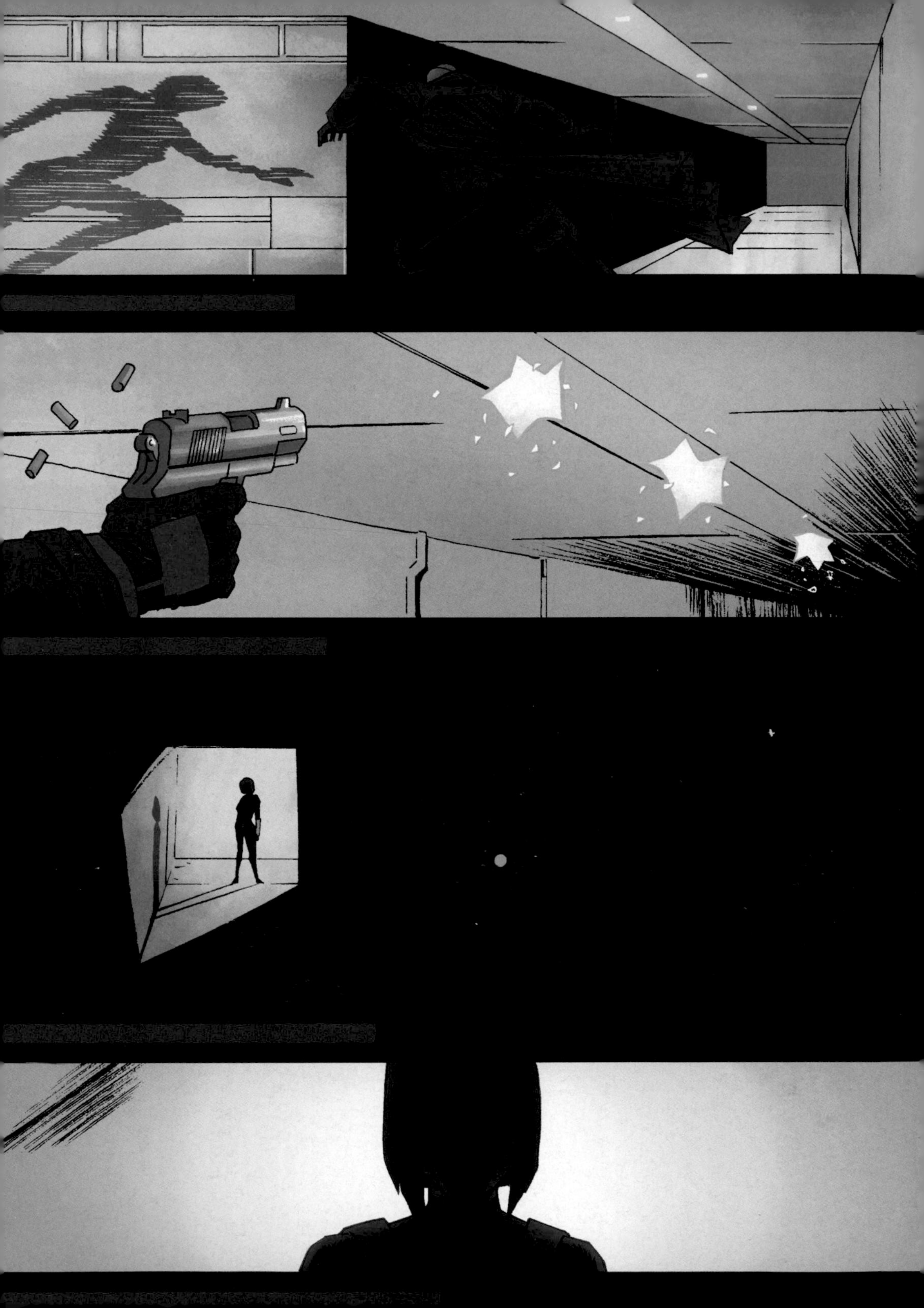

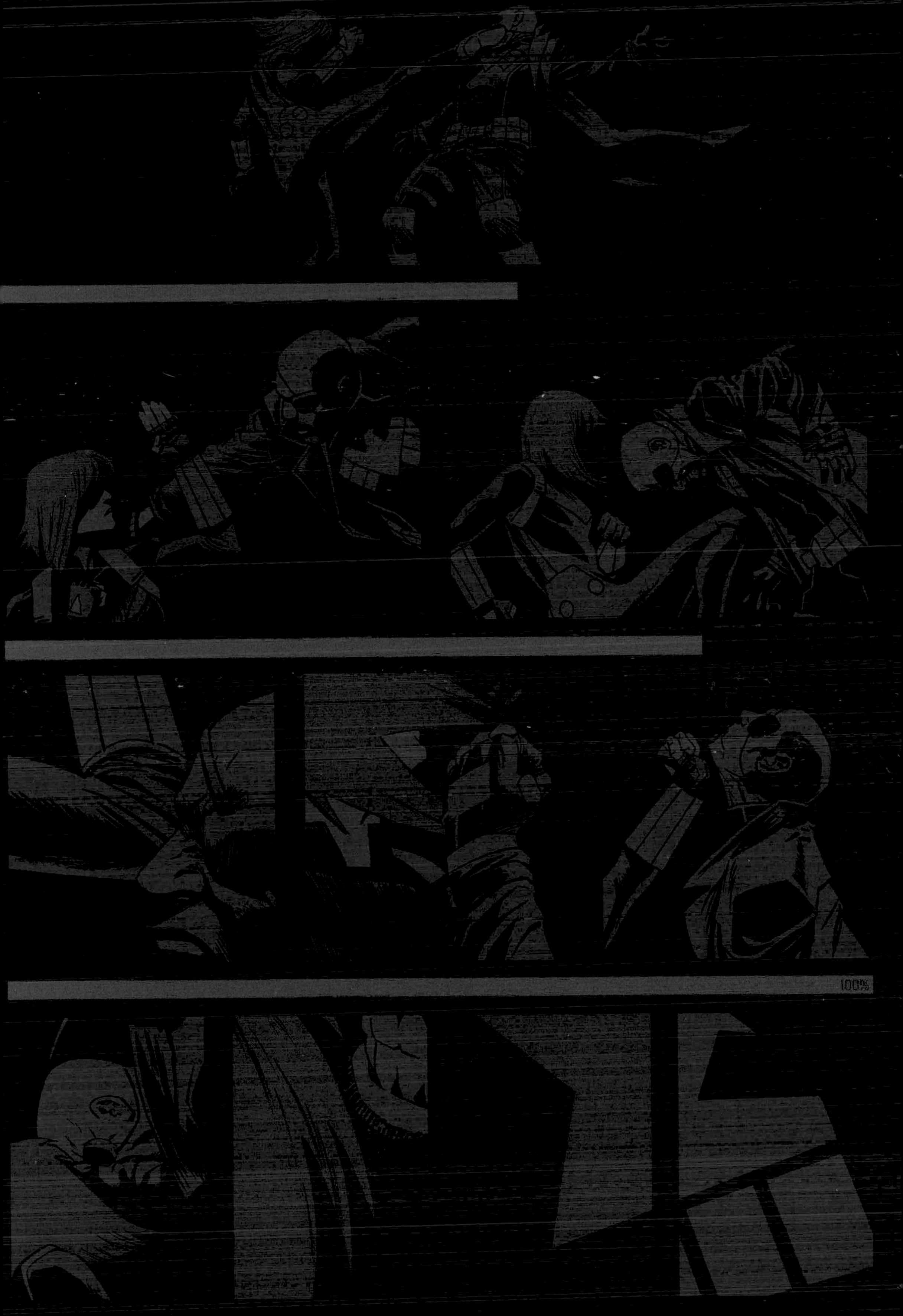
100%

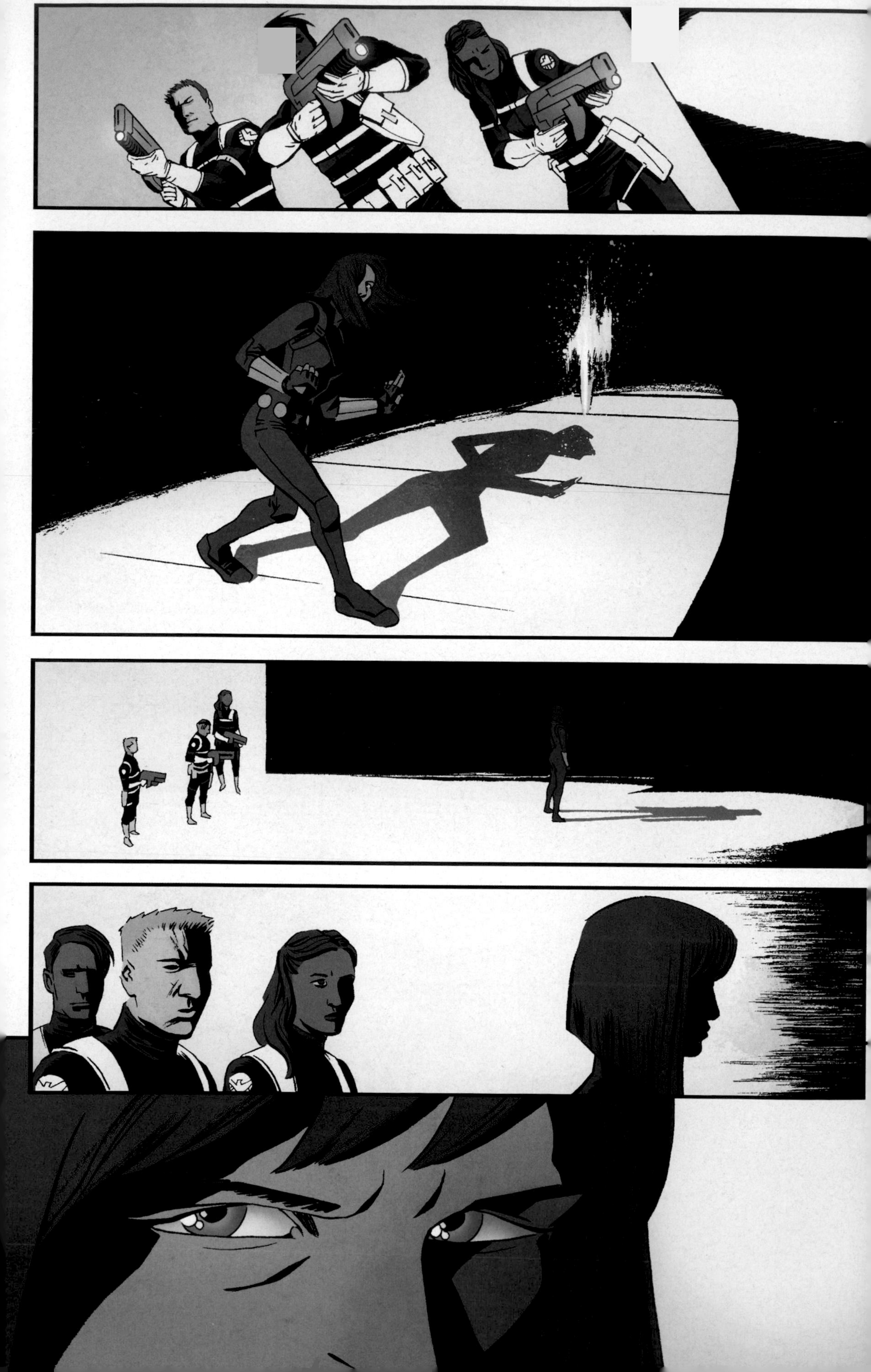

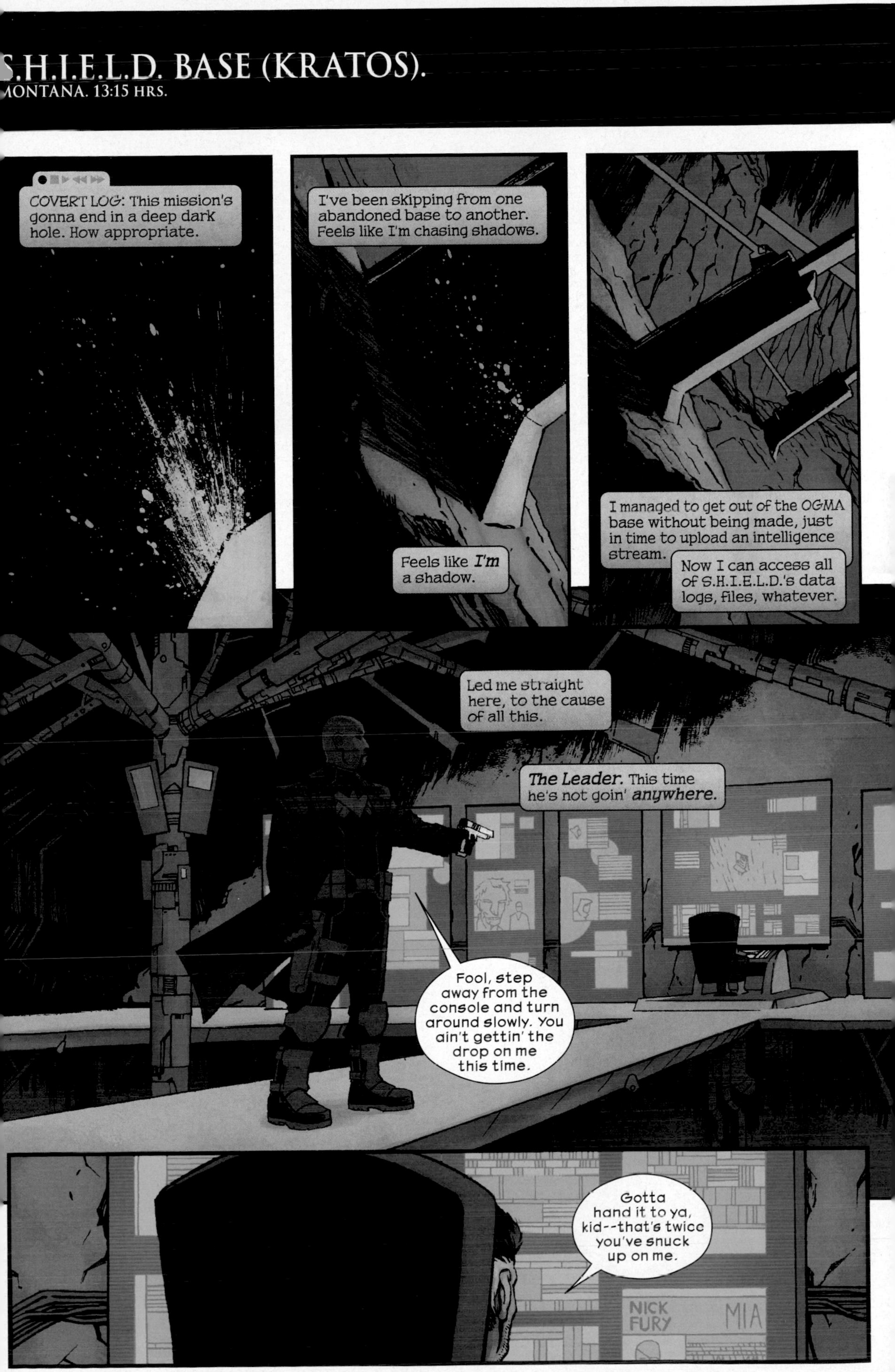
S.H.I.E.L.D. BASE (KRATOS).
MONTANA. 13:15 HRS.
COVERT LOG: This mission's gonna end in a deep dark hole. How appropriate.
I've been skipping from one abandoned base to another. Feels like I'm chasing shadows.
Feels like I'm a shadow.
I managed to get out of the OGMA base without being made, just in time to upload an intelligence stream.
Now I can access all of S.H.I.E.L.D.'s data logs, files, whatever.
Led me straight here, to the cause of all this.
The Leader. This time he's not goin' anywhere.
Fool, step away from the console and turn around slowly. You ain't gettin' the drop on me this time.
Gotta hand it to ya, kid--that's twice you've snuck up on me.
NICK FURY
MIA

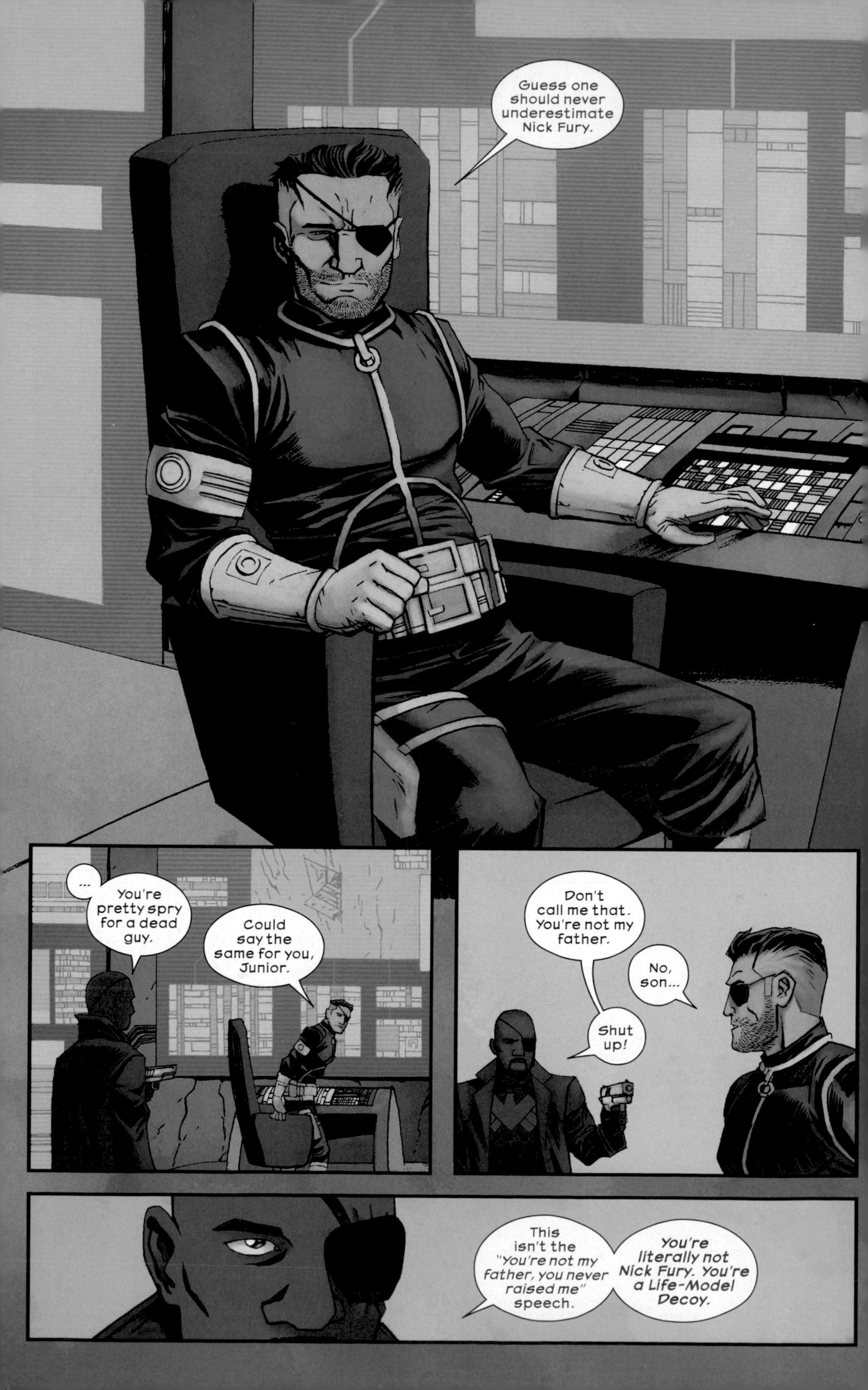
Guess one should never underestimate Nick Fury.
...
You're pretty spry for a dead guy.
Could say the same for you, Junior.
Don't call me that. You're not my father.
No, son...
Shut up!
This isn't the "You're not my father, you never raised me" speech.
You're literally not Nick Fury. You're a Life-Model Decoy.

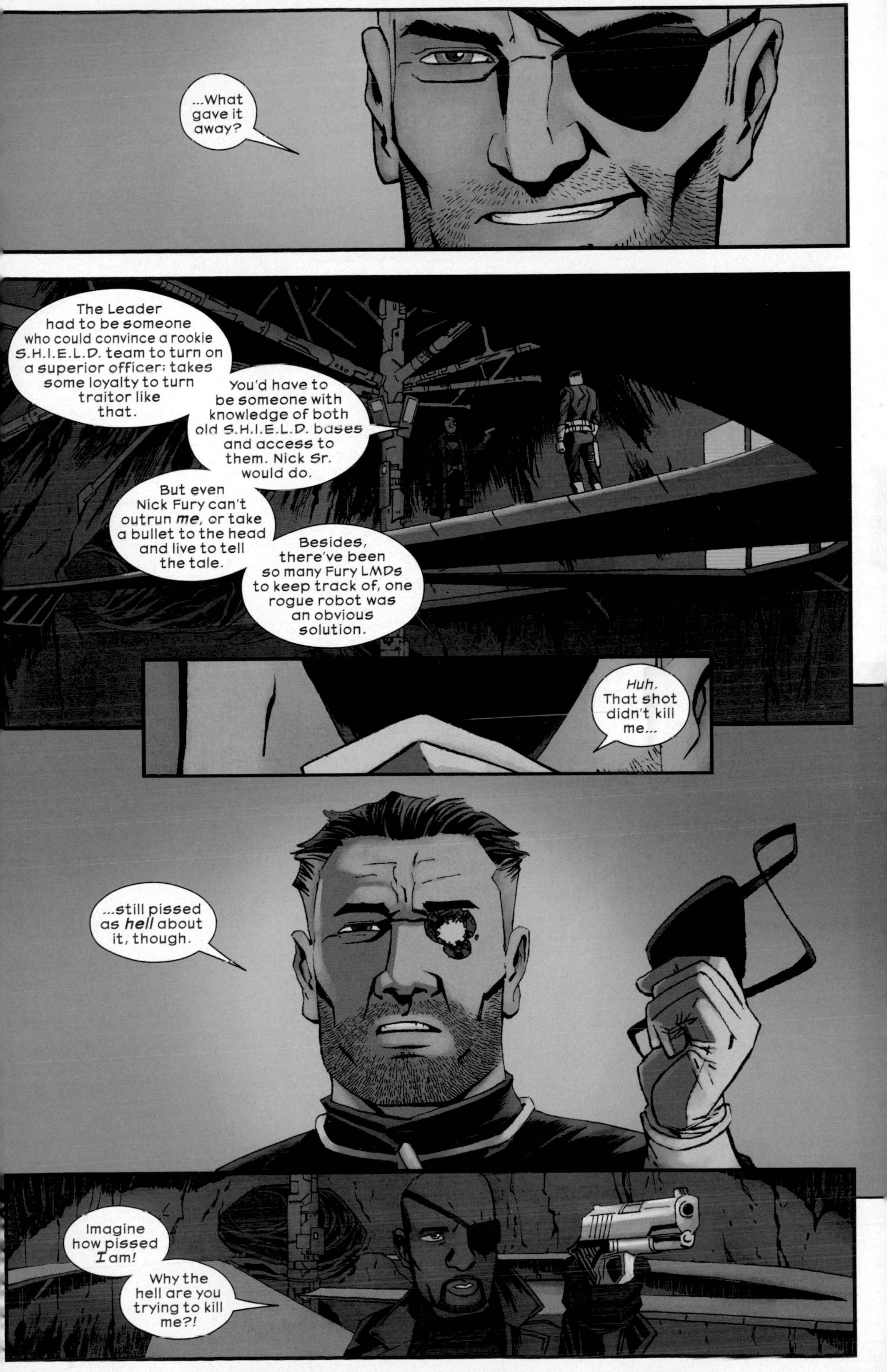
...What gave it away?
The Leader had to be someone who could convince a rookie S.H.I.E.L.D. team to turn on a superior officer; takes some loyalty to turn traitor like that.
You'd have to be someone with knowledge of both old S.H.I.E.L.D. bases and access to them. Nick Sr. would do.
But even Nick Fury can't outrun *me*, or take a bullet to the head and live to tell the tale.
Besides, there've been so many Fury LMDs to keep track of, one rogue robot was an obvious solution.
*Huh.* That shot didn't kill me...
...still pissed as *hell* about it, though.
Imagine how pissed *I* am!
Why the hell are you trying to kill me?!

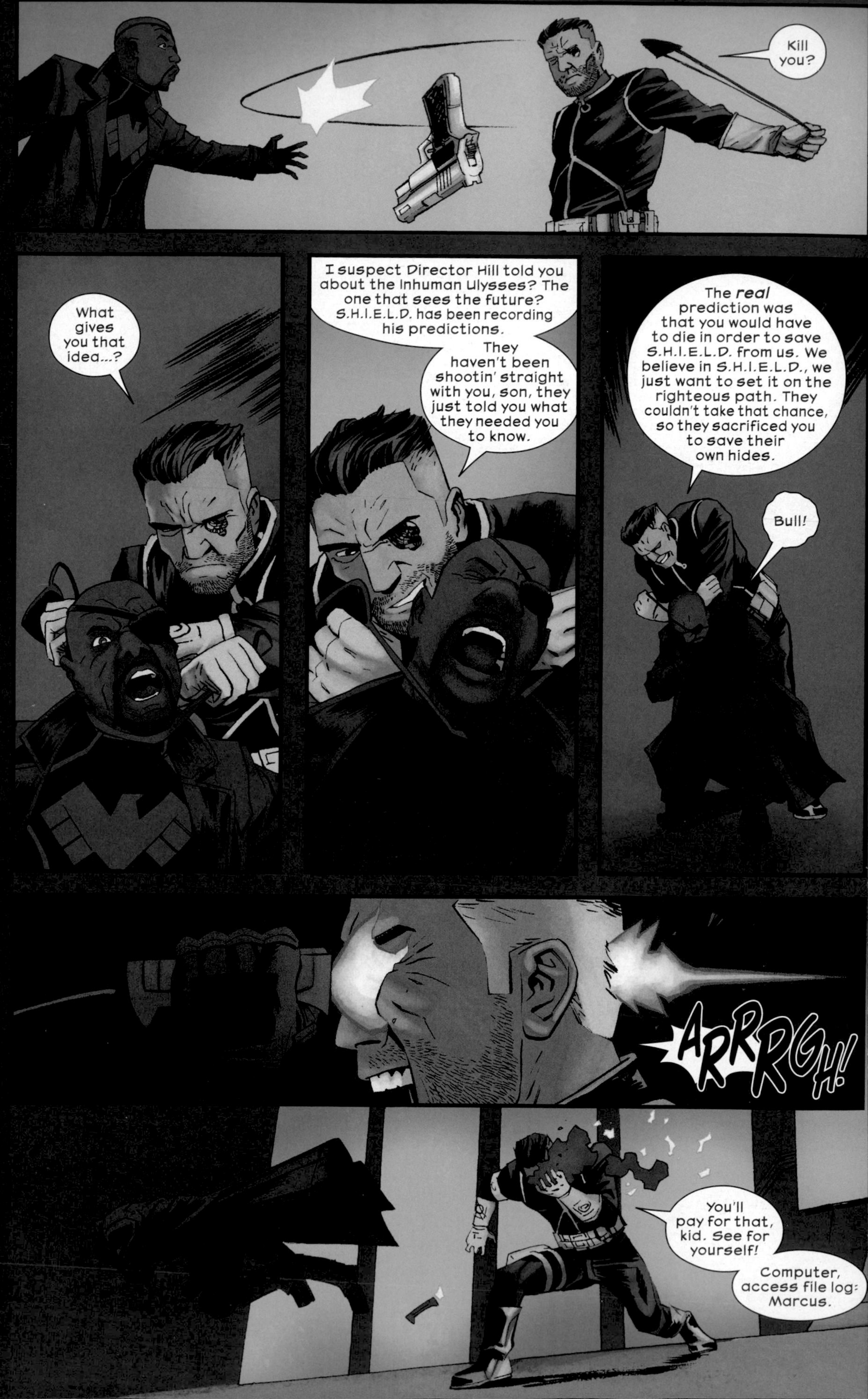
Kill you?
What gives you that idea...?
I suspect Director Hill told you about the Inhuman Ulysses? The one that sees the future? S.H.I.E.L.D. has been recording his predictions.
They haven't been shootin' straight with you, son, they just told you what they needed you to know.
The *real* prediction was that you would have to die in order to save S.H.I.E.L.D. from us. We believe in S.H.I.E.L.D., we just want to set it on the righteous path. They couldn't take that chance, so they sacrificed you to save their own hides.
Bull!
ARRRGH!
You'll pay for that, kid. See for yourself!
Computer, access file log: Marcus.

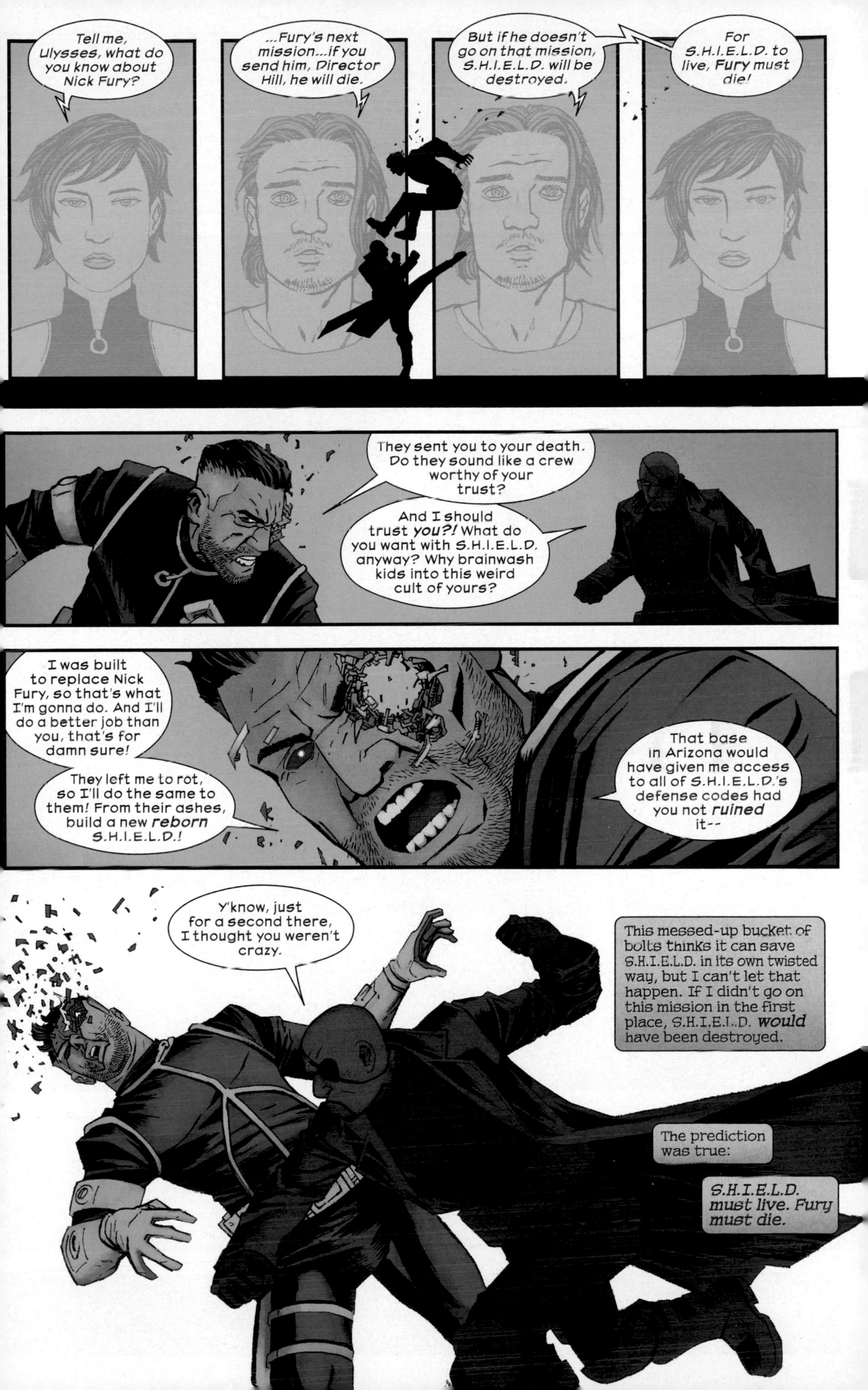

Tell me, Ulysses, what do you know about Nick Fury?
...Fury's next mission...if you send him, Director Hill, he will die.
But if he doesn't go on that mission, S.H.I.E.L.D. will be destroyed.
For S.H.I.E.L.D. to live, Fury must die!
They sent you to your death. Do they sound like a crew worthy of your trust?
And I should trust you?! What do you want with S.H.I.E.L.D. anyway? Why brainwash kids into this weird cult of yours?
I was built to replace Nick Fury, so that's what I'm gonna do. And I'll do a better job than you, that's for damn sure!
They left me to rot, so I'll do the same to them! From their ashes, build a new reborn S.H.I.E.L.D.!
That base in Arizona would have given me access to all of S.H.I.E.L.D.'s defense codes had you not ruined it--
Y'know, just for a second there, I thought you weren't crazy.
This messed-up bucket of bolts thinks it can save S.H.I.E.L.D. in its own twisted way, but I can't let that happen. If I didn't go on this mission in the first place, S.H.I.E.L.D. would have been destroyed.
The prediction was true:
S.H.I.E.L.D. must live. Fury must die.

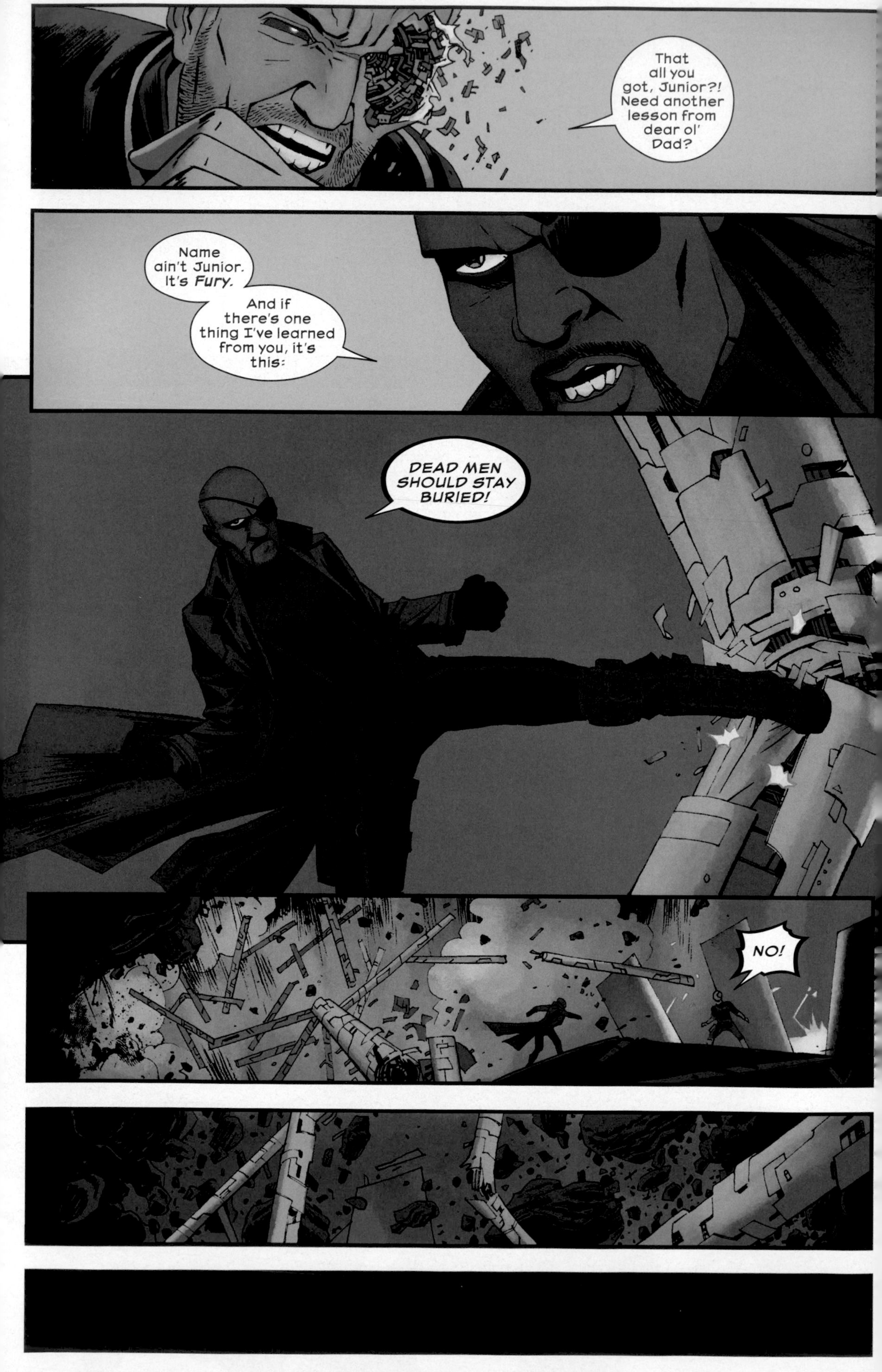
That all you got, Junior?! Need another lesson from dear ol' Dad?
Name ain't Junior. It's *Fury.*
And if there's one thing I've learned from you, it's this:
DEAD MEN SHOULD STAY BURIED!
NO!

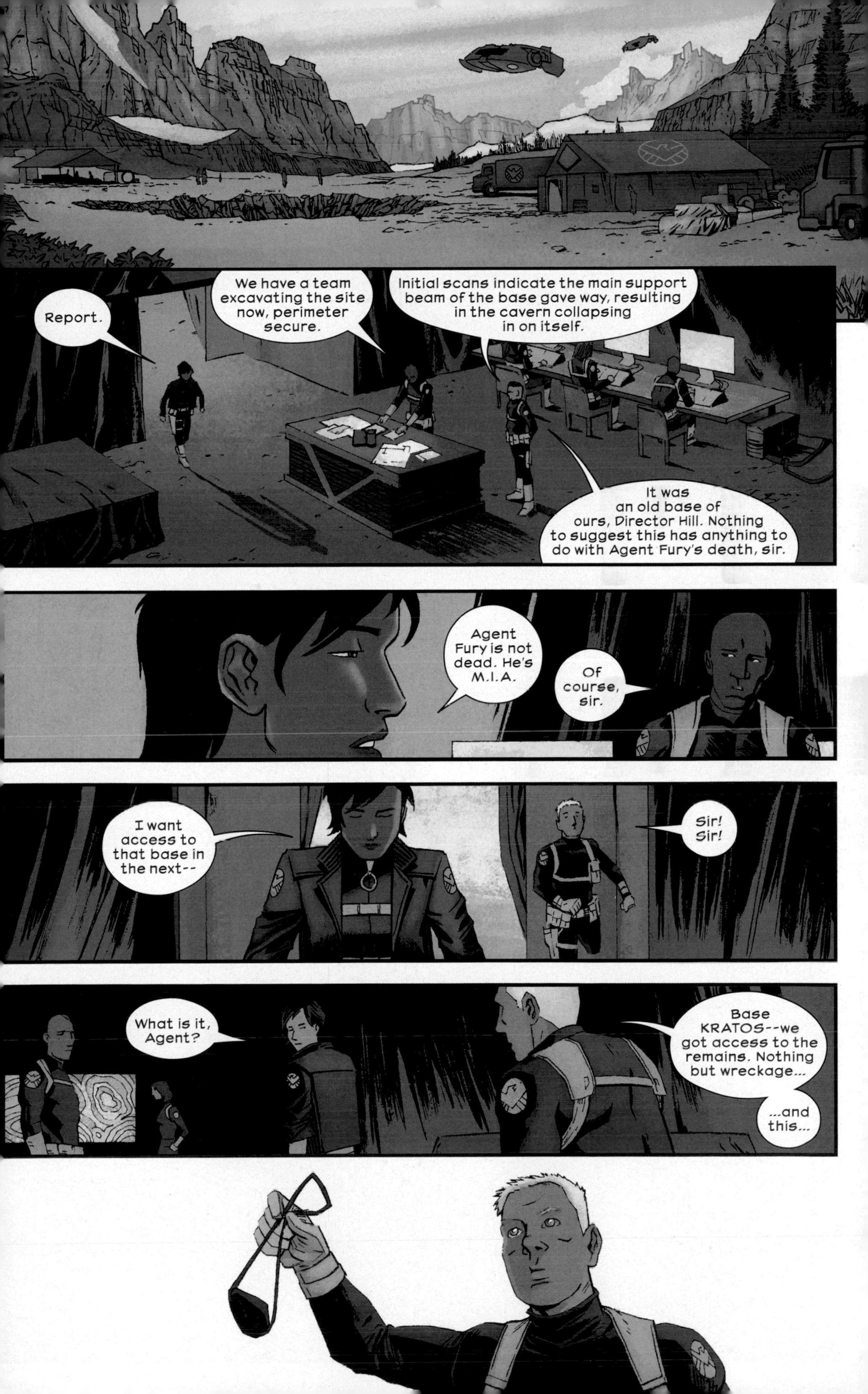
Report.
We have a team excavating the site now, perimeter secure.
Initial scans indicate the main support beam of the base gave way, resulting in the cavern collapsing in on itself.
It was an old base of ours, Director Hill. Nothing to suggest this has anything to do with Agent Fury's death, sir.
Agent Fury is not dead. He's M.I.A.
Of course, sir.
I want access to that base in the next--
Sir! Sir!
What is it, Agent?
Base KRATOS--we got access to the remains. Nothing but wreckage...
...and this...

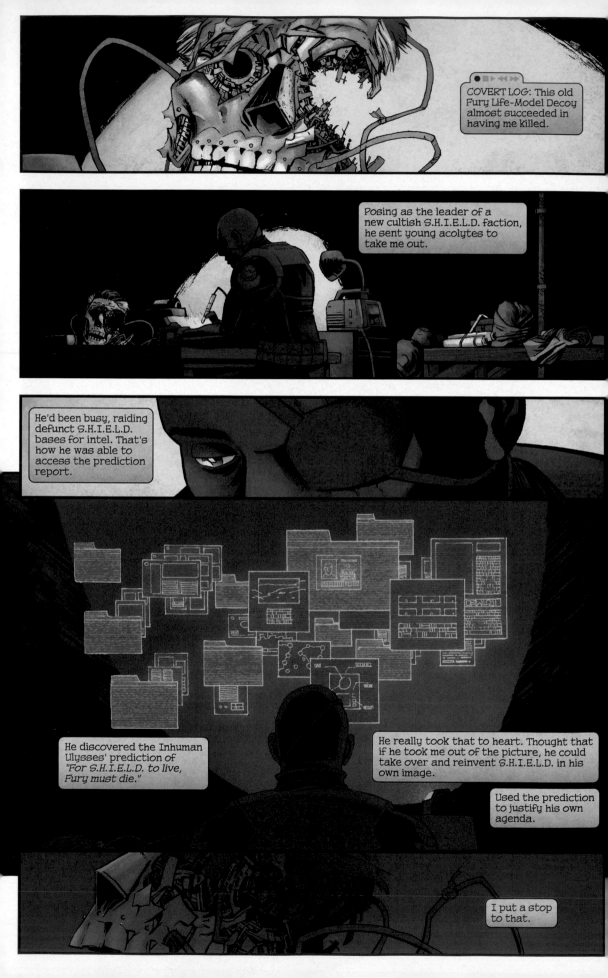

COVERT LOG: This old Fury Life-Model Decoy almost succeeded in having me killed.

Posing as the leader of a new cultish S.H.I.E.L.D. faction, he sent young acolytes to take me out.

He'd been busy, raiding defunct S.H.I.E.L.D. bases for intel. That's how he was able to access the prediction report.

He discovered the Inhuman Ulysses' prediction of "For S.H.I.E.L.D. to live, Fury must die."

He really took that to heart. Thought that if he took me out of the picture, he could take over and reinvent S.H.I.E.L.D. in his own image.

Used the prediction to justify his own agenda.

I put a stop to that.

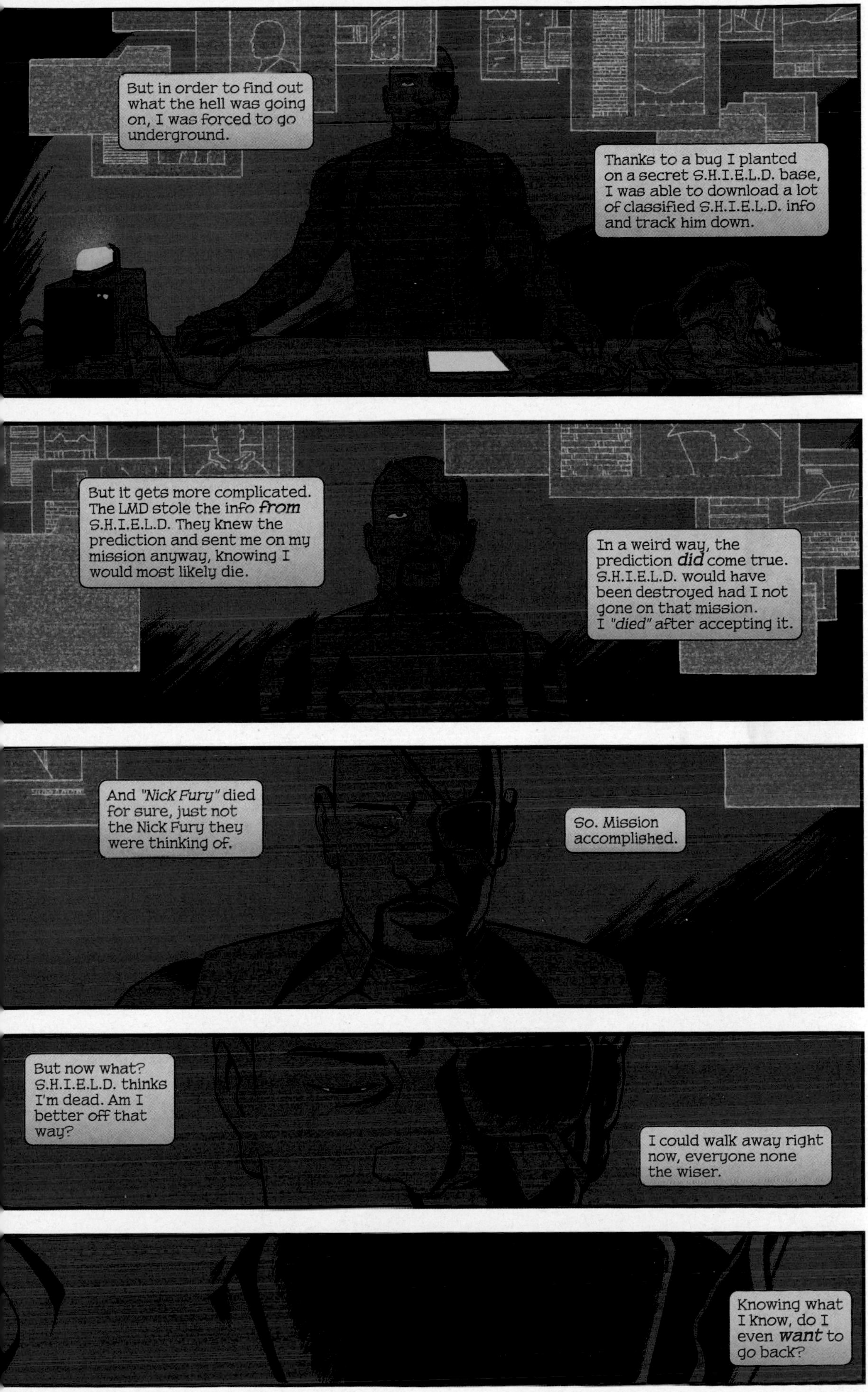
But in order to find out what the hell was going on, I was forced to go underground.
Thanks to a bug I planted on a secret S.H.I.E.L.D. base, I was able to download a lot of classified S.H.I.E.L.D. info and track him down.
But it gets more complicated. The LMD stole the info *from* S.H.I.E.L.D. They knew the prediction and sent me on my mission anyway, knowing I would most likely die.
In a weird way, the prediction *did* come true. S.H.I.E.L.D. would have been destroyed had I not gone on that mission. I *"died"* after accepting it.
And *"Nick Fury"* died for sure, just not the Nick Fury they were thinking of.
So. Mission accomplished.
But now what? S.H.I.E.L.D. thinks I'm dead. Am I better off that way?
I could walk away right now, everyone none the wiser.
Knowing what I know, do I even *want* to go back?

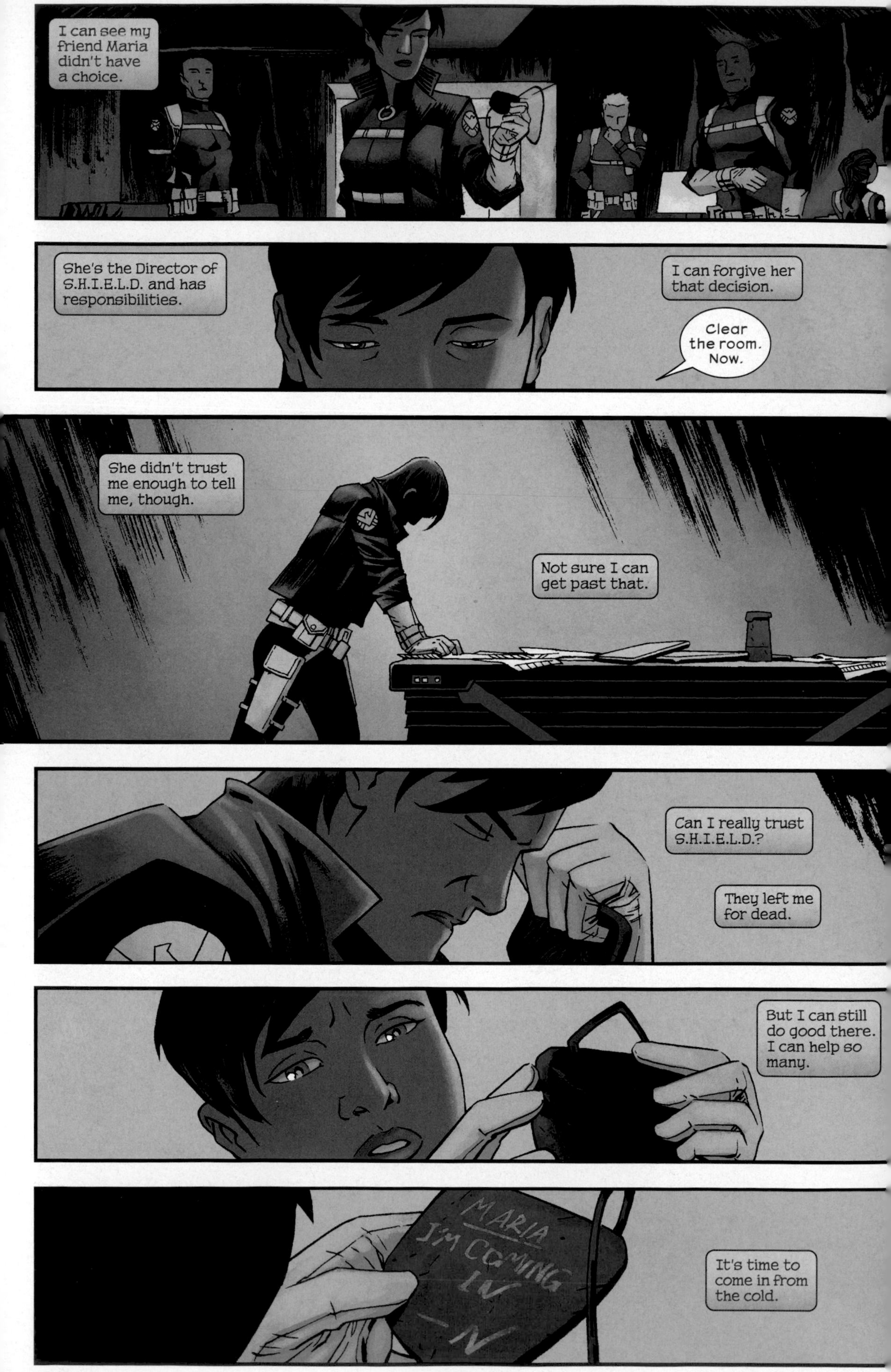
I can see my friend Maria didn't have a choice.
She's the Director of S.H.I.E.L.D. and has responsibilities.
I can forgive her that decision.
Clear the room. Now.
She didn't trust me enough to tell me, though.
Not sure I can get past that.
Can I really trust S.H.I.E.L.D.?
They left me for dead.
But I can still do good there. I can help so many.
MARIA
I'M COMING
IN
It's time to come in from the cold.

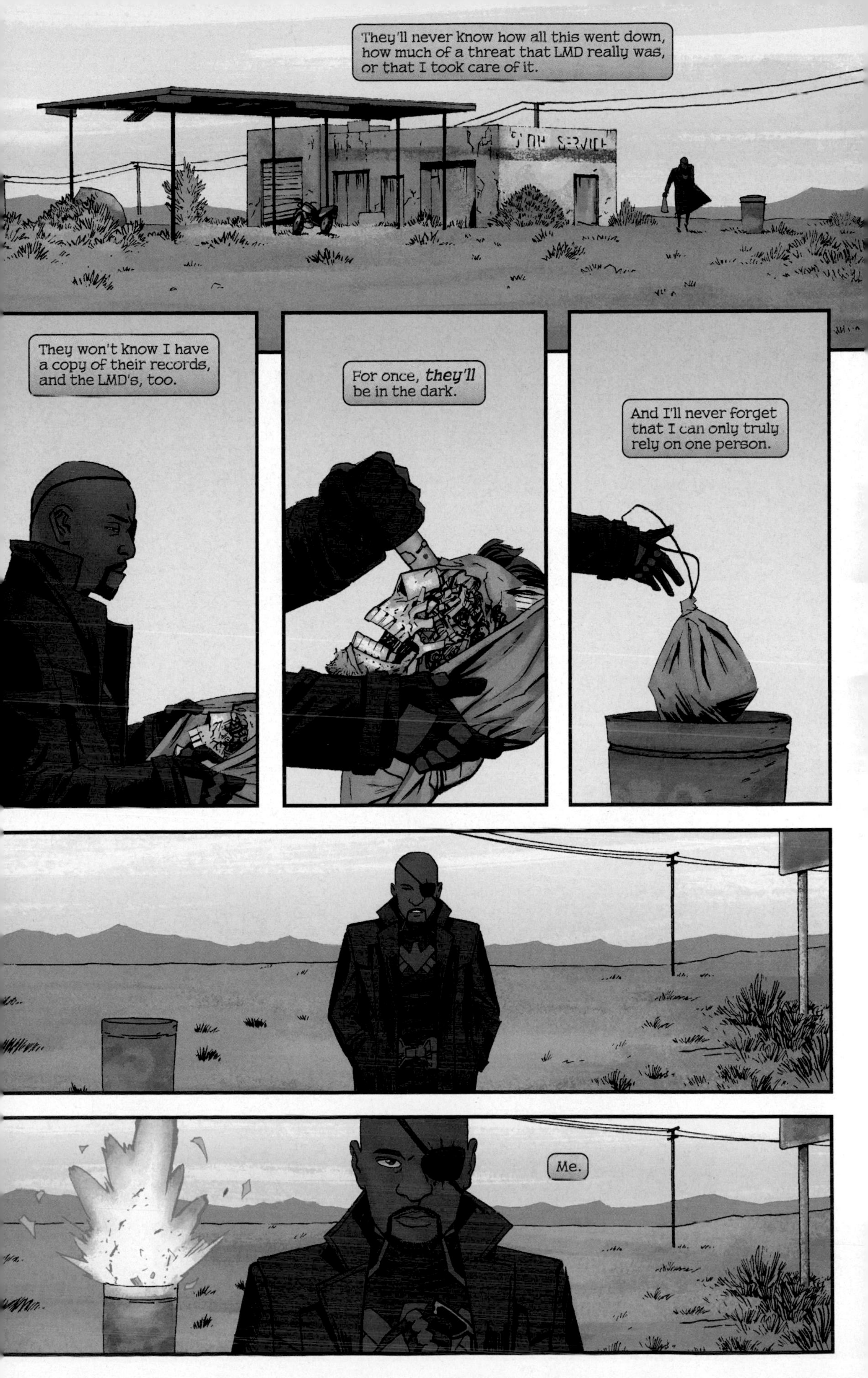
They'll never know how all this went down, how much of a threat that LMD really was, or that I took care of it.
S'ON SERVICE
They won't know I have a copy of their records, and the LMD's, too.
For once, they'll be in the dark.
And I'll never forget that I can only truly rely on one person.
Me.

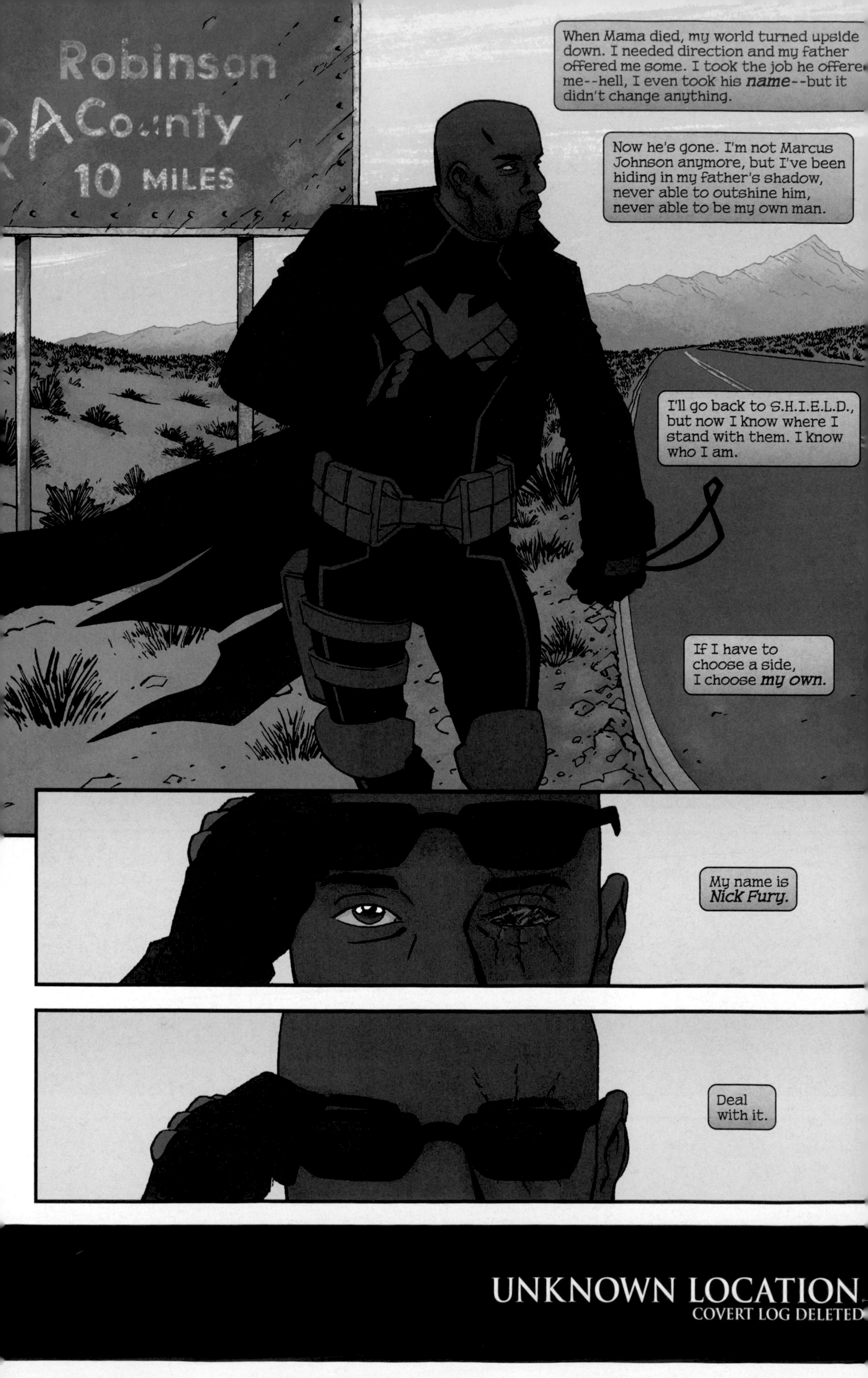
Robinson
County
10 MILES
When Mama died, my world turned upside down. I needed direction and my father offered me some. I took the job he offere me--hell, I even took his *name*--but it didn't change anything.
Now he's gone. I'm not Marcus Johnson anymore, but I've been hiding in my father's shadow, never able to outshine him, never able to be my own man.
I'll go back to S.H.I.E.L.D., but now I know where I stand with them. I know who I am.
If I have to choose a side, I choose *my own.*
My name is *Nick Fury.*
Deal with it.
UNKNOWN LOCATION
COVERT LOG DELETED

## NIGHT THRASHER

WRITER
**BRANDON EASTON**

ARTIST
**PAUL DAVIDSON**

COLOR ARTIST
**ANDREW CROSSLEY**

EDITOR
**CHRIS ROBINSON**

## DAMAGE CONTROL

WRITERS
**CHAD BOWERS & CHRIS SIMS**

ARTIST
**LEONARDO ROMERO**

COLOR ARTIST
**MIROSLAV MRVA**

ASSISTANT EDITOR
**CHARLES BEACHAM**

EDITOR
**WIL MOSS**

COVER ART BY
JIM CHEUNG &
JUSTIN PONSOR

# I

SAINT BERNARD OF CLAIRVAUX IS CREDITED WITH THE APHORISM *"THE ROAD TO HELL IS PAVED WITH GOOD INTENTIONS."*

WHENEVER WE STRIKE A BLOW AGAINST THE FORCES OF DARKNESS, THERE'S A SHOCKWAVE OF UNINTENDED CONSEQUENCES.

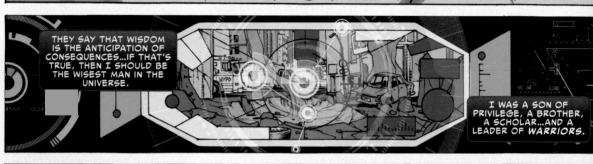

THEY SAY THAT WISDOM IS THE ANTICIPATION OF CONSEQUENCES...IF THAT'S TRUE, THEN I SHOULD BE THE WISEST MAN IN THE UNIVERSE.

I WAS A SON OF PRIVILEGE, A BROTHER, A SCHOLAR...AND A LEADER OF *WARRIORS*.

TKASSSHH TKASSSHH

YOU MIGHT SAY MY ENTIRE LIFE WAS SPENT MANAGING THE WAGES OF CONSEQUENCE. UNTIL MY LUCK RAN OUT.

THEN I REALIZED LUCK IS AN ILLUSION. IT'S ABOUT CONTROL.

RIGHT NOW, THE INVADER HAS LOST CONTROL OVER HIS FATE. IT'S A HARSH LESSON.

WHOOOOOOOOK

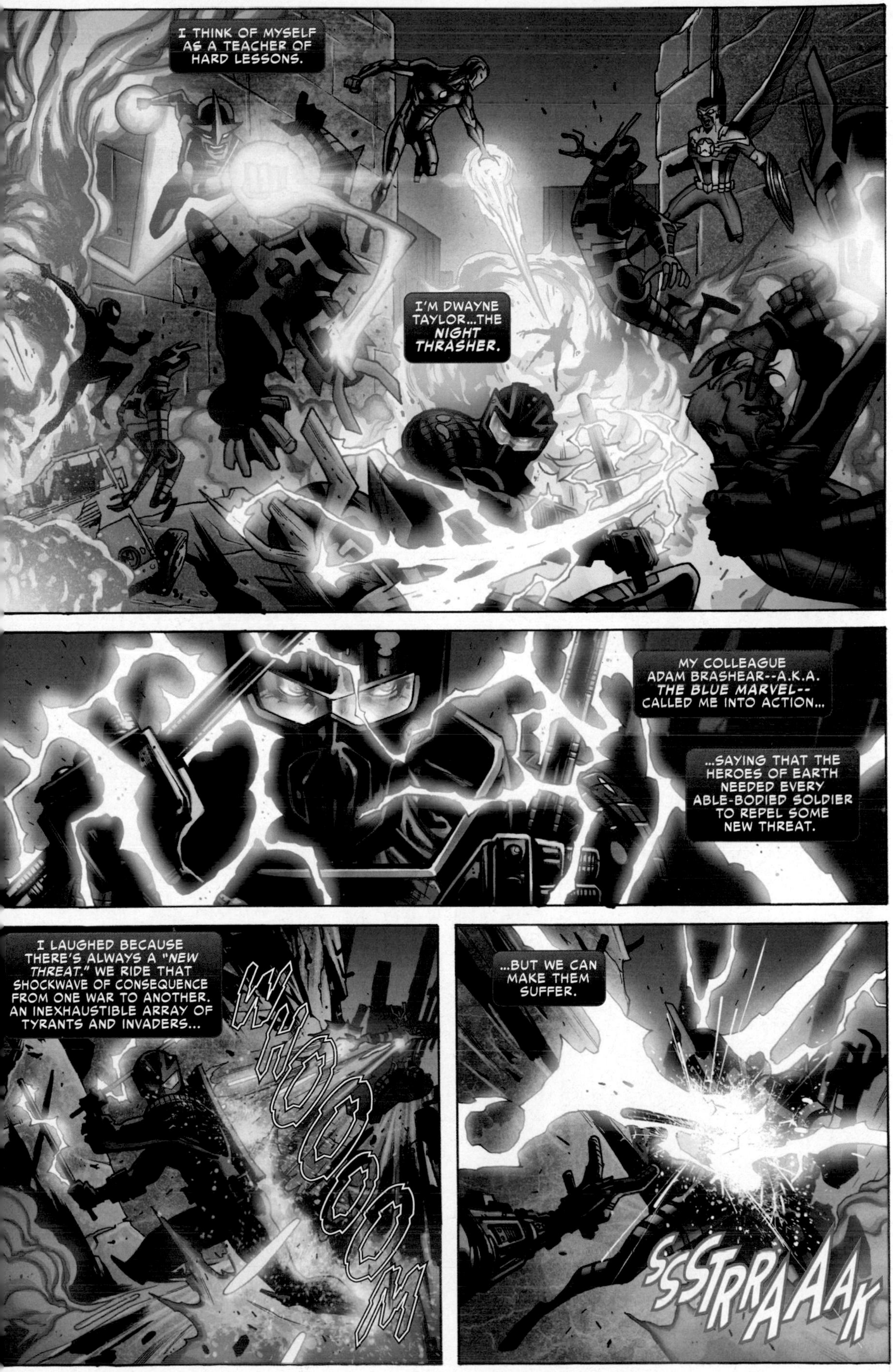
I THINK OF MYSELF AS A TEACHER OF HARD LESSONS.
I'M DWAYNE TAYLOR...THE NIGHT THRASHER.
MY COLLEAGUE ADAM BRASHEAR--A.K.A. THE BLUE MARVEL--CALLED ME INTO ACTION...
...SAYING THAT THE HEROES OF EARTH NEEDED EVERY ABLE-BODIED SOLDIER TO REPEL SOME NEW THREAT.
I LAUGHED BECAUSE THERE'S ALWAYS A "NEW THREAT." WE RIDE THAT SHOCKWAVE OF CONSEQUENCE FROM ONE WAR TO ANOTHER. AN INEXHAUSTIBLE ARRAY OF TYRANTS AND INVADERS...
WHOOOOOM
...BUT WE CAN MAKE THEM SUFFER.
SSSTRRAAAK

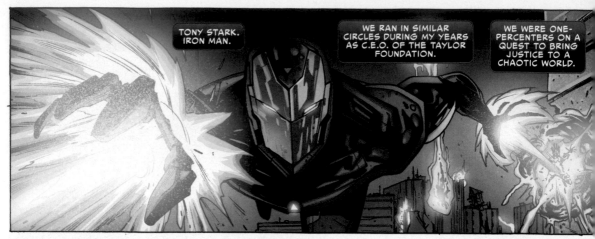

TONY STARK. IRON MAN.

WE RAN IN SIMILAR CIRCLES DURING MY YEARS AS C.E.O. OF THE TAYLOR FOUNDATION.

WE WERE ONE-PERCENTERS ON A QUEST TO BRING JUSTICE TO A CHAOTIC WORLD.

I FAILED. SOMEHOW, HE'S MAINTAINED THE FACADE OF STABILITY.

BILLIONAIRE WEAPONS MANUFACTURER. PLAYBOY. ALCOHOLIC. EGOMANIAC. A MANIC DEPRESSIVE WITH DELUSIONS OF GRANDEUR.

BEHIND YOU!

ZAAAARRRKKK

STILL, HE HAS HIS MOMENTS.

A REAL LEADER UNDERSTANDS THE STRATEGY OF NEUTRALIZING THE WEAPON FIRST.

THOOOM

I'M GETTING A HEARTBEAT FROM THAT WRECKAGE.

THIS AREA WAS SUPPOSED TO BE EVACUATED.

A REAL LEADER, HUH?

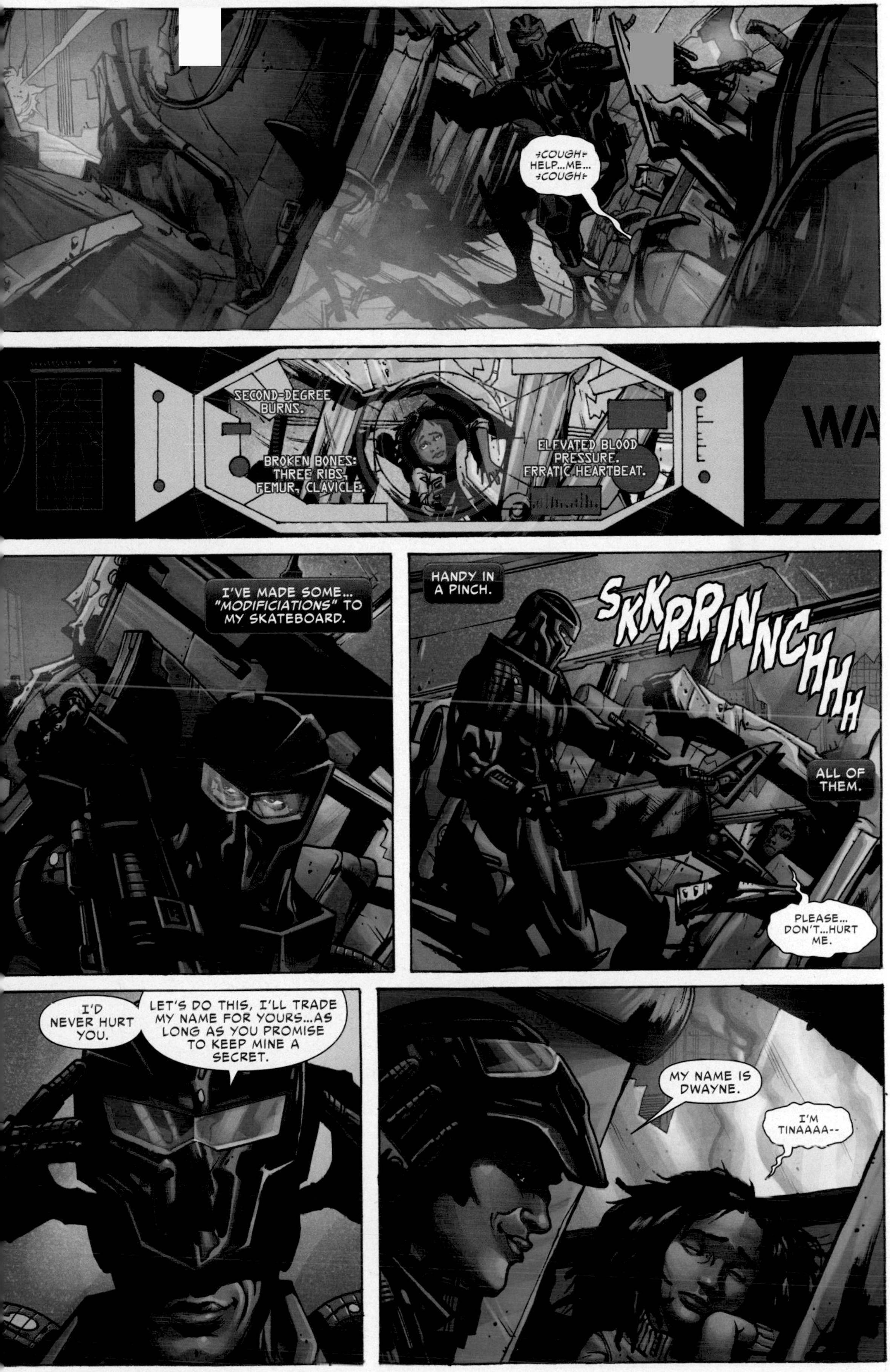
‡COUGH‡ HELP...ME... ‡COUGH‡
SECOND-DEGREE BURNS.
BROKEN BONES: THREE RIBS, FEMUR, CLAVICLE.
ELEVATED BLOOD PRESSURE. ERRATIC HEARTBEAT.
I'VE MADE SOME... "MODIFICIATIONS" TO MY SKATEBOARD.
HANDY IN A PINCH.
SKKRRINNCHHH
ALL OF THEM.
PLEASE... DON'T...HURT ME.
I'D NEVER HURT YOU.
LET'S DO THIS, I'LL TRADE MY NAME FOR YOURS...AS LONG AS YOU PROMISE TO KEEP MINE A SECRET.
MY NAME IS DWAYNE.
I'M TINAAAA--

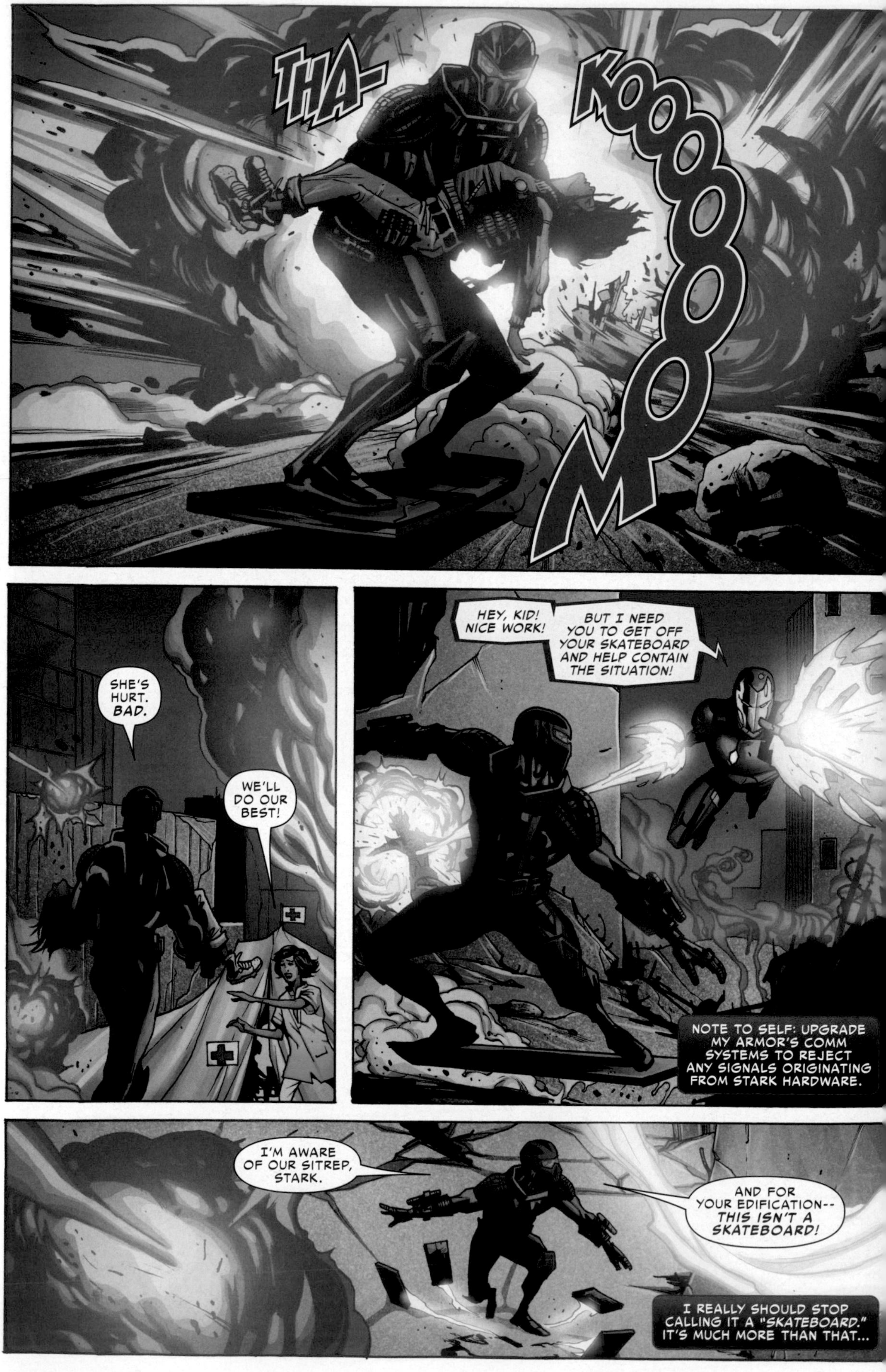
THA-
KOOOOOOOM
SHE'S HURT. BAD.
WE'LL DO OUR BEST!
HEY, KID! NICE WORK!
BUT I NEED YOU TO GET OFF YOUR SKATEBOARD AND HELP CONTAIN THE SITUATION!
NOTE TO SELF: UPGRADE MY ARMOR'S COMM SYSTEMS TO REJECT ANY SIGNALS ORIGINATING FROM STARK HARDWARE.
I'M AWARE OF OUR SITREP, STARK.
AND FOR YOUR EDIFICATION-- THIS ISN'T A SKATEBOARD!
I REALLY SHOULD STOP CALLING IT A "SKATEBOARD." IT'S MUCH MORE THAN THAT...

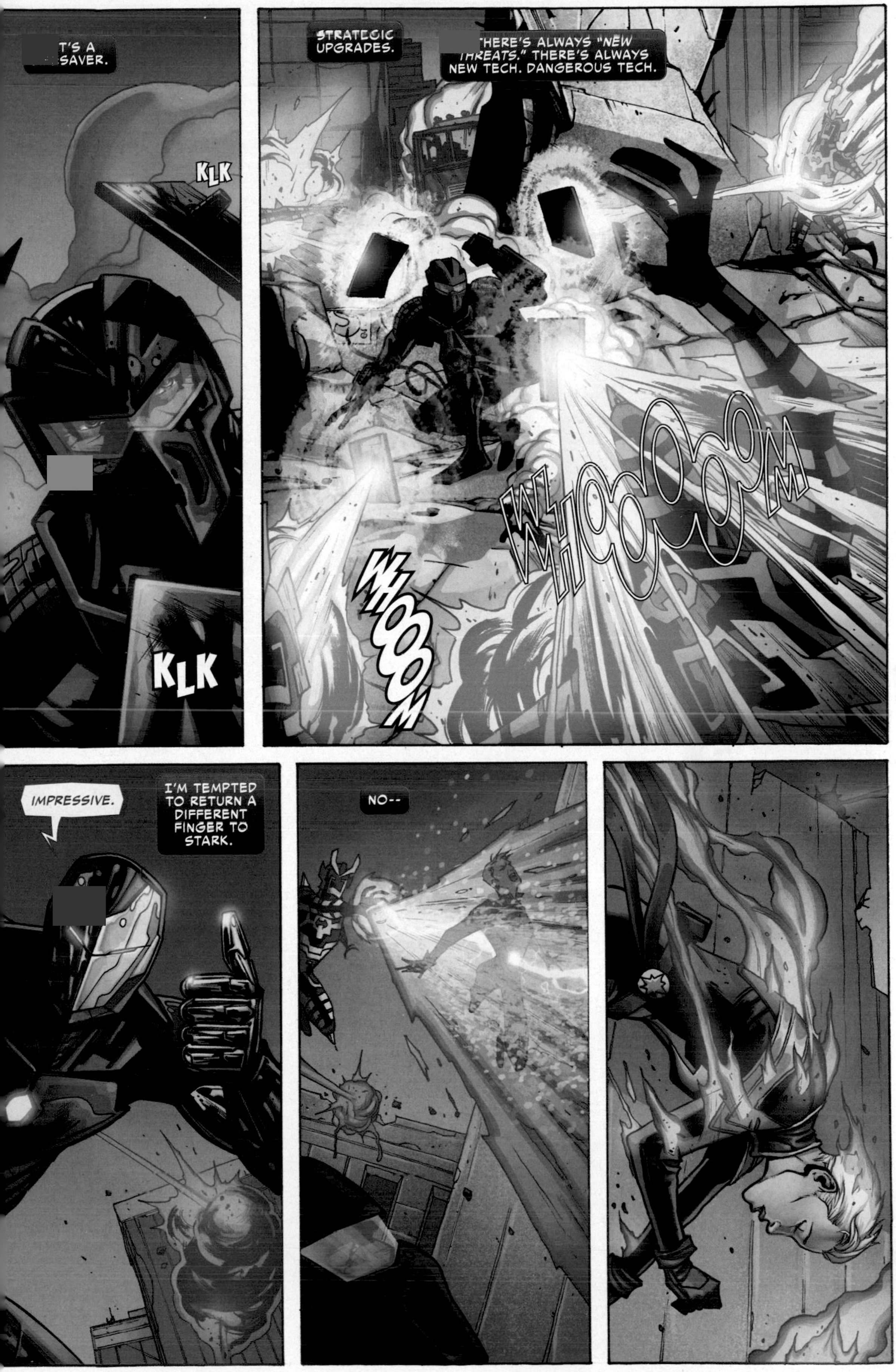
[redacted]T'S A [redacted]SAVER.
KLK
KLK
STRATEGIC UPGRADES.
[redacted]THERE'S ALWAYS "NEW THREATS." THERE'S ALWAYS NEW TECH. DANGEROUS TECH.
WHOOOOM
WHOOOOOM
IMPRESSIVE.
I'M TEMPTED TO RETURN A DIFFERENT FINGER TO STARK.
NO--

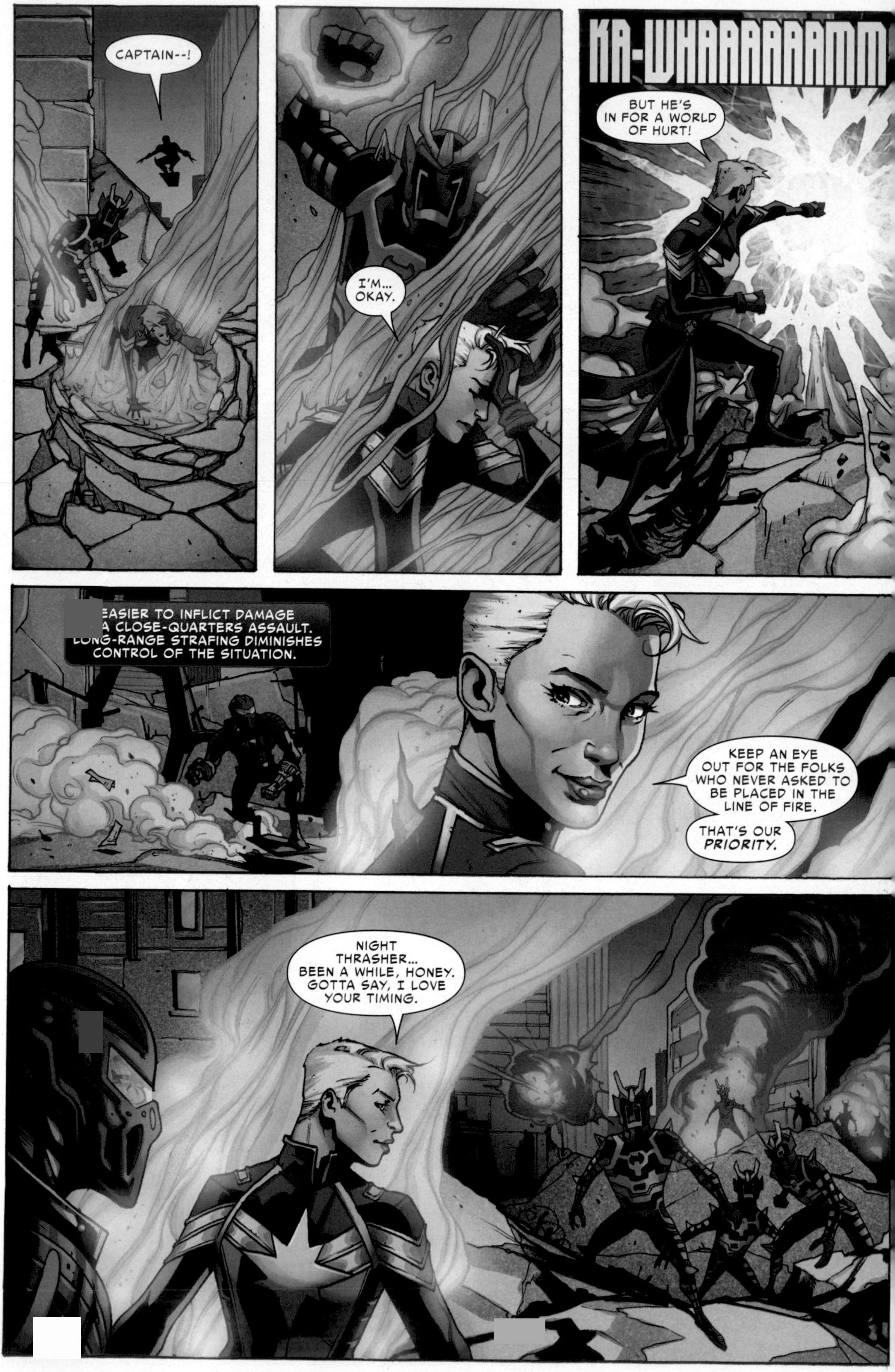

CAPTAIN--!
I'M... OKAY.
KA-WHAAAAAAMM
BUT HE'S IN FOR A WORLD OF HURT!
EASIER TO INFLICT DAMAGE
A CLOSE-QUARTERS ASSAULT.
LONG-RANGE STRAFING DIMINISHES CONTROL OF THE SITUATION.
KEEP AN EYE OUT FOR THE FOLKS WHO NEVER ASKED TO BE PLACED IN THE LINE OF FIRE.
THAT'S OUR PRIORITY.
NIGHT THRASHER... BEEN A WHILE, HONEY. GOTTA SAY, I LOVE YOUR TIMING.

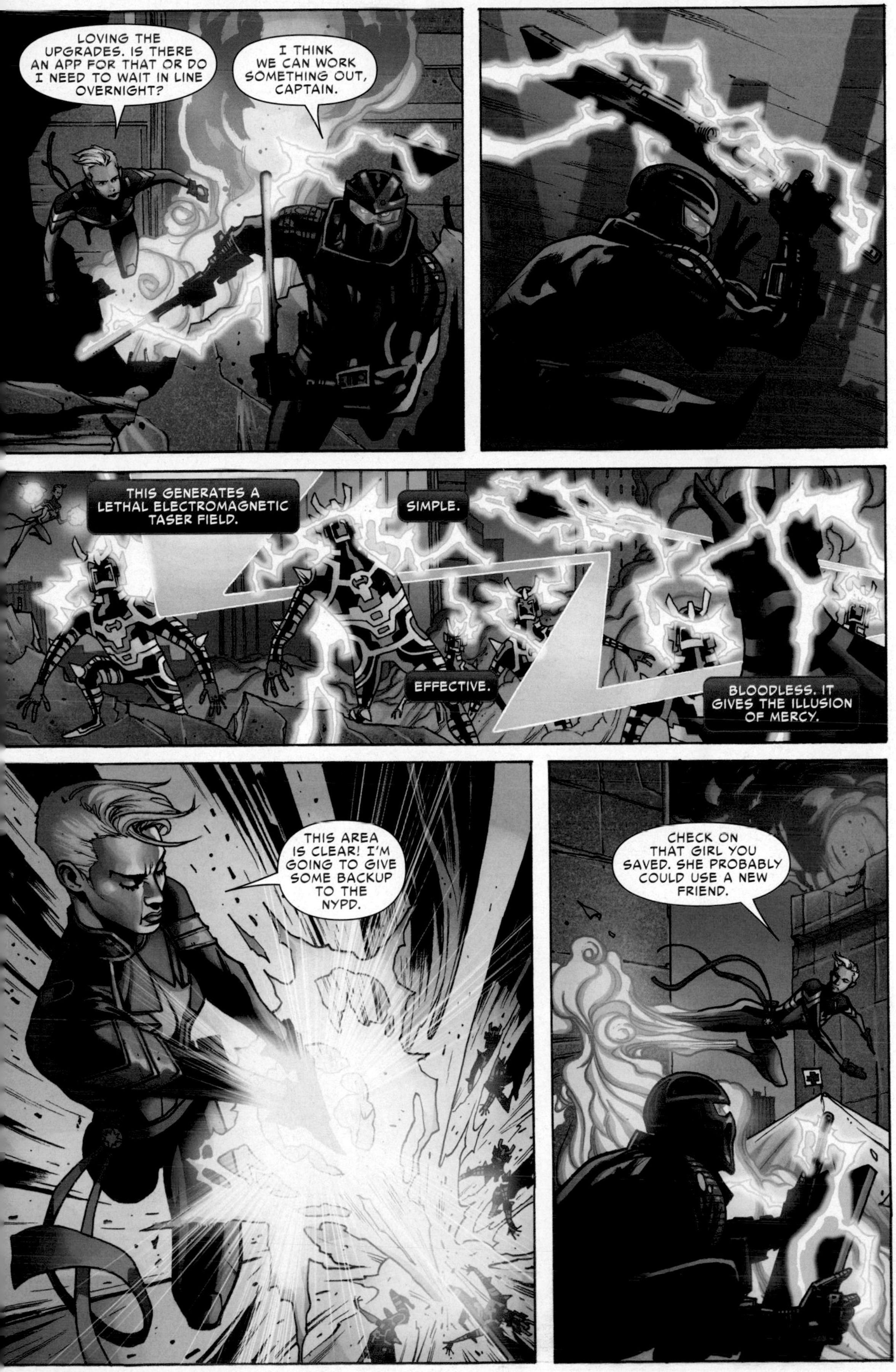
LOVING THE UPGRADES. IS THERE AN APP FOR THAT OR DO I NEED TO WAIT IN LINE OVERNIGHT?
I THINK WE CAN WORK SOMETHING OUT, CAPTAIN.
THIS GENERATES A LETHAL ELECTROMAGNETIC TASER FIELD.
SIMPLE.
EFFECTIVE.
BLOODLESS. IT GIVES THE ILLUSION OF MERCY.
THIS AREA IS CLEAR! I'M GOING TO GIVE SOME BACKUP TO THE NYPD.
CHECK ON THAT GIRL YOU SAVED. SHE PROBABLY COULD USE A NEW FRIEND.

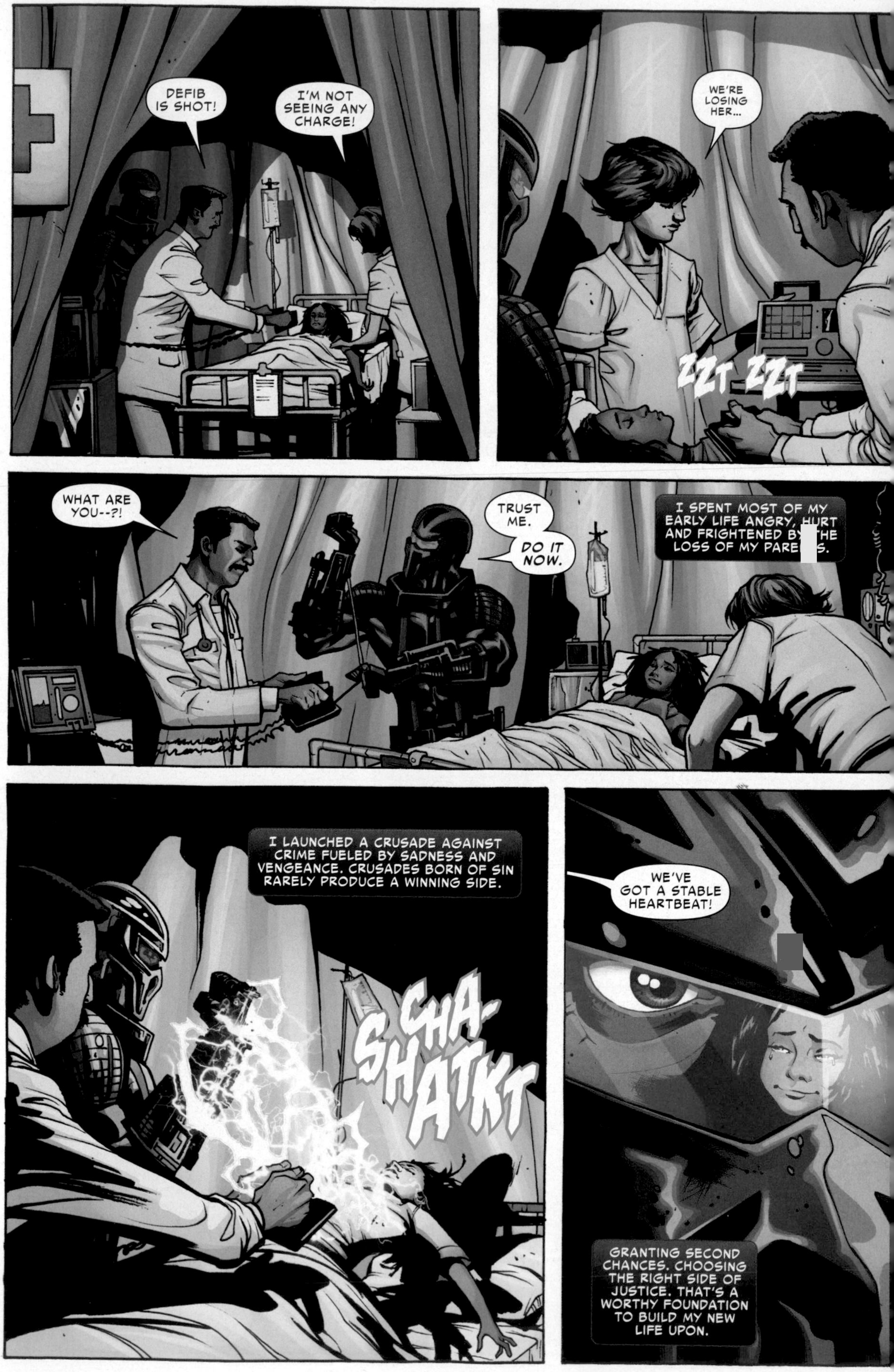
DEFIB IS SHOT!
I'M NOT SEEING ANY CHARGE!
WE'RE LOSING HER...
ZZT ZZT
WHAT ARE YOU--?!
TRUST ME.
DO IT NOW.
I SPENT MOST OF MY EARLY LIFE ANGRY, HURT AND FRIGHTENED BY THE LOSS OF MY PARENTS.
I LAUNCHED A CRUSADE AGAINST CRIME FUELED BY SADNESS AND VENGEANCE. CRUSADES BORN OF SIN RARELY PRODUCE A WINNING SIDE.
SHA-SHATKT
WE'VE GOT A STABLE HEARTBEAT!
GRANTING SECOND CHANCES. CHOOSING THE RIGHT SIDE OF JUSTICE. THAT'S A WORTHY FOUNDATION TO BUILD MY NEW LIFE UPON.

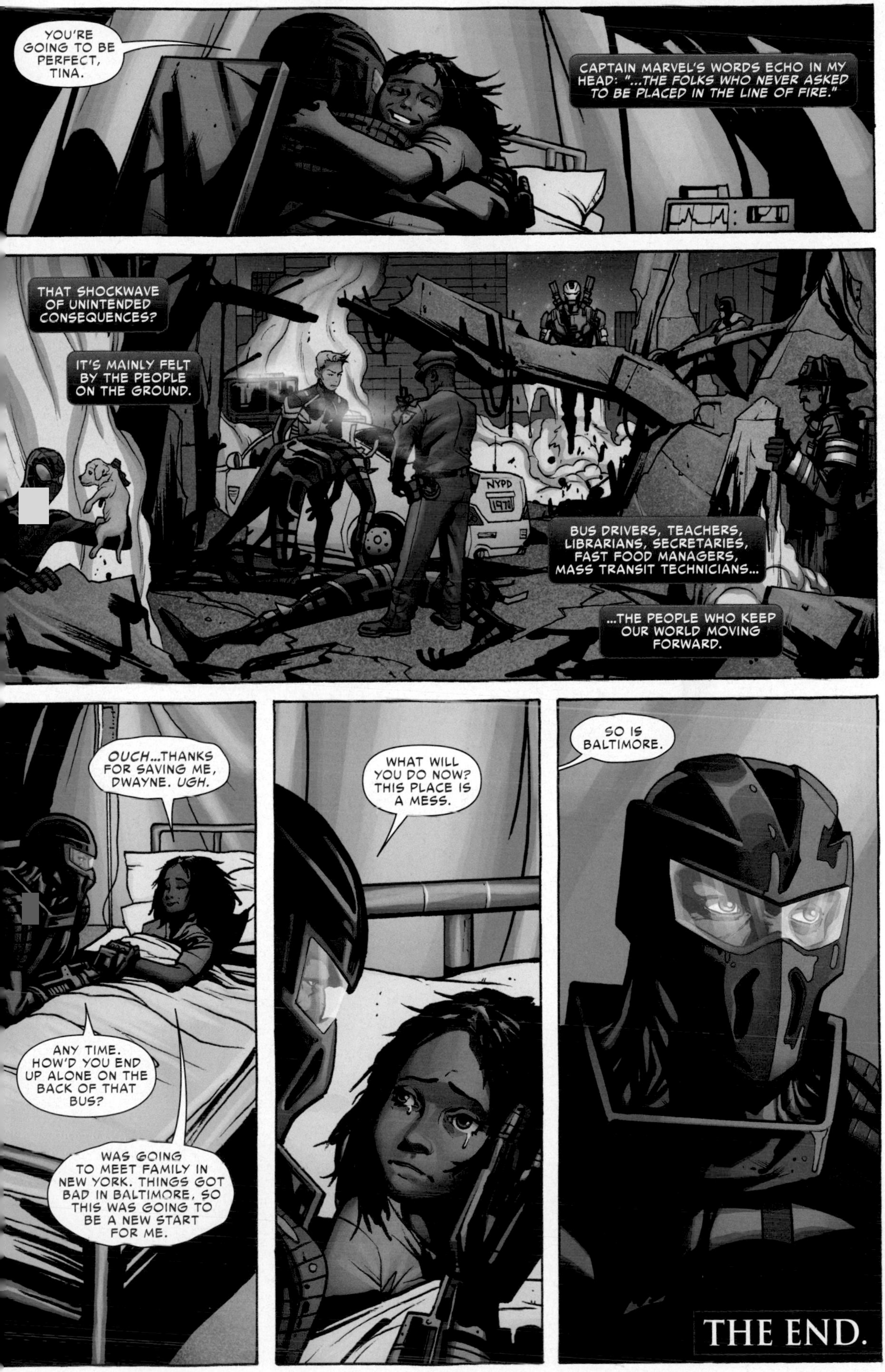
YOU'RE GOING TO BE PERFECT, TINA.
CAPTAIN MARVEL'S WORDS ECHO IN MY HEAD: "...THE FOLKS WHO NEVER ASKED TO BE PLACED IN THE LINE OF FIRE."
THAT SHOCKWAVE OF UNINTENDED CONSEQUENCES?
IT'S MAINLY FELT BY THE PEOPLE ON THE GROUND.
NYPD
BUS DRIVERS, TEACHERS, LIBRARIANS, SECRETARIES, FAST FOOD MANAGERS, MASS TRANSIT TECHNICIANS...
...THE PEOPLE WHO KEEP OUR WORLD MOVING FORWARD.
OUCH...THANKS FOR SAVING ME, DWAYNE. UGH.
ANY TIME. HOW'D YOU END UP ALONE ON THE BACK OF THAT BUS?
WAS GOING TO MEET FAMILY IN NEW YORK. THINGS GOT BAD IN BALTIMORE, SO THIS WAS GOING TO BE A NEW START FOR ME.
WHAT WILL YOU DO NOW? THIS PLACE IS A MESS.
SO IS BALTIMORE.
THE END.

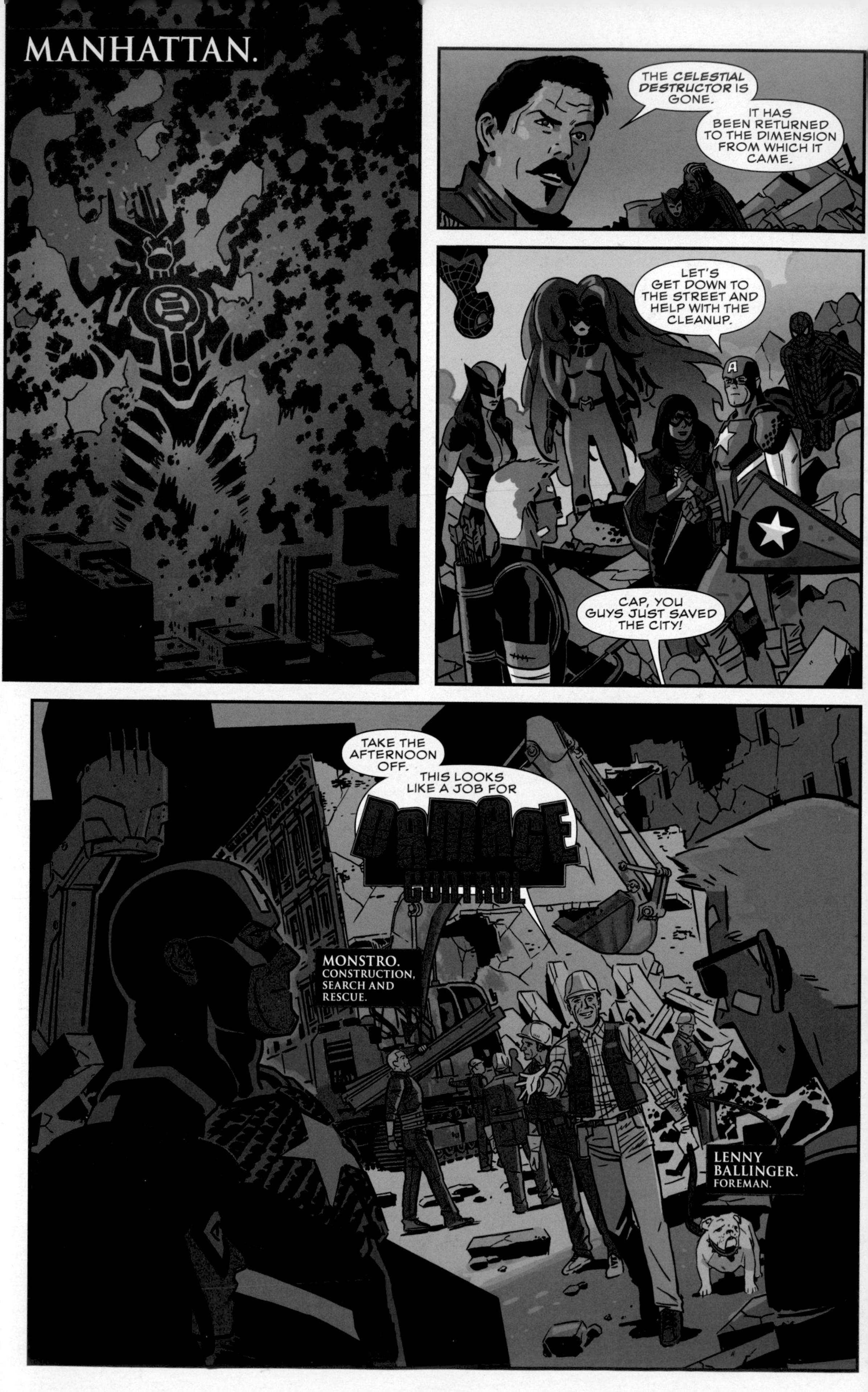
MANHATTAN.
THE CELESTIAL DESTRUCTOR IS GONE.
IT HAS BEEN RETURNED TO THE DIMENSION FROM WHICH IT CAME.
LET'S GET DOWN TO THE STREET AND HELP WITH THE CLEANUP.
CAP, YOU GUYS JUST SAVED THE CITY!
TAKE THE AFTERNOON OFF.
THIS LOOKS LIKE A JOB FOR
DAMAGE CONTROL
MONSTRO.
CONSTRUCTION, SEARCH AND RESCUE.
LENNY BALLINGER.
FOREMAN.

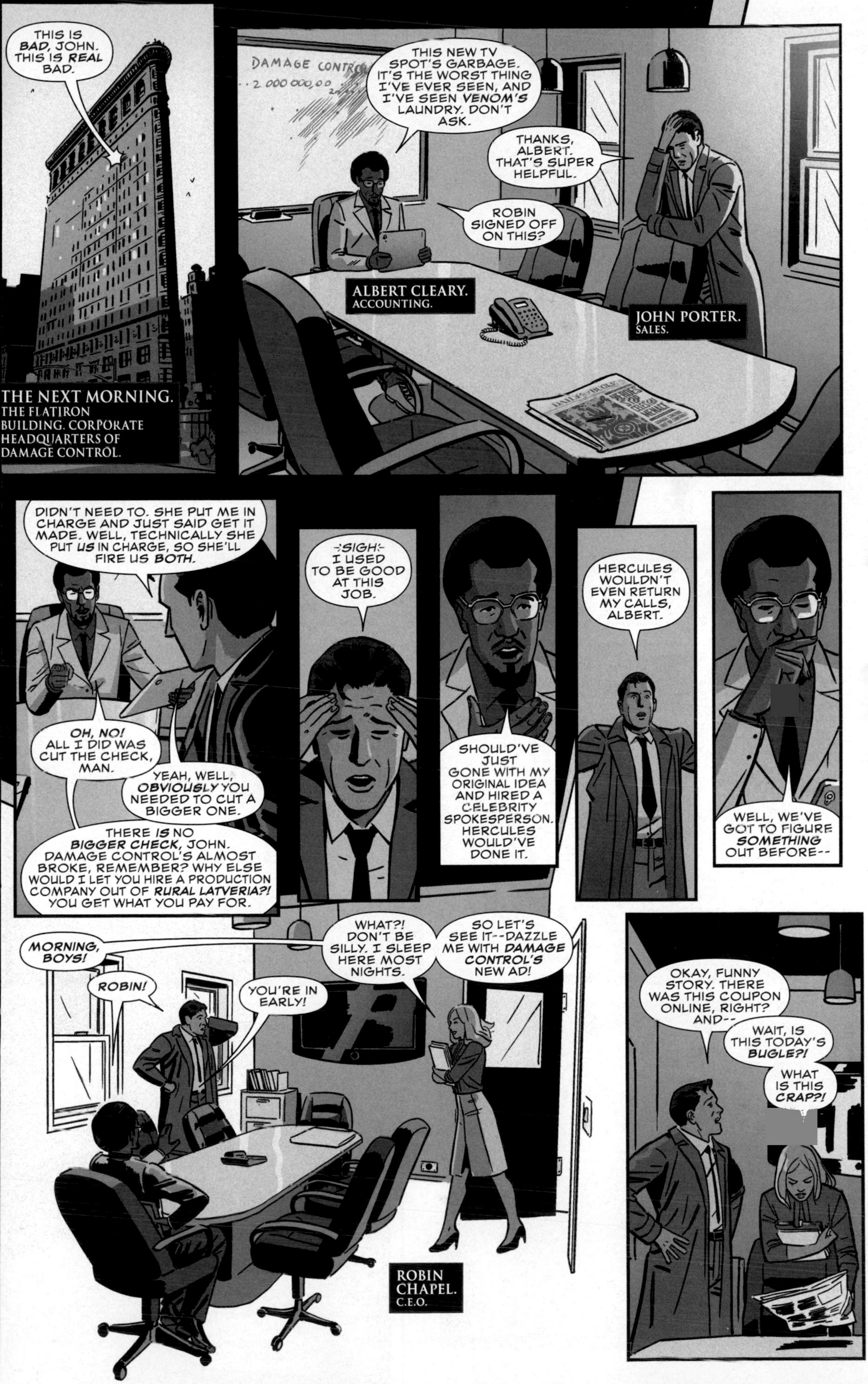
THIS IS BAD, JOHN. THIS IS REAL BAD.
THE NEXT MORNING. THE FLATIRON BUILDING. CORPORATE HEADQUARTERS OF DAMAGE CONTROL.
THIS NEW TV SPOT'S GARBAGE. IT'S THE WORST THING I'VE EVER SEEN, AND I'VE SEEN VENOM'S LAUNDRY. DON'T ASK.
THANKS, ALBERT. THAT'S SUPER HELPFUL.
ROBIN SIGNED OFF ON THIS?
ALBERT CLEARY. ACCOUNTING.
JOHN PORTER. SALES.
DIDN'T NEED TO. SHE PUT ME IN CHARGE AND JUST SAID GET IT MADE. WELL, TECHNICALLY SHE PUT US IN CHARGE, SO SHE'LL FIRE US BOTH.
OH, NO! ALL I DID WAS CUT THE CHECK, MAN.
YEAH, WELL, OBVIOUSLY YOU NEEDED TO CUT A BIGGER ONE.
THERE IS NO BIGGER CHECK, JOHN. DAMAGE CONTROL'S ALMOST BROKE, REMEMBER? WHY ELSE WOULD I LET YOU HIRE A PRODUCTION COMPANY OUT OF RURAL LATVERIA?! YOU GET WHAT YOU PAY FOR.
-SIGH- I USED TO BE GOOD AT THIS JOB.
SHOULD'VE JUST GONE WITH MY ORIGINAL IDEA AND HIRED A CELEBRITY SPOKESPERSON. HERCULES WOULD'VE DONE IT.
HERCULES WOULDN'T EVEN RETURN MY CALLS, ALBERT.
WELL, WE'VE GOT TO FIGURE SOMETHING OUT BEFORE--
MORNING, BOYS!
ROBIN!
YOU'RE IN EARLY!
WHAT?! DON'T BE SILLY. I SLEEP HERE MOST NIGHTS.
SO LET'S SEE IT--DAZZLE ME WITH DAMAGE CONTROL'S NEW AD!
ROBIN CHAPEL. C.E.O.
OKAY, FUNNY STORY. THERE WAS THIS COUPON ONLINE, RIGHT? AND--
WAIT, IS THIS TODAY'S BUGLE?!
WHAT IS THIS CRAP?!

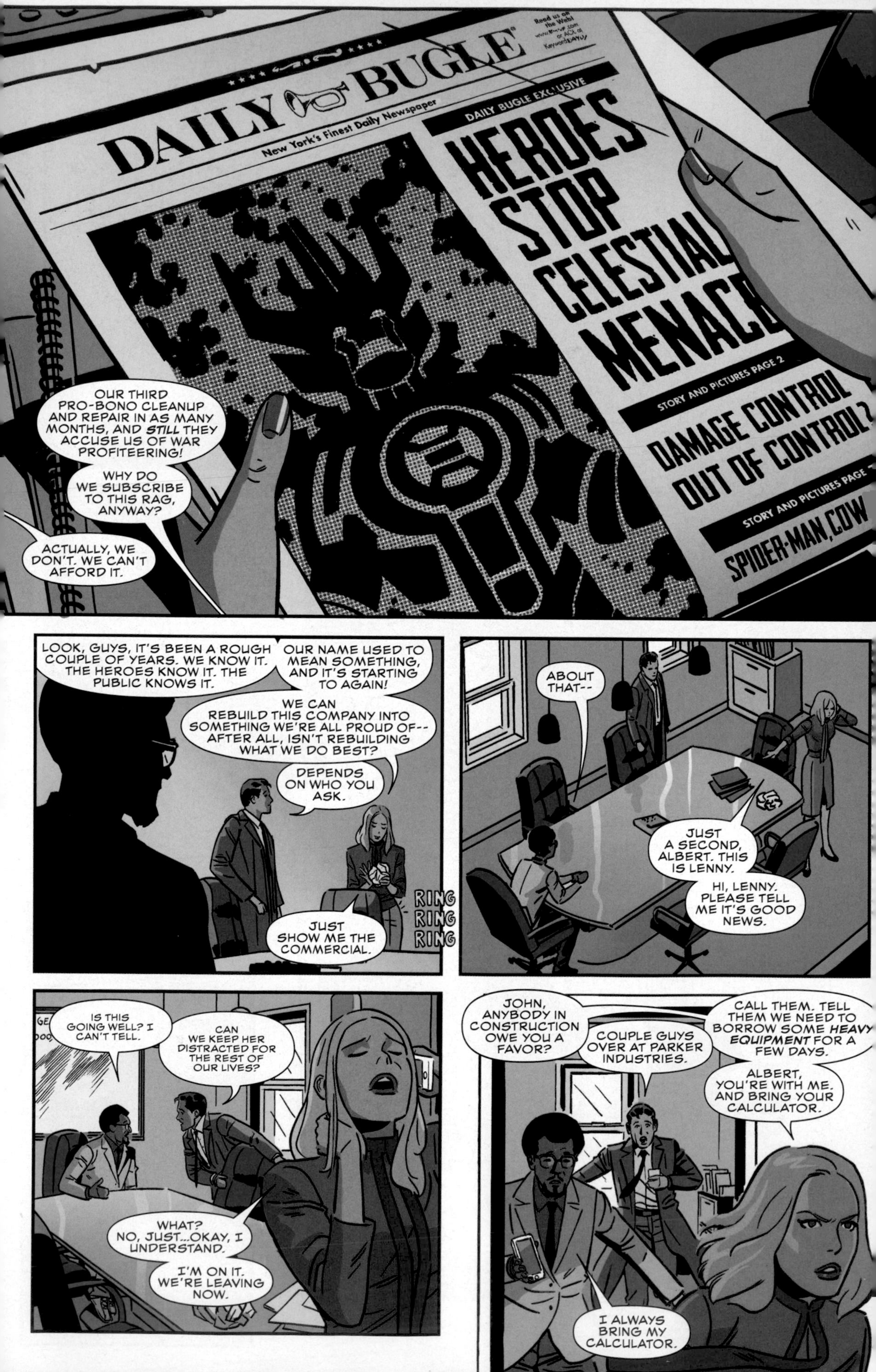
DAILY BUGLE
New York's Finest Daily Newspaper
DAILY BUGLE EXCLUSIVE
HEROES STOP CELESTIAL MENACE
STORY AND PICTURES PAGE 2
DAMAGE CONTROL OUT OF CONTROL?
STORY AND PICTURES PAGE
SPIDER-MAN, COW
OUR THIRD PRO-BONO CLEANUP AND REPAIR IN AS MANY MONTHS, AND STILL THEY ACCUSE US OF WAR PROFITEERING!
WHY DO WE SUBSCRIBE TO THIS RAG, ANYWAY?
ACTUALLY, WE DON'T. WE CAN'T AFFORD IT.
LOOK, GUYS, IT'S BEEN A ROUGH COUPLE OF YEARS. WE KNOW IT. THE HEROES KNOW IT. THE PUBLIC KNOWS IT.
OUR NAME USED TO MEAN SOMETHING, AND IT'S STARTING TO AGAIN!
WE CAN REBUILD THIS COMPANY INTO SOMETHING WE'RE ALL PROUD OF-- AFTER ALL, ISN'T REBUILDING WHAT WE DO BEST?
DEPENDS ON WHO YOU ASK.
JUST SHOW ME THE COMMERCIAL.
RING RING RING
ABOUT THAT--
JUST A SECOND, ALBERT. THIS IS LENNY.
HI, LENNY. PLEASE TELL ME IT'S GOOD NEWS.
IS THIS GOING WELL? I CAN'T TELL.
CAN WE KEEP HER DISTRACTED FOR THE REST OF OUR LIVES?
WHAT? NO, JUST...OKAY, I UNDERSTAND.
I'M ON IT. WE'RE LEAVING NOW.
JOHN, ANYBODY IN CONSTRUCTION OWE YOU A FAVOR?
COUPLE GUYS OVER AT PARKER INDUSTRIES.
CALL THEM. TELL THEM WE NEED TO BORROW SOME HEAVY EQUIPMENT FOR A FEW DAYS.
ALBERT, YOU'RE WITH ME. AND BRING YOUR CALCULATOR.
I ALWAYS BRING MY CALCULATOR.

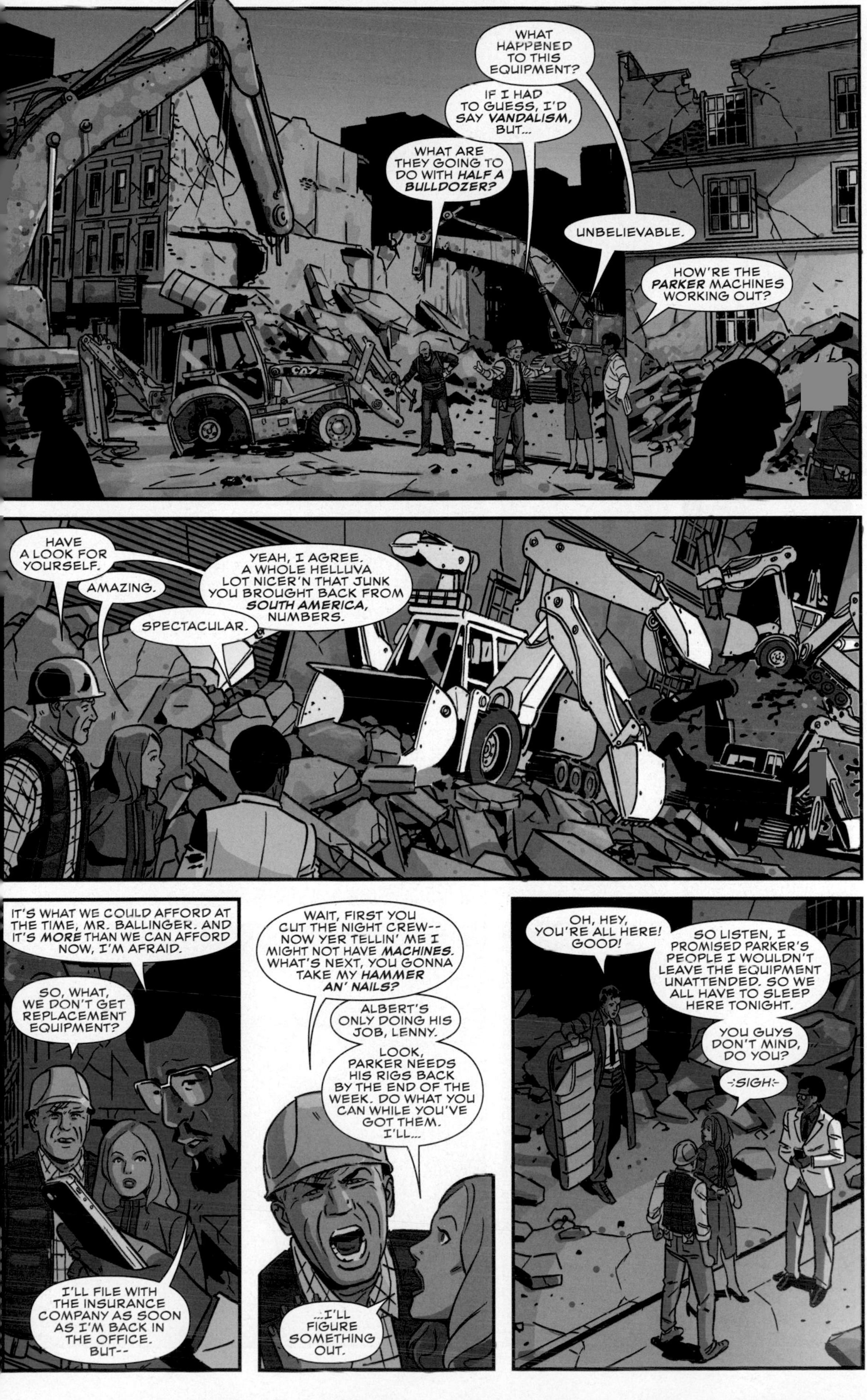
WHAT HAPPENED TO THIS EQUIPMENT?
IF I HAD TO GUESS, I'D SAY VANDALISM, BUT...
WHAT ARE THEY GOING TO DO WITH HALF A BULLDOZER?
UNBELIEVABLE.
HOW'RE THE PARKER MACHINES WORKING OUT?
HAVE A LOOK FOR YOURSELF.
AMAZING.
SPECTACULAR.
YEAH, I AGREE. A WHOLE HELLUVA LOT NICER'N THAT JUNK YOU BROUGHT BACK FROM SOUTH AMERICA, NUMBERS.
IT'S WHAT WE COULD AFFORD AT THE TIME, MR. BALLINGER. AND IT'S MORE THAN WE CAN AFFORD NOW, I'M AFRAID.
SO, WHAT, WE DON'T GET REPLACEMENT EQUIPMENT?
I'LL FILE WITH THE INSURANCE COMPANY AS SOON AS I'M BACK IN THE OFFICE. BUT--
WAIT, FIRST YOU CUT THE NIGHT CREW-- NOW YER TELLIN' ME I MIGHT NOT HAVE MACHINES. WHAT'S NEXT, YOU GONNA TAKE MY HAMMER AN' NAILS?
ALBERT'S ONLY DOING HIS JOB, LENNY.
LOOK, PARKER NEEDS HIS RIGS BACK BY THE END OF THE WEEK. DO WHAT YOU CAN WHILE YOU'VE GOT THEM. I'LL...
...I'LL FIGURE SOMETHING OUT.
OH, HEY, YOU'RE ALL HERE! GOOD!
SO LISTEN, I PROMISED PARKER'S PEOPLE I WOULDN'T LEAVE THE EQUIPMENT UNATTENDED. SO WE ALL HAVE TO SLEEP HERE TONIGHT.
YOU GUYS DON'T MIND, DO YOU?
-SIGH-

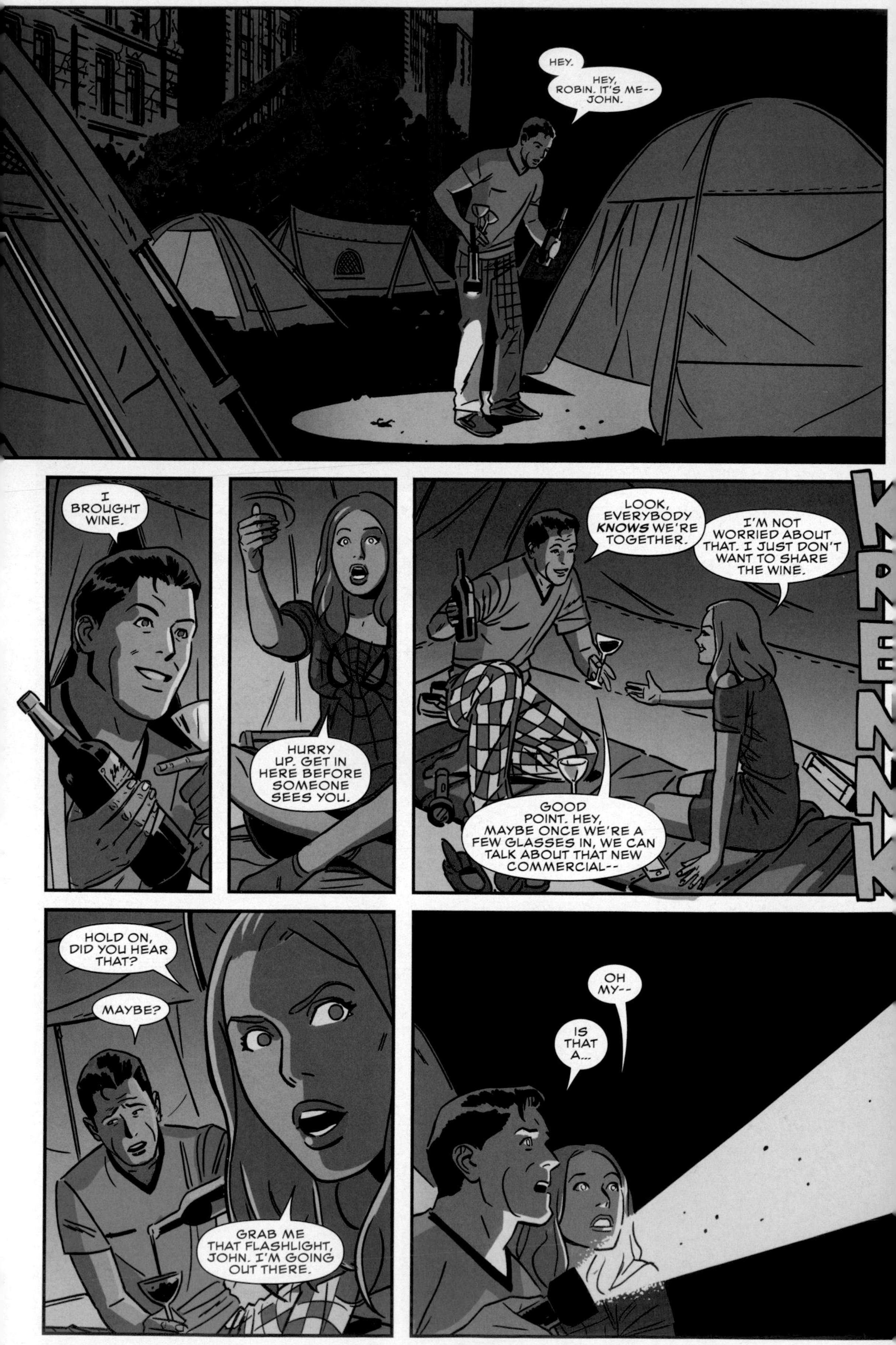
HEY.
HEY, ROBIN. IT'S ME-- JOHN.
I BROUGHT WINE.
HURRY UP. GET IN HERE BEFORE SOMEONE SEES YOU.
LOOK, EVERYBODY KNOWS WE'RE TOGETHER.
I'M NOT WORRIED ABOUT THAT. I JUST DON'T WANT TO SHARE THE WINE.
GOOD POINT. HEY, MAYBE ONCE WE'RE A FEW GLASSES IN, WE CAN TALK ABOUT THAT NEW COMMERCIAL--
KRENNK
HOLD ON, DID YOU HEAR THAT?
MAYBE?
GRAB ME THAT FLASHLIGHT, JOHN. I'M GOING OUT THERE.
OH MY--
IS THAT A...

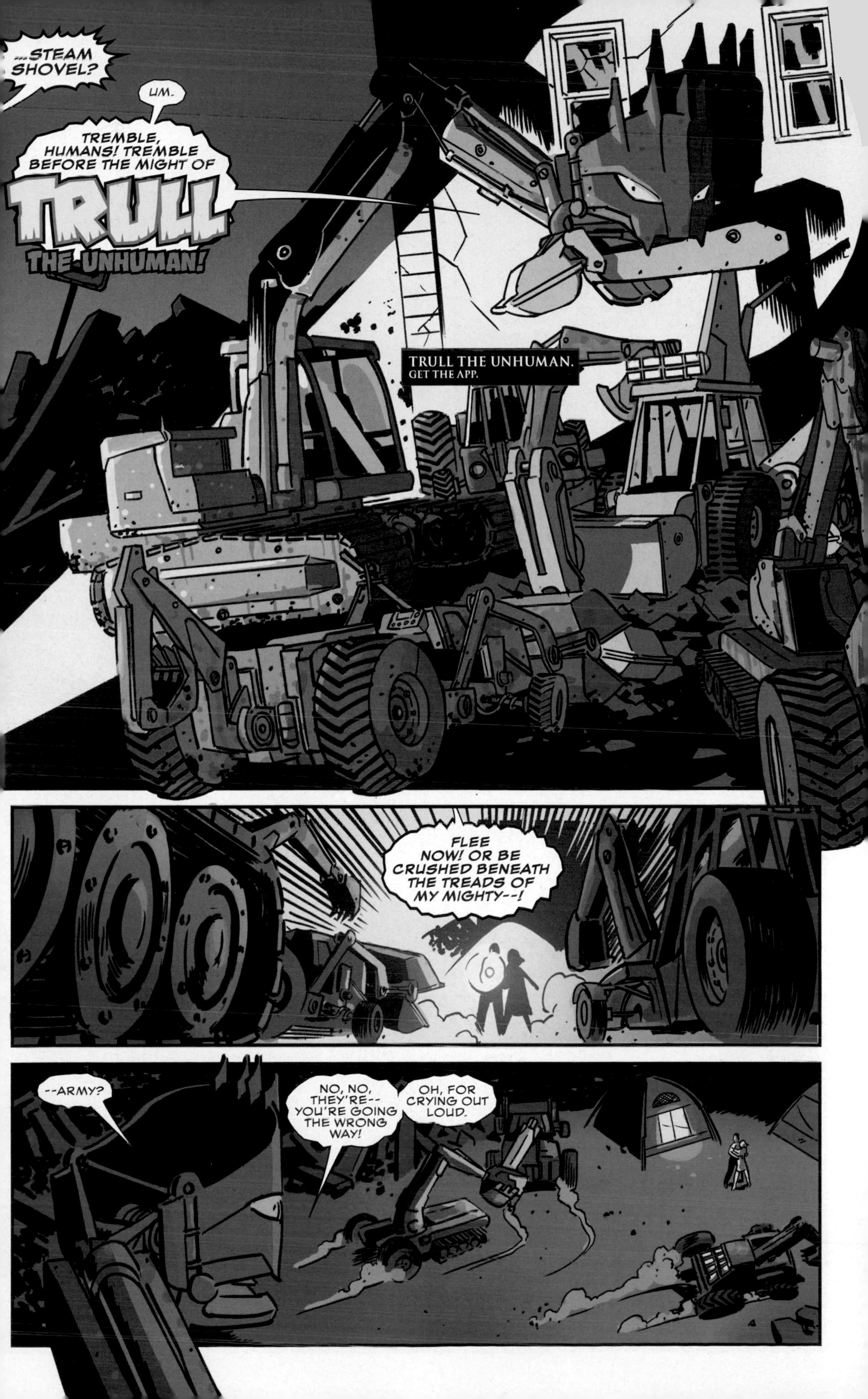
...STEAM SHOVEL?
UM.
TREMBLE, HUMANS! TREMBLE BEFORE THE MIGHT OF
TRULL
THE UNHUMAN!
TRULL THE UNHUMAN.
GET THE APP.
FLEE NOW! OR BE CRUSHED BENEATH THE TREADS OF MY MIGHTY--!
--ARMY?
NO, NO, THEY'RE-- YOU'RE GOING THE WRONG WAY!
OH, FOR CRYING OUT LOUD.

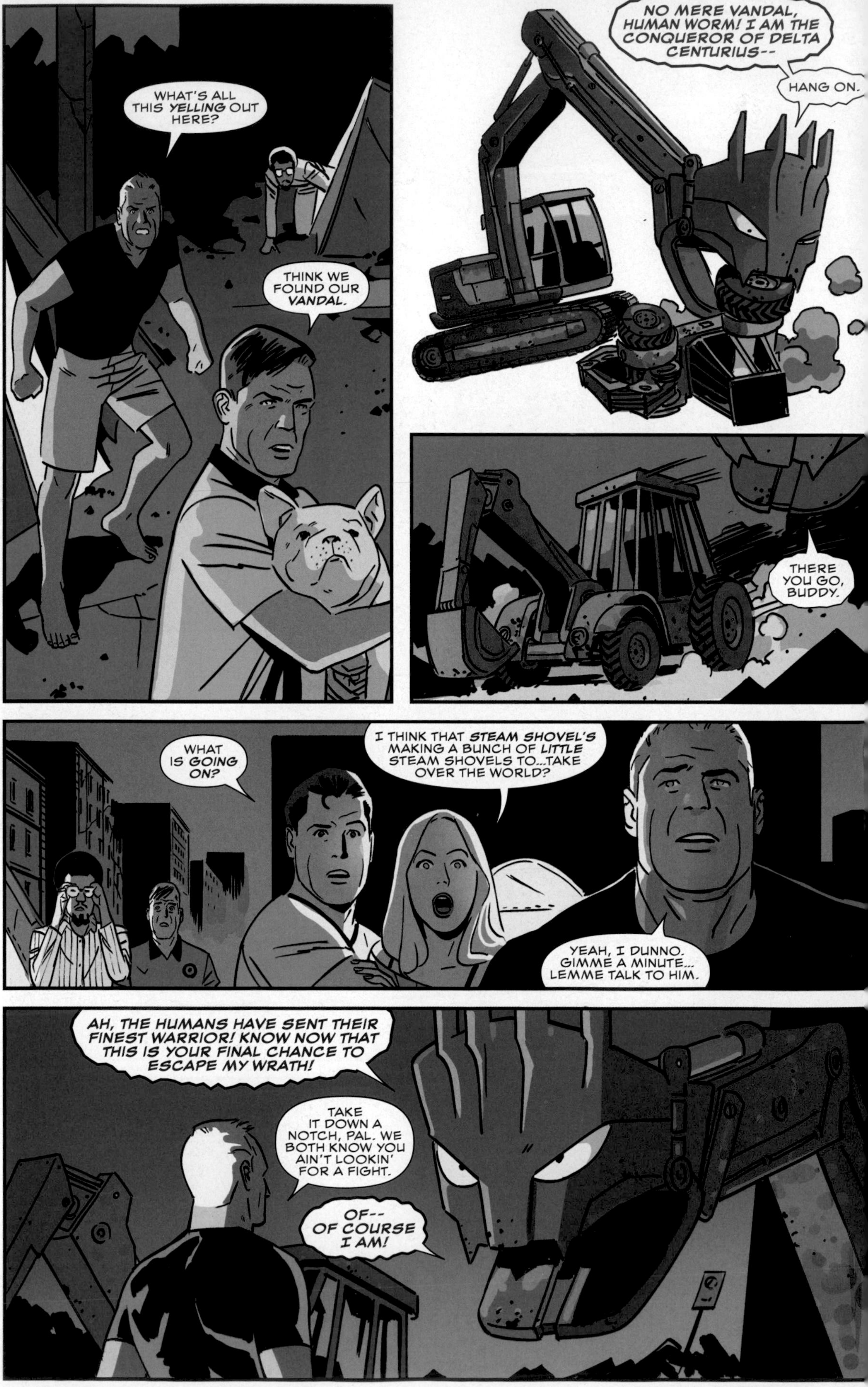
WHAT'S ALL THIS YELLING OUT HERE?
THINK WE FOUND OUR VANDAL.
NO MERE VANDAL, HUMAN WORM! I AM THE CONQUEROR OF DELTA CENTURIUS--
HANG ON.
THERE YOU GO, BUDDY.
WHAT IS GOING ON?
I THINK THAT STEAM SHOVEL'S MAKING A BUNCH OF LITTLE STEAM SHOVELS TO...TAKE OVER THE WORLD?
YEAH, I DUNNO. GIMME A MINUTE... LEMME TALK TO HIM.
AH, THE HUMANS HAVE SENT THEIR FINEST WARRIOR! KNOW NOW THAT THIS IS YOUR FINAL CHANCE TO ESCAPE MY WRATH!
TAKE IT DOWN A NOTCH, PAL. WE BOTH KNOW YOU AIN'T LOOKIN' FOR A FIGHT.
OF-- OF COURSE I AM!

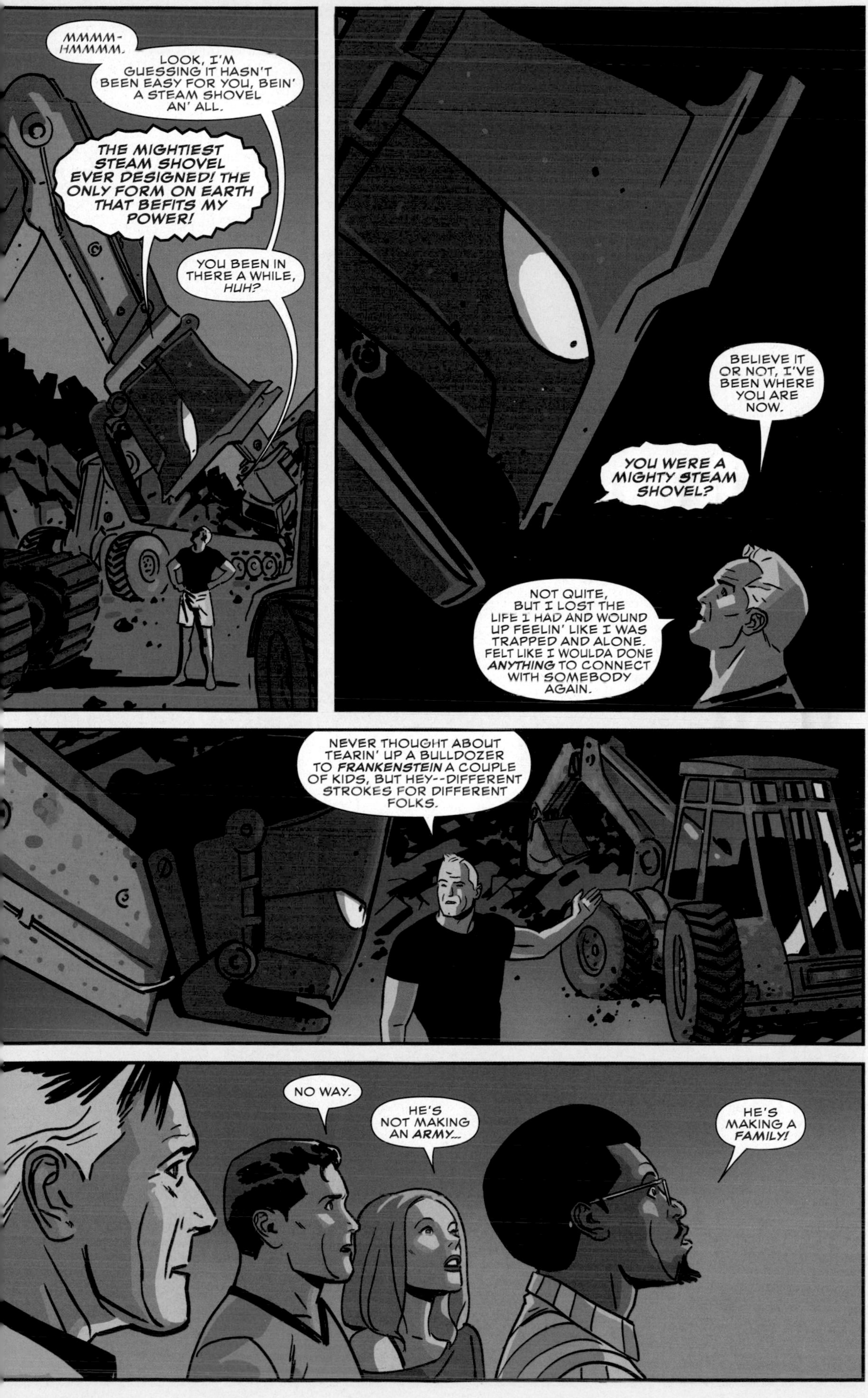
MMMM-HMMMM.
LOOK, I'M GUESSING IT HASN'T BEEN EASY FOR YOU, BEIN' A STEAM SHOVEL AN' ALL.
THE MIGHTIEST STEAM SHOVEL EVER DESIGNED! THE ONLY FORM ON EARTH THAT BEFITS MY POWER!
YOU BEEN IN THERE A WHILE, HUH?
BELIEVE IT OR NOT, I'VE BEEN WHERE YOU ARE NOW.
YOU WERE A MIGHTY STEAM SHOVEL?
NOT QUITE, BUT I LOST THE LIFE I HAD AND WOUND UP FEELIN' LIKE I WAS TRAPPED AND ALONE. FELT LIKE I WOULDA DONE ANYTHING TO CONNECT WITH SOMEBODY AGAIN.
NEVER THOUGHT ABOUT TEARIN' UP A BULLDOZER TO FRANKENSTEIN A COUPLE OF KIDS, BUT HEY--DIFFERENT STROKES FOR DIFFERENT FOLKS.
NO WAY.
HE'S NOT MAKING AN ARMY...
HE'S MAKING A FAMILY!

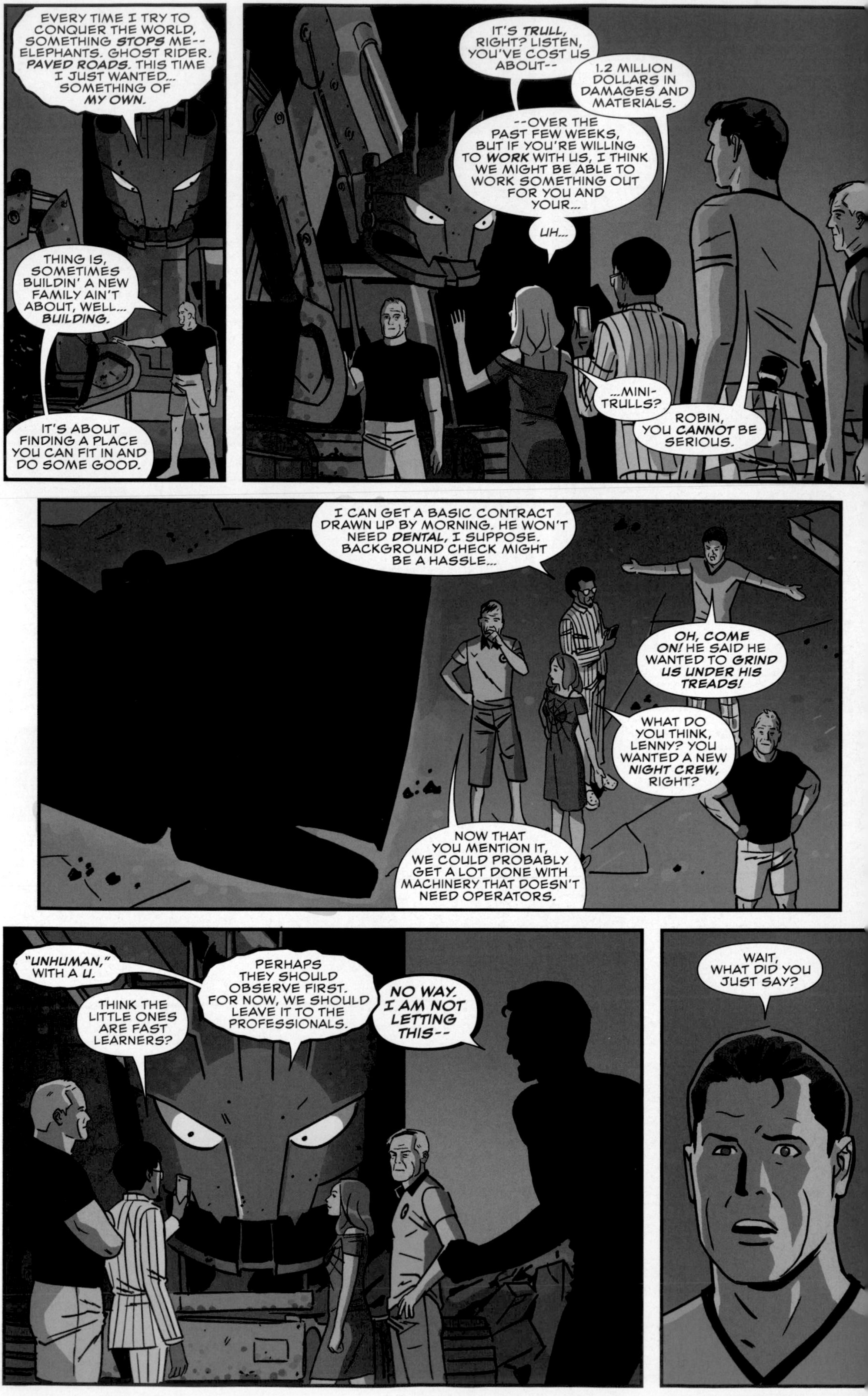
EVERY TIME I TRY TO CONQUER THE WORLD, SOMETHING STOPS ME-- ELEPHANTS. GHOST RIDER. PAVED ROADS. THIS TIME I JUST WANTED... SOMETHING OF MY OWN.
THING IS, SOMETIMES BUILDIN' A NEW FAMILY AIN'T ABOUT, WELL... BUILDING.
IT'S ABOUT FINDING A PLACE YOU CAN FIT IN AND DO SOME GOOD.
IT'S TRULL, RIGHT? LISTEN, YOU'VE COST US ABOUT--
1.2 MILLION DOLLARS IN DAMAGES AND MATERIALS.
--OVER THE PAST FEW WEEKS, BUT IF YOU'RE WILLING TO WORK WITH US, I THINK WE MIGHT BE ABLE TO WORK SOMETHING OUT FOR YOU AND YOUR...
UH...
...MINI-TRULLS?
ROBIN, YOU CANNOT BE SERIOUS.
I CAN GET A BASIC CONTRACT DRAWN UP BY MORNING. HE WON'T NEED DENTAL, I SUPPOSE. BACKGROUND CHECK MIGHT BE A HASSLE...
OH, COME ON! HE SAID HE WANTED TO GRIND US UNDER HIS TREADS!
WHAT DO YOU THINK, LENNY? YOU WANTED A NEW NIGHT CREW, RIGHT?
NOW THAT YOU MENTION IT, WE COULD PROBABLY GET A LOT DONE WITH MACHINERY THAT DOESN'T NEED OPERATORS.
"UNHUMAN," WITH A U.
THINK THE LITTLE ONES ARE FAST LEARNERS?
PERHAPS THEY SHOULD OBSERVE FIRST. FOR NOW, WE SHOULD LEAVE IT TO THE PROFESSIONALS.
NO WAY. I AM NOT LETTING THIS--
WAIT, WHAT DID YOU JUST SAY?

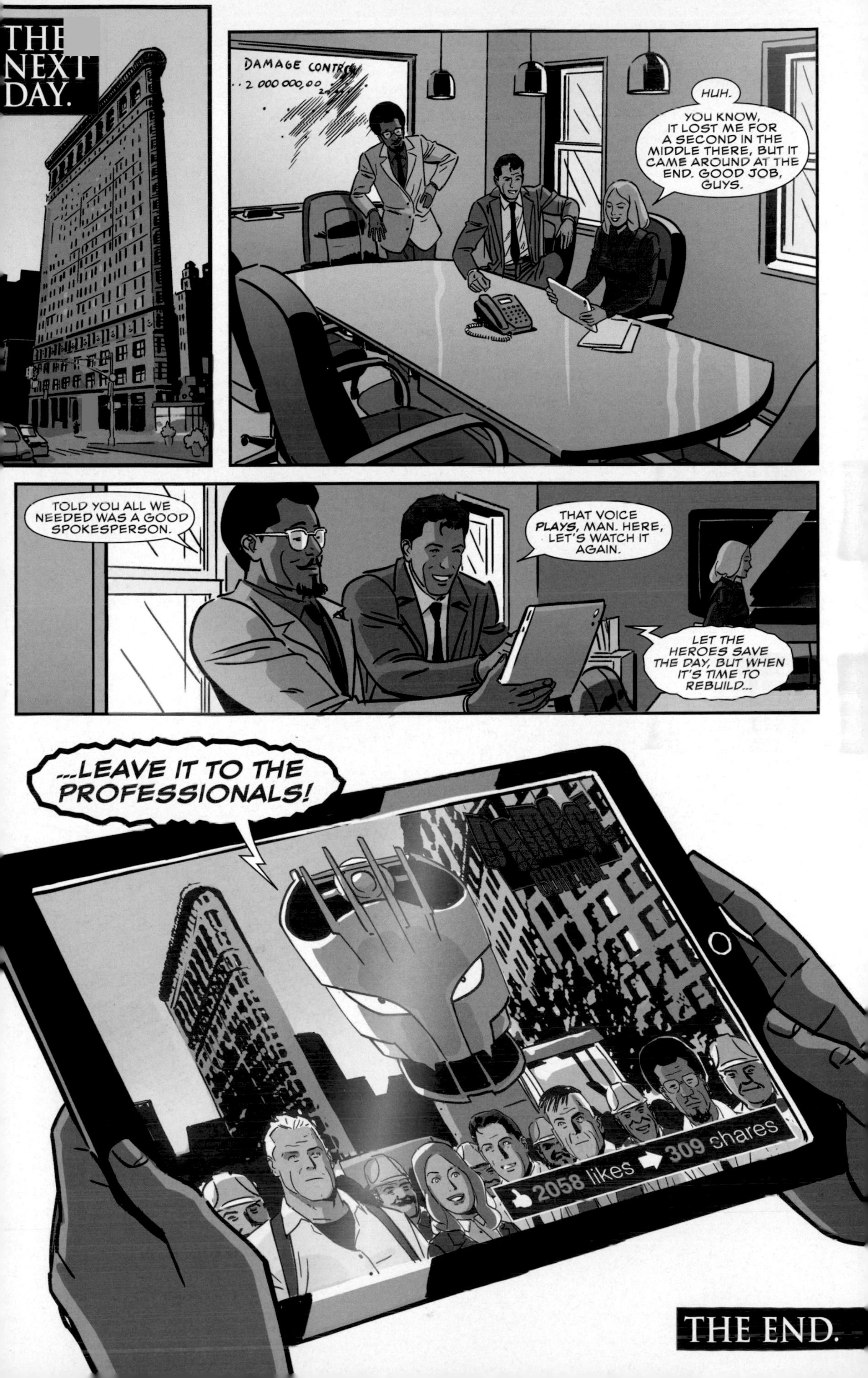
THE NEXT DAY.
HUH.
YOU KNOW, IT LOST ME FOR A SECOND IN THE MIDDLE THERE, BUT IT CAME AROUND AT THE END. GOOD JOB, GUYS.
TOLD YOU ALL WE NEEDED WAS A GOOD SPOKESPERSON.
THAT VOICE *PLAYS*, MAN. HERE, LET'S WATCH IT AGAIN.
LET THE HEROES SAVE THE DAY, BUT WHEN IT'S TIME TO REBUILD...
...LEAVE IT TO THE PROFESSIONALS!
2058 likes
309 shares
THE END.

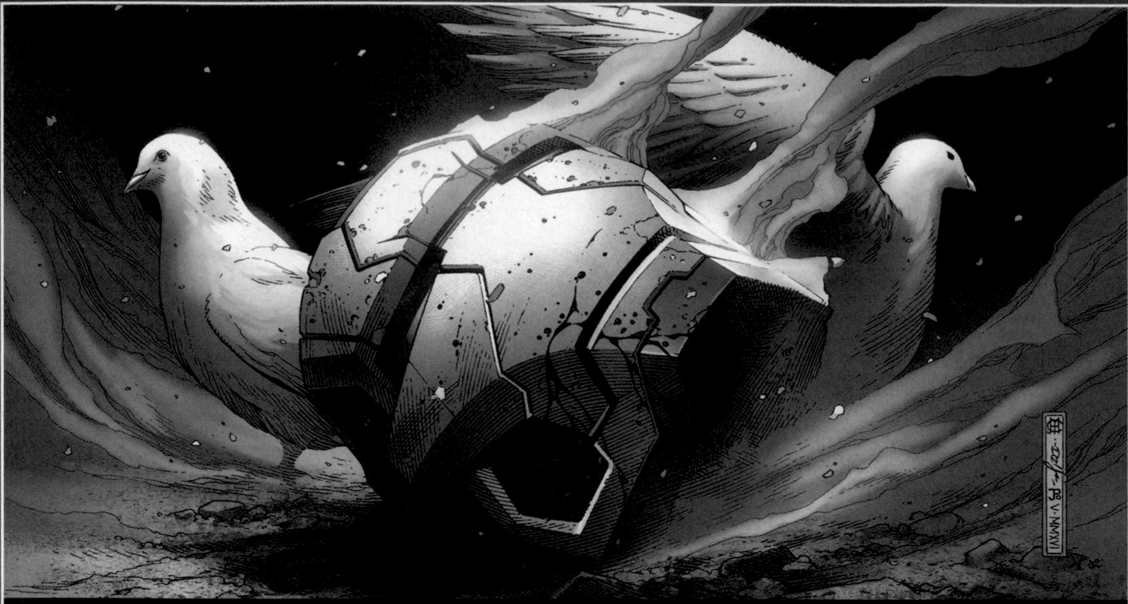

COVER ART BY JIM CHEUNG & JUSTIN PONSOR

# WAR MACHINE

WRITER
JEREMY WHITLEY

ARTIST
MARGUERITE SAUVAGE

ASSISTANT EDITOR
CHARLES BEACHAM

EDITOR
WIL MOSS

# GOLIATH

WRITER
BRANDON THOMAS

ARTIST
MARCO RUDY

EDITOR
CHRIS ROBINSON

COVER ART BY DECLAN SHALVEY & JORDIE BELLAIRE

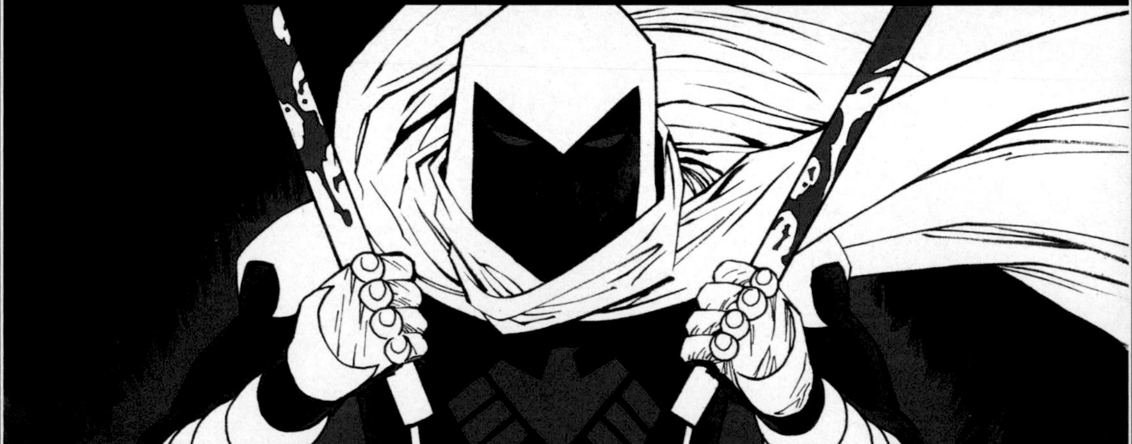

# II

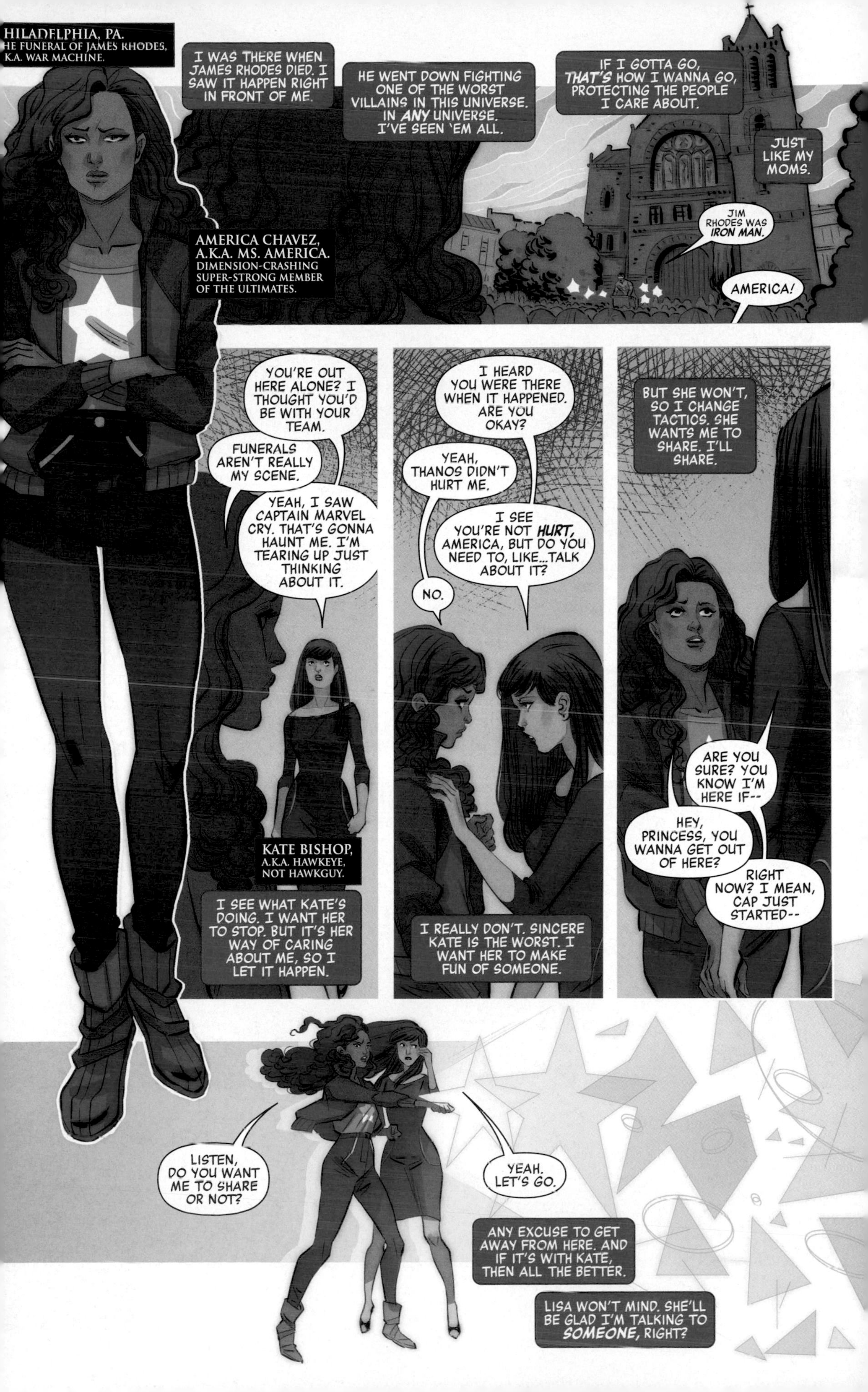
HILADELPHIA, PA.
HE FUNERAL OF JAMES RHODES, K.A. WAR MACHINE.
I WAS THERE WHEN JAMES RHODES DIED. I SAW IT HAPPEN RIGHT IN FRONT OF ME.
HE WENT DOWN FIGHTING ONE OF THE WORST VILLAINS IN THIS UNIVERSE. IN ANY UNIVERSE. I'VE SEEN 'EM ALL.
IF I GOTTA GO, THAT'S HOW I WANNA GO, PROTECTING THE PEOPLE I CARE ABOUT.
JUST LIKE MY MOMS.
JIM RHODES WAS IRON MAN.
AMERICA CHAVEZ, A.K.A. MS. AMERICA. DIMENSION-CRASHING SUPER-STRONG MEMBER OF THE ULTIMATES.
AMERICA!
YOU'RE OUT HERE ALONE? I THOUGHT YOU'D BE WITH YOUR TEAM.
FUNERALS AREN'T REALLY MY SCENE.
YEAH, I SAW CAPTAIN MARVEL CRY. THAT'S GONNA HAUNT ME. I'M TEARING UP JUST THINKING ABOUT IT.
KATE BISHOP, A.K.A. HAWKEYE, NOT HAWKGUY.
I SEE WHAT KATE'S DOING. I WANT HER TO STOP. BUT IT'S HER WAY OF CARING ABOUT ME, SO I LET IT HAPPEN.
I HEARD YOU WERE THERE WHEN IT HAPPENED. ARE YOU OKAY?
YEAH, THANOS DIDN'T HURT ME.
I SEE YOU'RE NOT HURT, AMERICA, BUT DO YOU NEED TO, LIKE...TALK ABOUT IT?
NO.
I REALLY DON'T. SINCERE KATE IS THE WORST. I WANT HER TO MAKE FUN OF SOMEONE.
BUT SHE WON'T, SO I CHANGE TACTICS. SHE WANTS ME TO SHARE. I'LL SHARE.
ARE YOU SURE? YOU KNOW I'M HERE IF--
HEY, PRINCESS, YOU WANNA GET OUT OF HERE?
RIGHT NOW? I MEAN, CAP JUST STARTED--
LISTEN, DO YOU WANT ME TO SHARE OR NOT?
YEAH. LET'S GO.
ANY EXCUSE TO GET AWAY FROM HERE. AND IF IT'S WITH KATE, THEN ALL THE BETTER.
LISA WON'T MIND. SHE'LL BE GLAD I'M TALKING TO SOMEONE, RIGHT?

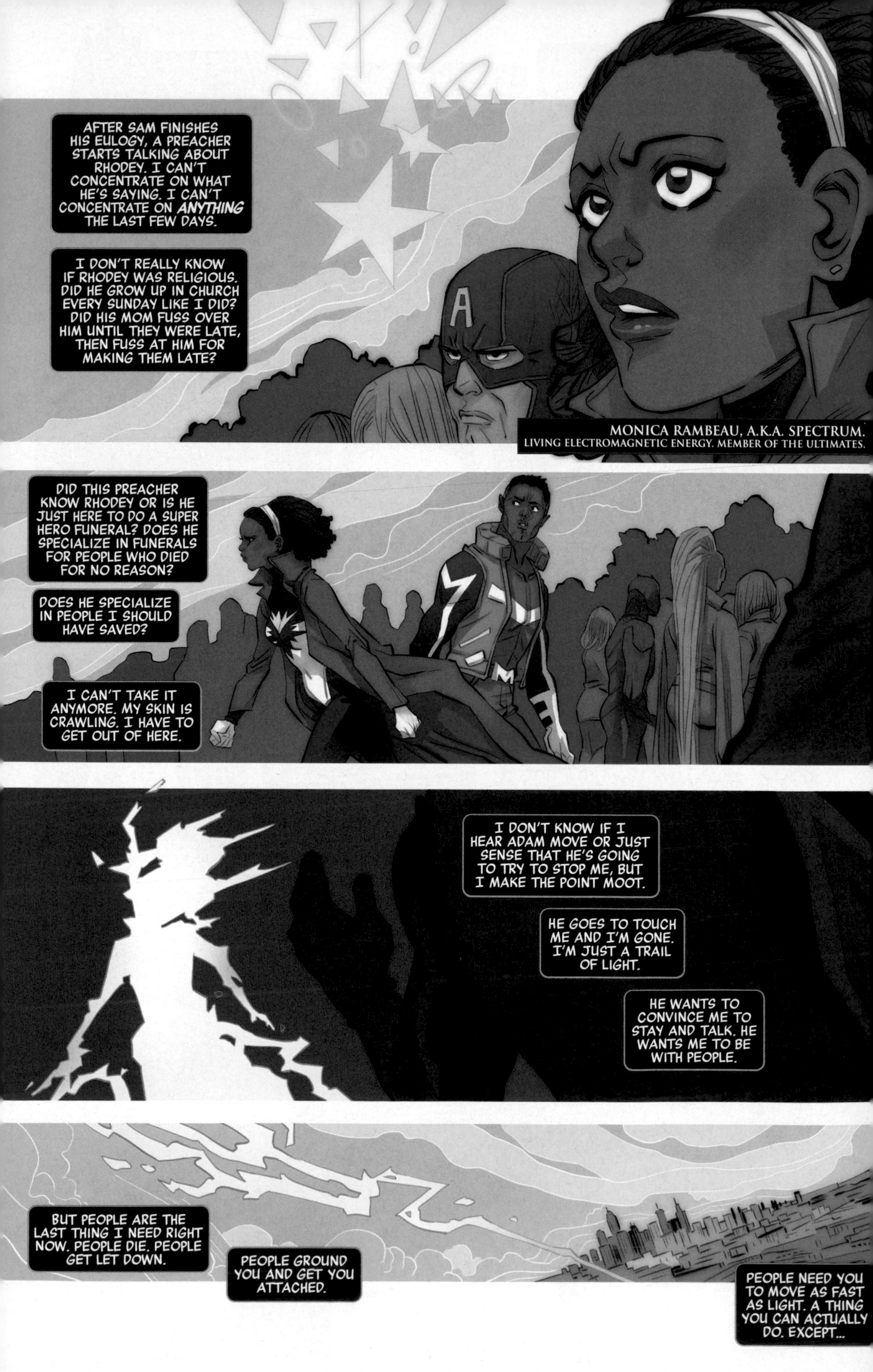
AFTER SAM FINISHES HIS EULOGY, A PREACHER STARTS TALKING ABOUT RHODEY. I CAN'T CONCENTRATE ON WHAT HE'S SAYING. I CAN'T CONCENTRATE ON *ANYTHING* THE LAST FEW DAYS.
I DON'T REALLY KNOW IF RHODEY WAS RELIGIOUS. DID HE GROW UP IN CHURCH EVERY SUNDAY LIKE I DID? DID HIS MOM FUSS OVER HIM UNTIL THEY WERE LATE, THEN FUSS AT HIM FOR MAKING THEM LATE?
MONICA RAMBEAU, A.K.A. SPECTRUM.
LIVING ELECTROMAGNETIC ENERGY. MEMBER OF THE ULTIMATES.
DID THIS PREACHER KNOW RHODEY OR IS HE JUST HERE TO DO A SUPER HERO FUNERAL? DOES HE SPECIALIZE IN FUNERALS FOR PEOPLE WHO DIED FOR NO REASON?
DOES HE SPECIALIZE IN PEOPLE I SHOULD HAVE SAVED?
I CAN'T TAKE IT ANYMORE. MY SKIN IS CRAWLING. I HAVE TO GET OUT OF HERE.
I DON'T KNOW IF I HEAR ADAM MOVE OR JUST SENSE THAT HE'S GOING TO TRY TO STOP ME, BUT I MAKE THE POINT MOOT.
HE GOES TO TOUCH ME AND I'M GONE. I'M JUST A TRAIL OF LIGHT.
HE WANTS TO CONVINCE ME TO STAY AND TALK. HE WANTS ME TO BE WITH PEOPLE.
BUT PEOPLE ARE THE LAST THING I NEED RIGHT NOW. PEOPLE DIE. PEOPLE GET LET DOWN.
PEOPLE GROUND YOU AND GET YOU ATTACHED.
PEOPLE NEED YOU TO MOVE AS FAST AS LIGHT. A THING YOU CAN ACTUALLY DO. EXCEPT...

...NOT WHEN THEY NEED YOU TO. NOT WHEN THEY'RE RIGHT IN FRONT OF YOU AND THEY'RE ABOUT TO DIE AND YOU COULD SAVE THEM.
BUT YOU DON'T MOVE FAST ENOUGH. YOU DON'T SAVE RHODEY. YOU DIDN'T SAVE MARRINA ALL THOSE YEARS AGO. HOW MANY SINCE THEN? YOU HAD A CHANCE TO SAVE YOUR ENTIRE WORLD AND YOU COULDN'T.
WHEN WILL IT END?
WHEN WILL WE STOP LOSING?
WHEN WILL I STOP LETTING PEOPLE DIE THAT I CAN SAVE?
I COULD DO IT NOW. I COULD END IT. IT WOULD BE SO EASY.
I DON'T TELL PEOPLE THIS BECAUSE I DON'T WANT THEM TRYING TO FIX ME, BUT...
I HAVE TO WILL MYSELF TO STAY TOGETHER THESE DAYS.
I'VE SPENT SO MUCH TIME AS ENERGY, IF I DON'T CONCENTRATE I FIND MYSELF FADING AWAY.
I COULD STOP FIGHTING IT. I COULD HELP IT ALONG. I COULD LET THE LIGHT DISSIPATE.
JUST LET MONICA RAMBEAU FADE OUT OF EXISTENCE LIKE THE LIGHT OF A SETTING SUN.
BUT I WON'T. NOT TODAY.
THAT'S NOT WHO I AM. I DON'T KNOW WHO I AM HALF THE TIME, BUT I KNOW IT'S NOT THAT.
THIS ISN'T THE END OF MONICA RAMBEAU'S STORY. THIS IS THE END OF THE STORY OF JAMES RHODES.
I'M SORRY I COULDN'T SAVE YOU, JAMES, BUT I'LL GET BETTER.
AND I'LL SAVE THE NEXT ONE. I SWEAR I WILL.
BETTER GET TO THE BAR BEFORE PEOPLE MISS ME.

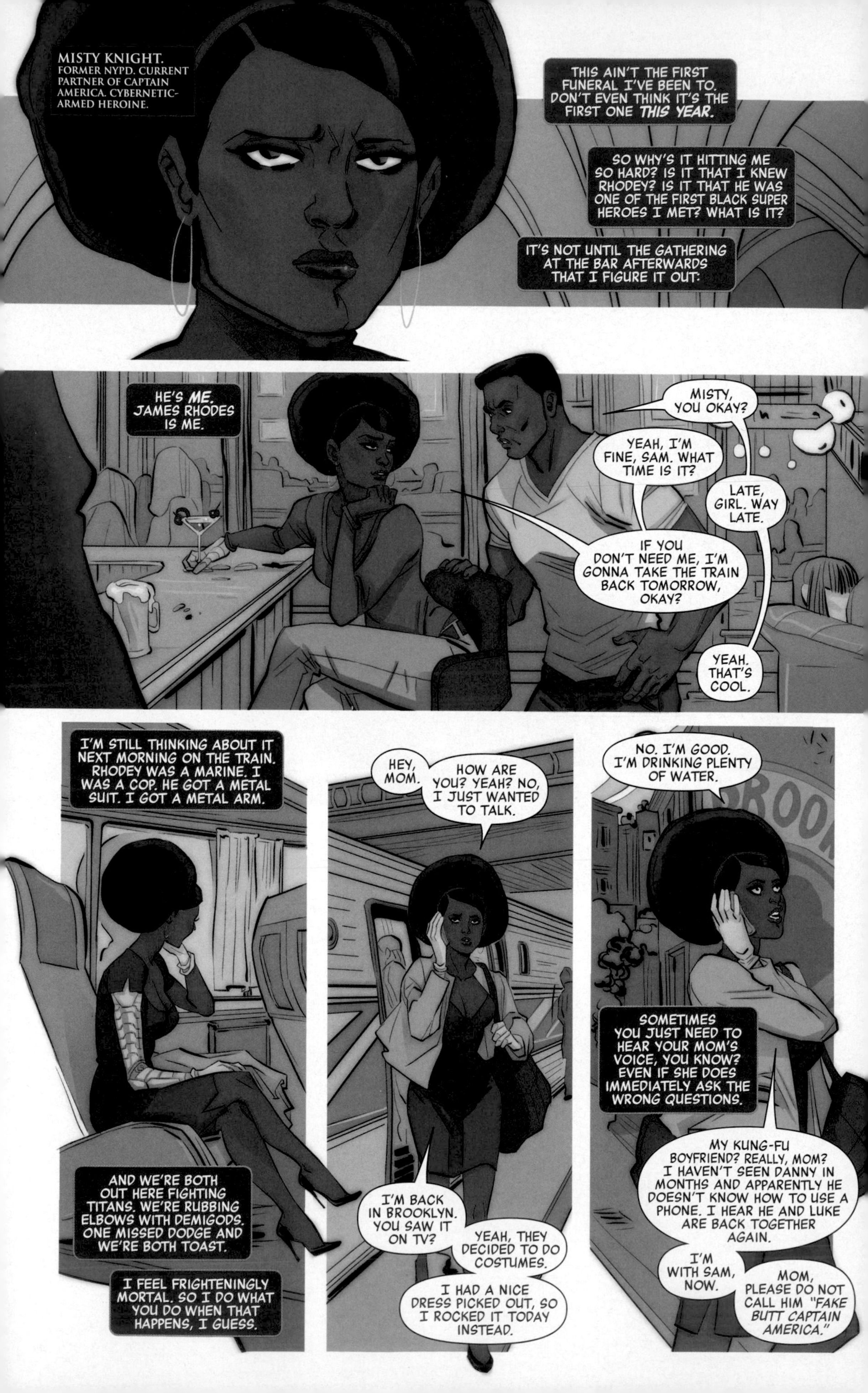

MISTY KNIGHT. FORMER NYPD. CURRENT PARTNER OF CAPTAIN AMERICA. CYBERNETIC-ARMED HEROINE.
THIS AIN'T THE FIRST FUNERAL I'VE BEEN TO. DON'T EVEN THINK IT'S THE FIRST ONE THIS YEAR.
SO WHY'S IT HITTING ME SO HARD? IS IT THAT I KNEW RHODEY? IS IT THAT HE WAS ONE OF THE FIRST BLACK SUPER HEROES I MET? WHAT IS IT?
IT'S NOT UNTIL THE GATHERING AT THE BAR AFTERWARDS THAT I FIGURE IT OUT:
HE'S ME. JAMES RHODES IS ME.
MISTY, YOU OKAY?
YEAH, I'M FINE, SAM. WHAT TIME IS IT?
LATE, GIRL. WAY LATE.
IF YOU DON'T NEED ME, I'M GONNA TAKE THE TRAIN BACK TOMORROW, OKAY?
YEAH. THAT'S COOL.
I'M STILL THINKING ABOUT IT NEXT MORNING ON THE TRAIN. RHODEY WAS A MARINE. I WAS A COP. HE GOT A METAL SUIT. I GOT A METAL ARM.
AND WE'RE BOTH OUT HERE FIGHTING TITANS. WE'RE RUBBING ELBOWS WITH DEMIGODS. ONE MISSED DODGE AND WE'RE BOTH TOAST.
I FEEL FRIGHTENINGLY MORTAL. SO I DO WHAT YOU DO WHEN THAT HAPPENS, I GUESS.
HEY, MOM.
HOW ARE YOU? YEAH? NO, I JUST WANTED TO TALK.
I'M BACK IN BROOKLYN. YOU SAW IT ON TV?
YEAH, THEY DECIDED TO DO COSTUMES.
I HAD A NICE DRESS PICKED OUT, SO I ROCKED IT TODAY INSTEAD.
NO. I'M GOOD. I'M DRINKING PLENTY OF WATER.
SOMETIMES YOU JUST NEED TO HEAR YOUR MOM'S VOICE, YOU KNOW? EVEN IF SHE DOES IMMEDIATELY ASK THE WRONG QUESTIONS.
MY KUNG-FU BOYFRIEND? REALLY, MOM? I HAVEN'T SEEN DANNY IN MONTHS AND APPARENTLY HE DOESN'T KNOW HOW TO USE A PHONE. I HEAR HE AND LUKE ARE BACK TOGETHER AGAIN.
I'M WITH SAM, NOW.
MOM, PLEASE DO NOT CALL HIM "FAKE BUTT CAPTAIN AMERICA."

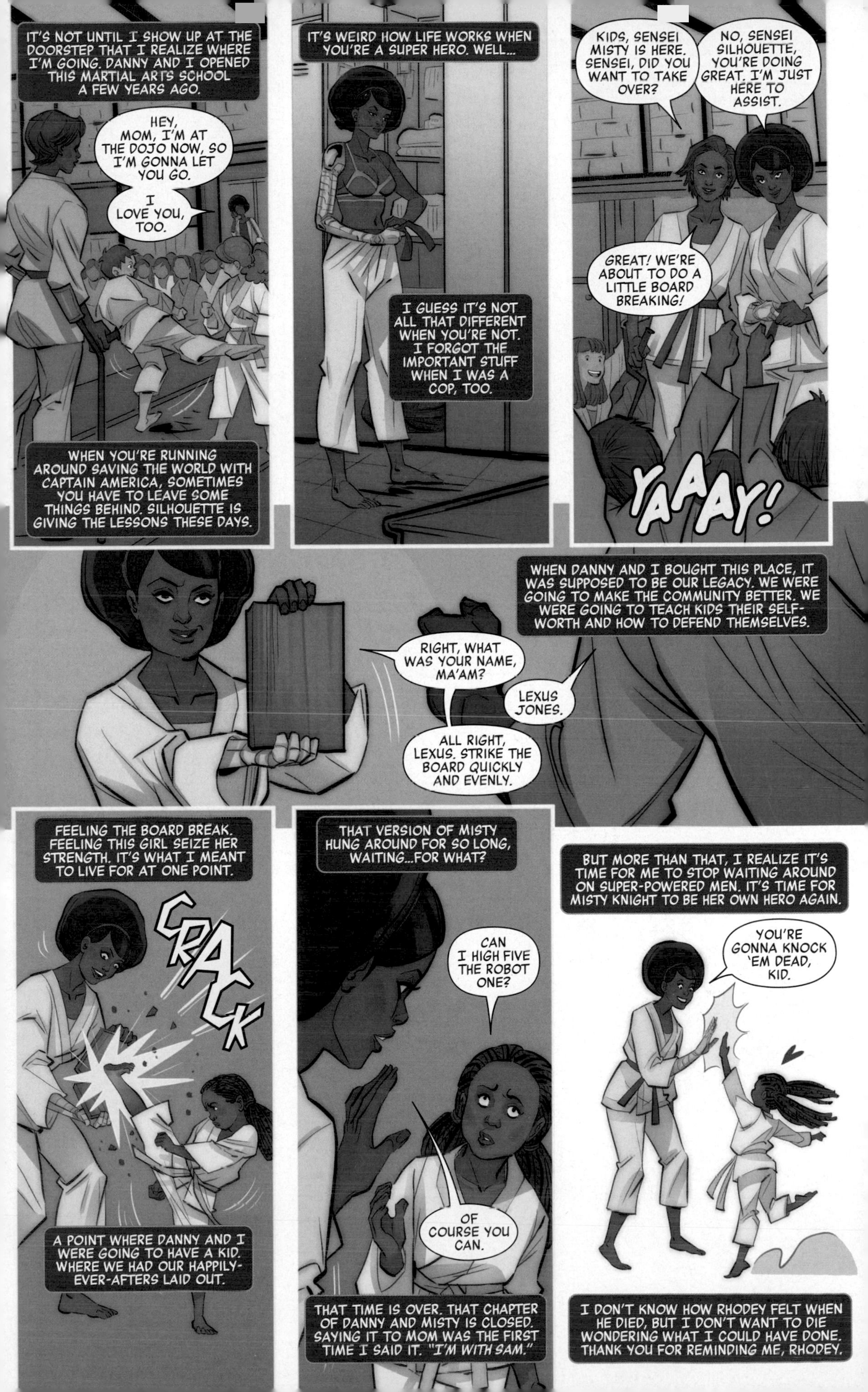
IT'S NOT UNTIL I SHOW UP AT THE DOORSTEP THAT I REALIZE WHERE I'M GOING. DANNY AND I OPENED THIS MARTIAL ARTS SCHOOL A FEW YEARS AGO.
HEY, MOM, I'M AT THE DOJO NOW, SO I'M GONNA LET YOU GO.
I LOVE YOU, TOO.
WHEN YOU'RE RUNNING AROUND SAVING THE WORLD WITH CAPTAIN AMERICA, SOMETIMES YOU HAVE TO LEAVE SOME THINGS BEHIND. SILHOUETTE IS GIVING THE LESSONS THESE DAYS.
IT'S WEIRD HOW LIFE WORKS WHEN YOU'RE A SUPER HERO. WELL...
I GUESS IT'S NOT ALL THAT DIFFERENT WHEN YOU'RE NOT. I FORGOT THE IMPORTANT STUFF WHEN I WAS A COP, TOO.
KIDS, SENSEI MISTY IS HERE. SENSEI, DID YOU WANT TO TAKE OVER?
NO, SENSEI SILHOUETTE, YOU'RE DOING GREAT. I'M JUST HERE TO ASSIST.
GREAT! WE'RE ABOUT TO DO A LITTLE BOARD BREAKING!
YAAAAY!
WHEN DANNY AND I BOUGHT THIS PLACE, IT WAS SUPPOSED TO BE OUR LEGACY. WE WERE GOING TO MAKE THE COMMUNITY BETTER. WE WERE GOING TO TEACH KIDS THEIR SELF-WORTH AND HOW TO DEFEND THEMSELVES.
RIGHT, WHAT WAS YOUR NAME, MA'AM?
LEXUS JONES.
ALL RIGHT, LEXUS. STRIKE THE BOARD QUICKLY AND EVENLY.
FEELING THE BOARD BREAK. FEELING THIS GIRL SEIZE HER STRENGTH. IT'S WHAT I MEANT TO LIVE FOR AT ONE POINT.
CRACK
A POINT WHERE DANNY AND I WERE GOING TO HAVE A KID. WHERE WE HAD OUR HAPPILY-EVER-AFTERS LAID OUT.
THAT VERSION OF MISTY HUNG AROUND FOR SO LONG, WAITING...FOR WHAT?
CAN I HIGH FIVE THE ROBOT ONE?
OF COURSE YOU CAN.
THAT TIME IS OVER. THAT CHAPTER OF DANNY AND MISTY IS CLOSED. SAYING IT TO MOM WAS THE FIRST TIME I SAID IT. "I'M WITH SAM."
BUT MORE THAN THAT, I REALIZE IT'S TIME FOR ME TO STOP WAITING AROUND ON SUPER-POWERED MEN. IT'S TIME FOR MISTY KNIGHT TO BE HER OWN HERO AGAIN.
YOU'RE GONNA KNOCK 'EM DEAD, KID.
I DON'T KNOW HOW RHODEY FELT WHEN HE DIED, BUT I DON'T WANT TO DIE WONDERING WHAT I COULD HAVE DONE. THANK YOU FOR REMINDING ME, RHODEY.

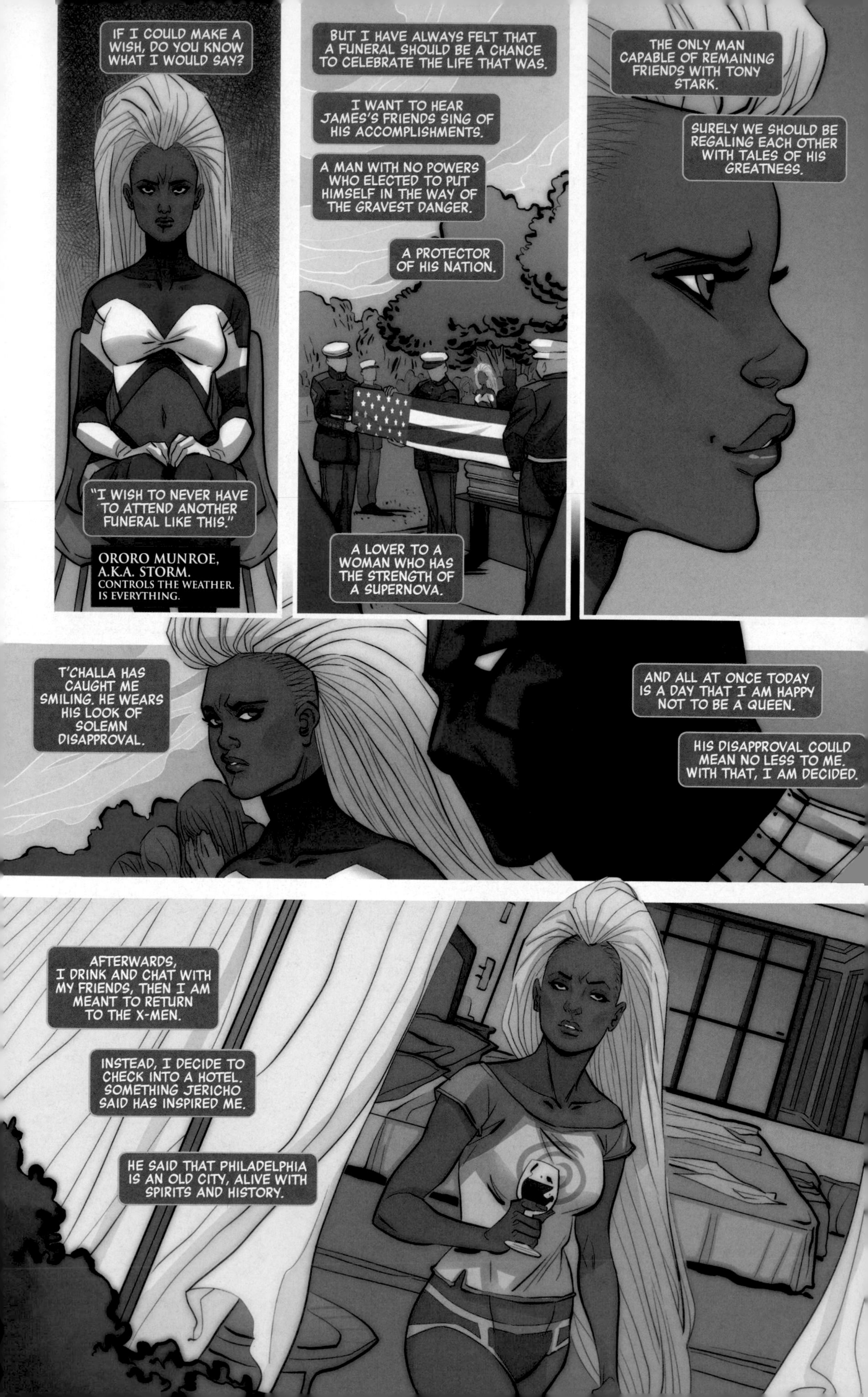
IF I COULD MAKE A WISH, DO YOU KNOW WHAT I WOULD SAY?
"I WISH TO NEVER HAVE TO ATTEND ANOTHER FUNERAL LIKE THIS."
ORORO MUNROE, A.K.A. STORM. CONTROLS THE WEATHER. IS EVERYTHING.
BUT I HAVE ALWAYS FELT THAT A FUNERAL SHOULD BE A CHANCE TO CELEBRATE THE LIFE THAT WAS.
I WANT TO HEAR JAMES'S FRIENDS SING OF HIS ACCOMPLISHMENTS.
A MAN WITH NO POWERS WHO ELECTED TO PUT HIMSELF IN THE WAY OF THE GRAVEST DANGER.
A PROTECTOR OF HIS NATION.
A LOVER TO A WOMAN WHO HAS THE STRENGTH OF A SUPERNOVA.
THE ONLY MAN CAPABLE OF REMAINING FRIENDS WITH TONY STARK.
SURELY WE SHOULD BE REGALING EACH OTHER WITH TALES OF HIS GREATNESS.
T'CHALLA HAS CAUGHT ME SMILING. HE WEARS HIS LOOK OF SOLEMN DISAPPROVAL.
AND ALL AT ONCE TODAY IS A DAY THAT I AM HAPPY NOT TO BE A QUEEN.
HIS DISAPPROVAL COULD MEAN NO LESS TO ME. WITH THAT, I AM DECIDED.
AFTERWARDS, I DRINK AND CHAT WITH MY FRIENDS, THEN I AM MEANT TO RETURN TO THE X-MEN.
INSTEAD, I DECIDE TO CHECK INTO A HOTEL. SOMETHING JERICHO SAID HAS INSPIRED ME.
HE SAID THAT PHILADELPHIA IS AN OLD CITY, ALIVE WITH SPIRITS AND HISTORY.

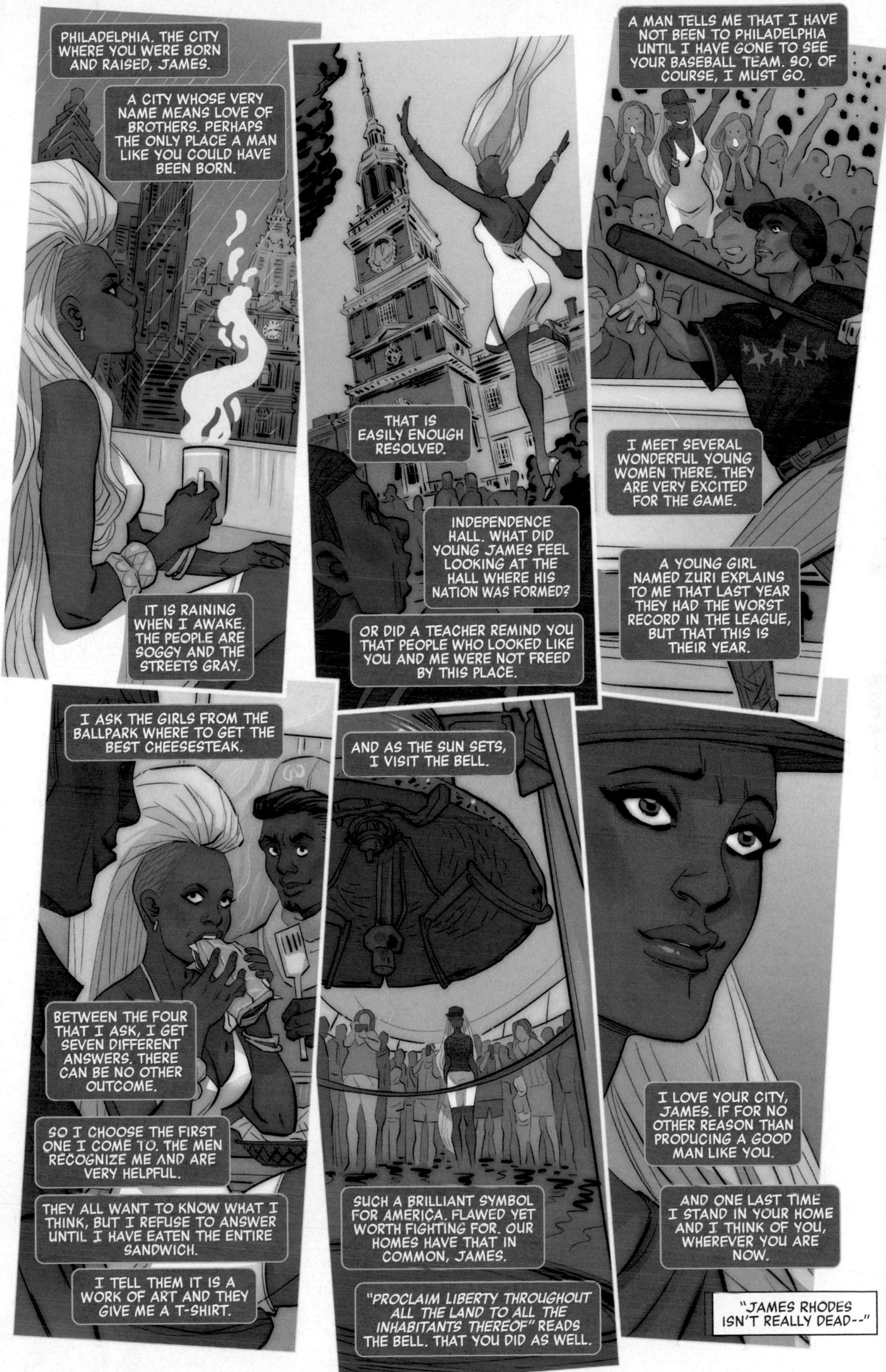
PHILADELPHIA. THE CITY WHERE YOU WERE BORN AND RAISED, JAMES.
A CITY WHOSE VERY NAME MEANS LOVE OF BROTHERS. PERHAPS THE ONLY PLACE A MAN LIKE YOU COULD HAVE BEEN BORN.
IT IS RAINING WHEN I AWAKE. THE PEOPLE ARE SOGGY AND THE STREETS GRAY.
THAT IS EASILY ENOUGH RESOLVED.
INDEPENDENCE HALL. WHAT DID YOUNG JAMES FEEL LOOKING AT THE HALL WHERE HIS NATION WAS FORMED?
OR DID A TEACHER REMIND YOU THAT PEOPLE WHO LOOKED LIKE YOU AND ME WERE NOT FREED BY THIS PLACE.
A MAN TELLS ME THAT I HAVE NOT BEEN TO PHILADELPHIA UNTIL I HAVE GONE TO SEE YOUR BASEBALL TEAM. SO, OF COURSE, I MUST GO.
I MEET SEVERAL WONDERFUL YOUNG WOMEN THERE. THEY ARE VERY EXCITED FOR THE GAME.
A YOUNG GIRL NAMED ZURI EXPLAINS TO ME THAT LAST YEAR THEY HAD THE WORST RECORD IN THE LEAGUE, BUT THAT THIS IS THEIR YEAR.
I ASK THE GIRLS FROM THE BALLPARK WHERE TO GET THE BEST CHEESESTEAK.
BETWEEN THE FOUR THAT I ASK, I GET SEVEN DIFFERENT ANSWERS. THERE CAN BE NO OTHER OUTCOME.
SO I CHOOSE THE FIRST ONE I COME TO. THE MEN RECOGNIZE ME AND ARE VERY HELPFUL.
THEY ALL WANT TO KNOW WHAT I THINK, BUT I REFUSE TO ANSWER UNTIL I HAVE EATEN THE ENTIRE SANDWICH.
I TELL THEM IT IS A WORK OF ART AND THEY GIVE ME A T-SHIRT.
AND AS THE SUN SETS, I VISIT THE BELL.
SUCH A BRILLIANT SYMBOL FOR AMERICA. FLAWED YET WORTH FIGHTING FOR. OUR HOMES HAVE THAT IN COMMON, JAMES.
"PROCLAIM LIBERTY THROUGHOUT ALL THE LAND TO ALL THE INHABITANTS THEREOF" READS THE BELL. THAT YOU DID AS WELL.
I LOVE YOUR CITY, JAMES. IF FOR NO OTHER REASON THAN PRODUCING A GOOD MAN LIKE YOU.
AND ONE LAST TIME I STAND IN YOUR HOME AND I THINK OF YOU, WHEREVER YOU ARE NOW.
"JAMES RHODES ISN'T REALLY DEAD--"

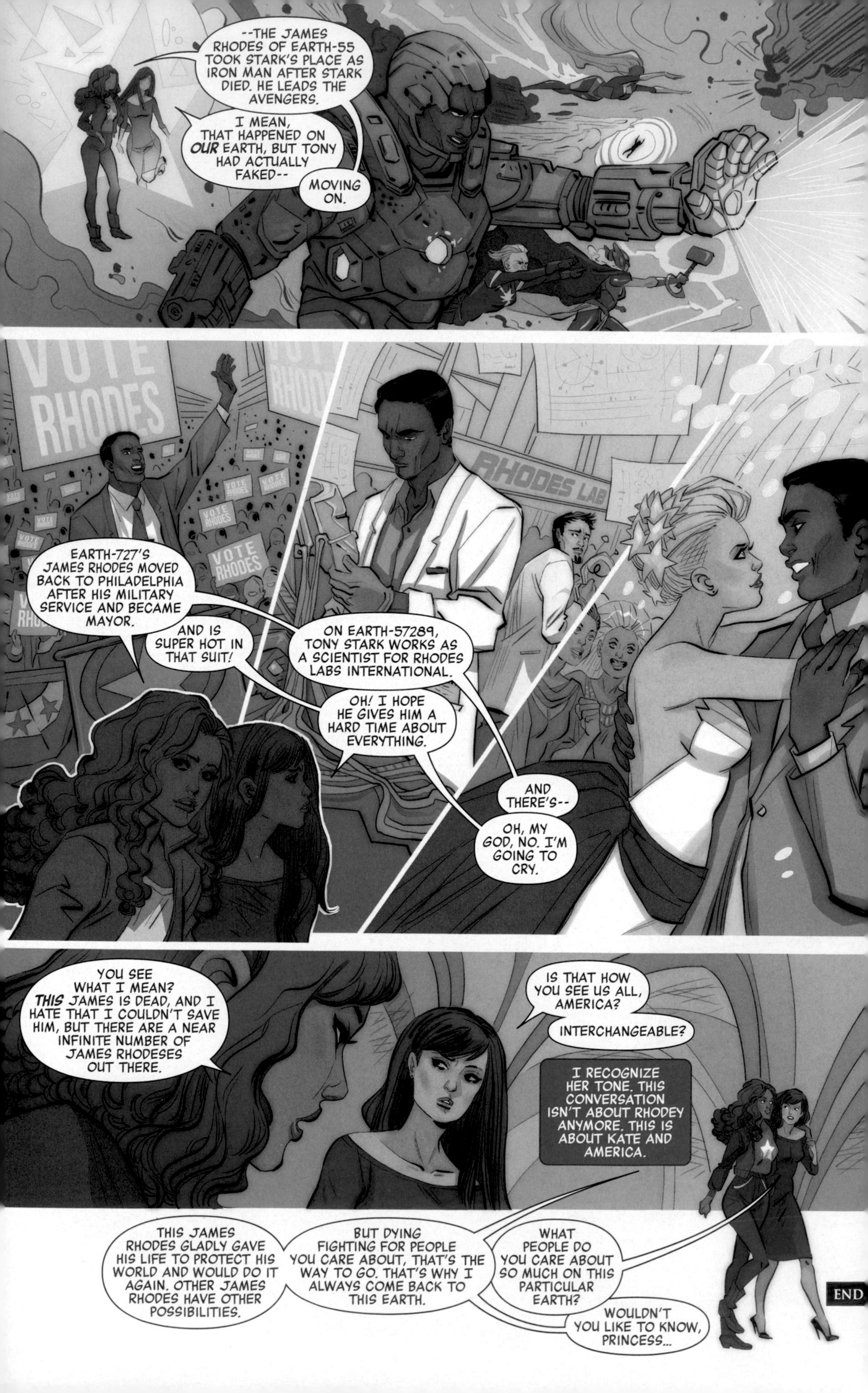
--THE JAMES RHODES OF EARTH-55 TOOK STARK'S PLACE AS IRON MAN AFTER STARK DIED. HE LEADS THE AVENGERS.
I MEAN, THAT HAPPENED ON OUR EARTH, BUT TONY HAD ACTUALLY FAKED--
MOVING ON.
VOTE RHODES
RHODES LAB
EARTH-727'S JAMES RHODES MOVED BACK TO PHILADELPHIA AFTER HIS MILITARY SERVICE AND BECAME MAYOR.
AND IS SUPER HOT IN THAT SUIT!
ON EARTH-57289, TONY STARK WORKS AS A SCIENTIST FOR RHODES LABS INTERNATIONAL.
OH! I HOPE HE GIVES HIM A HARD TIME ABOUT EVERYTHING.
AND THERE'S--
OH, MY GOD, NO. I'M GOING TO CRY.
YOU SEE WHAT I MEAN? THIS JAMES IS DEAD, AND I HATE THAT I COULDN'T SAVE HIM, BUT THERE ARE A NEAR INFINITE NUMBER OF JAMES RHODESES OUT THERE.
IS THAT HOW YOU SEE US ALL, AMERICA?
INTERCHANGEABLE?
I RECOGNIZE HER TONE. THIS CONVERSATION ISN'T ABOUT RHODEY ANYMORE. THIS IS ABOUT KATE AND AMERICA.
THIS JAMES RHODES GLADLY GAVE HIS LIFE TO PROTECT HIS WORLD AND WOULD DO IT AGAIN. OTHER JAMES RHODES HAVE OTHER POSSIBILITIES.
BUT DYING FIGHTING FOR PEOPLE YOU CARE ABOUT, THAT'S THE WAY TO GO. THAT'S WHY I ALWAYS COME BACK TO THIS EARTH.
WHAT PEOPLE DO YOU CARE ABOUT SO MUCH ON THIS PARTICULAR EARTH?
WOULDN'T YOU LIKE TO KNOW, PRINCESS...
END

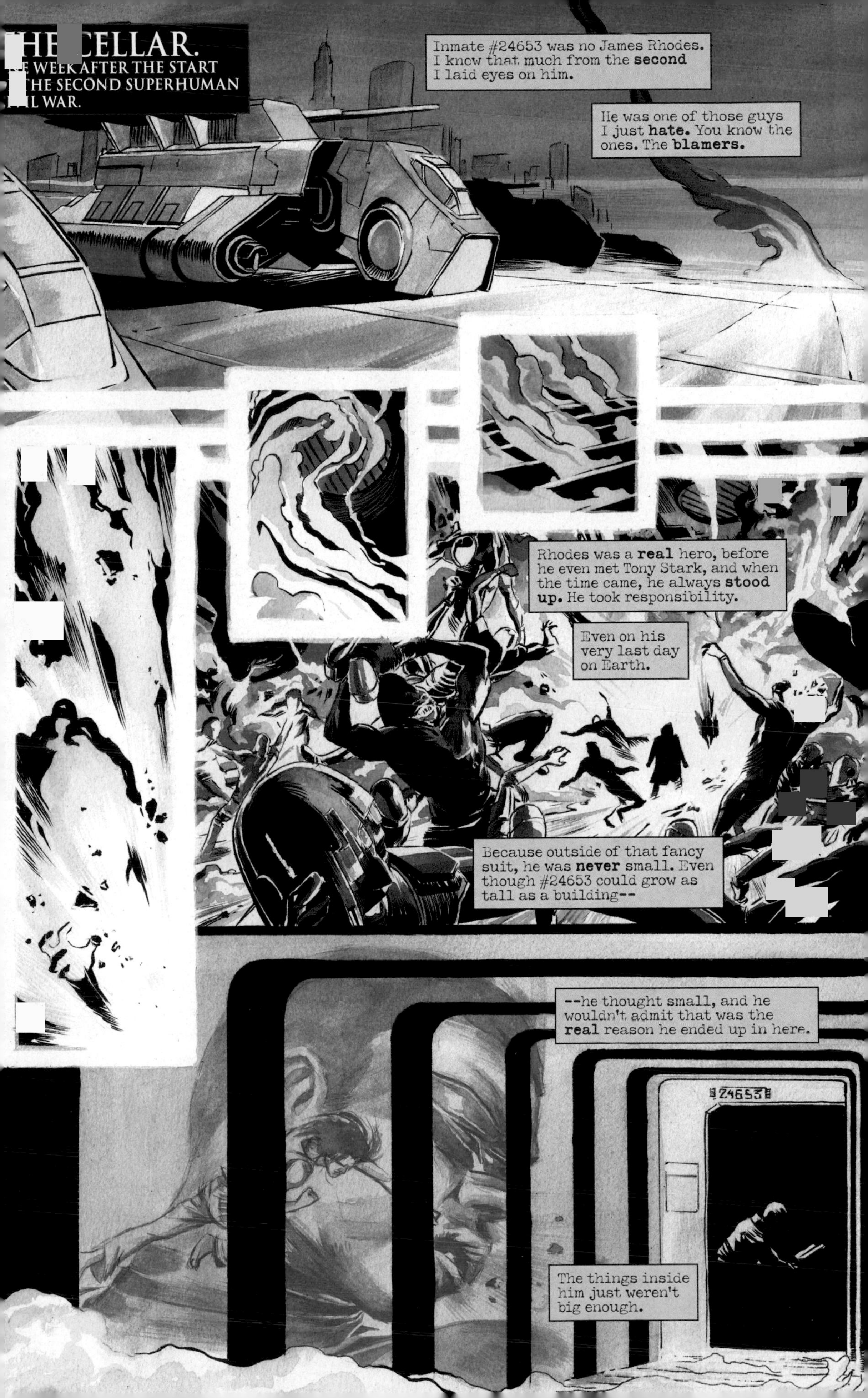
HE CELLAR.
NE WEEK AFTER THE START
THE SECOND SUPERHUMAN
IL WAR.
Inmate #24653 was no James Rhodes. I know that much from the second I laid eyes on him.
He was one of those guys I just hate. You know the ones. The blamers.
Rhodes was a real hero, before he even met Tony Stark, and when the time came, he always stood up. He took responsibility.
Even on his very last day on Earth.
Because outside of that fancy suit, he was never small. Even though #24653 could grow as tall as a building--
--he thought small, and he wouldn't admit that was the real reason he ended up in here.
24653
The things inside him just weren't big enough.

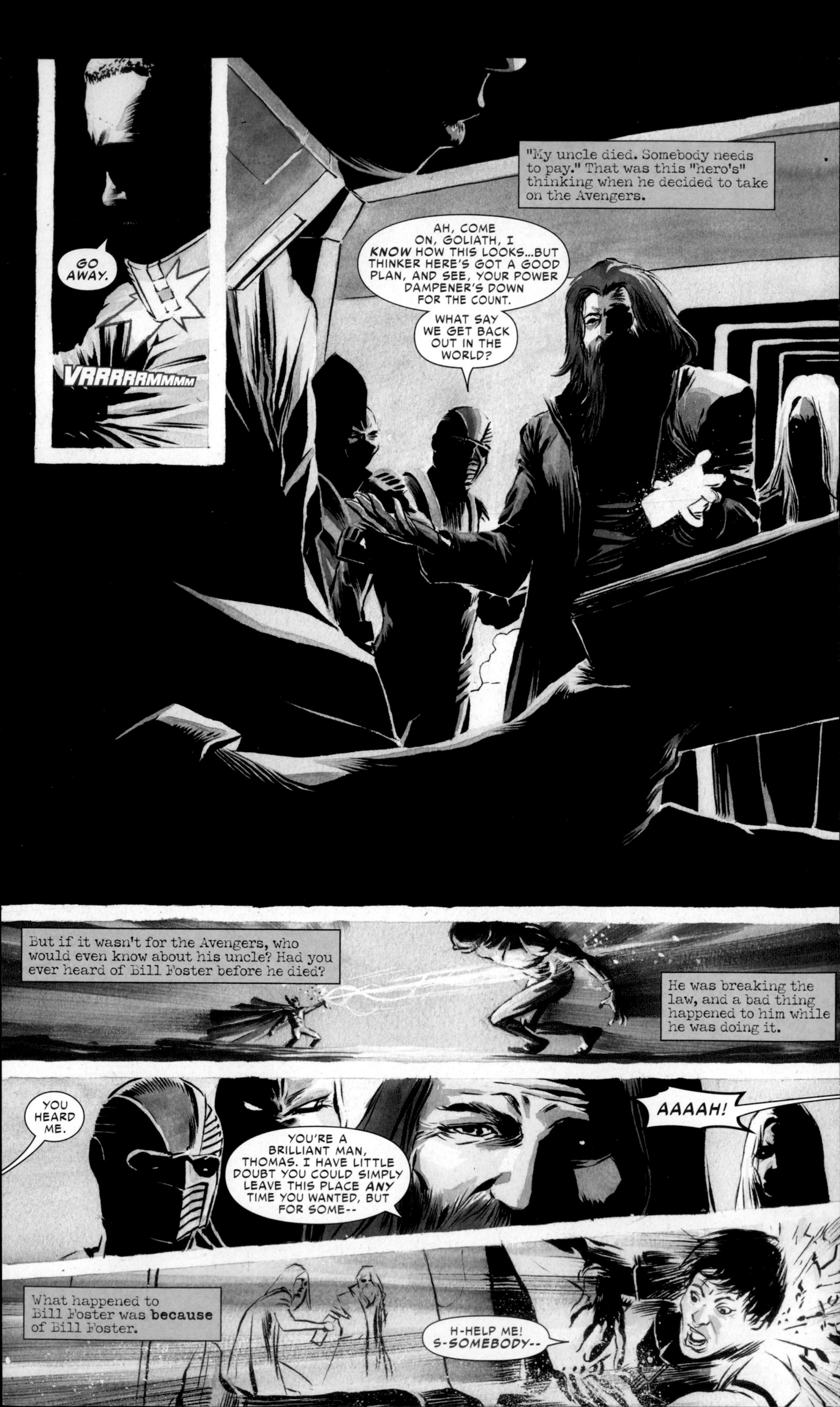
GO AWAY.
VRRRRRMMMM
"My uncle died. Somebody needs to pay." That was this "hero's" thinking when he decided to take on the Avengers.
AH, COME ON, GOLIATH, I KNOW HOW THIS LOOKS...BUT THINKER HERE'S GOT A GOOD PLAN, AND SEE, YOUR POWER DAMPENER'S DOWN FOR THE COUNT.
WHAT SAY WE GET BACK OUT IN THE WORLD?
But if it wasn't for the Avengers, who would even know about his uncle? Had you ever heard of Bill Foster before he died?
He was breaking the law, and a bad thing happened to him while he was doing it.
YOU HEARD ME.
YOU'RE A BRILLIANT MAN, THOMAS. I HAVE LITTLE DOUBT YOU COULD SIMPLY LEAVE THIS PLACE ANY TIME YOU WANTED, BUT FOR SOME--
AAAAH!
What happened to Bill Foster was because of Bill Foster.
H-HELP ME! S-SOMEBODY--

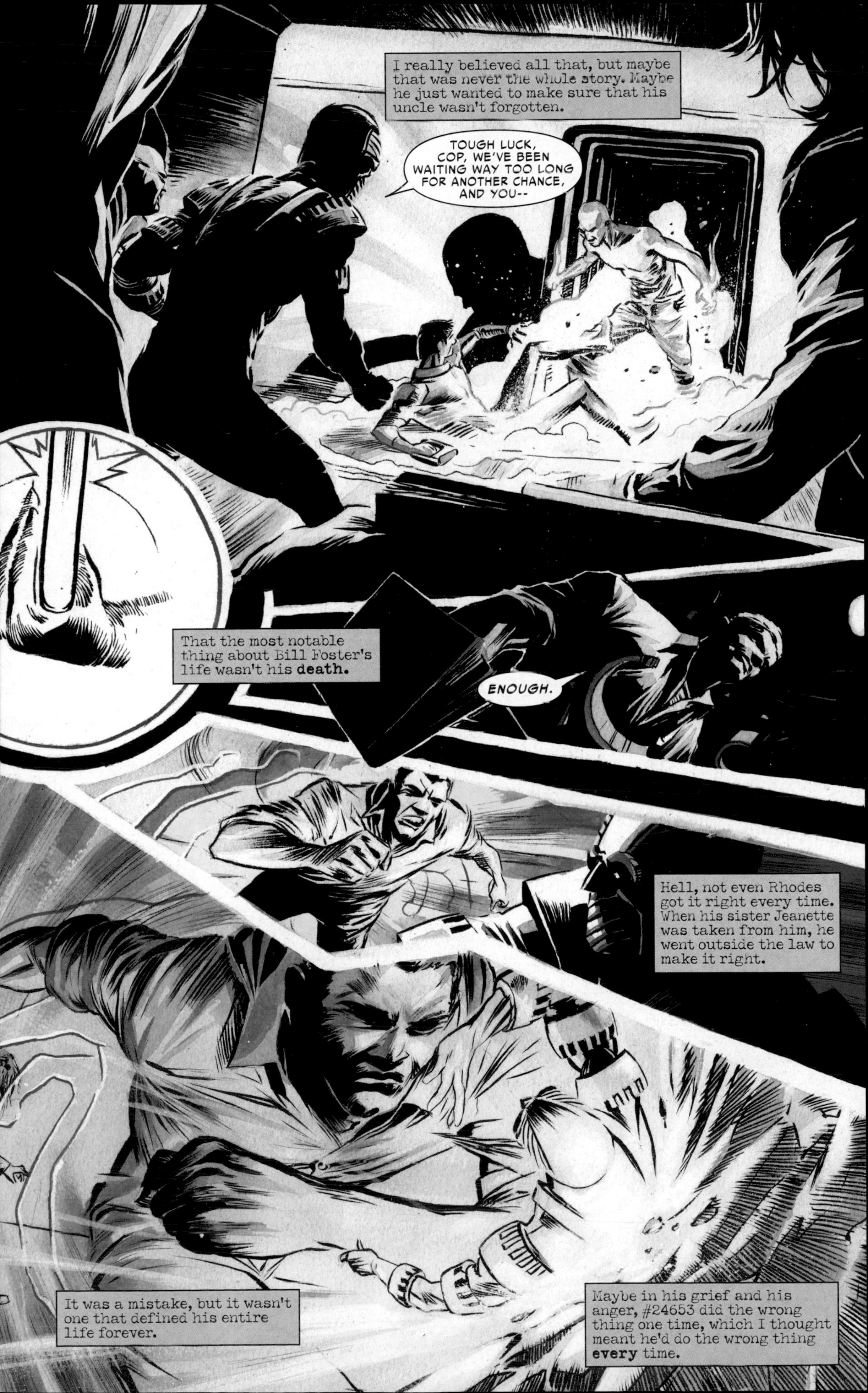
I really believed all that, but maybe that was never the whole story. Maybe he just wanted to make sure that his uncle wasn't forgotten.
TOUGH LUCK, COP, WE'VE BEEN WAITING WAY TOO LONG FOR ANOTHER CHANCE, AND YOU--
That the most notable thing about Bill Foster's life wasn't his **death.**
ENOUGH.
Hell, not even Rhodes got it right every time. When his sister Jeanette was taken from him, he went outside the law to make it right.
It was a mistake, but it wasn't one that defined his entire life forever.
Maybe in his grief and his anger, #24653 did the wrong thing one time, which I thought meant he'd do the wrong thing **every** time.

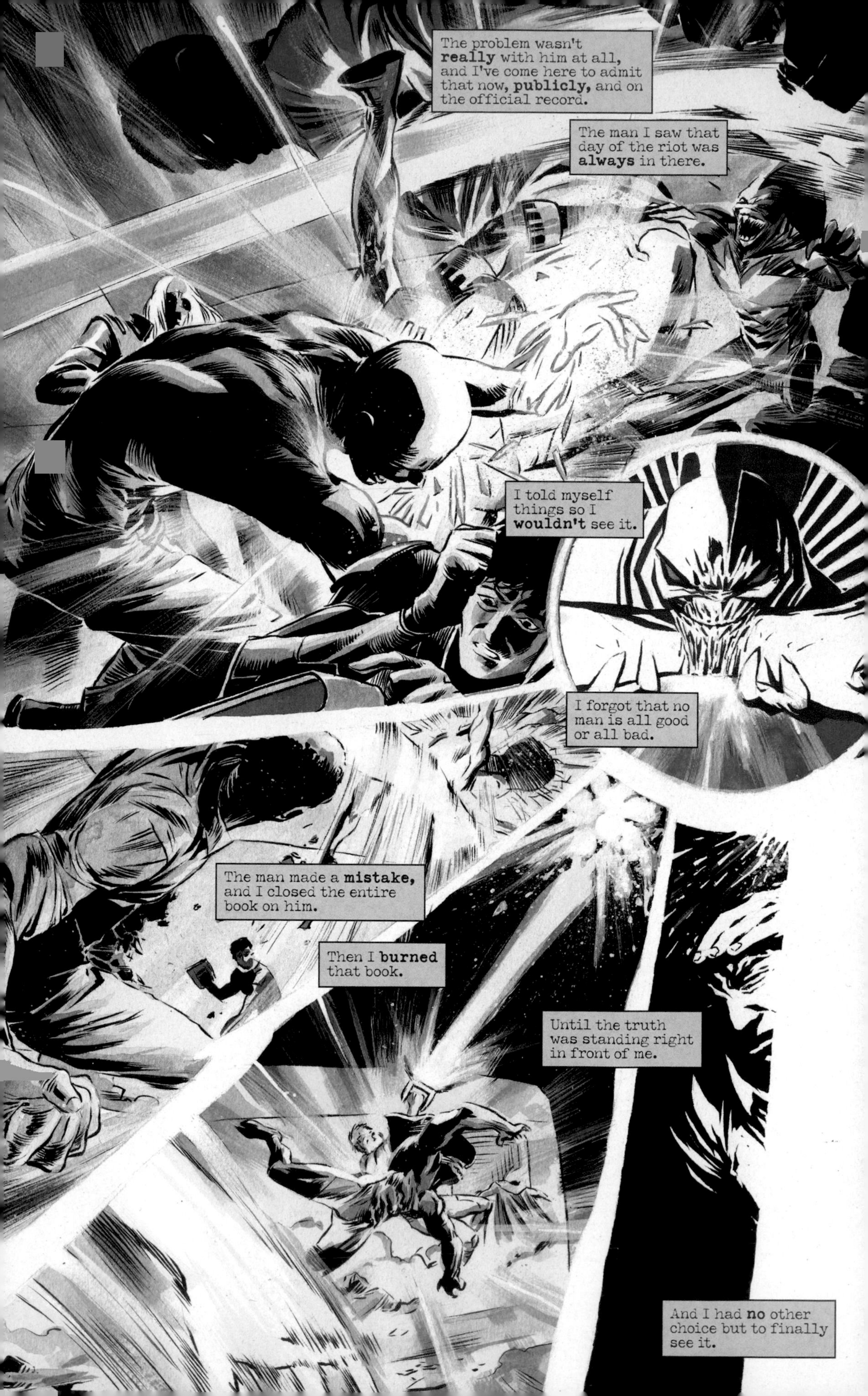

The problem wasn't **really** with him at all, and I've come here to admit that now, **publicly,** and on the official record.
The man I saw that day of the riot was **always** in there.
I told myself things so I **wouldn't** see it.
I forgot that no man is all good or all bad.
The man made a **mistake,** and I closed the entire book on him.
Then I **burned** that book.
Until the truth was standing right in front of me.
And I had **no** other choice but to finally see it.

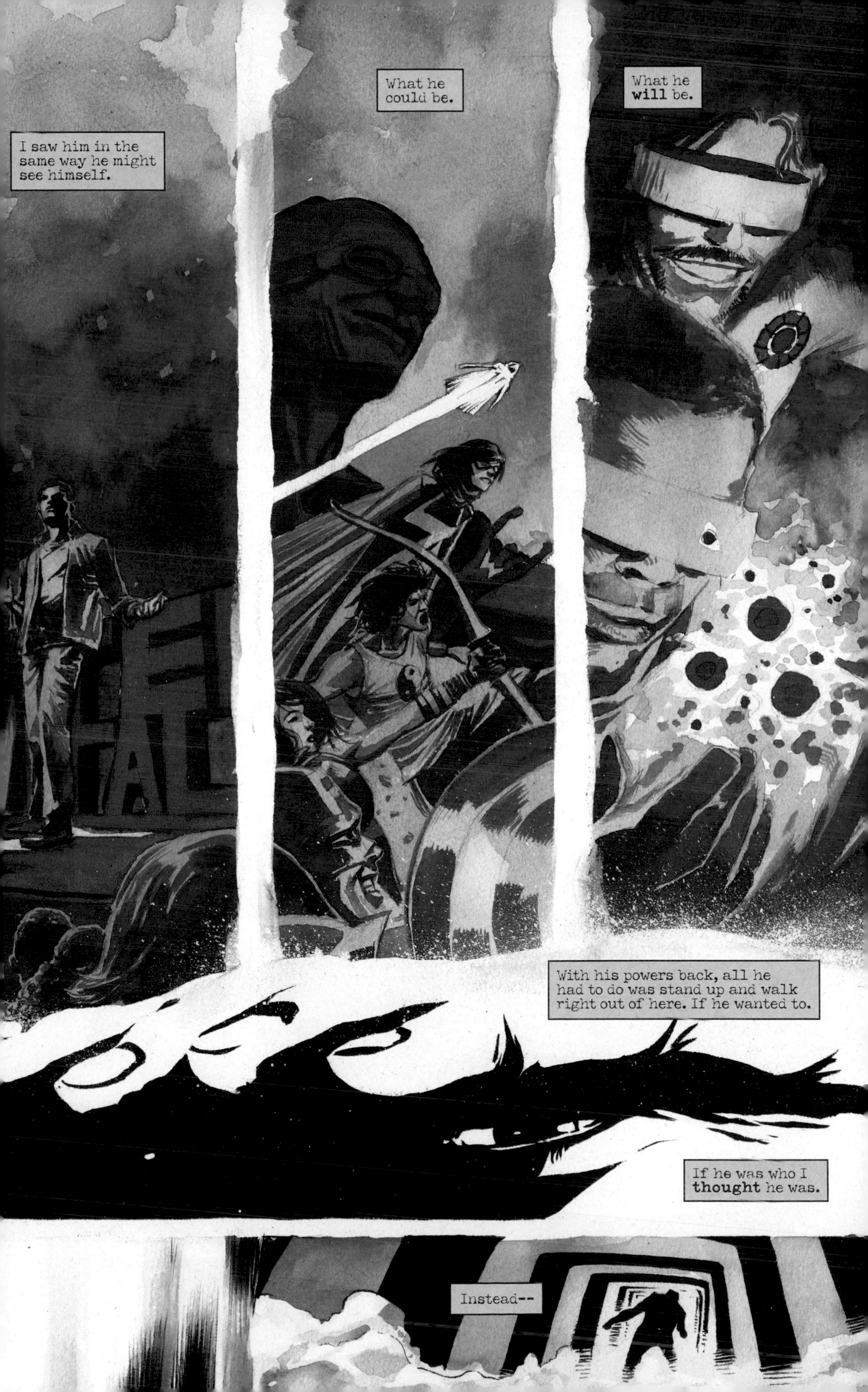
I saw him in the same way he might see himself.
What he could be.
What he **will** be.
With his powers back, all he had to do was stand up and walk right out of here. If he wanted to.
If he was who I **thought** he was.
Instead--

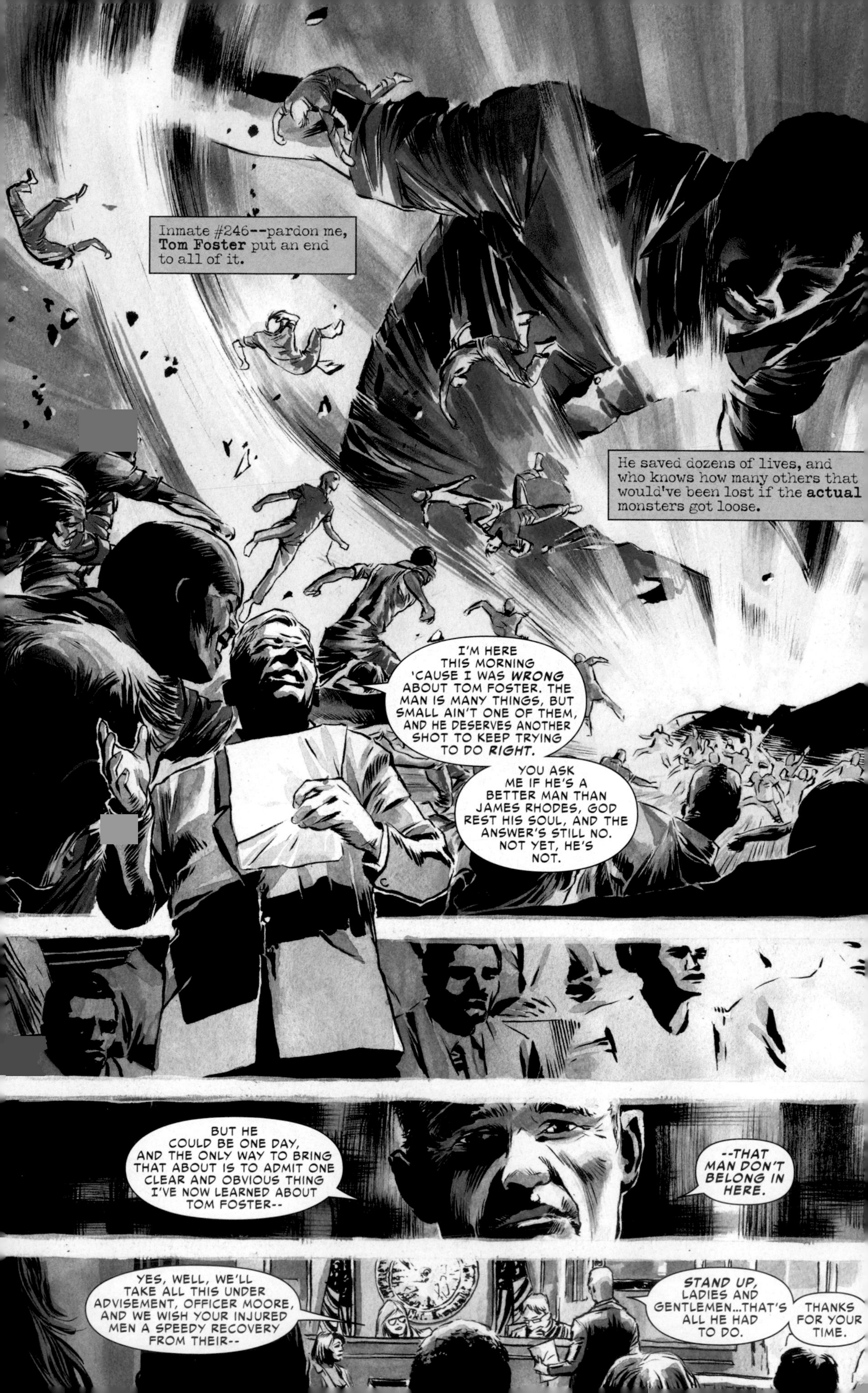
Inmate #246--pardon me, **Tom Foster** put an end to all of it.
He saved dozens of lives, and who knows how many others that would've been lost if the **actual** monsters got loose.
I'M HERE THIS MORNING 'CAUSE I WAS *WRONG* ABOUT TOM FOSTER. THE MAN IS MANY THINGS, BUT SMALL AIN'T ONE OF THEM, AND HE DESERVES ANOTHER SHOT TO KEEP TRYING TO DO *RIGHT*.
YOU ASK ME IF HE'S A BETTER MAN THAN JAMES RHODES, GOD REST HIS SOUL, AND THE ANSWER'S STILL NO. NOT YET, HE'S NOT.
BUT HE COULD BE ONE DAY, AND THE ONLY WAY TO BRING THAT ABOUT IS TO ADMIT ONE CLEAR AND OBVIOUS THING I'VE NOW LEARNED ABOUT TOM FOSTER--
--THAT MAN DON'T BELONG IN HERE.
YES, WELL, WE'LL TAKE ALL THIS UNDER ADVISEMENT, OFFICER MOORE, AND WE WISH YOUR INJURED MEN A SPEEDY RECOVERY FROM THEIR--
*STAND UP,* LADIES AND GENTLEMEN...THAT'S ALL HE HAD TO DO.
THANKS FOR YOUR TIME.

PA-PING

PA-PING

PA-PING

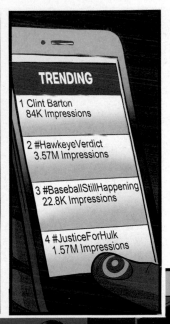

TRENDING

1 Clint Barton
84K Impressions

2 #HawkeyeVerdict
3.57M Impressions

3 #BaseballStillHappening
22.8K Impressions

4 #JusticeForHulk
1.57M Impressions

Super H
Questio

**Latest Update**

10 Things
Didn't Know
ut Hawkeye

**Guilty?**

**Motivations to kill?**

**Avengers Controversy**

**Innocent?**

UGH!

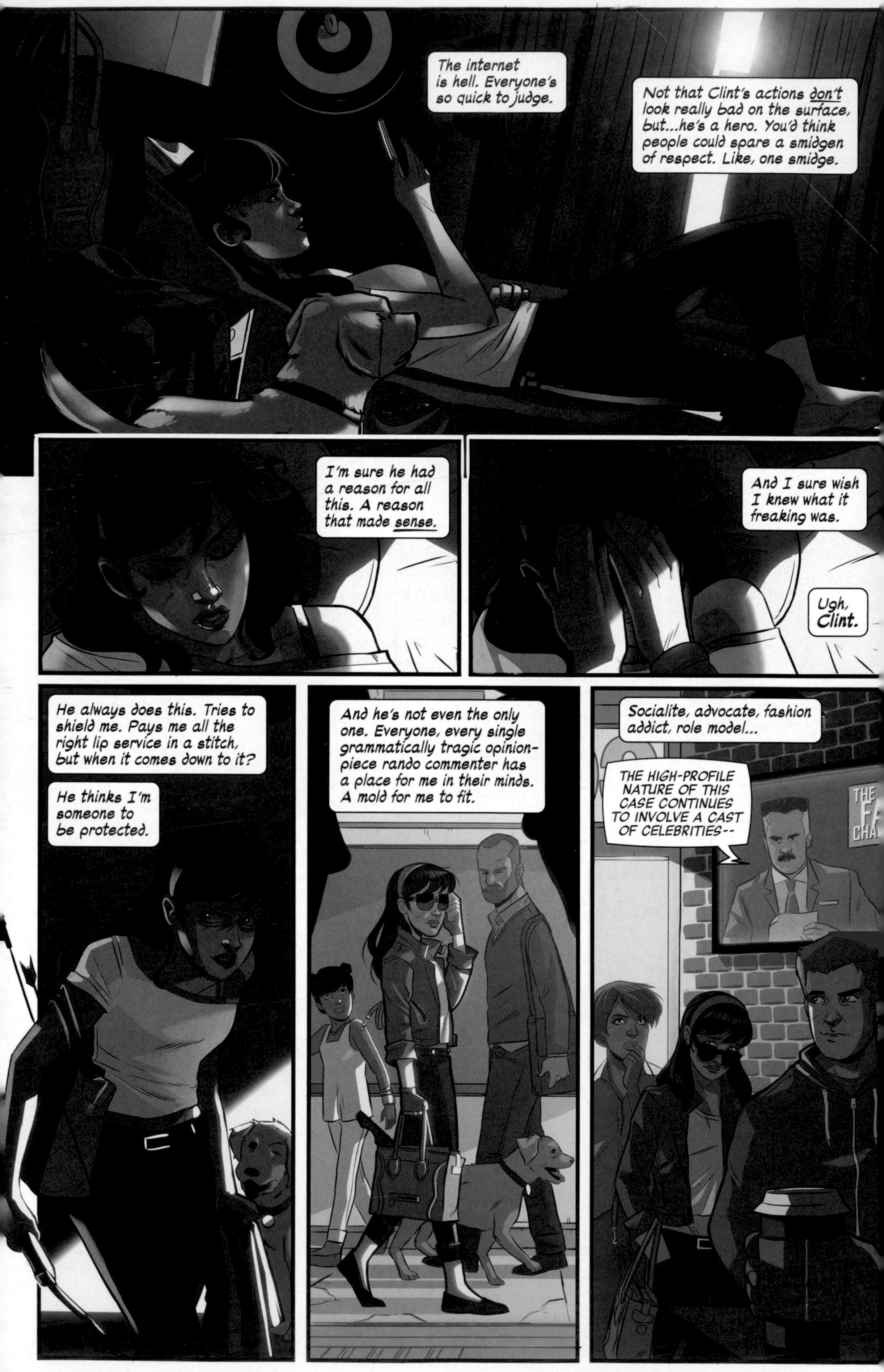
The internet is hell. Everyone's so quick to judge.
Not that Clint's actions don't look really bad on the surface, but...he's a hero. You'd think people could spare a smidgen of respect. Like, one smidge.
I'm sure he had a reason for all this. A reason that made sense.
And I sure wish I knew what it freaking was.
Ugh, Clint.
He always does this. Tries to shield me. Pays me all the right lip service in a stitch, but when it comes down to it?
He thinks I'm someone to be protected.
And he's not even the only one. Everyone, every single grammatically tragic opinion-piece rando commenter has a place for me in their minds. A mold for me to fit.
Socialite, advocate, fashion addict, role model...
THE HIGH-PROFILE NATURE OF THIS CASE CONTINUES TO INVOLVE A CAST OF CELEBRITIES--

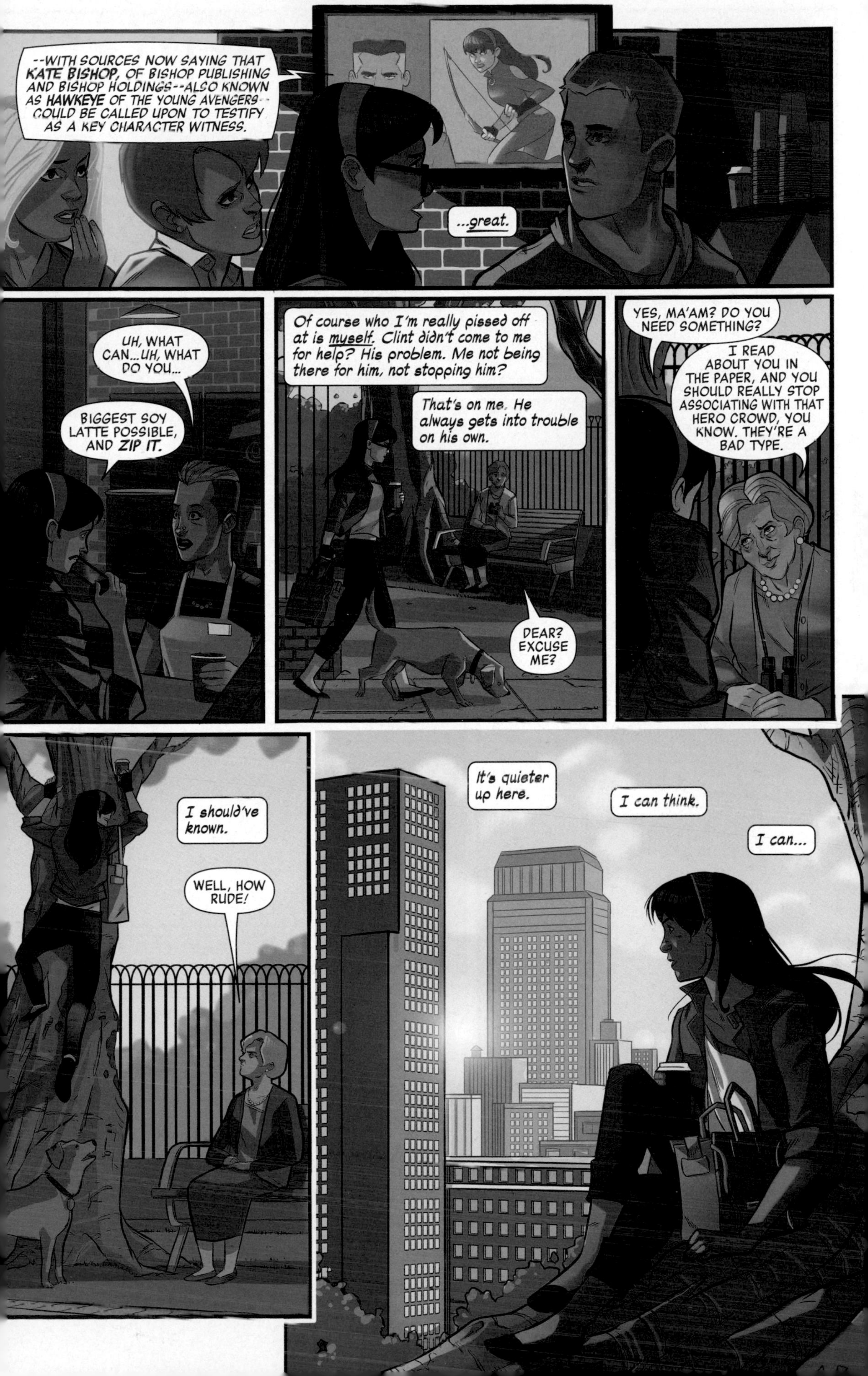
--WITH SOURCES NOW SAYING THAT KATE BISHOP, OF BISHOP PUBLISHING AND BISHOP HOLDINGS--ALSO KNOWN AS HAWKEYE OF THE YOUNG AVENGERS--COULD BE CALLED UPON TO TESTIFY AS A KEY CHARACTER WITNESS.
...great.
UH, WHAT CAN...UH, WHAT DO YOU...
BIGGEST SOY LATTE POSSIBLE, AND ZIP IT.
Of course who I'm really pissed off at is myself. Clint didn't come to me for help? His problem. Me not being there for him, not stopping him?
That's on me. He always gets into trouble on his own.
DEAR? EXCUSE ME?
YES, MA'AM? DO YOU NEED SOMETHING?
I READ ABOUT YOU IN THE PAPER, AND YOU SHOULD REALLY STOP ASSOCIATING WITH THAT HERO CROWD, YOU KNOW. THEY'RE A BAD TYPE.
I should've known.
WELL, HOW RUDE!
It's quieter up here.
I can think.
I can...

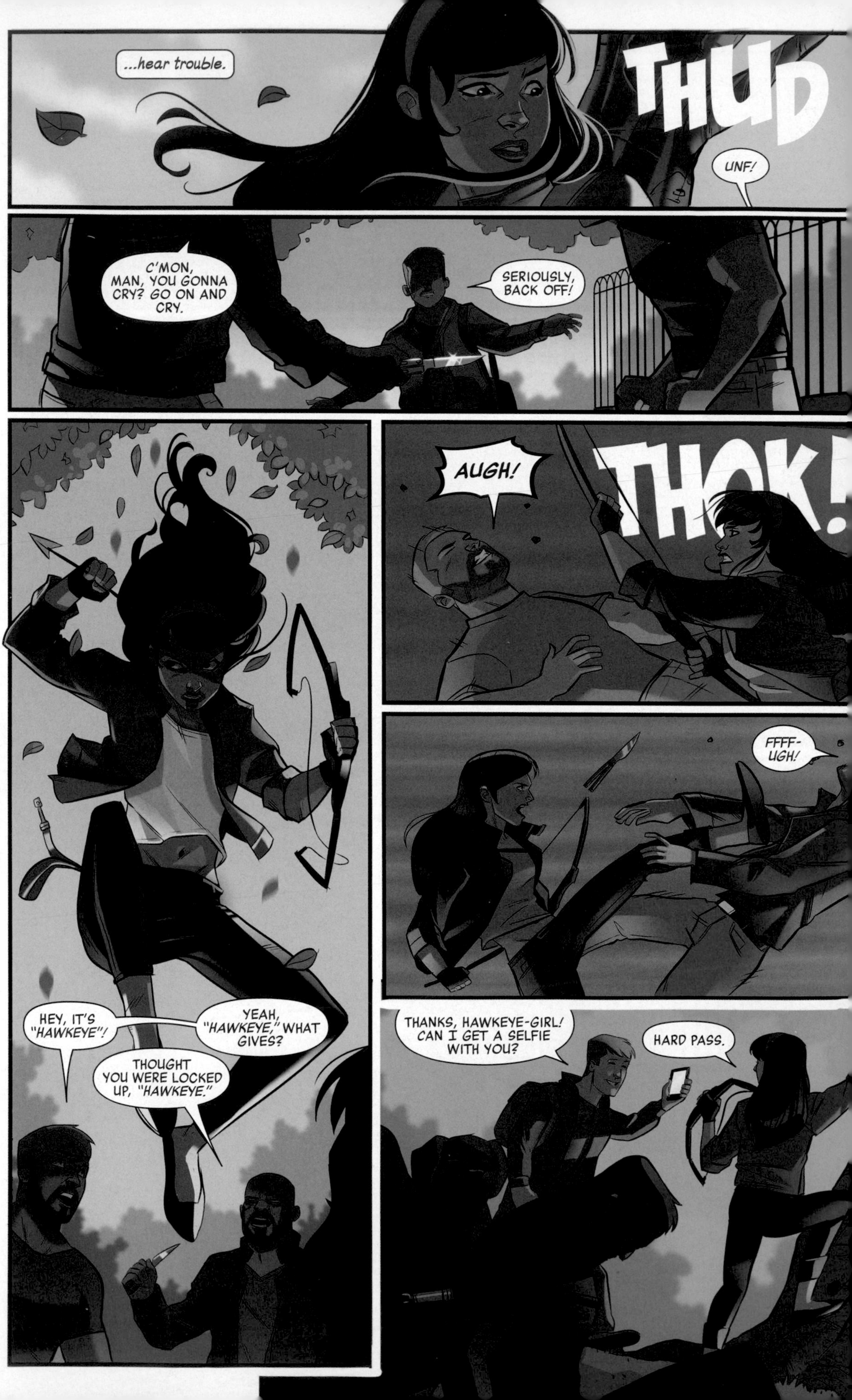
...hear trouble.
THUD
UNF!
C'MON, MAN, YOU GONNA CRY? GO ON AND CRY.
SERIOUSLY, BACK OFF!
AUGH!
THOK!
FFFF-UGH!
HEY, IT'S "HAWKEYE"!
YEAH, "HAWKEYE," WHAT GIVES?
THOUGHT YOU WERE LOCKED UP, "HAWKEYE."
THANKS, HAWKEYE-GIRL! CAN I GET A SELFIE WITH YOU?
HARD PASS.

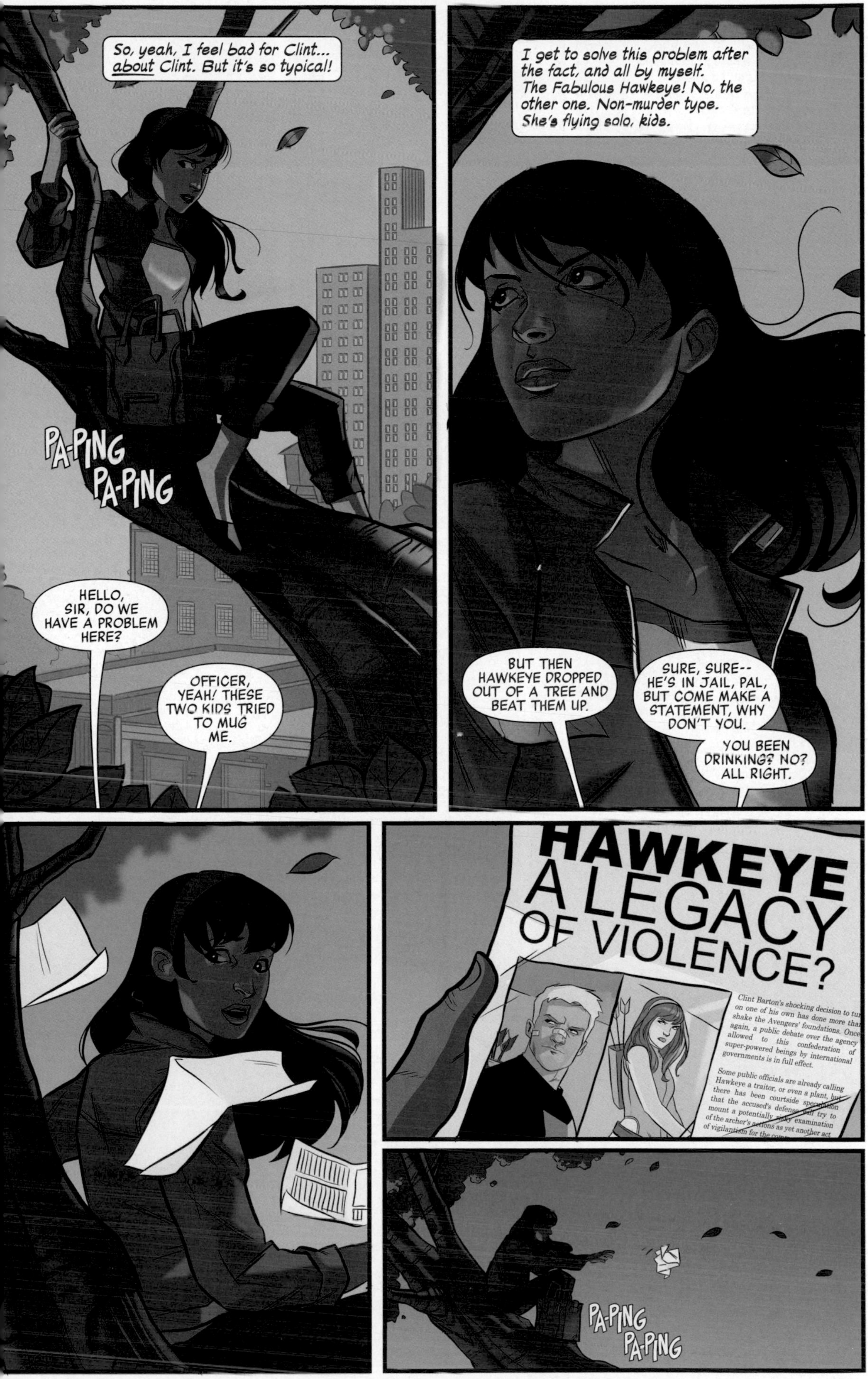

So, yeah, I feel bad for Clint... about Clint. But it's so typical!
PA-PING PA-PING
HELLO, SIR, DO WE HAVE A PROBLEM HERE?
OFFICER, YEAH! THESE TWO KIDS TRIED TO MUG ME.
I get to solve this problem after the fact, and all by myself. The Fabulous Hawkeye! No, the other one. Non-murder type. She's flying solo, kids.
BUT THEN HAWKEYE DROPPED OUT OF A TREE AND BEAT THEM UP.
SURE, SURE-- HE'S IN JAIL, PAL, BUT COME MAKE A STATEMENT, WHY DON'T YOU.
YOU BEEN DRINKING? NO? ALL RIGHT.
HAWKEYE
A LEGACY OF VIOLENCE?
Clint Barton's shocking decision to tu on one of his own has done more tha shake the Avengers' foundations. Once again, a public debate over the agency allowed to this confederation of super-powered beings by international governments is in full effect.
Some public officials are already calling Hawkeye a traitor, or even a plant, but there has been courtside speculation that the accused's defense will try to mount a potentially risky examination of the archer's actions as yet another act of vigilantism for the com
PA-PING PA-PING

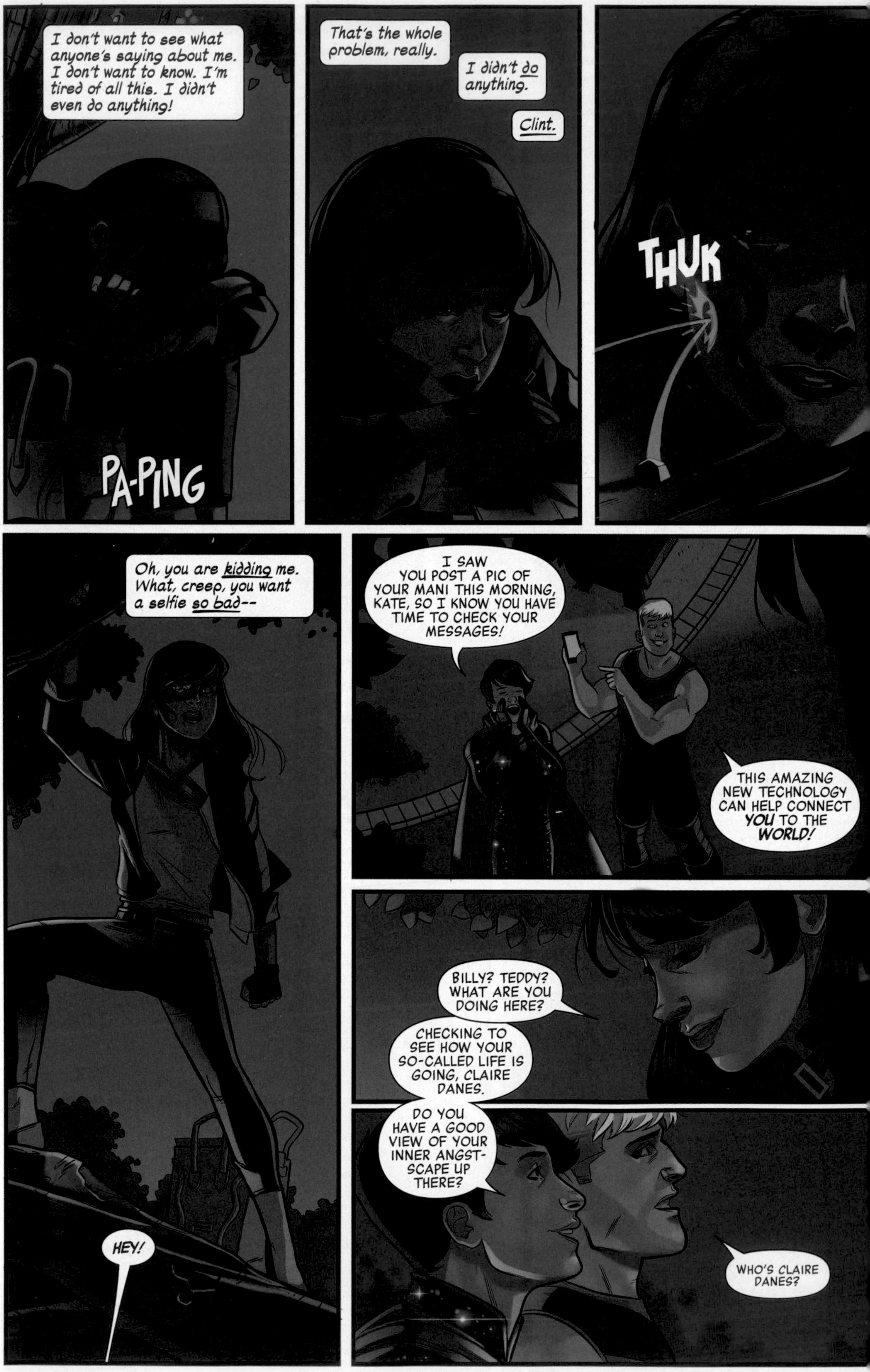
I don't want to see what anyone's saying about me. I don't want to know. I'm tired of all this. I didn't even do anything!
PA-PING
That's the whole problem, really.
I didn't do anything.
Clint.
THUK
Oh, you are kidding me. What, creep, you want a selfie so bad--
HEY!
I SAW YOU POST A PIC OF YOUR MANI THIS MORNING, KATE, SO I KNOW YOU HAVE TIME TO CHECK YOUR MESSAGES!
THIS AMAZING NEW TECHNOLOGY CAN HELP CONNECT YOU TO THE WORLD!
BILLY? TEDDY? WHAT ARE YOU DOING HERE?
CHECKING TO SEE HOW YOUR SO-CALLED LIFE IS GOING, CLAIRE DANES.
DO YOU HAVE A GOOD VIEW OF YOUR INNER ANGST-SCAPE UP THERE?
WHO'S CLAIRE DANES?

SO AMERICA HERE TEXTED AROUND THAT YOU MIGHT BE GOING THROUGH A ROUGH PATCH, AND--

WE'RE HERE TO LOVE AND SUPPORT YOU, OBVIOUSLY.

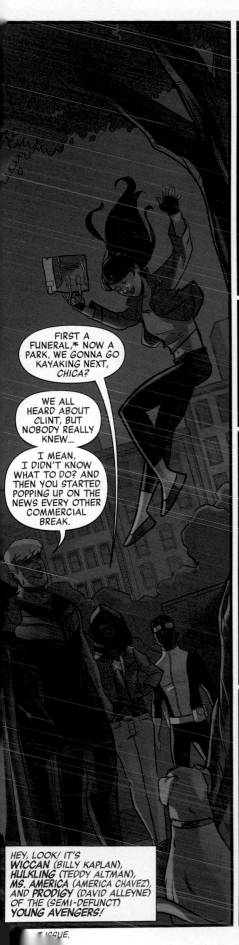

FIRST A FUNERAL,* NOW A PARK. WE GONNA GO KAYAKING NEXT, CHICA?

WE ALL HEARD ABOUT CLINT, BUT NOBODY REALLY KNEW...

I MEAN, I DIDN'T KNOW WHAT TO DO? AND THEN YOU STARTED POPPING UP ON THE NEWS EVERY OTHER COMMERCIAL BREAK.

HEY, LOOK! IT'S WICCAN (BILLY KAPLAN), HULKLING (TEDDY ALTMAN), MS. AMERICA (AMERICA CHAVEZ), AND PRODIGY (DAVID ALLEYNE) OF THE (SEMI-DEFUNCT) YOUNG AVENGERS!

* ISSUE.

WOW... YOU GUYS, THIS IS SO...

...SO EXACTLY WHAT I NEEDED. YOU'RE RIGHT, I'VE BEEN FEELING LIKE THIS WHOLE THING WAS CRUSHING DOWN ON ME, AND LIKE I WAS TOTALLY ALONE.

I DON'T REALLY KNOW WHAT'S UP WITH CLINT EITHER, AND, LIKE... AM I A BAD GUY? IS HE? I DON'T KNOW, BUT I'VE JUST BEEN FEELING SO BAD.

HEY.

IT'S ALL GOOD. EVERYONE GETS IT, WE'VE ALL BEEN THERE.

WE GOT YOUR BACK, PRINCESS.

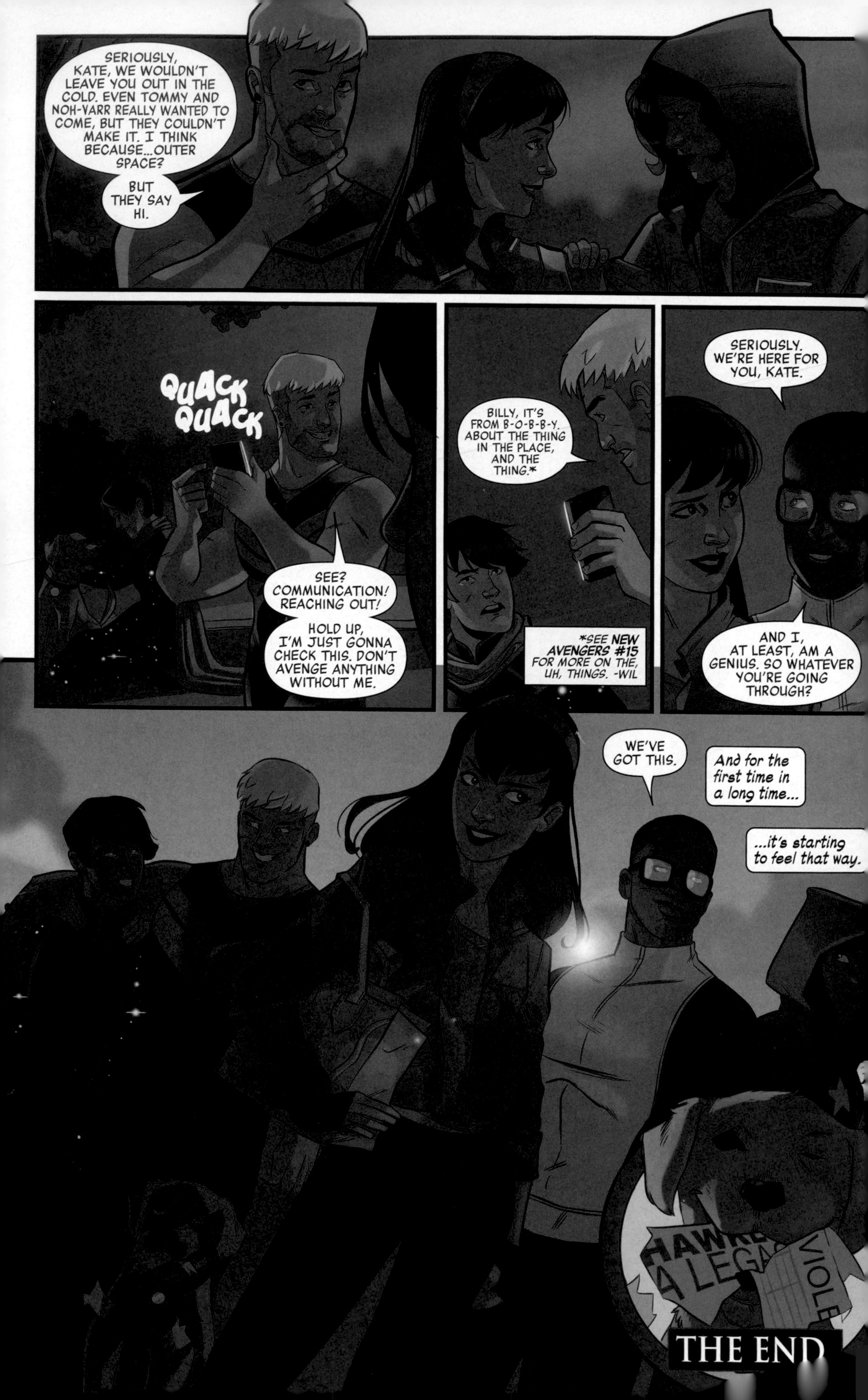
SERIOUSLY, KATE, WE WOULDN'T LEAVE YOU OUT IN THE COLD. EVEN TOMMY AND NOH-VARR REALLY WANTED TO COME, BUT THEY COULDN'T MAKE IT. I THINK BECAUSE...OUTER SPACE?
BUT THEY SAY HI.
QUACK QUACK
SEE? COMMUNICATION! REACHING OUT!
HOLD UP, I'M JUST GONNA CHECK THIS. DON'T AVENGE ANYTHING WITHOUT ME.
BILLY, IT'S FROM B-O-B-B-Y. ABOUT THE THING IN THE PLACE, AND THE THING.*
*SEE NEW AVENGERS #15 FOR MORE ON THE, UH, THINGS. -WIL
SERIOUSLY. WE'RE HERE FOR YOU, KATE.
AND I, AT LEAST, AM A GENIUS. SO WHATEVER YOU'RE GOING THROUGH?
WE'VE GOT THIS.
And for the first time in a long time...
...it's starting to feel that way.
THE END

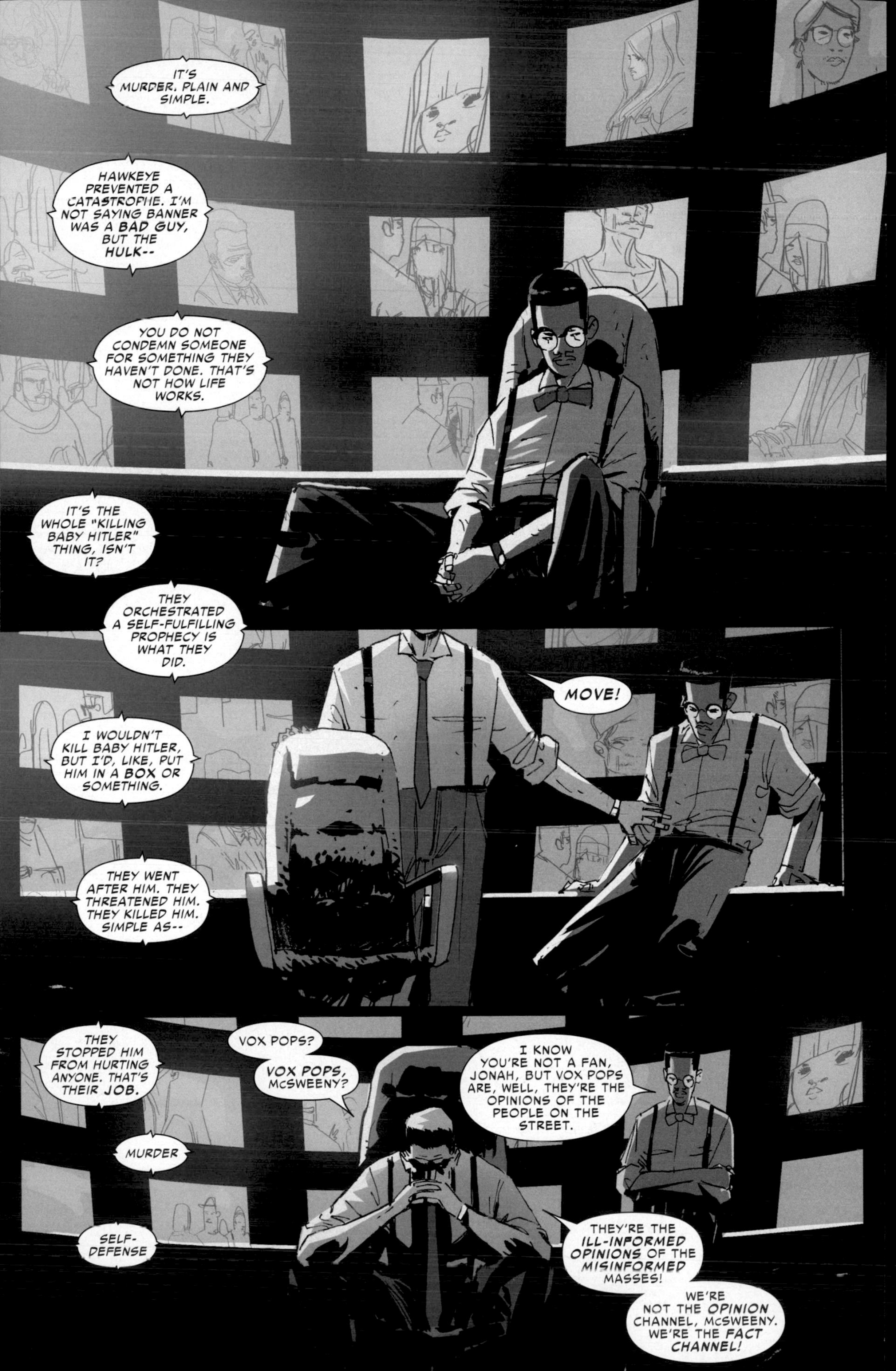
IT'S MURDER. PLAIN AND SIMPLE.
HAWKEYE PREVENTED A CATASTROPHE. I'M NOT SAYING BANNER WAS A BAD GUY, BUT THE HULK--
YOU DO NOT CONDEMN SOMEONE FOR SOMETHING THEY HAVEN'T DONE. THAT'S NOT HOW LIFE WORKS.
IT'S THE WHOLE "KILLING BABY HITLER" THING, ISN'T IT?
THEY ORCHESTRATED A SELF-FULFILLING PROPHECY IS WHAT THEY DID.
MOVE!
I WOULDN'T KILL BABY HITLER, BUT I'D, LIKE, PUT HIM IN A BOX OR SOMETHING.
THEY WENT AFTER HIM. THEY THREATENED HIM. THEY KILLED HIM. SIMPLE AS--
THEY STOPPED HIM FROM HURTING ANYONE. THAT'S THEIR JOB.
VOX POPS?
VOX POPS, McSWEENY?
I KNOW YOU'RE NOT A FAN, JONAH, BUT VOX POPS ARE, WELL, THEY'RE THE OPINIONS OF THE PEOPLE ON THE STREET.
MURDER
SELF-DEFENSE
THEY'RE THE ILL-INFORMED OPINIONS OF THE MISINFORMED MASSES!
WE'RE NOT THE OPINION CHANNEL, McSWEENY. WE'RE THE FACT CHANNEL!

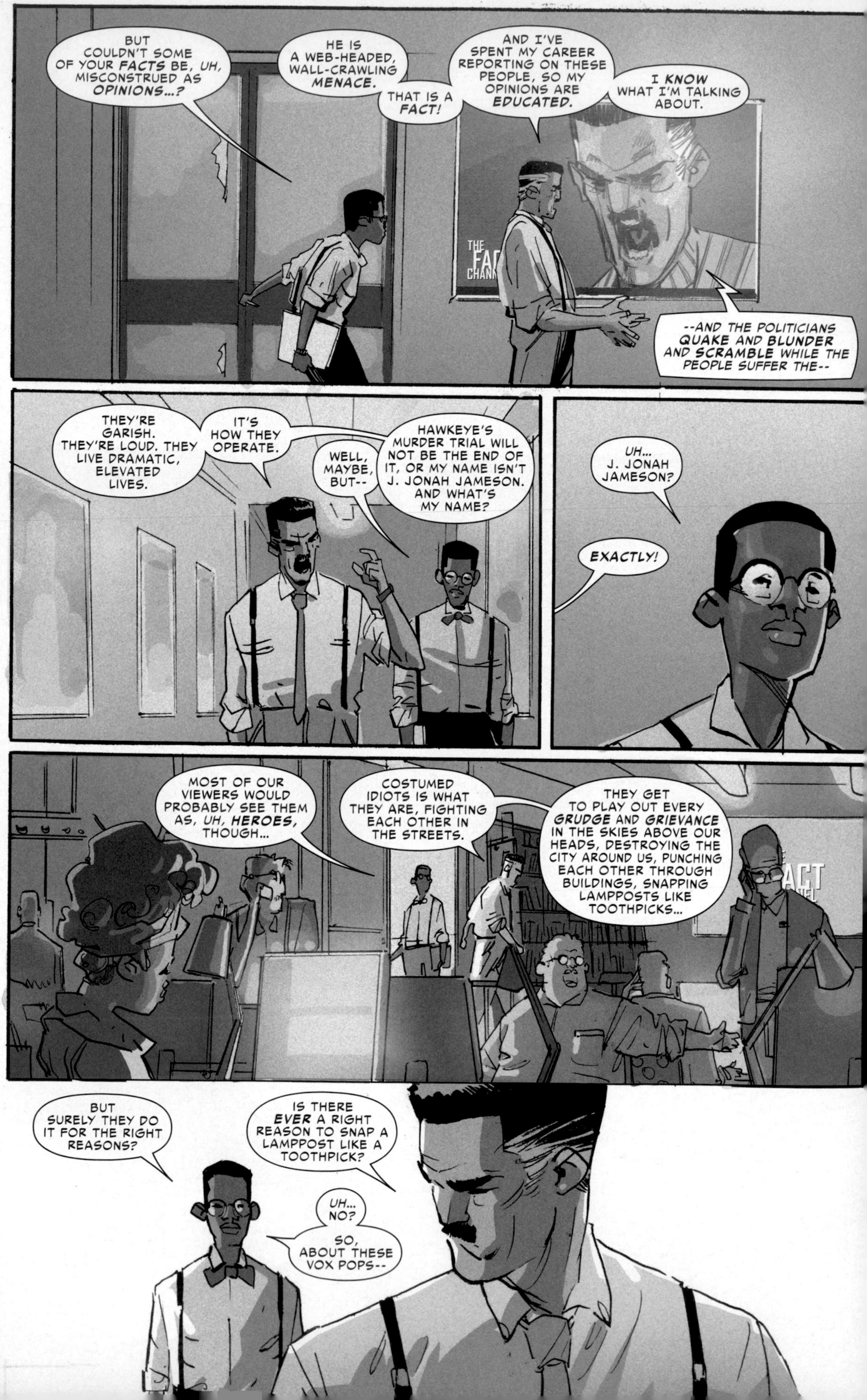
BUT COULDN'T SOME OF YOUR FACTS BE, UH, MISCONSTRUED AS OPINIONS...?
HE IS A WEB-HEADED, WALL-CRAWLING MENACE.
THAT IS A FACT!
AND I'VE SPENT MY CAREER REPORTING ON THESE PEOPLE, SO MY OPINIONS ARE EDUCATED.
I KNOW WHAT I'M TALKING ABOUT.
THE FACT CHANNEL
--AND THE POLITICIANS QUAKE AND BLUNDER AND SCRAMBLE WHILE THE PEOPLE SUFFER THE--
THEY'RE GARISH. THEY'RE LOUD. THEY LIVE DRAMATIC, ELEVATED LIVES.
IT'S HOW THEY OPERATE.
WELL, MAYBE, BUT--
HAWKEYE'S MURDER TRIAL WILL NOT BE THE END OF IT, OR MY NAME ISN'T J. JONAH JAMESON. AND WHAT'S MY NAME?
UH... J. JONAH JAMESON?
EXACTLY!
MOST OF OUR VIEWERS WOULD PROBABLY SEE THEM AS, UH, HEROES, THOUGH...
COSTUMED IDIOTS IS WHAT THEY ARE, FIGHTING EACH OTHER IN THE STREETS.
THEY GET TO PLAY OUT EVERY GRUDGE AND GRIEVANCE IN THE SKIES ABOVE OUR HEADS, DESTROYING THE CITY AROUND US, PUNCHING EACH OTHER THROUGH BUILDINGS, SNAPPING LAMPPOSTS LIKE TOOTHPICKS...
BUT SURELY THEY DO IT FOR THE RIGHT REASONS?
IS THERE EVER A RIGHT REASON TO SNAP A LAMPPOST LIKE A TOOTHPICK?
UH... NO?
SO, ABOUT THESE VOX POPS--

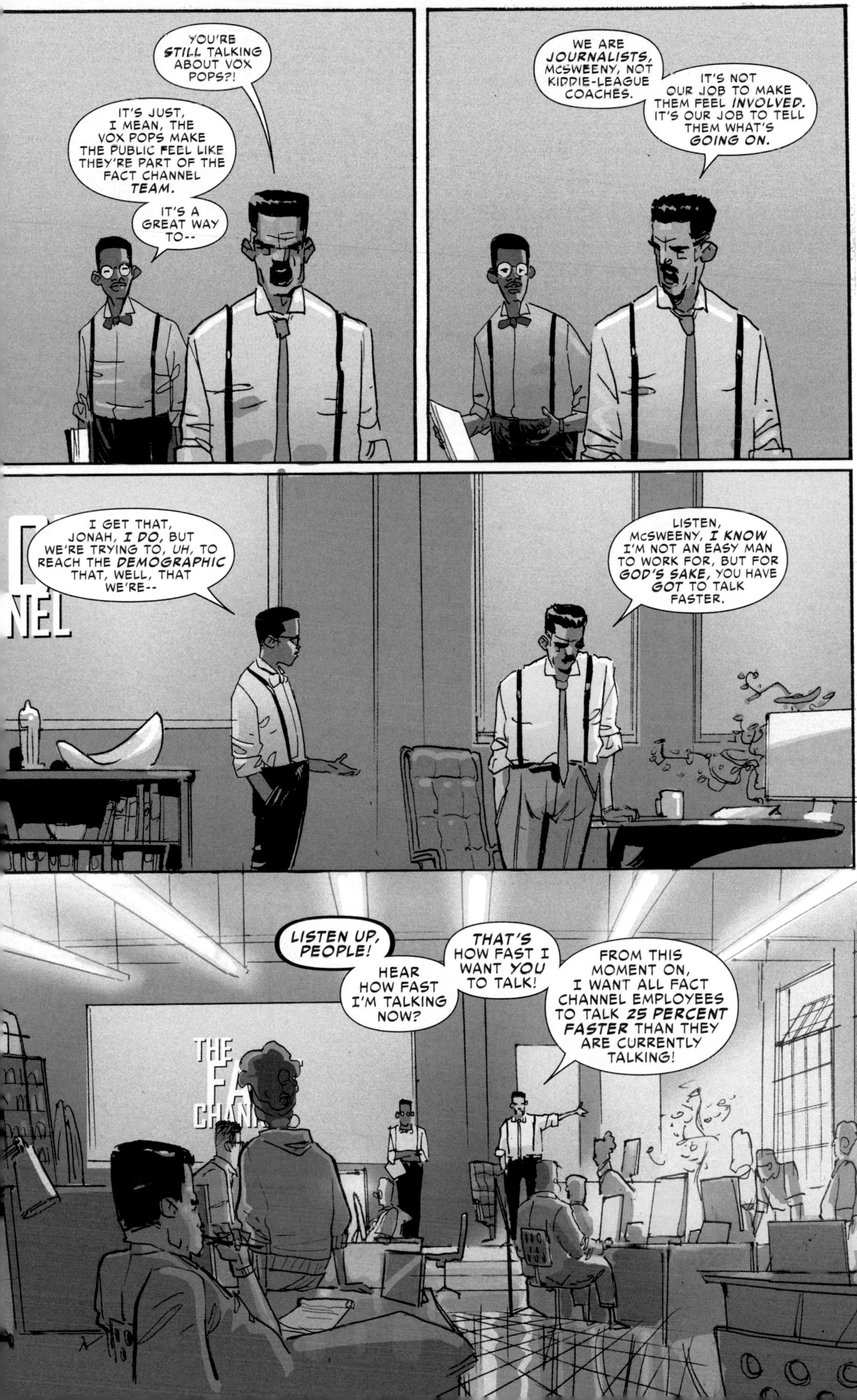
IT'S JUST, I MEAN, THE VOX POPS MAKE THE PUBLIC FEEL LIKE THEY'RE PART OF THE FACT CHANNEL TEAM.
IT'S A GREAT WAY TO--
YOU'RE STILL TALKING ABOUT VOX POPS?!
WE ARE JOURNALISTS, McSWEENY, NOT KIDDIE-LEAGUE COACHES.
IT'S NOT OUR JOB TO MAKE THEM FEEL INVOLVED. IT'S OUR JOB TO TELL THEM WHAT'S GOING ON.
I GET THAT, JONAH, I DO, BUT WE'RE TRYING TO, UH, TO REACH THE DEMOGRAPHIC THAT, WELL, THAT WE'RE--
LISTEN, McSWEENY, I KNOW I'M NOT AN EASY MAN TO WORK FOR, BUT FOR GOD'S SAKE, YOU HAVE GOT TO TALK FASTER.
LISTEN UP, PEOPLE!
HEAR HOW FAST I'M TALKING NOW?
THAT'S HOW FAST I WANT YOU TO TALK!
FROM THIS MOMENT ON, I WANT ALL FACT CHANNEL EMPLOYEES TO TALK 25 PERCENT FASTER THAN THEY ARE CURRENTLY TALKING!

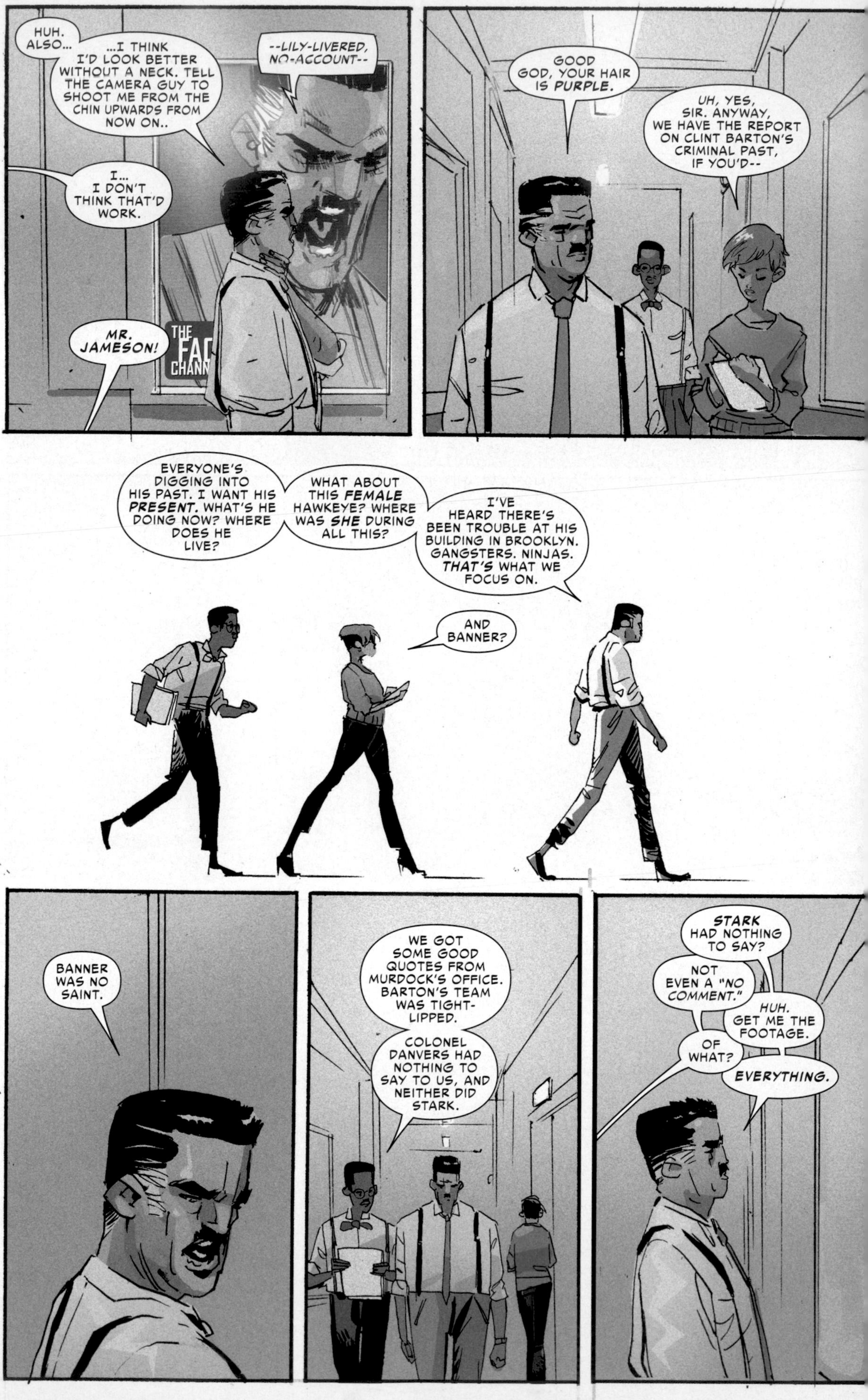
HUH. ALSO...
...I THINK I'D LOOK BETTER WITHOUT A NECK. TELL THE CAMERA GUY TO SHOOT ME FROM THE CHIN UPWARDS FROM NOW ON..
--LILY-LIVERED, NO-ACCOUNT--
I... I DON'T THINK THAT'D WORK.
MR. JAMESON!
THE FAC
CHANN
GOOD GOD, YOUR HAIR IS PURPLE.
UH, YES, SIR. ANYWAY, WE HAVE THE REPORT ON CLINT BARTON'S CRIMINAL PAST, IF YOU'D--
EVERYONE'S DIGGING INTO HIS PAST. I WANT HIS PRESENT. WHAT'S HE DOING NOW? WHERE DOES HE LIVE?
WHAT ABOUT THIS FEMALE HAWKEYE? WHERE WAS SHE DURING ALL THIS?
I'VE HEARD THERE'S BEEN TROUBLE AT HIS BUILDING IN BROOKLYN. GANGSTERS. NINJAS. THAT'S WHAT WE FOCUS ON.
AND BANNER?
BANNER WAS NO SAINT.
WE GOT SOME GOOD QUOTES FROM MURDOCK'S OFFICE. BARTON'S TEAM WAS TIGHT-LIPPED.
COLONEL DANVERS HAD NOTHING TO SAY TO US, AND NEITHER DID STARK.
STARK HAD NOTHING TO SAY?
NOT EVEN A "NO COMMENT."
HUH. GET ME THE FOOTAGE.
OF WHAT?
EVERYTHING.

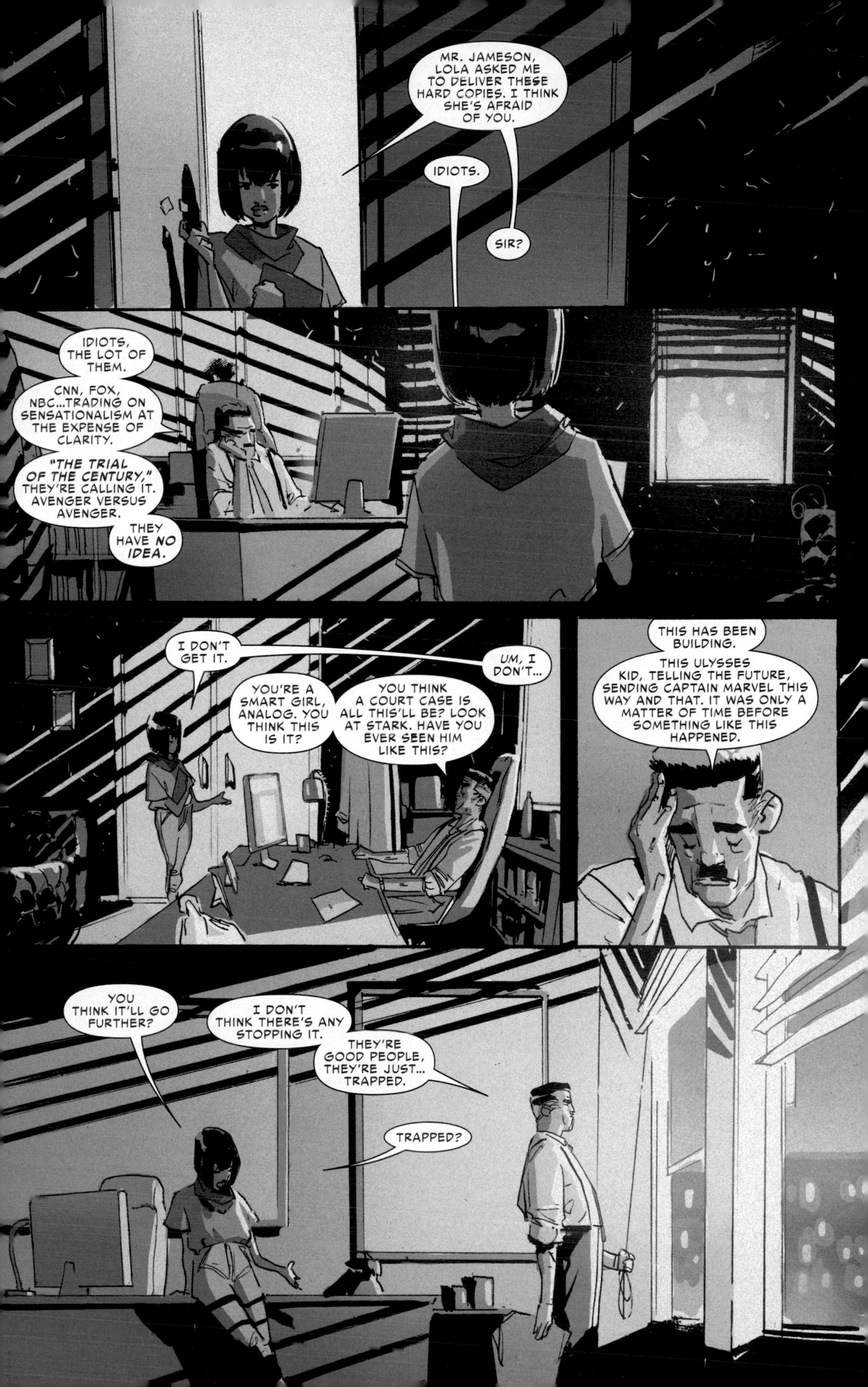
MR. JAMESON, LOLA ASKED ME TO DELIVER THESE HARD COPIES. I THINK SHE'S AFRAID OF YOU.
IDIOTS.
SIR?
IDIOTS, THE LOT OF THEM.
CNN, FOX, NBC...TRADING ON SENSATIONALISM AT THE EXPENSE OF CLARITY.
"THE TRIAL OF THE CENTURY," THEY'RE CALLING IT. AVENGER VERSUS AVENGER.
THEY HAVE NO IDEA.
I DON'T GET IT.
UM, I DON'T...
YOU'RE A SMART GIRL, ANALOG. YOU THINK THIS IS IT?
YOU THINK A COURT CASE IS ALL THIS'LL BE? LOOK AT STARK. HAVE YOU EVER SEEN HIM LIKE THIS?
THIS HAS BEEN BUILDING.
THIS ULYSSES KID, TELLING THE FUTURE, SENDING CAPTAIN MARVEL THIS WAY AND THAT. IT WAS ONLY A MATTER OF TIME BEFORE SOMETHING LIKE THIS HAPPENED.
YOU THINK IT'LL GO FURTHER?
I DON'T THINK THERE'S ANY STOPPING IT.
THEY'RE GOOD PEOPLE, THEY'RE JUST... TRAPPED.
TRAPPED?

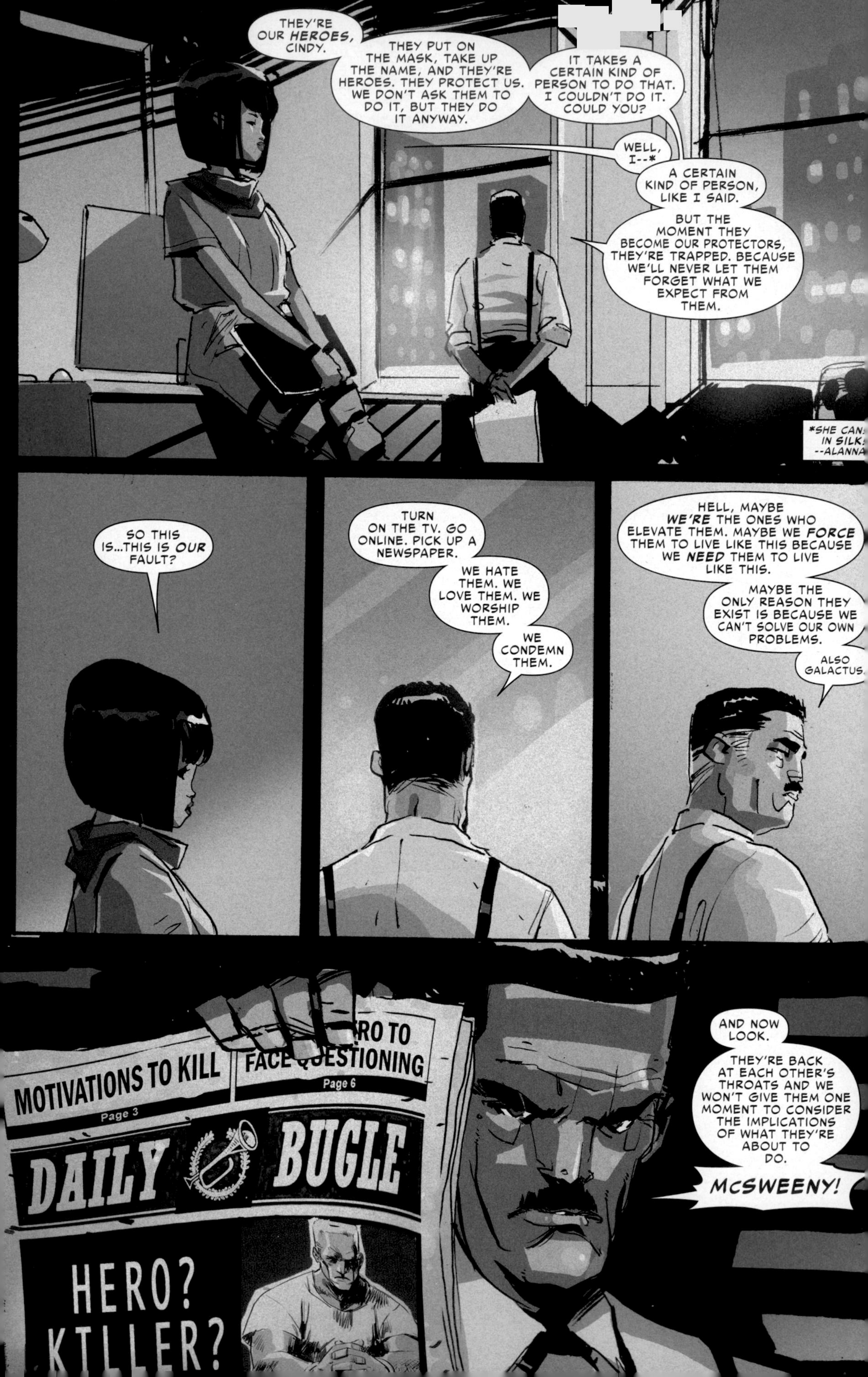
THEY'RE OUR *HEROES*, CINDY.
THEY PUT ON THE MASK, TAKE UP THE NAME, AND THEY'RE HEROES. THEY PROTECT US. WE DON'T ASK THEM TO DO IT, BUT THEY DO IT ANYWAY.
IT TAKES A CERTAIN KIND OF PERSON TO DO THAT. I COULDN'T DO IT. COULD YOU?
WELL, I--*
A CERTAIN KIND OF PERSON, LIKE I SAID.
BUT THE MOMENT THEY BECOME OUR PROTECTORS, THEY'RE TRAPPED. BECAUSE WE'LL NEVER LET THEM FORGET WHAT WE EXPECT FROM THEM.
SO THIS IS...THIS IS *OUR* FAULT?
TURN ON THE TV. GO ONLINE. PICK UP A NEWSPAPER.
WE HATE THEM. WE LOVE THEM. WE WORSHIP THEM.
WE CONDEMN THEM.
HELL, MAYBE *WE'RE* THE ONES WHO ELEVATE THEM. MAYBE WE *FORCE* THEM TO LIVE LIKE THIS BECAUSE WE *NEED* THEM TO LIVE LIKE THIS.
MAYBE THE ONLY REASON THEY EXIST IS BECAUSE WE CAN'T SOLVE OUR OWN PROBLEMS.
ALSO GALACTUS.
MOTIVATIONS TO KILL
Page 3
FACE QUESTIONING
Page 6
DAILY BUGLE
HERO? KILLER?
AND NOW LOOK.
THEY'RE BACK AT EACH OTHER'S THROATS AND WE WON'T GIVE THEM ONE MOMENT TO CONSIDER THE IMPLICATIONS OF WHAT THEY'RE ABOUT TO DO.
McSWEENY!

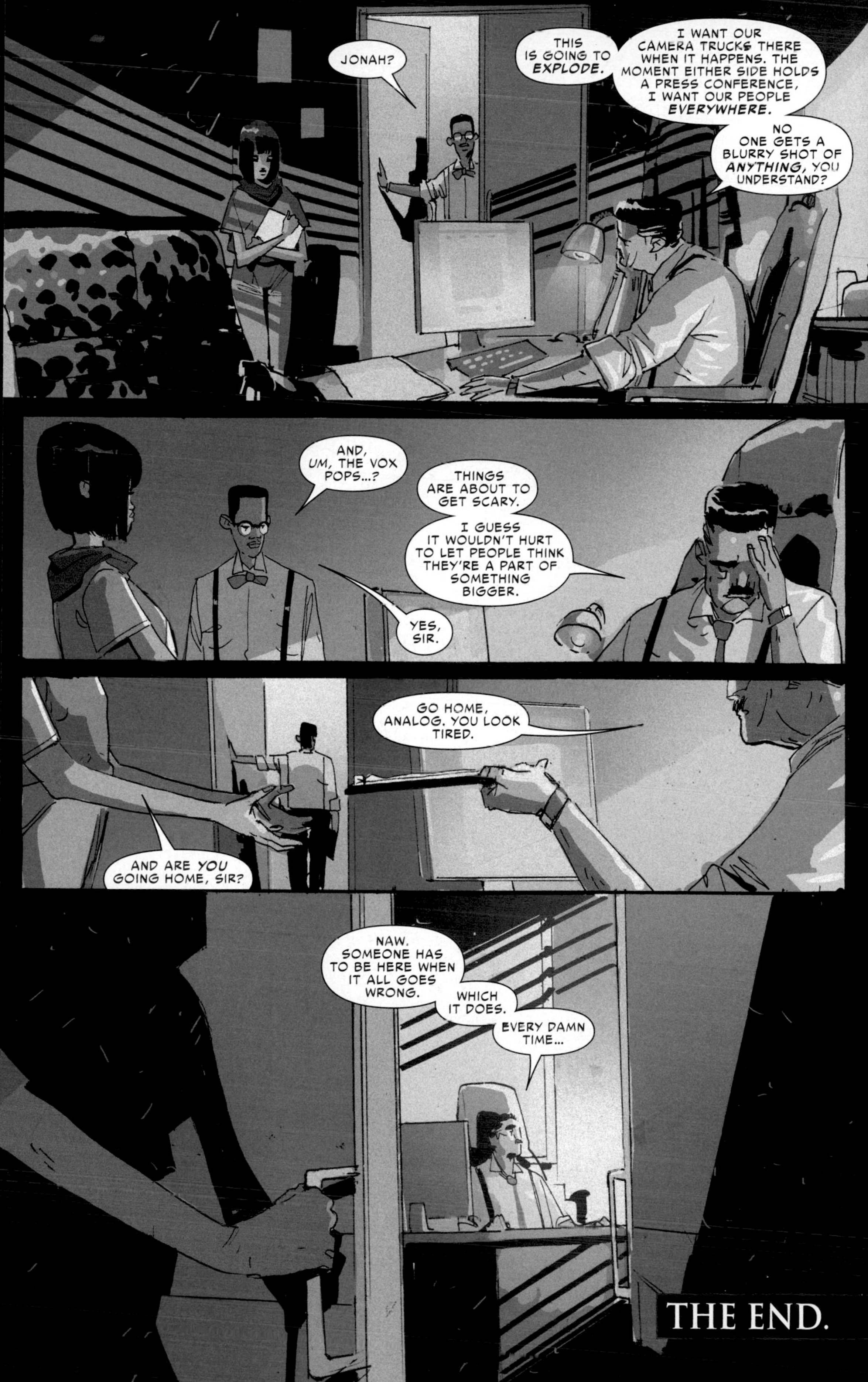
JONAH?
THIS IS GOING TO *EXPLODE.*
I WANT OUR CAMERA TRUCKS THERE WHEN IT HAPPENS. THE MOMENT EITHER SIDE HOLDS A PRESS CONFERENCE, I WANT OUR PEOPLE *EVERYWHERE.*
NO ONE GETS A BLURRY SHOT OF *ANYTHING*, YOU UNDERSTAND?
AND, UM, THE VOX POPS...?
THINGS ARE ABOUT TO GET SCARY.
I GUESS IT WOULDN'T HURT TO LET PEOPLE THINK THEY'RE A PART OF SOMETHING BIGGER.
YES, SIR.
GO HOME, ANALOG. YOU LOOK TIRED.
AND ARE *YOU* GOING HOME, SIR?
NAW. SOMEONE HAS TO BE HERE WHEN IT ALL GOES WRONG.
WHICH IT DOES.
EVERY DAMN TIME...
THE END.

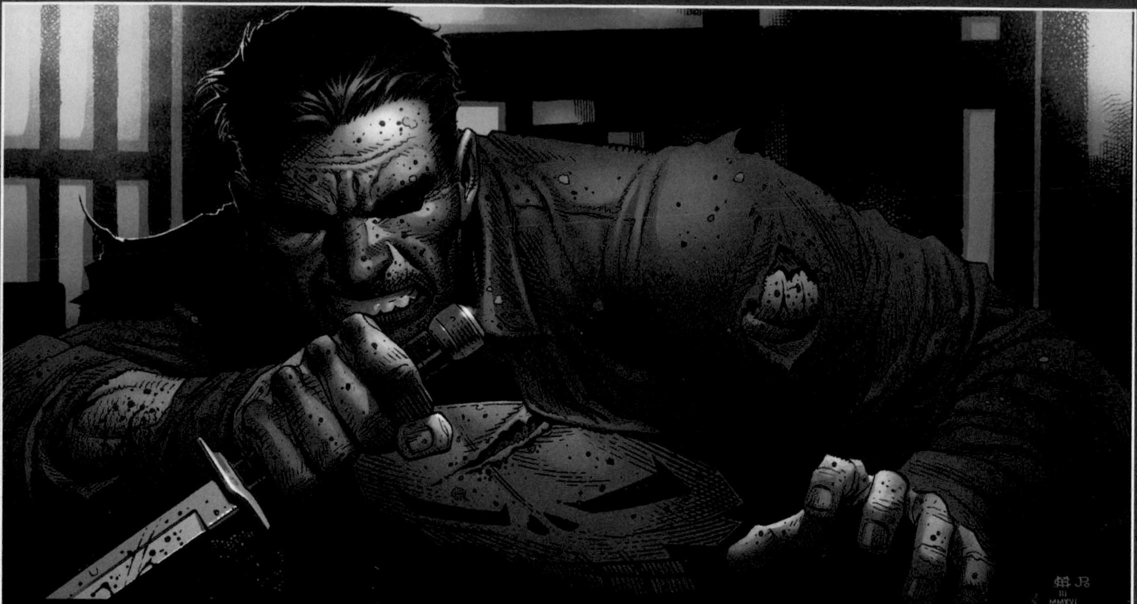

COVER ART BY JIM CHEUNG & JUSTIN PONSOR

# THE PUNISHER

WRITER
CHUCK BROWN

ARTIST
CHRIS VISIONS

COLOR ARTIST
MEGAN WILSON

EDITOR
CHRIS ROBINSON

# POWER PACK

WRITER
JOHN ALLISON

ARTIST
ROSI KÄMPE

COLOR ARTIST
MEGAN WILSON

ASSISTANT EDITOR
CHARLES BEACHAM

EDITOR
WIL MOSS

COVER ART BY DECLAN SHALVEY & JORDIE BELLAIRE

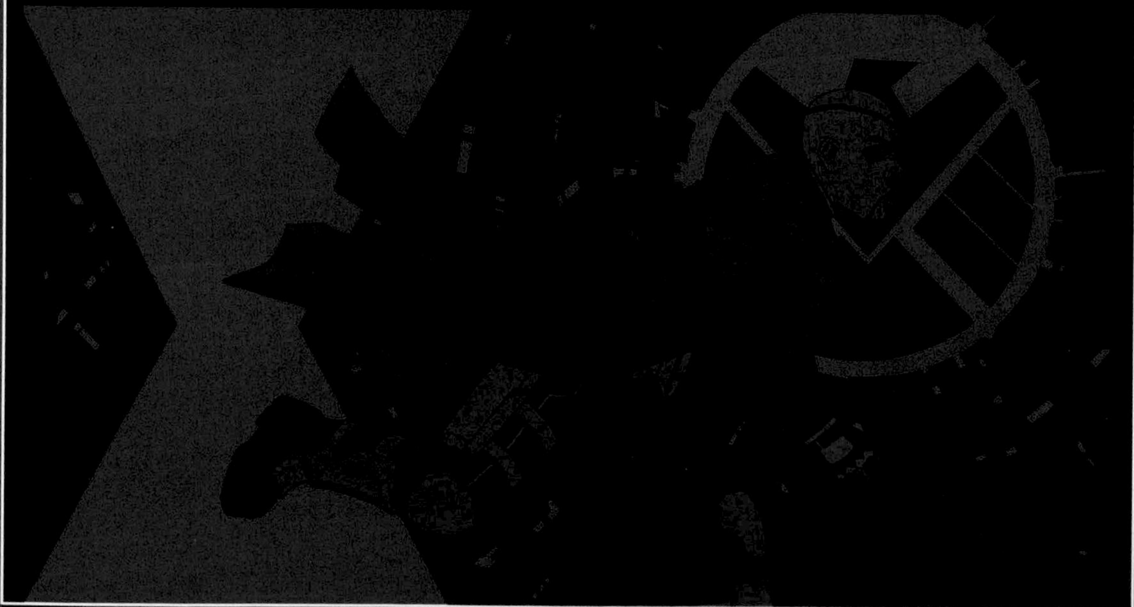

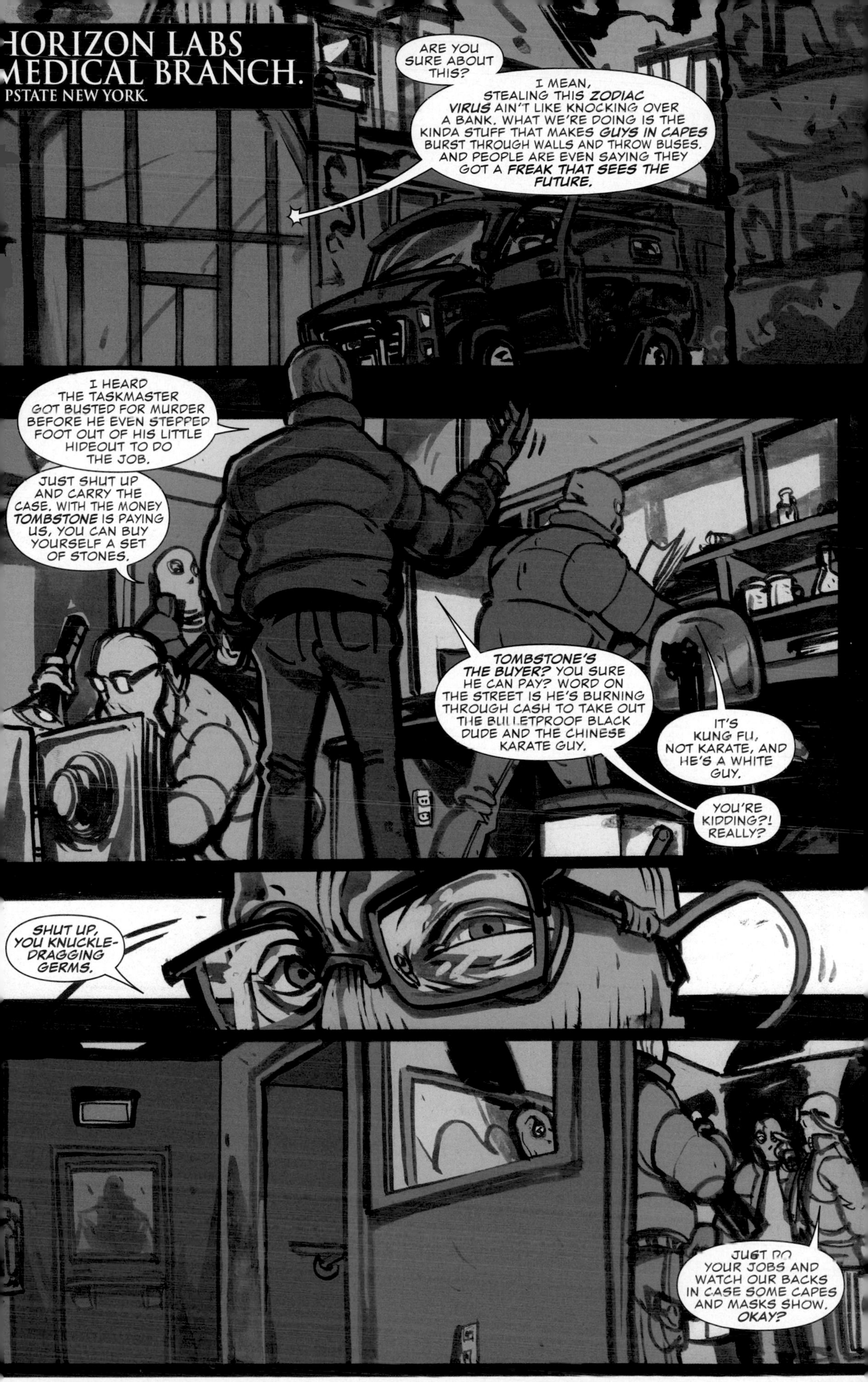
HORIZON LABS MEDICAL BRANCH.
UPSTATE NEW YORK.
ARE YOU SURE ABOUT THIS?
I MEAN, STEALING THIS ZODIAC VIRUS AIN'T LIKE KNOCKING OVER A BANK. WHAT WE'RE DOING IS THE KINDA STUFF THAT MAKES GUYS IN CAPES BURST THROUGH WALLS AND THROW BUSES. AND PEOPLE ARE EVEN SAYING THEY GOT A FREAK THAT SEES THE FUTURE.
I HEARD THE TASKMASTER GOT BUSTED FOR MURDER BEFORE HE EVEN STEPPED FOOT OUT OF HIS LITTLE HIDEOUT TO DO THE JOB.
JUST SHUT UP AND CARRY THE CASE. WITH THE MONEY TOMBSTONE IS PAYING US, YOU CAN BUY YOURSELF A SET OF STONES.
TOMBSTONE'S THE BUYER? YOU SURE HE CAN PAY? WORD ON THE STREET IS HE'S BURNING THROUGH CASH TO TAKE OUT THE BULLETPROOF BLACK DUDE AND THE CHINESE KARATE GUY.
IT'S KUNG FU, NOT KARATE, AND HE'S A WHITE GUY.
YOU'RE KIDDING?! REALLY?
SHUT UP, YOU KNUCKLE-DRAGGING GERMS.
JUST DO YOUR JOBS AND WATCH OUR BACKS IN CASE SOME CAPES AND MASKS SHOW. OKAY?

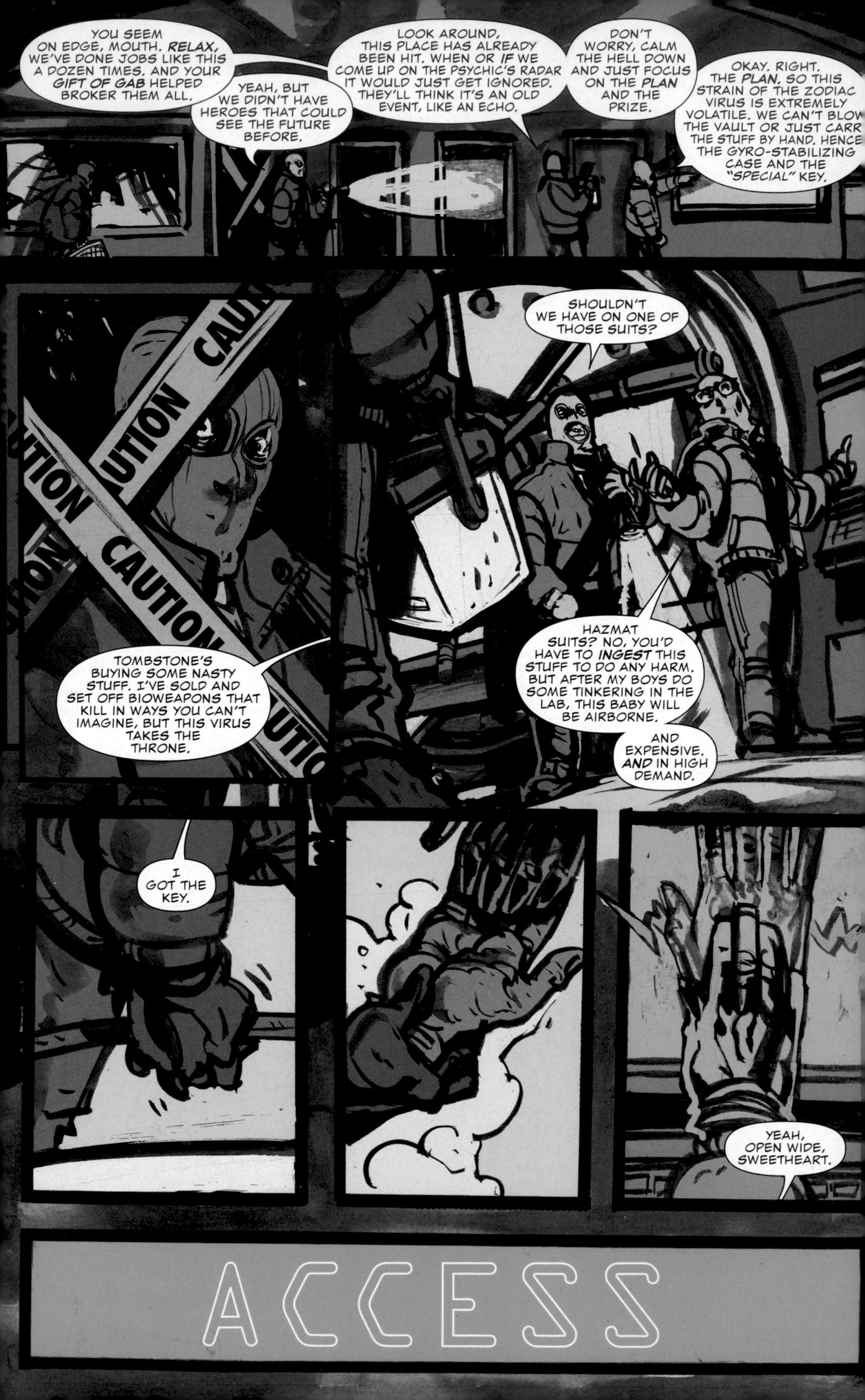
YOU SEEM ON EDGE, MOUTH. RELAX, WE'VE DONE JOBS LIKE THIS A DOZEN TIMES. AND YOUR GIFT OF GAB HELPED BROKER THEM ALL.
YEAH, BUT WE DIDN'T HAVE HEROES THAT COULD SEE THE FUTURE BEFORE.
LOOK AROUND, THIS PLACE HAS ALREADY BEEN HIT. WHEN OR IF WE COME UP ON THE PSYCHIC'S RADAR IT WOULD JUST GET IGNORED. THEY'LL THINK IT'S AN OLD EVENT, LIKE AN ECHO.
DON'T WORRY, CALM THE HELL DOWN AND JUST FOCUS ON THE PLAN AND THE PRIZE.
OKAY. RIGHT. THE PLAN. SO THIS STRAIN OF THE ZODIAC VIRUS IS EXTREMELY VOLATILE. WE CAN'T BLOW THE VAULT OR JUST CARR THE STUFF BY HAND. HENCE THE GYRO-STABILIZING CASE AND THE "SPECIAL" KEY.
CAUTION
CAUTION
TOMBSTONE'S BUYING SOME NASTY STUFF. I'VE SOLD AND SET OFF BIOWEAPONS THAT KILL IN WAYS YOU CAN'T IMAGINE, BUT THIS VIRUS TAKES THE THRONE.
SHOULDN'T WE HAVE ON ONE OF THOSE SUITS?
HAZMAT SUITS? NO, YOU'D HAVE TO INGEST THIS STUFF TO DO ANY HARM. BUT AFTER MY BOYS DO SOME TINKERING IN THE LAB, THIS BABY WILL BE AIRBORNE.
AND EXPENSIVE. AND IN HIGH DEMAND.
I GOT THE KEY.
YEAH, OPEN WIDE, SWEETHEART.
ACCESS

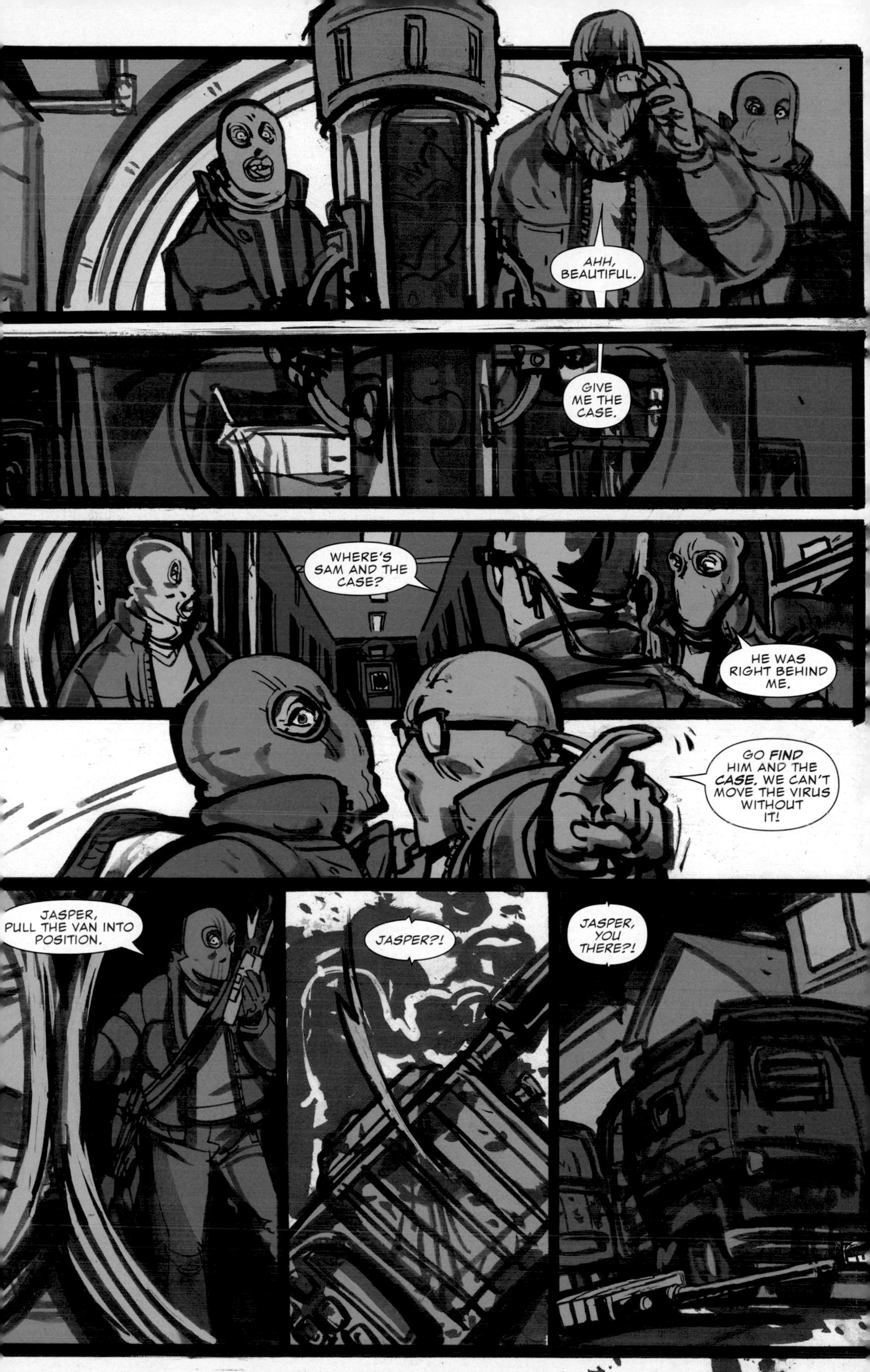
AHH, BEAUTIFUL.
GIVE ME THE CASE.
WHERE'S SAM AND THE CASE?
HE WAS RIGHT BEHIND ME.
GO **FIND** HIM AND THE **CASE.** WE CAN'T MOVE THE VIRUS WITHOUT IT!
JASPER, PULL THE VAN INTO POSITION.
JASPER?!
JASPER, YOU THERE?!

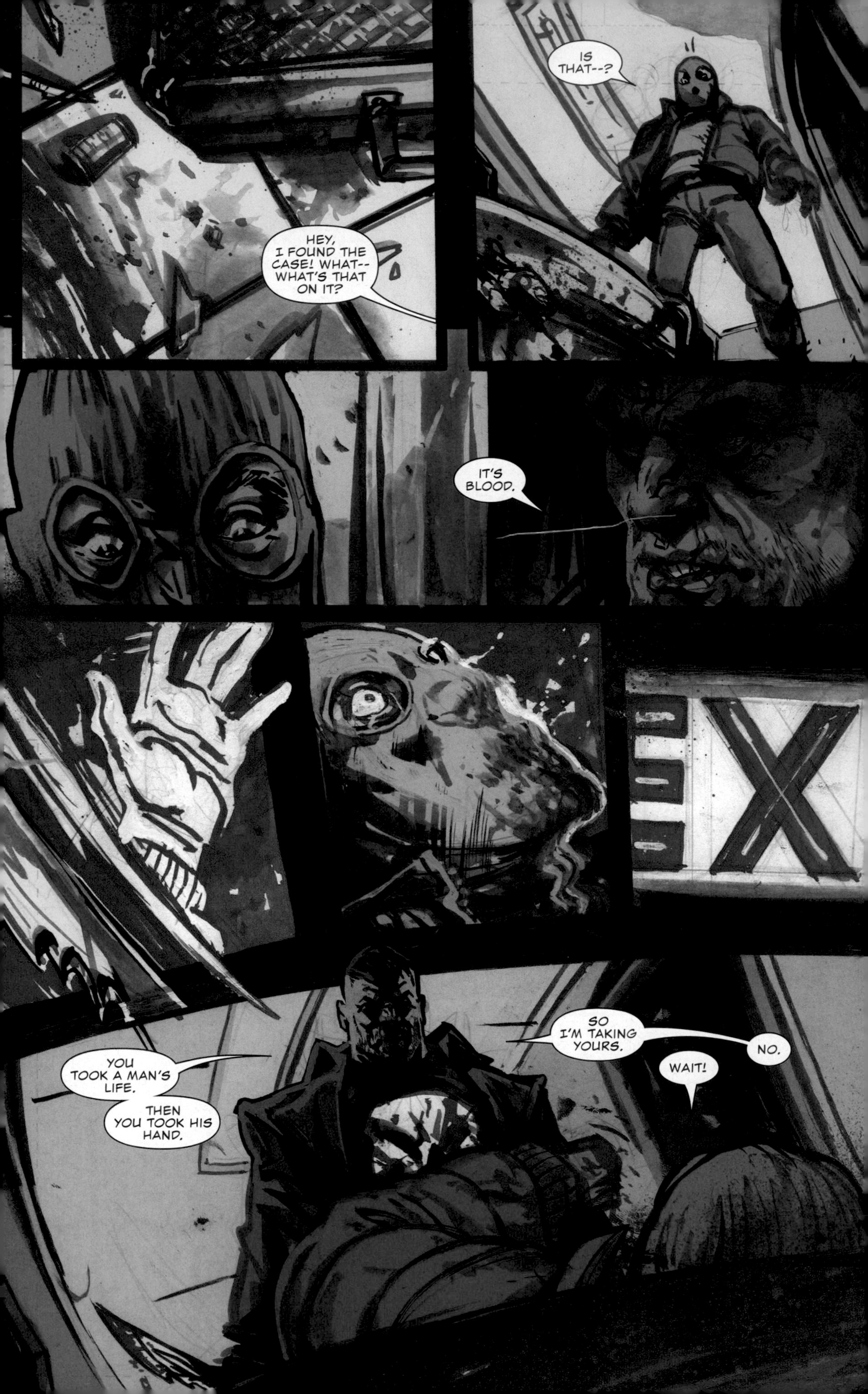
HEY, I FOUND THE CASE! WHAT-- WHAT'S THAT ON IT?
IS THAT--?
IT'S BLOOD.
YOU TOOK A MAN'S LIFE.
THEN YOU TOOK HIS HAND.
SO I'M TAKING YOURS.
NO.
WAIT!

AHHHHRRRRAAAUUUGGHHH!
SOMETHING'S GOT 'EM, WE GOTTA GET OUT OF HERE!
CALM DOWN, JUST STICK TO THE PLAN!
YOU'RE RUNNING AWAY FROM MILLIONS!
IT'S ONE OF THEM! THE FREAK SAW US COMING!

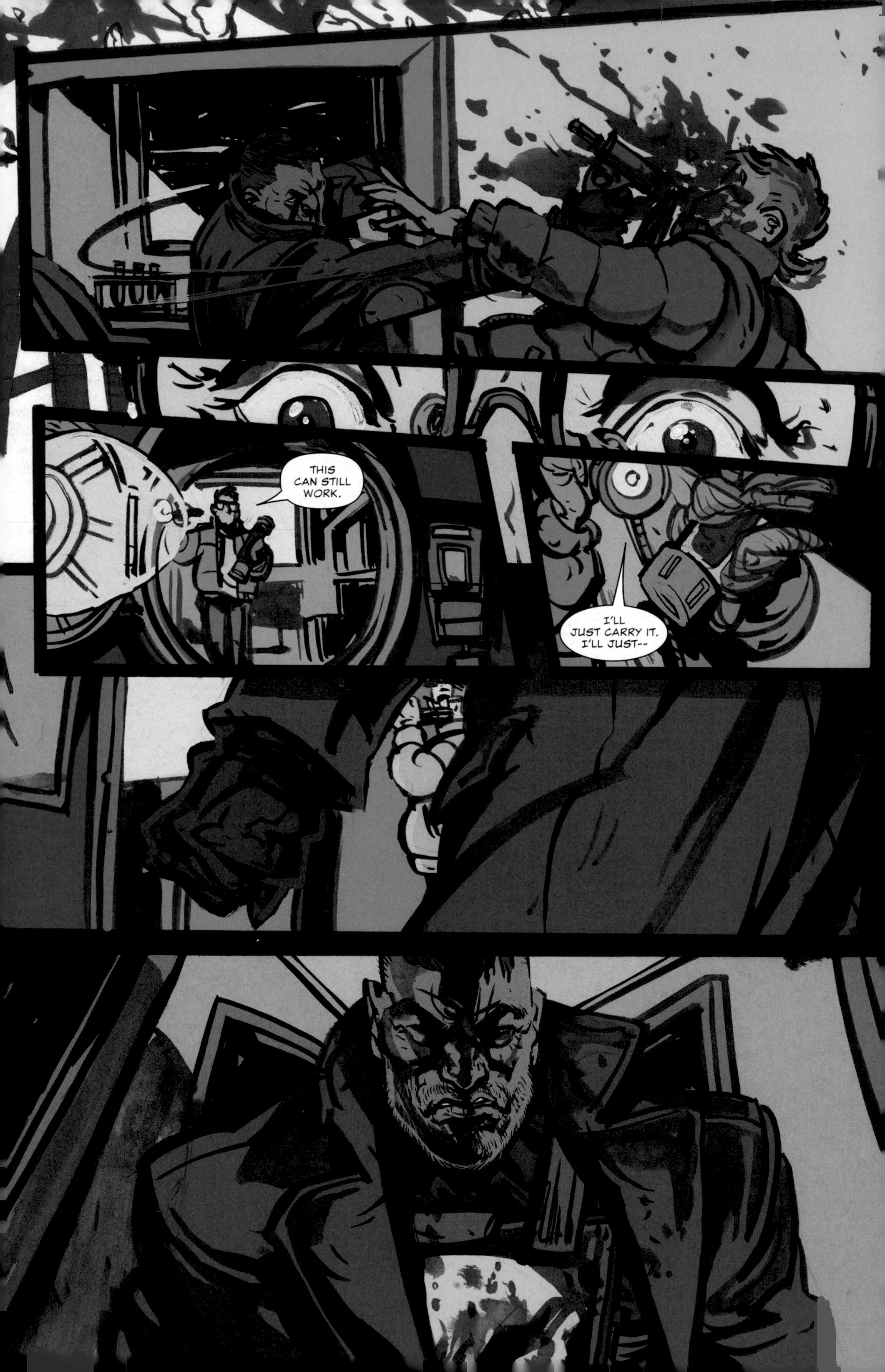
THIS CAN STILL WORK.
I'LL JUST CARRY IT. I'LL JUST--

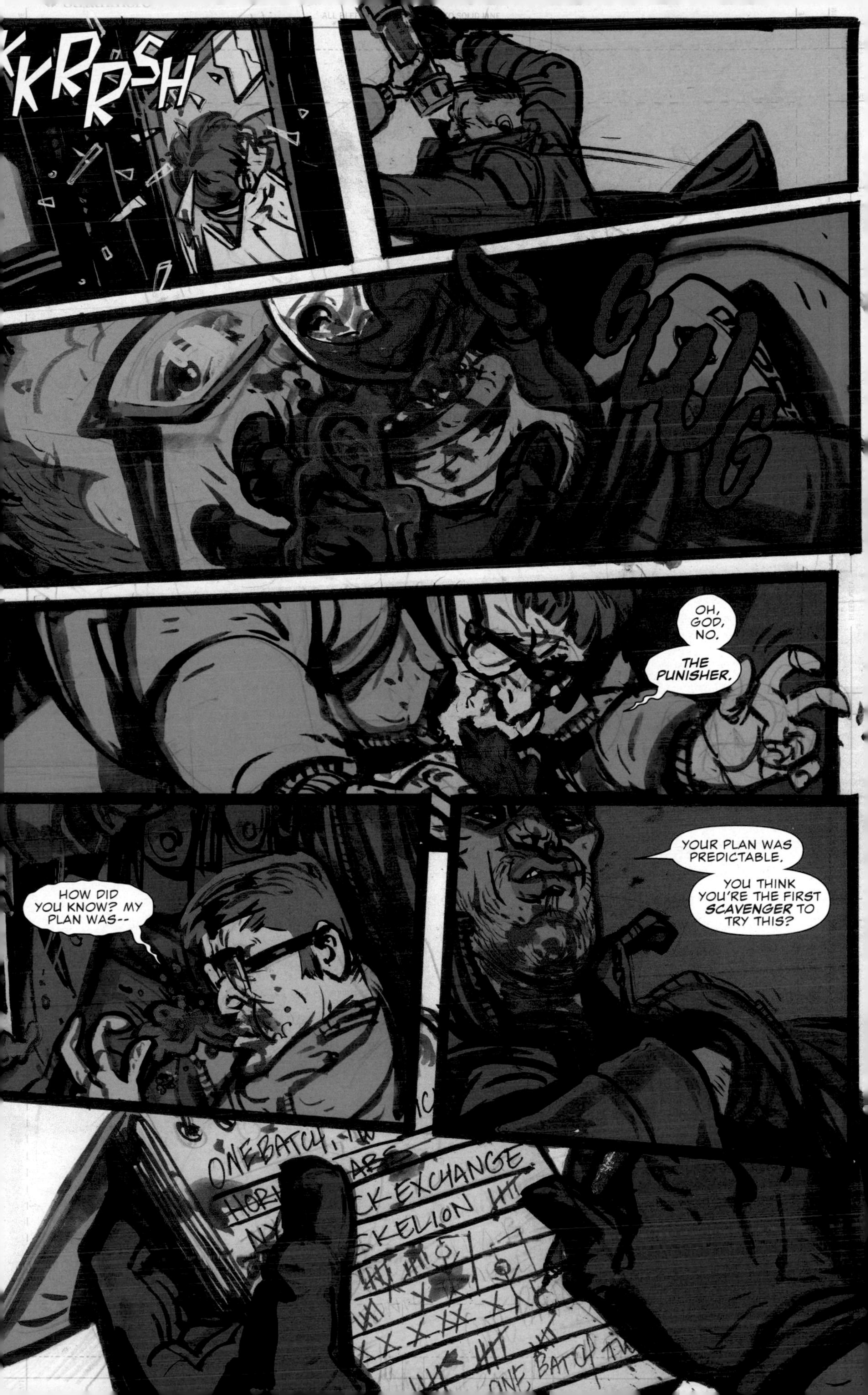
KKRRSH
GLUG
OH, GOD, NO.
THE PUNISHER.
HOW DID YOU KNOW? MY PLAN WAS--
YOUR PLAN WAS PREDICTABLE.
YOU THINK YOU'RE THE FIRST SCAVENGER TO TRY THIS?

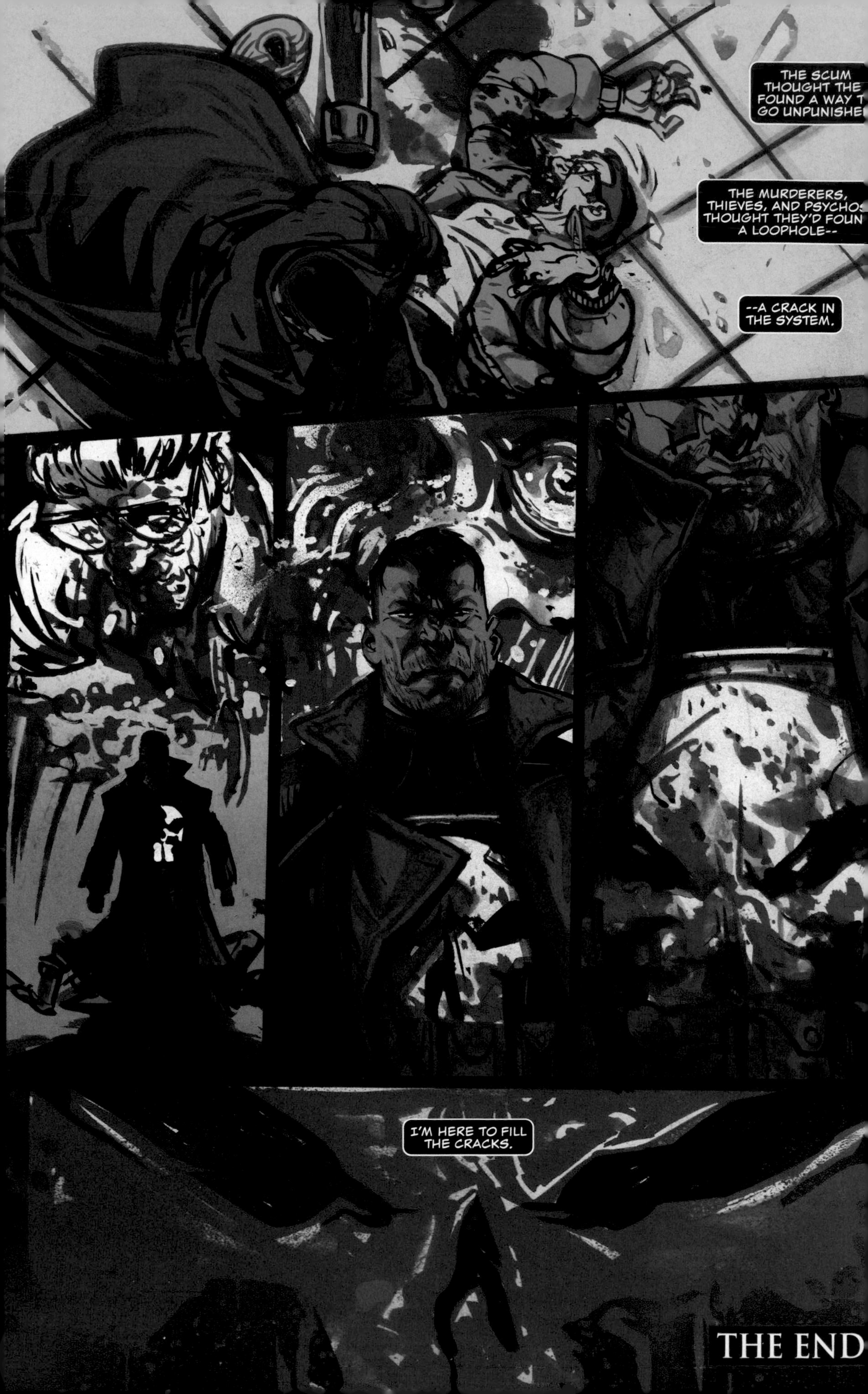
THE SCUM THOUGHT THE FOUND A WAY T GO UNPUNISHE
THE MURDERERS, THIEVES, AND PSYCHOS THOUGHT THEY'D FOUN A LOOPHOLE--
--A CRACK IN THE SYSTEM.
I'M HERE TO FILL THE CRACKS.
THE END

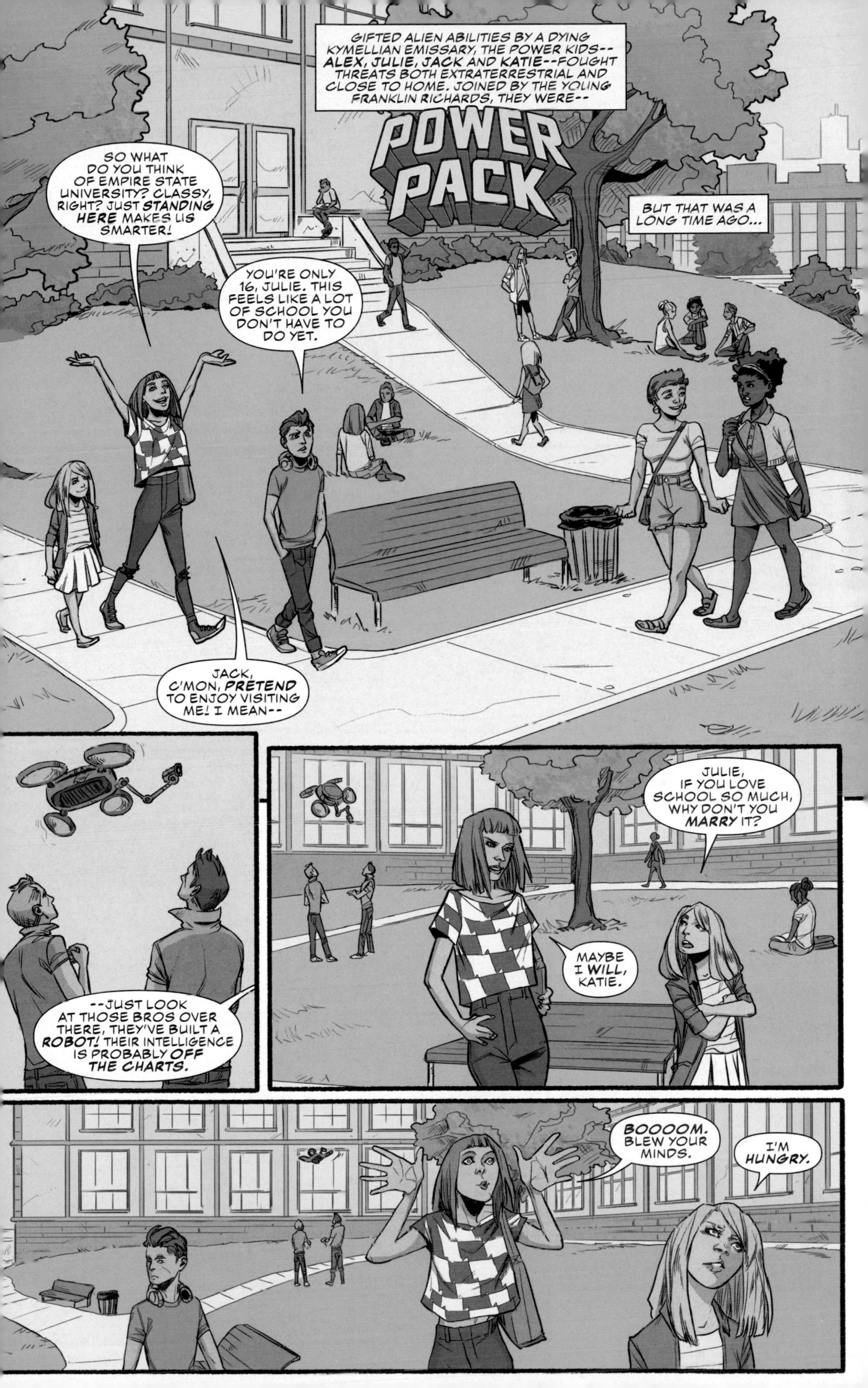
GIFTED ALIEN ABILITIES BY A DYING KYMELLIAN EMISSARY, THE POWER KIDS--ALEX, JULIE, JACK AND KATIE--FOUGHT THREATS BOTH EXTRATERRESTRIAL AND CLOSE TO HOME. JOINED BY THE YOUNG FRANKLIN RICHARDS, THEY WERE--
POWER PACK
BUT THAT WAS A LONG TIME AGO...
SO WHAT DO YOU THINK OF EMPIRE STATE UNIVERSITY? CLASSY, RIGHT? JUST STANDING HERE MAKES US SMARTER!
YOU'RE ONLY 16, JULIE. THIS FEELS LIKE A LOT OF SCHOOL YOU DON'T HAVE TO DO YET.
JACK, C'MON, PRETEND TO ENJOY VISITING ME! I MEAN--
--JUST LOOK AT THOSE BROS OVER THERE, THEY'VE BUILT A ROBOT! THEIR INTELLIGENCE IS PROBABLY OFF THE CHARTS.
JULIE, IF YOU LOVE SCHOOL SO MUCH, WHY DON'T YOU MARRY IT?
MAYBE I WILL, KATIE.
BOOOOM. BLEW YOUR MINDS.
I'M HUNGRY.

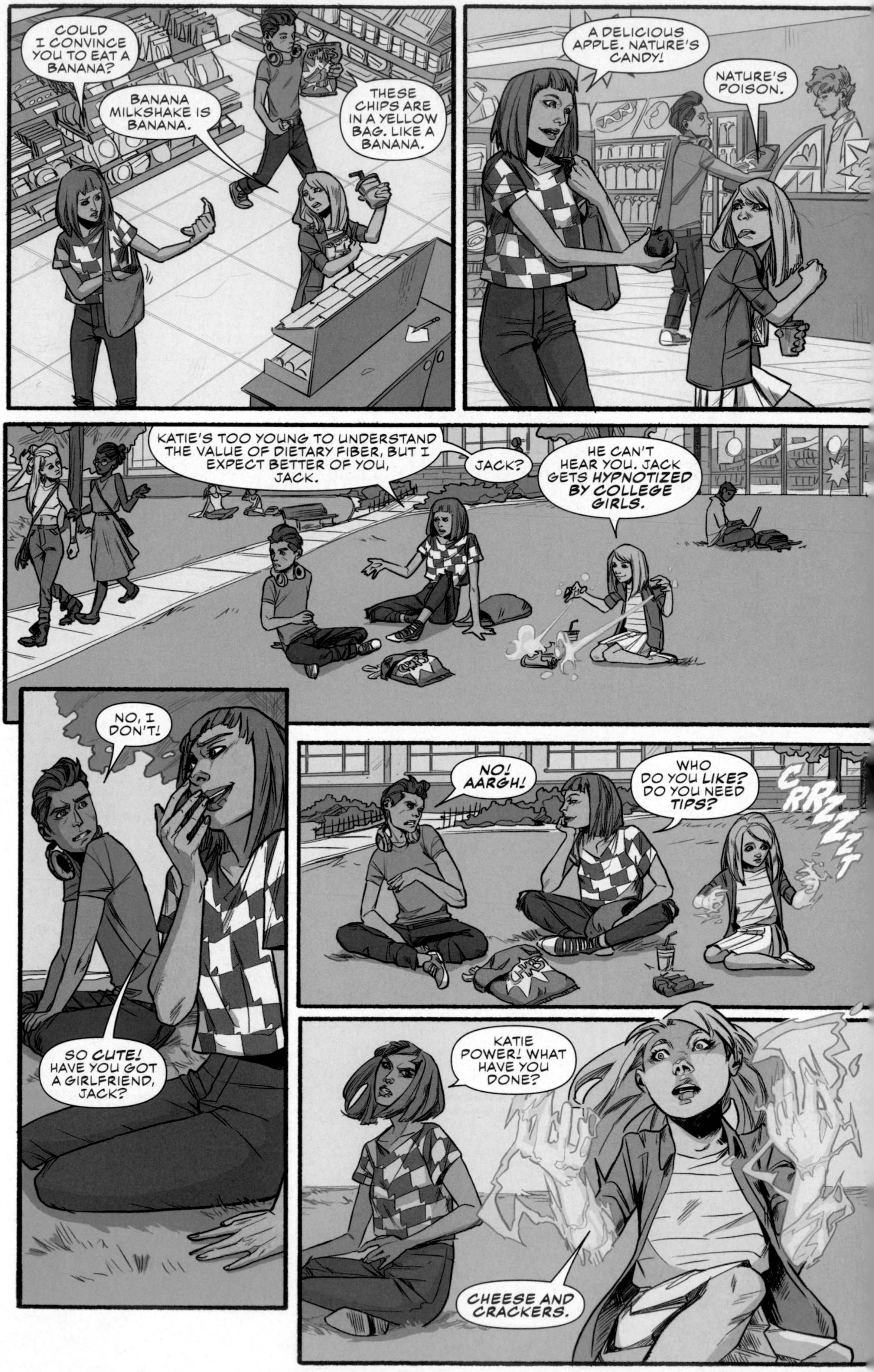
COULD I CONVINCE YOU TO EAT A BANANA?
BANANA MILKSHAKE IS BANANA.
THESE CHIPS ARE IN A YELLOW BAG. LIKE A BANANA.
A DELICIOUS APPLE. NATURE'S CANDY!
NATURE'S POISON.
KATIE'S TOO YOUNG TO UNDERSTAND THE VALUE OF DIETARY FIBER, BUT I EXPECT BETTER OF YOU, JACK.
JACK?
HE CAN'T HEAR YOU. JACK GETS HYPNOTIZED BY COLLEGE GIRLS.
NO, I DON'T!
SO CUTE! HAVE YOU GOT A GIRLFRIEND, JACK?
NO! AARGH!
WHO DO YOU LIKE? DO YOU NEED TIPS?
CRRZZZT
KATIE POWER! WHAT HAVE YOU DONE?
CHEESE AND CRACKERS.

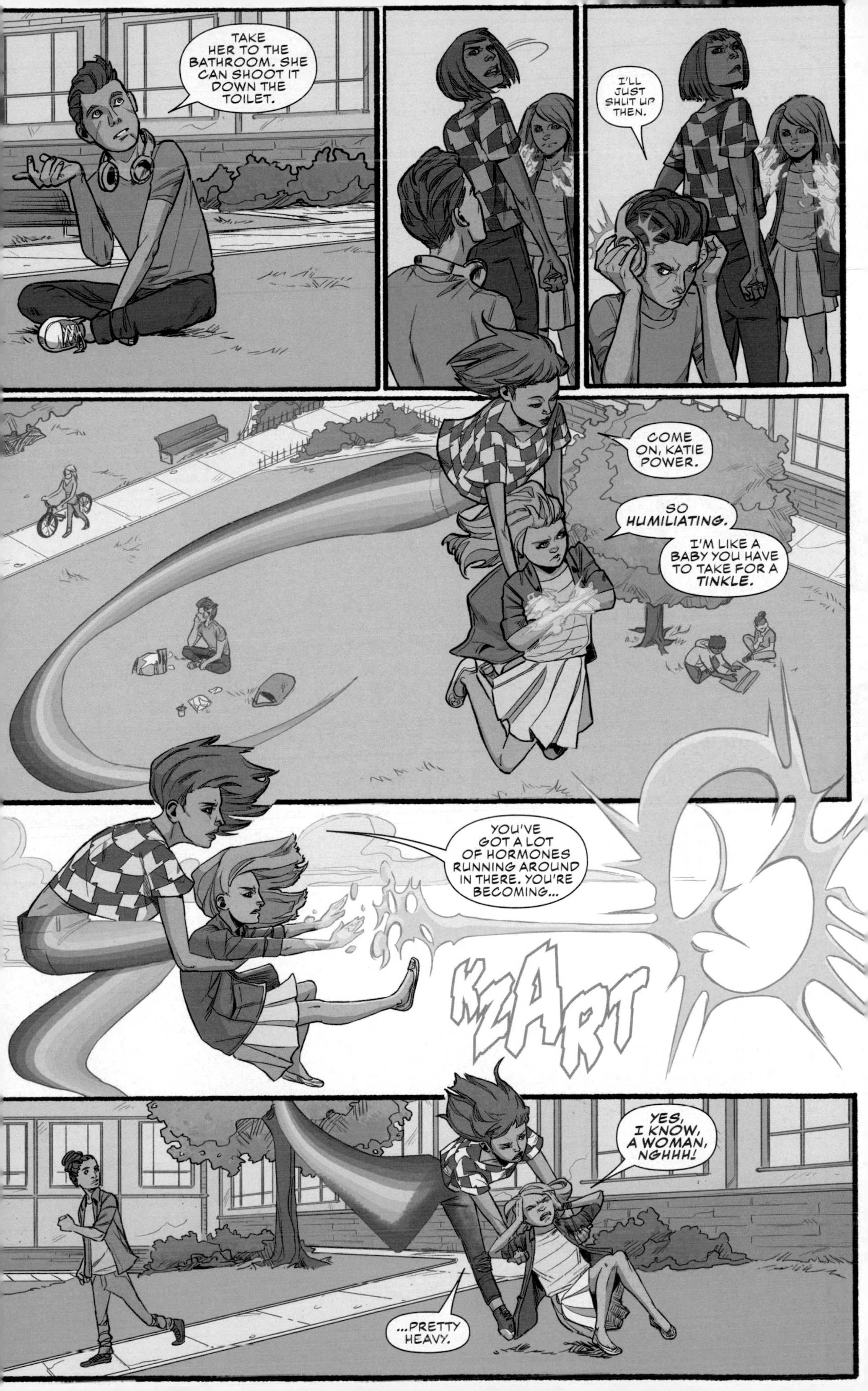
TAKE HER TO THE BATHROOM. SHE CAN SHOOT IT DOWN THE TOILET.
I'LL JUST SHUT UP THEN.
COME ON, KATIE POWER.
SO HUMILIATING.
I'M LIKE A BABY YOU HAVE TO TAKE FOR A TINKLE.
YOU'VE GOT A LOT OF HORMONES RUNNING AROUND IN THERE. YOU'RE BECOMING...
KZART
...PRETTY HEAVY.
YES, I KNOW, A WOMAN, NGHHH!

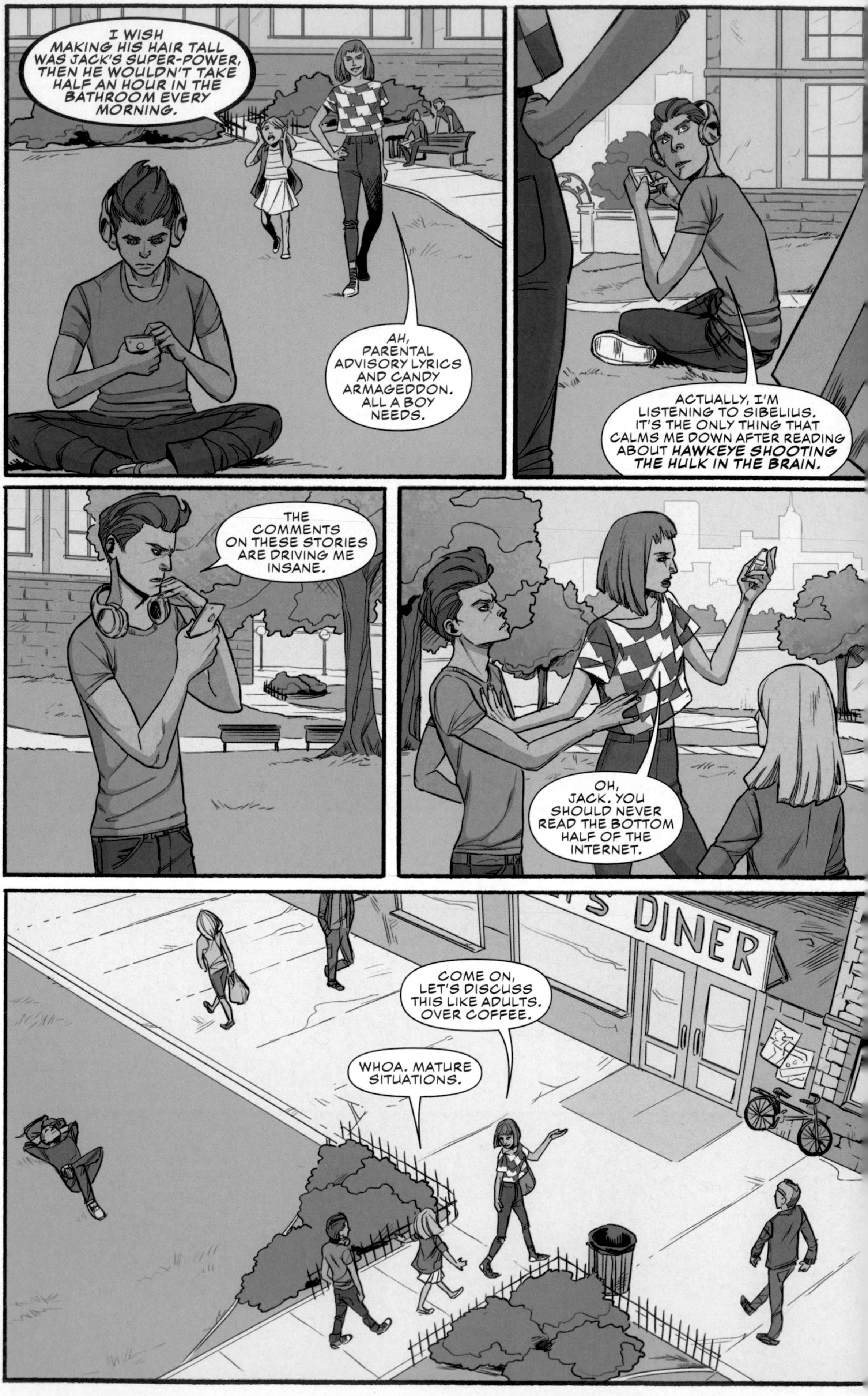
I WISH MAKING HIS HAIR TALL WAS JACK'S SUPER-POWER, THEN HE WOULDN'T TAKE HALF AN HOUR IN THE BATHROOM EVERY MORNING.
AH, PARENTAL ADVISORY LYRICS AND CANDY ARMAGEDDON. ALL A BOY NEEDS.
ACTUALLY, I'M LISTENING TO SIBELIUS. IT'S THE ONLY THING THAT CALMS ME DOWN AFTER READING ABOUT **HAWKEYE SHOOTING THE HULK IN THE BRAIN.**
THE COMMENTS ON THESE STORIES ARE DRIVING ME INSANE.
OH, JACK. YOU SHOULD NEVER READ THE BOTTOM HALF OF THE INTERNET.
DINER
COME ON, LET'S DISCUSS THIS LIKE ADULTS. OVER COFFEE.
WHOA. MATURE SITUATIONS.

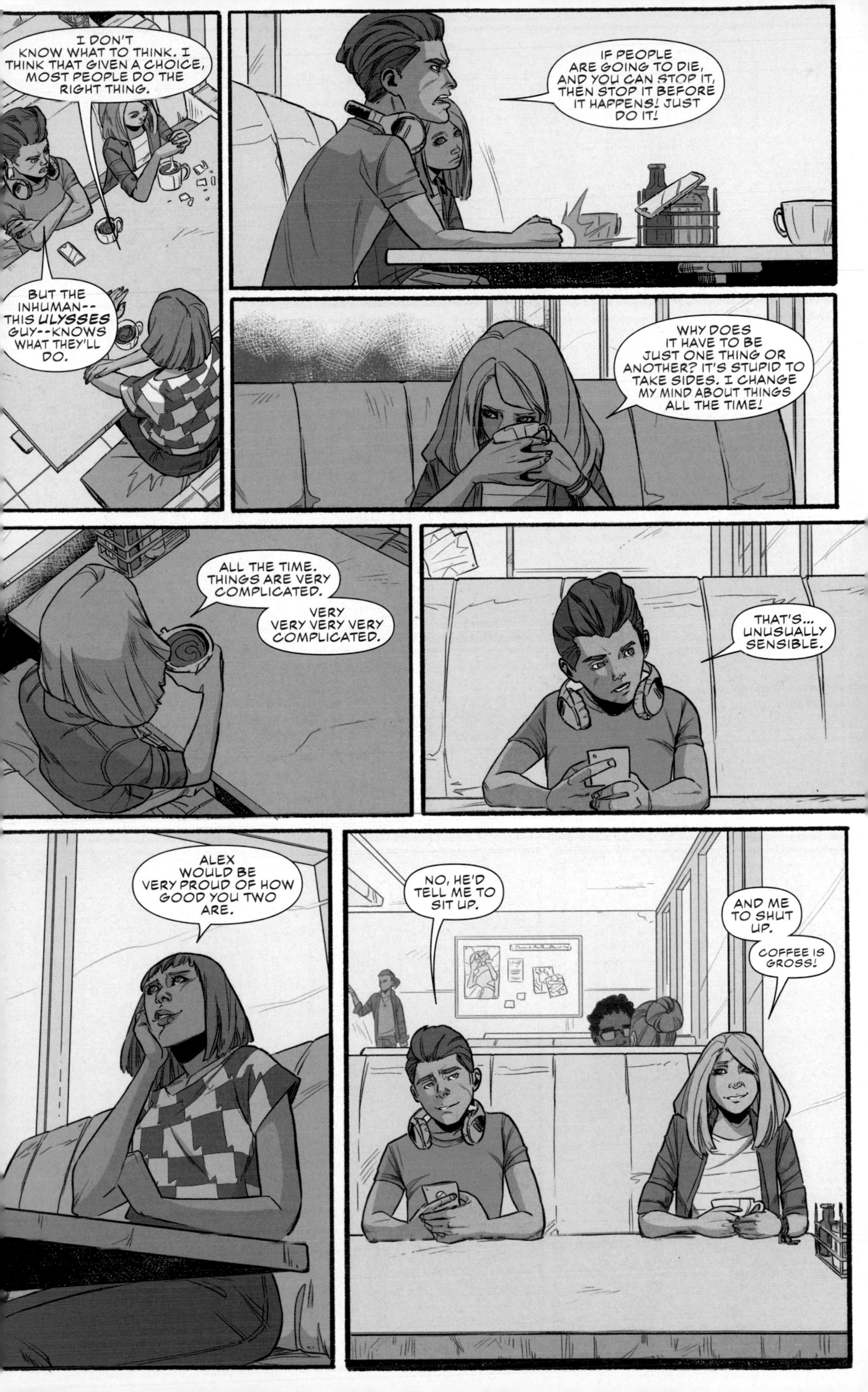
I DON'T KNOW WHAT TO THINK. I THINK THAT GIVEN A CHOICE, MOST PEOPLE DO THE RIGHT THING.
BUT THE INHUMAN-- THIS ULYSSES GUY--KNOWS WHAT THEY'LL DO.
IF PEOPLE ARE GOING TO DIE, AND YOU CAN STOP IT, THEN STOP IT BEFORE IT HAPPENS! JUST DO IT!
WHY DOES IT HAVE TO BE JUST ONE THING OR ANOTHER? IT'S STUPID TO TAKE SIDES. I CHANGE MY MIND ABOUT THINGS ALL THE TIME!
ALL THE TIME. THINGS ARE VERY COMPLICATED.
VERY VERY VERY VERY COMPLICATED.
THAT'S... UNUSUALLY SENSIBLE.
ALEX WOULD BE VERY PROUD OF HOW GOOD YOU TWO ARE.
NO, HE'D TELL ME TO SIT UP.
AND ME TO SHUT UP.
COFFEE IS GROSS!

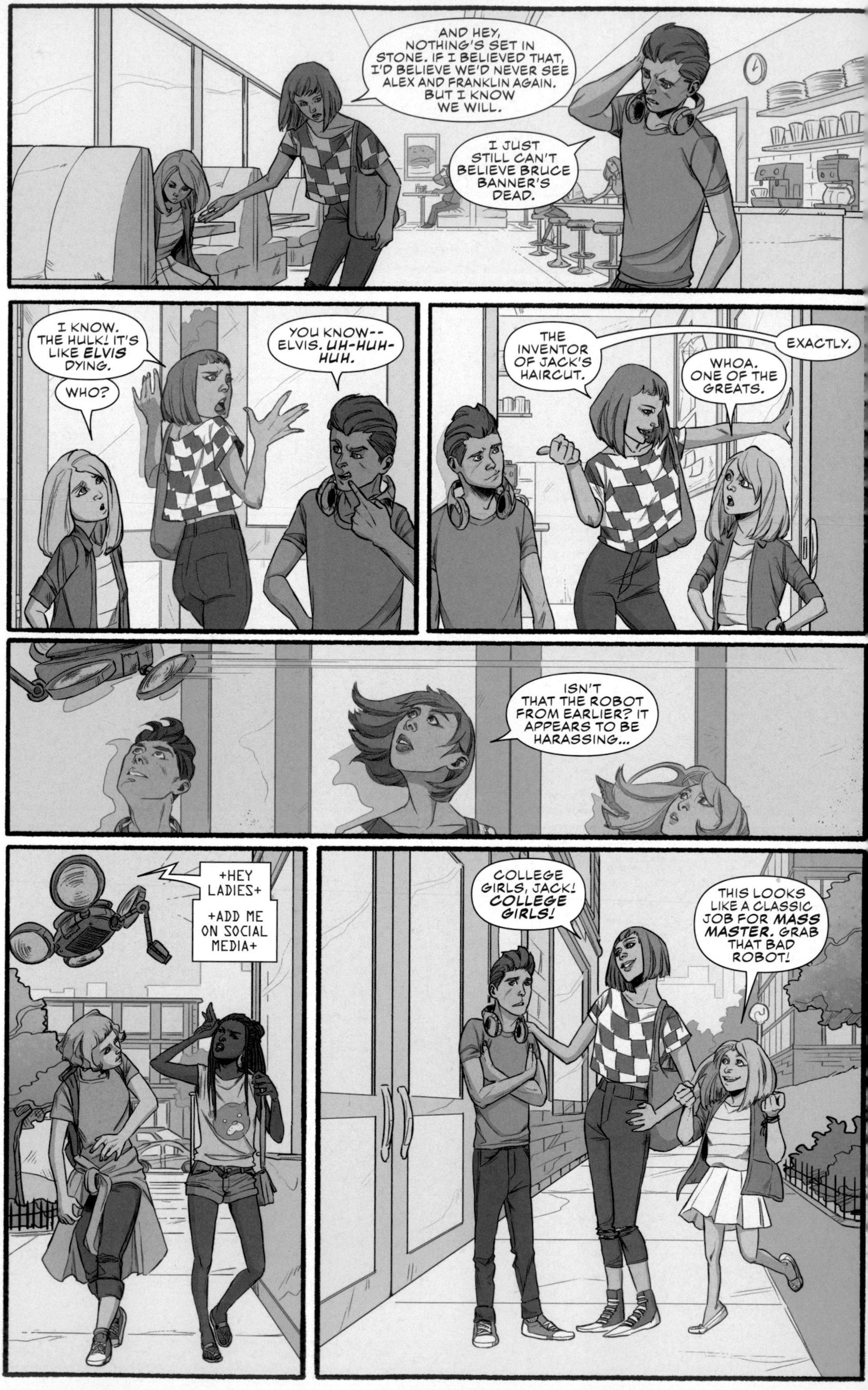
AND HEY, NOTHING'S SET IN STONE. IF I BELIEVED THAT, I'D BELIEVE WE'D NEVER SEE ALEX AND FRANKLIN AGAIN. BUT I KNOW WE WILL.
I JUST STILL CAN'T BELIEVE BRUCE BANNER'S DEAD.
I KNOW. THE HULK! IT'S LIKE ELVIS DYING.
WHO?
YOU KNOW-- ELVIS. UH-HUH-HUH.
THE INVENTOR OF JACK'S HAIRCUT.
EXACTLY.
WHOA. ONE OF THE GREATS.
ISN'T THAT THE ROBOT FROM EARLIER? IT APPEARS TO BE HARASSING...
+HEY LADIES+
+ADD ME ON SOCIAL MEDIA+
COLLEGE GIRLS, JACK! COLLEGE GIRLS!
THIS LOOKS LIKE A CLASSIC JOB FOR MASS MASTER. GRAB THAT BAD ROBOT!

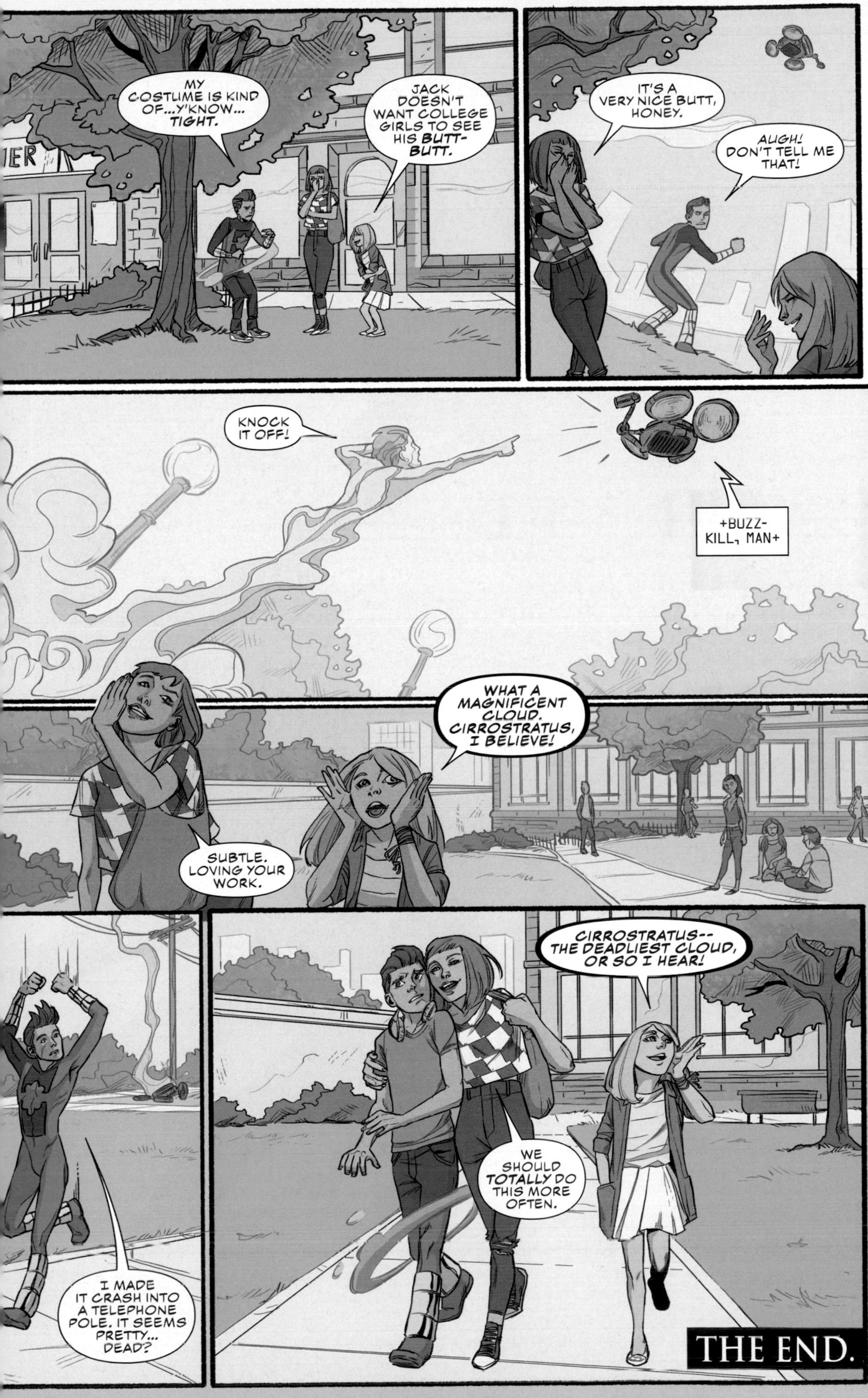

MY COSTUME IS KIND OF...Y'KNOW... TIGHT.
JACK DOESN'T WANT COLLEGE GIRLS TO SEE HIS BUTT-BUTT.
IT'S A VERY NICE BUTT, HONEY.
AUGH! DON'T TELL ME THAT!
KNOCK IT OFF!
+BUZZ-KILL, MAN+
WHAT A MAGNIFICENT CLOUD. CIRROSTRATUS, I BELIEVE!
SUBTLE. LOVING YOUR WORK.
I MADE IT CRASH INTO A TELEPHONE POLE. IT SEEMS PRETTY... DEAD?
CIRROSTRATUS-- THE DEADLIEST CLOUD, OR SO I HEAR!
WE SHOULD TOTALLY DO THIS MORE OFTEN.
THE END.

COVER ART BY CAMERON STEWART & MATTHEW WILSON

# ALPHA FLIGHT

WRITER
**CHIP ZDARSKY**

ARTIST
**RAMÓN PÉREZ**

ASSISTANT EDITOR
**CHARLES BEACHAM**

EDITOR
**WIL MOSS**

# COLLEEN WING

WRITER
**ENRIQUE CARRION**

ARTIST
**ANNAPAOLA MARTELLO**

COLOR ARTIST
**NOLAN WOODARD**

EDITOR
**CHRIS ROBINSON**

COVER ART BY DECLAN SHALVEY

V

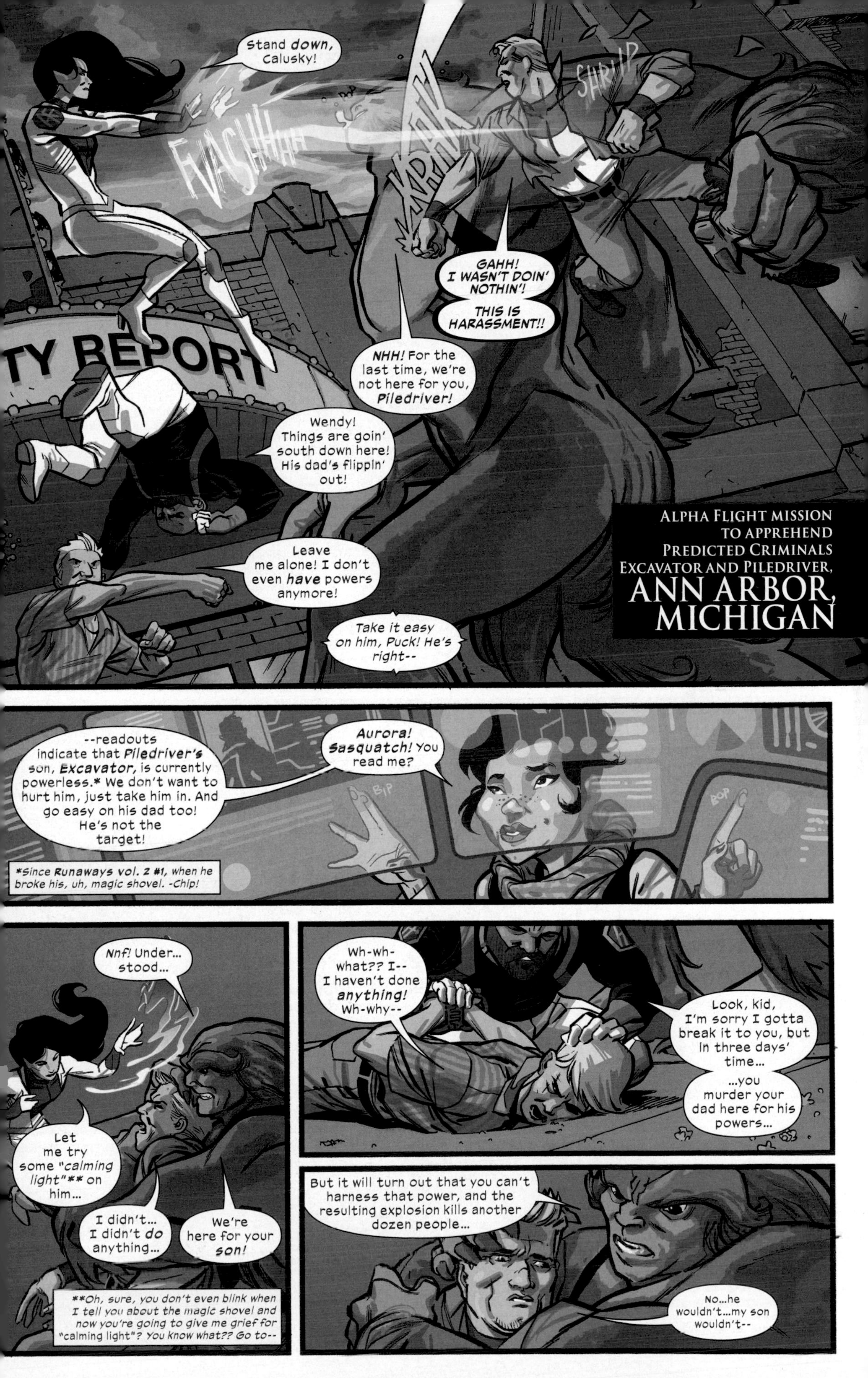

Stand down, Calusky!
GAHH! I WASN'T DOIN' NOTHIN'!
THIS IS HARASSMENT!!
NHH! For the last time, we're not here for you, Piledriver!
Wendy! Things are goin' south down here! His dad's flippin' out!
Leave me alone! I don't even have powers anymore!
Take it easy on him, Puck! He's right--
ALPHA FLIGHT MISSION TO APPREHEND PREDICTED CRIMINALS EXCAVATOR AND PILEDRIVER, ANN ARBOR, MICHIGAN
TY REPORT
Aurora! Sasquatch! You read me?
--readouts indicate that Piledriver's son, Excavator, is currently powerless.* We don't want to hurt him, just take him in. And go easy on his dad too! He's not the target!
*Since Runaways vol. 2 #1, when he broke his, uh, magic shovel. -Chip!
BIP
BOP
Nnf! Under... stood...
Let me try some "calming light"** on him...
I didn't... I didn't do anything...
We're here for your son!
**Oh, sure, you don't even blink when I tell you about the magic shovel and now you're going to give me grief for "calming light"? You know what?? Go to--
Wh-wh-what?? I-- I haven't done anything! Wh-why--
Look, kid, I'm sorry I gotta break it to you, but in three days' time...
...you murder your dad here for his powers...
But it will turn out that you can't harness that power, and the resulting explosion kills another dozen people...
No...he wouldn't...my son wouldn't--

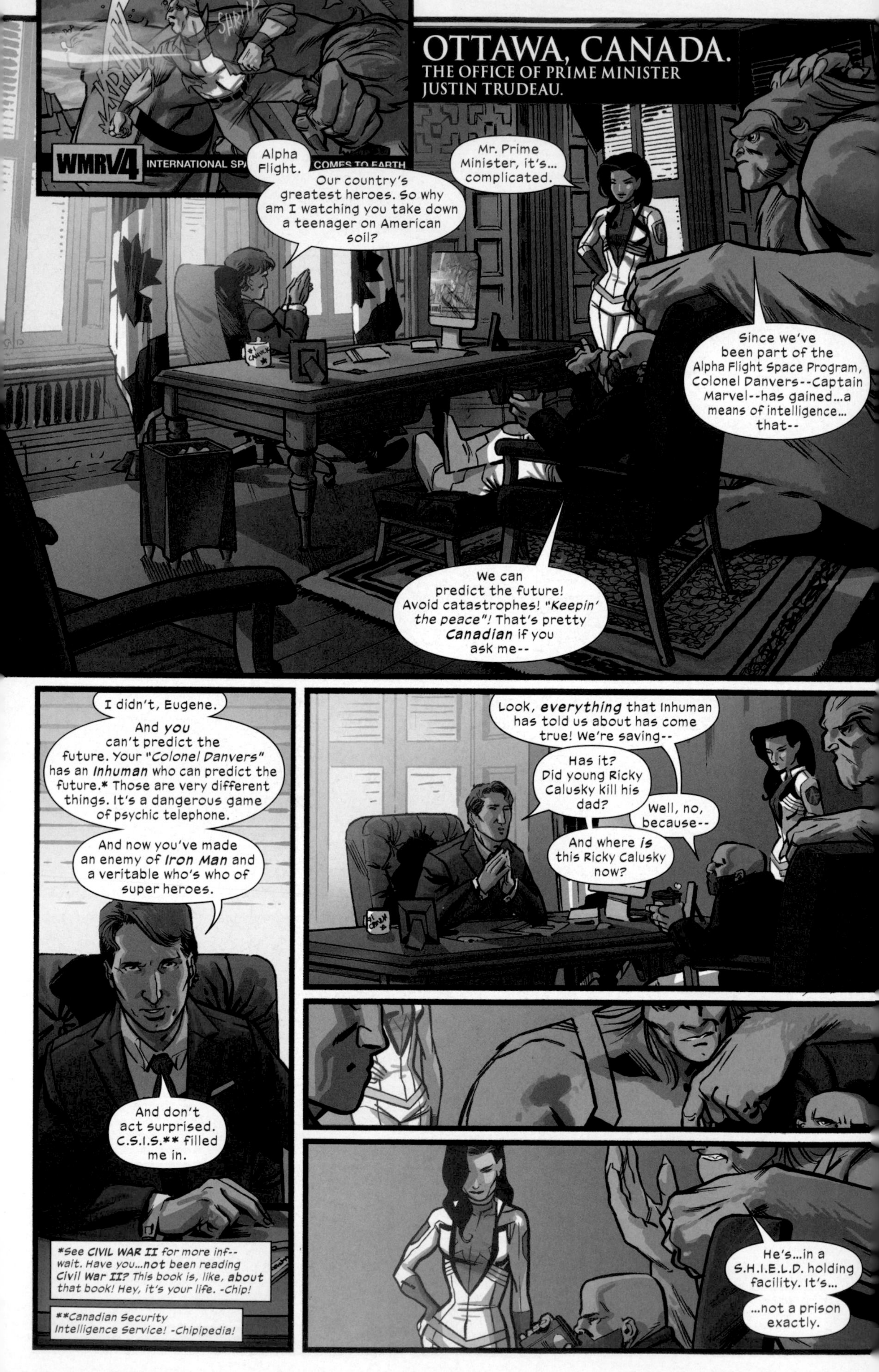
OTTAWA, CANADA.
THE OFFICE OF PRIME MINISTER JUSTIN TRUDEAU.
WMRV4
Alpha Flight.
Our country's greatest heroes. So why am I watching you take down a teenager on American soil?
Mr. Prime Minister, it's... complicated.
Since we've been part of the Alpha Flight Space Program, Colonel Danvers--Captain Marvel--has gained...a means of intelligence... that--
We can predict the future! Avoid catastrophes! "Keepin' the peace"! That's pretty Canadian if you ask me--
I didn't, Eugene.
And you can't predict the future. Your "Colonel Danvers" has an Inhuman who can predict the future.* Those are very different things. It's a dangerous game of psychic telephone.
And now you've made an enemy of Iron Man and a veritable who's who of super heroes.
And don't act surprised. C.S.I.S.** filled me in.
*See CIVIL WAR II for more inf-- wait. Have you...not been reading Civil War II? This book is, like, about that book! Hey, it's your life. -Chip!
**Canadian Security Intelligence Service! -Chipipedia!
Look, everything that Inhuman has told us about has come true! We're saving--
Has it? Did young Ricky Calusky kill his dad?
Well, no, because--
And where is this Ricky Calusky now?
He's...in a S.H.I.E.L.D. holding facility. It's...
...not a prison exactly.

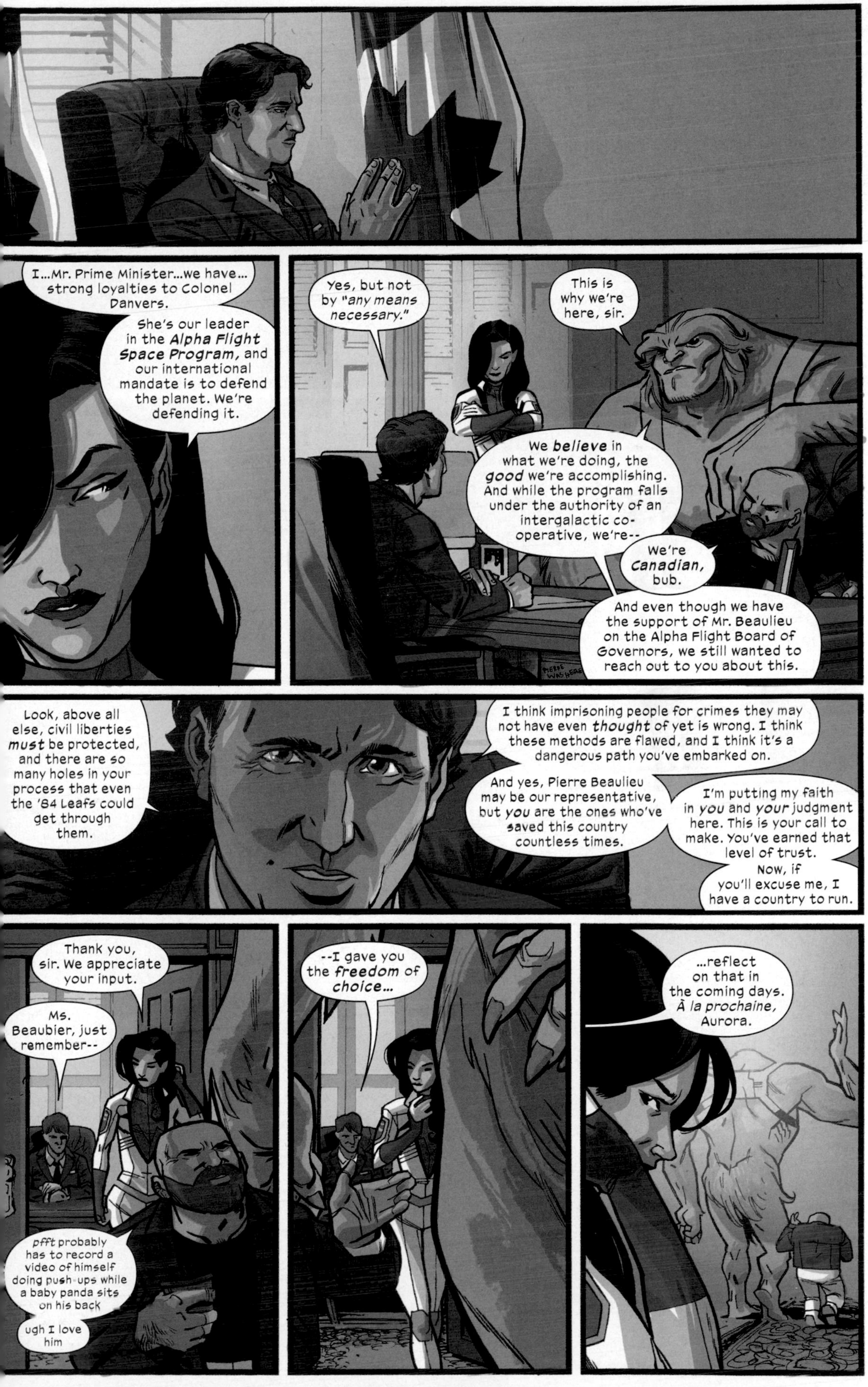
I...Mr. Prime Minister...we have... strong loyalties to Colonel Danvers.
She's our leader in the Alpha Flight Space Program, and our international mandate is to defend the planet. We're defending it.
Yes, but not by "any means necessary."
This is why we're here, sir.
We believe in what we're doing, the good we're accomplishing. And while the program falls under the authority of an intergalactic co-operative, we're--
We're Canadian, bub.
And even though we have the support of Mr. Beaulieu on the Alpha Flight Board of Governors, we still wanted to reach out to you about this.
PIERRE WAS HERE
Look, above all else, civil liberties must be protected, and there are so many holes in your process that even the '84 Leafs could get through them.
I think imprisoning people for crimes they may not have even thought of yet is wrong. I think these methods are flawed, and I think it's a dangerous path you've embarked on.
And yes, Pierre Beaulieu may be our representative, but you are the ones who've saved this country countless times.
I'm putting my faith in you and your judgment here. This is your call to make. You've earned that level of trust.
Now, if you'll excuse me, I have a country to run.
Thank you, sir. We appreciate your input.
Ms. Beaubier, just remember--
pfft probably has to record a video of himself doing push-ups while a baby panda sits on his back
ugh I love him
--I gave you the freedom of choice...
...reflect on that in the coming days. À la prochaine, Aurora.

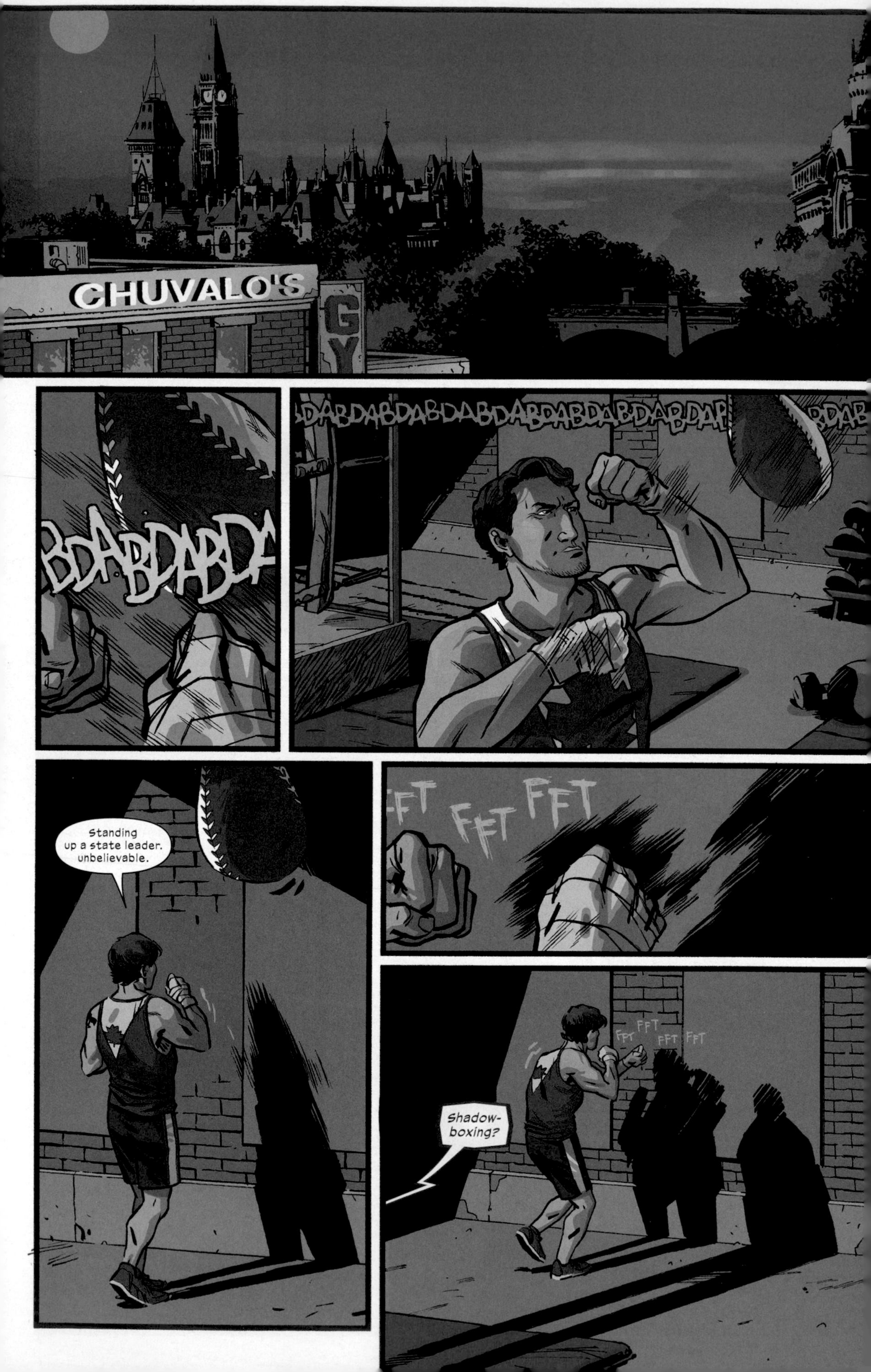
CHUVALO'S
GY
BDABDABDA
DABDABDABDABDABDABDABDABDABDAB
BDAB
Standing up a state leader. unbelievable.
FFT FFT FFT
FFT FFT FFT FFT
Shadow-boxing?

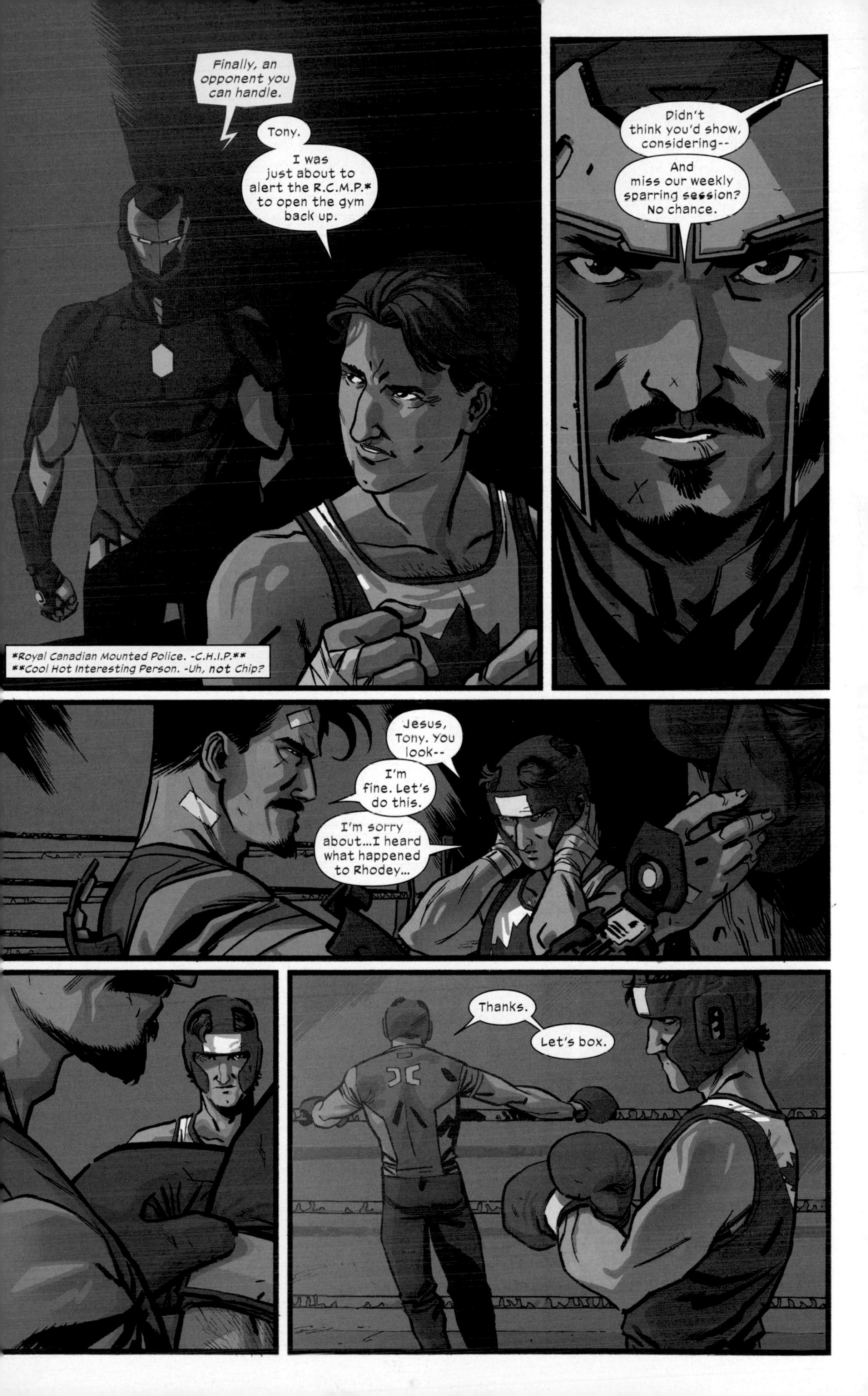
Finally, an opponent you can handle.
Tony.
I was just about to alert the R.C.M.P.* to open the gym back up.
*Royal Canadian Mounted Police. -C.H.I.P.**
**Cool Hot Interesting Person. -Uh, not Chip?
Didn't think you'd show, considering--
And miss our weekly sparring session? No chance.
Jesus, Tony. You look--
I'm fine. Let's do this.
I'm sorry about...I heard what happened to Rhodey...
Thanks.
Let's box.

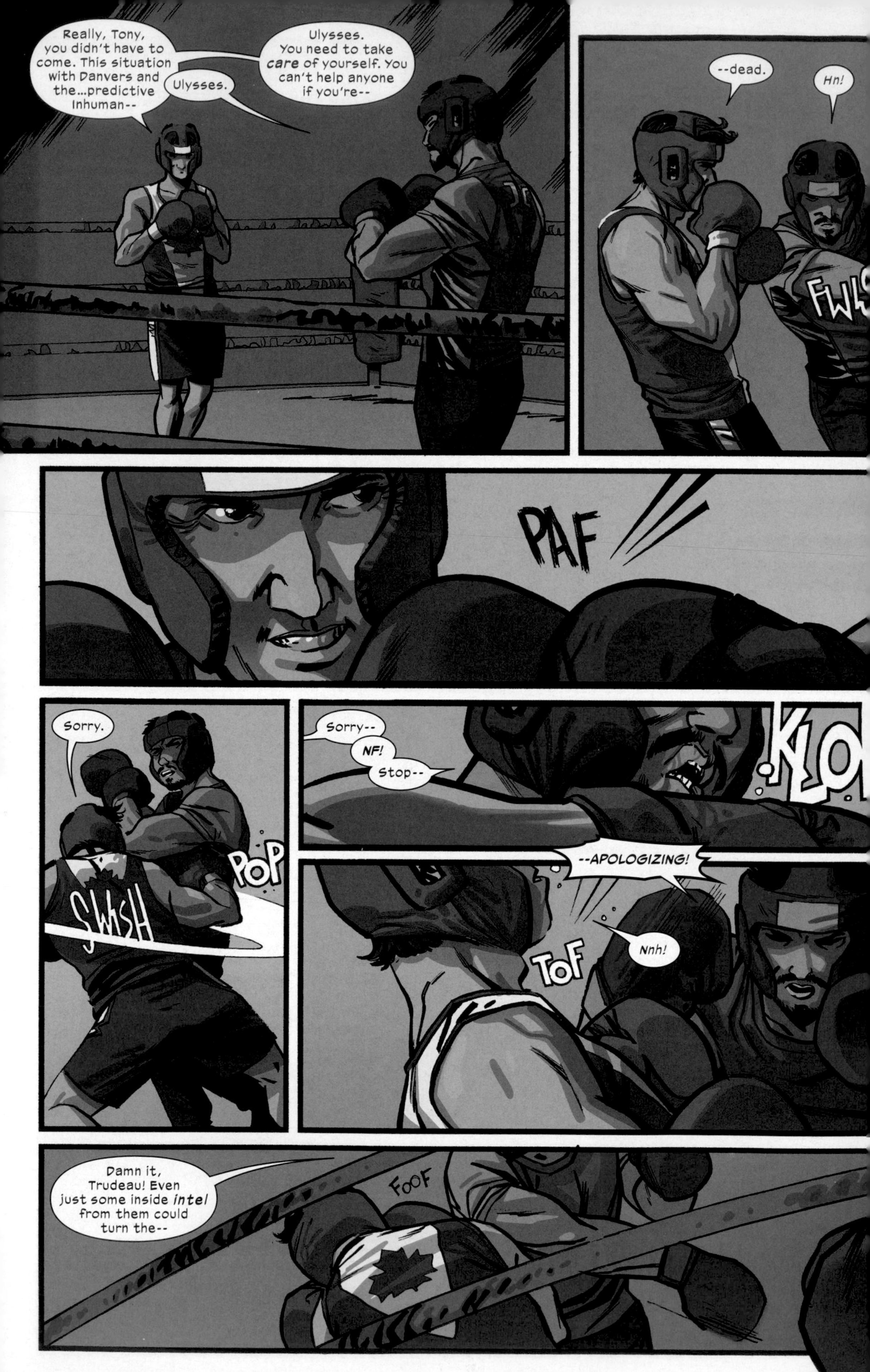
Really, Tony, you didn't have to come. This situation with Danvers and the...predictive Inhuman--
Ulysses.
Ulysses. You need to take care of yourself. You can't help anyone if you're--
--dead.
Hn!
FWISH
PAF
Sorry.
POP
SWISH
Sorry--
NF!
Stop--
KLOK
--APOLOGIZING!
Nnh!
TOF
Damn it, Trudeau! Even just some inside intel from them could turn the--
FOOF

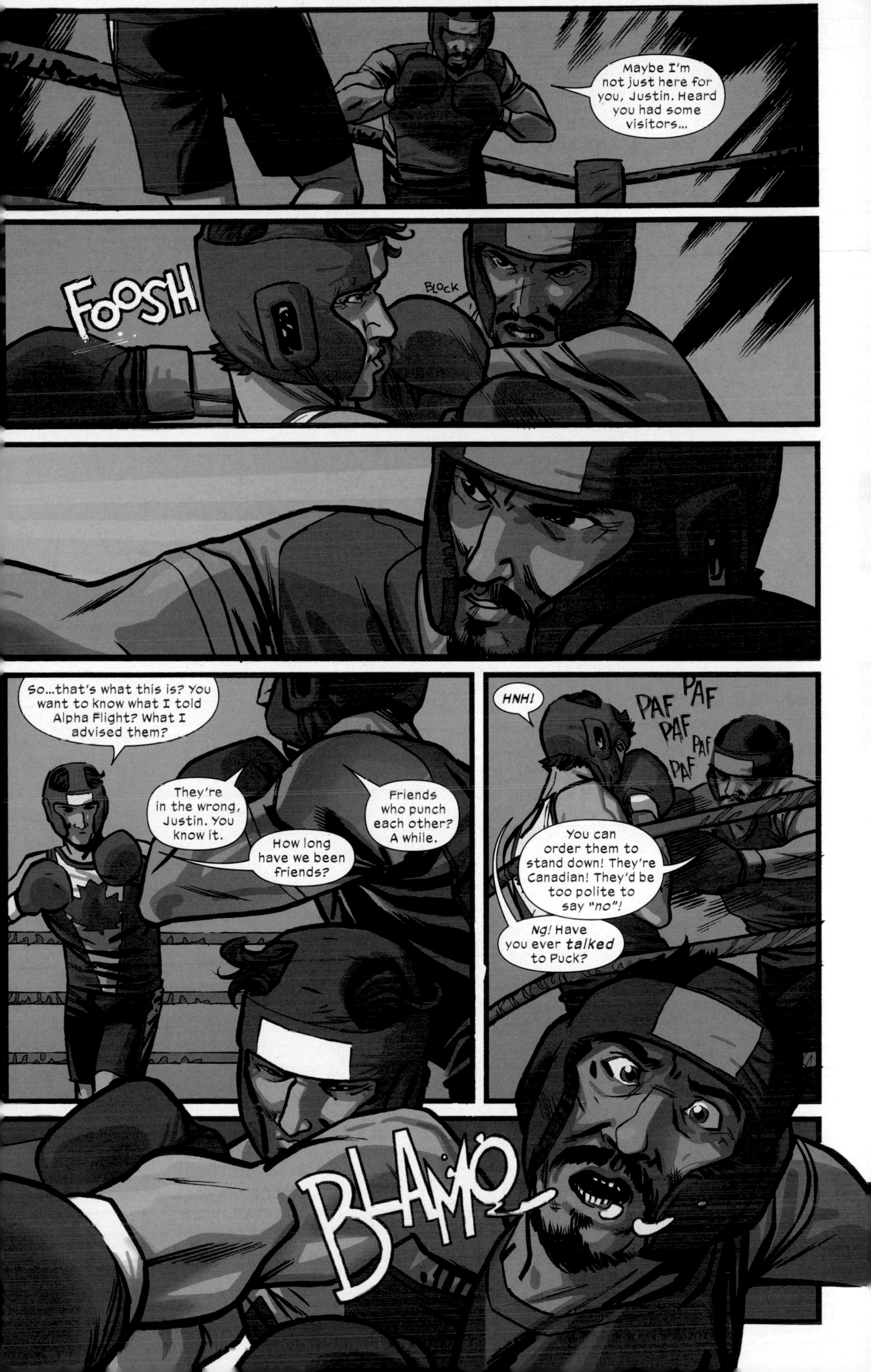
Maybe I'm not just here for you, Justin. Heard you had some visitors...
FOOSH
BLOCK
So...that's what this is? You want to know what I told Alpha Flight? What I advised them?
They're in the wrong, Justin. You know it.
How long have we been friends?
Friends who punch each other? A while.
HNH!
PAF PAF PAF PAF PAF
You can order them to stand down! They're Canadian! They'd be too polite to say "no"!
Ng! Have you ever talked to Puck?
BLAMO

Sorry.

Cheap shot.

Tony, I don't think they're in the right here.

Exactly! Then just--

But neither are you.

There's a middle ground. There always is.

This isn't some *bill* to be negotiated and passed on "Canadian Capitol Hill"--

Parliament.

Justin, they killed my best friend...

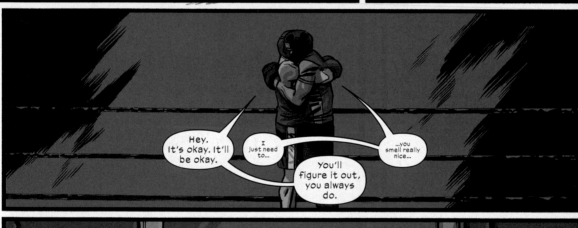

Hey. It's okay. It'll be okay.

I just need to...

...you smell really nice...

You'll figure it out, you always do.

No more fighting tonight, Tony. You fight enough.

You all fight too much...

CHU

"...with the wrong opponents."

END.

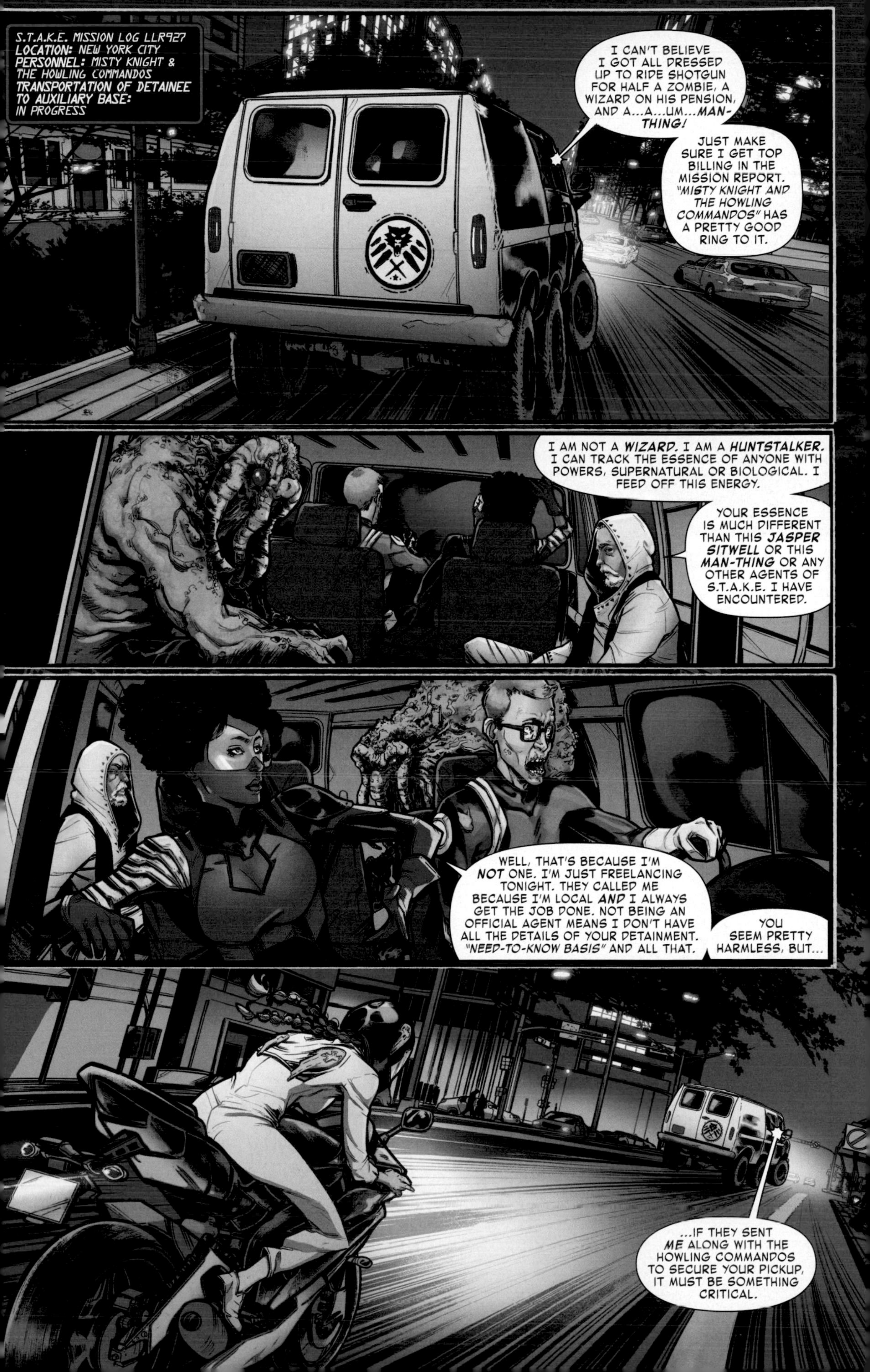
S.T.A.K.E. MISSION LOG LLR927
LOCATION: NEW YORK CITY
PERSONNEL: MISTY KNIGHT & THE HOWLING COMMANDOS
TRANSPORTATION OF DETAINEE TO AUXILIARY BASE: IN PROGRESS
I CAN'T BELIEVE I GOT ALL DRESSED UP TO RIDE SHOTGUN FOR HALF A ZOMBIE, A WIZARD ON HIS PENSION, AND A...A...UM...MAN-THING!
JUST MAKE SURE I GET TOP BILLING IN THE MISSION REPORT. "MISTY KNIGHT AND THE HOWLING COMMANDOS" HAS A PRETTY GOOD RING TO IT.
I AM NOT A WIZARD. I AM A HUNTSTALKER. I CAN TRACK THE ESSENCE OF ANYONE WITH POWERS, SUPERNATURAL OR BIOLOGICAL. I FEED OFF THIS ENERGY.
YOUR ESSENCE IS MUCH DIFFERENT THAN THIS JASPER SITWELL OR THIS MAN-THING OR ANY OTHER AGENTS OF S.T.A.K.E. I HAVE ENCOUNTERED.
WELL, THAT'S BECAUSE I'M NOT ONE. I'M JUST FREELANCING TONIGHT. THEY CALLED ME BECAUSE I'M LOCAL AND I ALWAYS GET THE JOB DONE. NOT BEING AN OFFICIAL AGENT MEANS I DON'T HAVE ALL THE DETAILS OF YOUR DETAINMENT. "NEED-TO-KNOW BASIS" AND ALL THAT.
YOU SEEM PRETTY HARMLESS, BUT...
...IF THEY SENT ME ALONG WITH THE HOWLING COMMANDOS TO SECURE YOUR PICKUP, IT MUST BE SOMETHING CRITICAL.

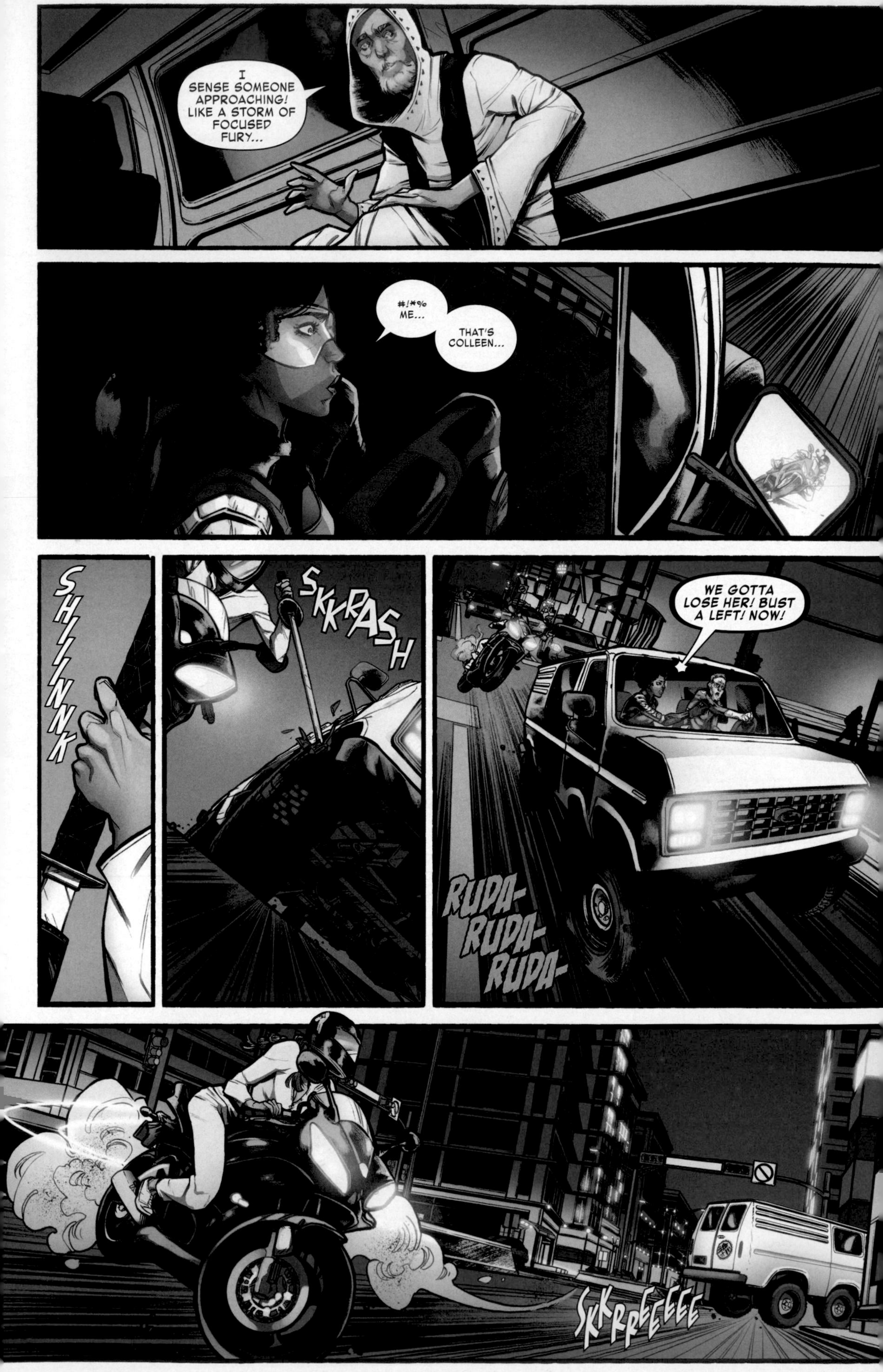
I SENSE SOMEONE APPROACHING! LIKE A STORM OF FOCUSED FURY...
#!*% ME...
THAT'S COLLEEN...
SHIIINNK
SKKRASH
WE GOTTA LOSE HER! BUST A LEFT! NOW!
RUDA-RUDA-RUDA-
SKKRREEEEE

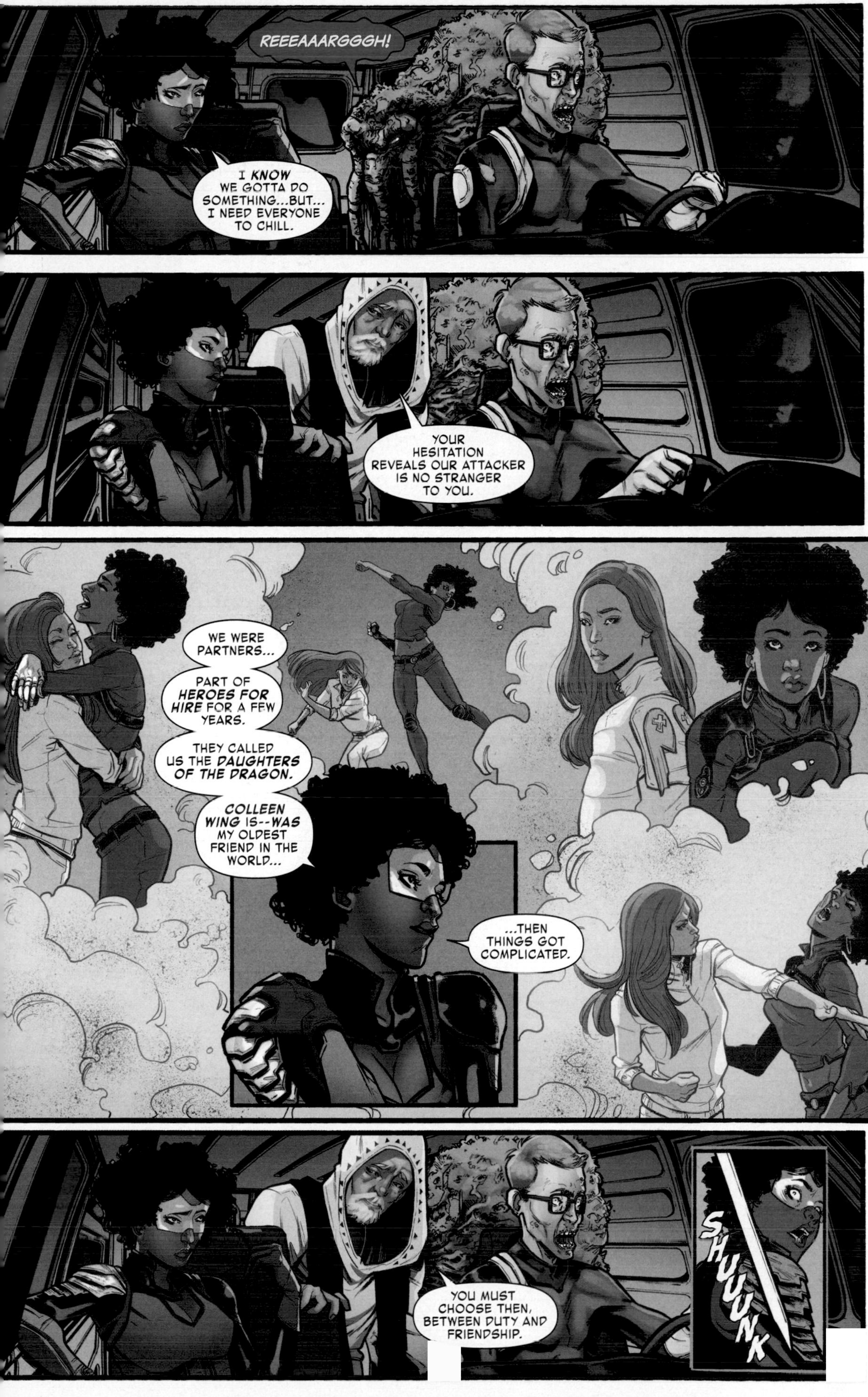
REEEAAARGGGH!
I KNOW WE GOTTA DO SOMETHING...BUT... I NEED EVERYONE TO CHILL.
YOUR HESITATION REVEALS OUR ATTACKER IS NO STRANGER TO YOU.
WE WERE PARTNERS...
PART OF HEROES FOR HIRE FOR A FEW YEARS.
THEY CALLED US THE DAUGHTERS OF THE DRAGON.
COLLEEN WING IS--WAS MY OLDEST FRIEND IN THE WORLD...
...THEN THINGS GOT COMPLICATED.
YOU MUST CHOOSE THEN, BETWEEN DUTY AND FRIENDSHIP.
SHUUUNK

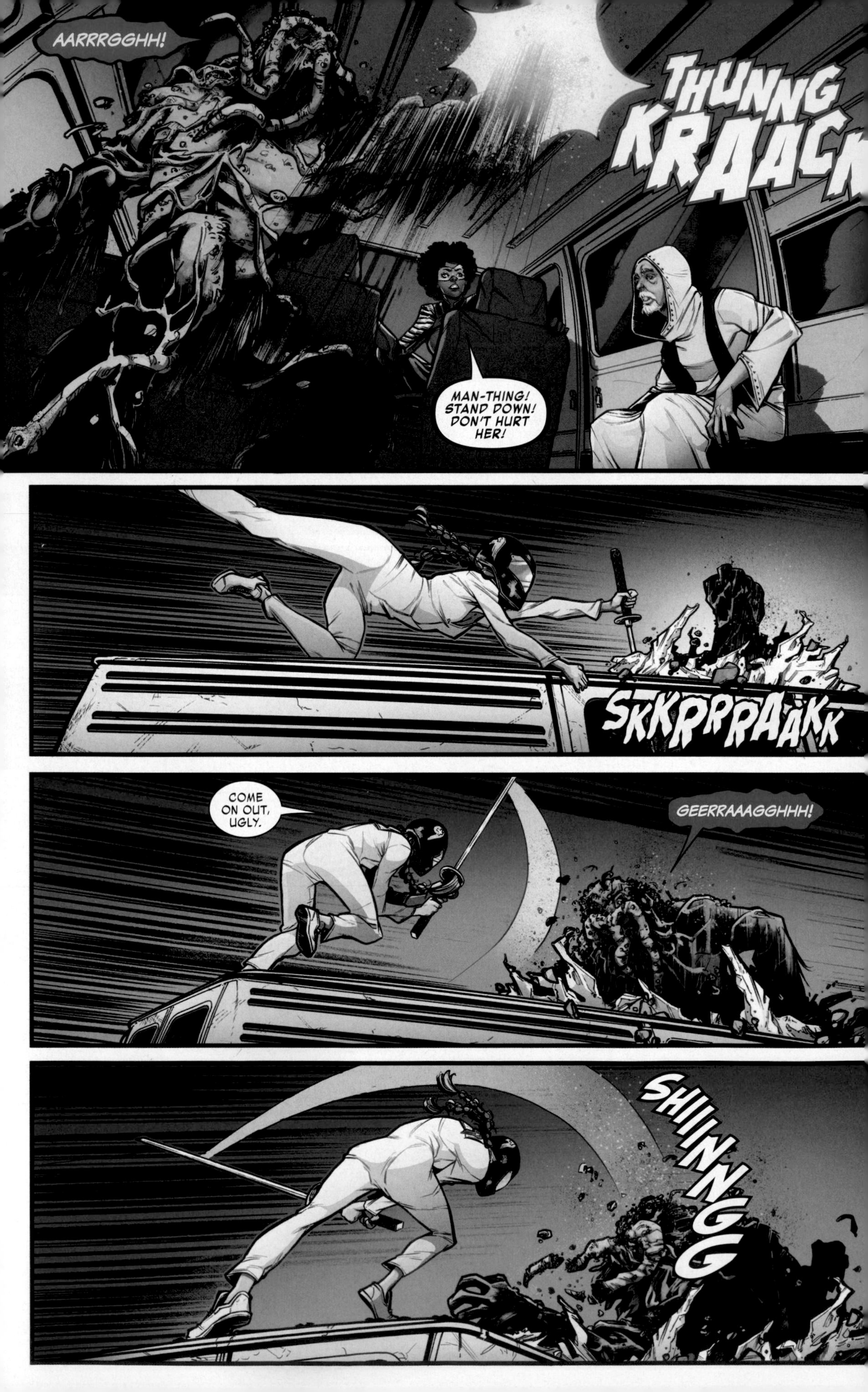
AARRRGGHH!
THUNNG
KRAACK
MAN-THING! STAND DOWN! DON'T HURT HER!
SKKRRRAAKK
COME ON OUT, UGLY.
GEERRAAAGGHHH!
SHIIINNGG

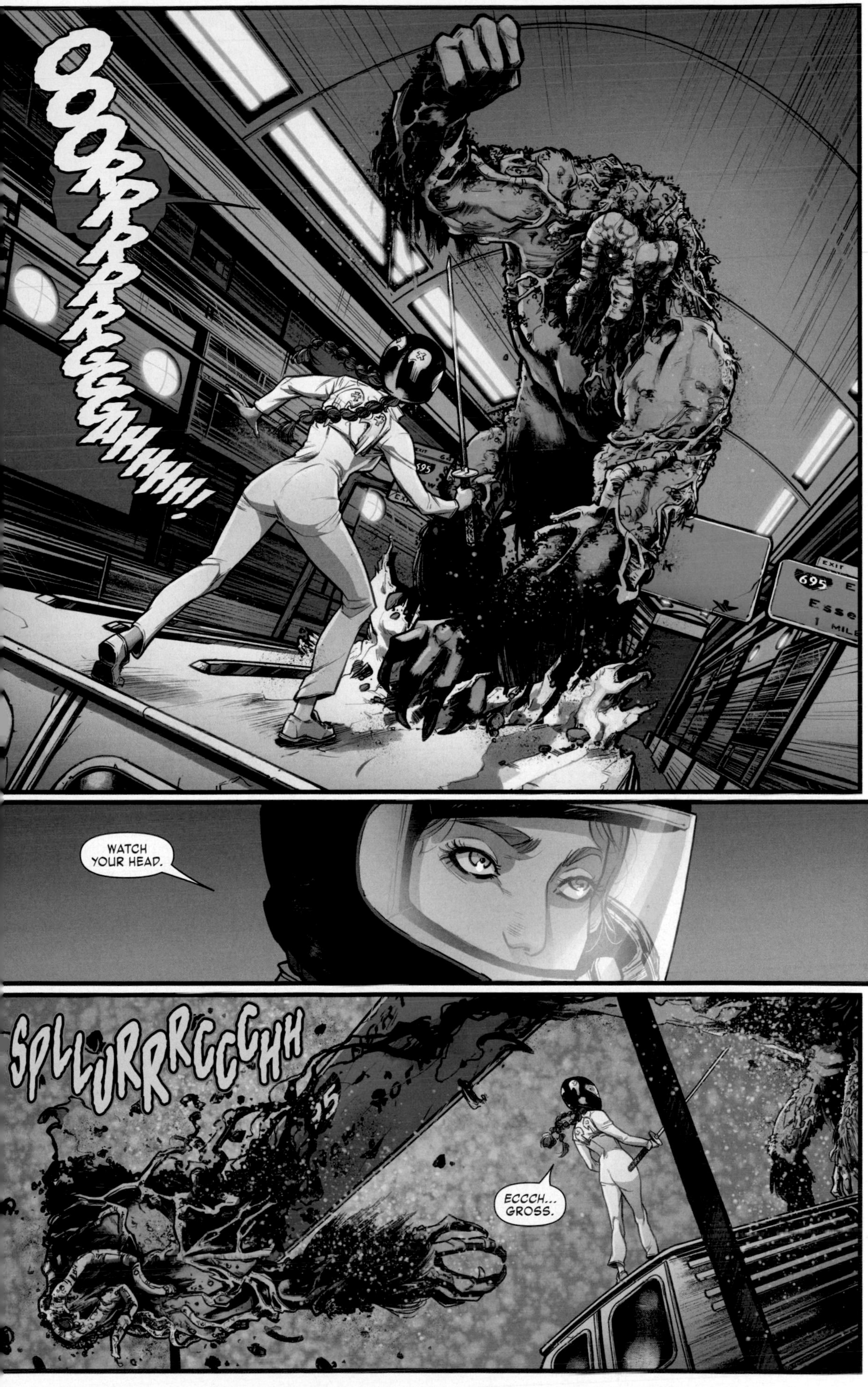
OOORRRRGGGHHHHH!
WATCH YOUR HEAD.
SPLLURRRCCCHH
ECCCH... GROSS.

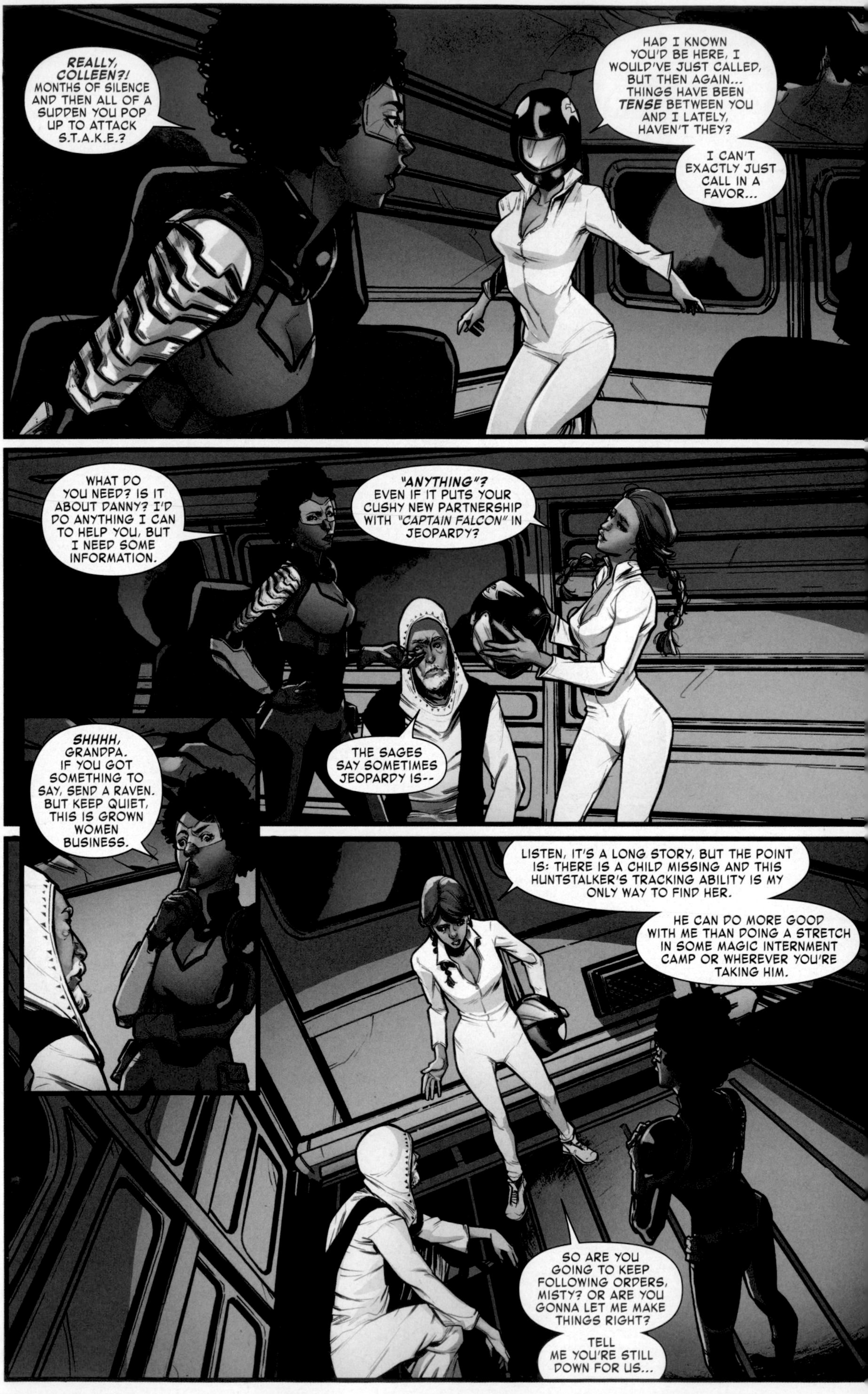
REALLY, COLLEEN?! MONTHS OF SILENCE AND THEN ALL OF A SUDDEN YOU POP UP TO ATTACK S.T.A.K.E.?
HAD I KNOWN YOU'D BE HERE, I WOULD'VE JUST CALLED, BUT THEN AGAIN... THINGS HAVE BEEN TENSE BETWEEN YOU AND I LATELY, HAVEN'T THEY?
I CAN'T EXACTLY JUST CALL IN A FAVOR...
WHAT DO YOU NEED? IS IT ABOUT DANNY? I'D DO ANYTHING I CAN TO HELP YOU, BUT I NEED SOME INFORMATION.
"ANYTHING"? EVEN IF IT PUTS YOUR CUSHY NEW PARTNERSHIP WITH "CAPTAIN FALCON" IN JEOPARDY?
THE SAGES SAY SOMETIMES JEOPARDY IS--
SHHHH, GRANDPA. IF YOU GOT SOMETHING TO SAY, SEND A RAVEN. BUT KEEP QUIET, THIS IS GROWN WOMEN BUSINESS.
LISTEN, IT'S A LONG STORY, BUT THE POINT IS: THERE IS A CHILD MISSING AND THIS HUNTSTALKER'S TRACKING ABILITY IS MY ONLY WAY TO FIND HER.
HE CAN DO MORE GOOD WITH ME THAN DOING A STRETCH IN SOME MAGIC INTERNMENT CAMP OR WHEREVER YOU'RE TAKING HIM.
SO ARE YOU GOING TO KEEP FOLLOWING ORDERS, MISTY? OR ARE YOU GONNA LET ME MAKE THINGS RIGHT?
TELL ME YOU'RE STILL DOWN FOR US...

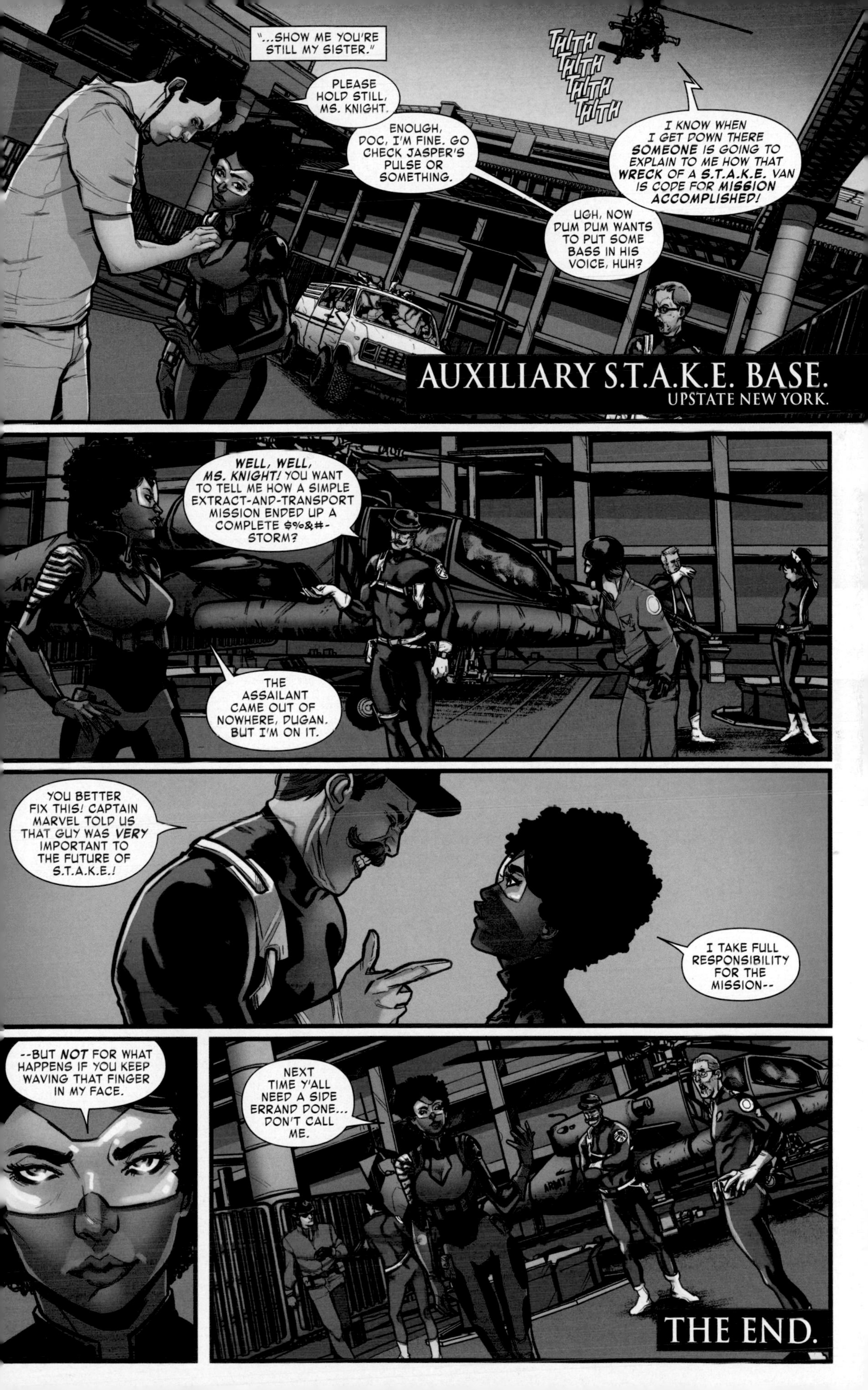
"...SHOW ME YOU'RE STILL MY SISTER."
PLEASE HOLD STILL, MS. KNIGHT.
ENOUGH, DOC, I'M FINE. GO CHECK JASPER'S PULSE OR SOMETHING.
THTH THTH THTH THTH
I KNOW WHEN I GET DOWN THERE SOMEONE IS GOING TO EXPLAIN TO ME HOW THAT WRECK OF A S.T.A.K.E. VAN IS CODE FOR MISSION ACCOMPLISHED!
UGH, NOW DUM DUM WANTS TO PUT SOME BASS IN HIS VOICE, HUH?
AUXILIARY S.T.A.K.E. BASE.
UPSTATE NEW YORK.
WELL, WELL, MS. KNIGHT! YOU WANT TO TELL ME HOW A SIMPLE EXTRACT-AND-TRANSPORT MISSION ENDED UP A COMPLETE $%&#-STORM?
THE ASSAILANT CAME OUT OF NOWHERE, DUGAN. BUT I'M ON IT.
YOU BETTER FIX THIS! CAPTAIN MARVEL TOLD US THAT GUY WAS VERY IMPORTANT TO THE FUTURE OF S.T.A.K.E.!
I TAKE FULL RESPONSIBILITY FOR THE MISSION--
--BUT NOT FOR WHAT HAPPENS IF YOU KEEP WAVING THAT FINGER IN MY FACE.
NEXT TIME Y'ALL NEED A SIDE ERRAND DONE... DON'T CALL ME.
THE END.

ALIAS
INVESTIGATIONS
NEW YORK BULLETIN
IT'S WAR!

COVER ART BY
CAMERON STEWART
& MATTHEW WILSON

# JESSICA JONES

THIS STORY TAKES PLACE BEFORE CIVIL WAR II #3

WRITER
CHELSEA CAIN

ARTIST
ALISON SAMPSON

COLOR ARTIST
JORDIE BELLAIRE

ASSISTANT EDITOR
CHARLES BEACHAM

EDITOR
WIL MOSS

# WHITE FOX

WRITER
CHRISTINA STRAIN

ARTIST
SANA TAKEDA

EDITOR
CHRIS ROBINSON

COVER ART BY
DECLAN SHALVEY &
JORDIE BELLAIRE

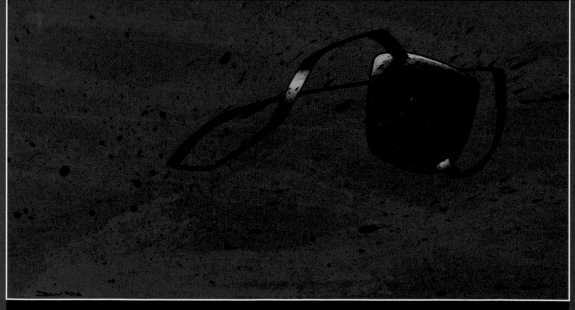

VI

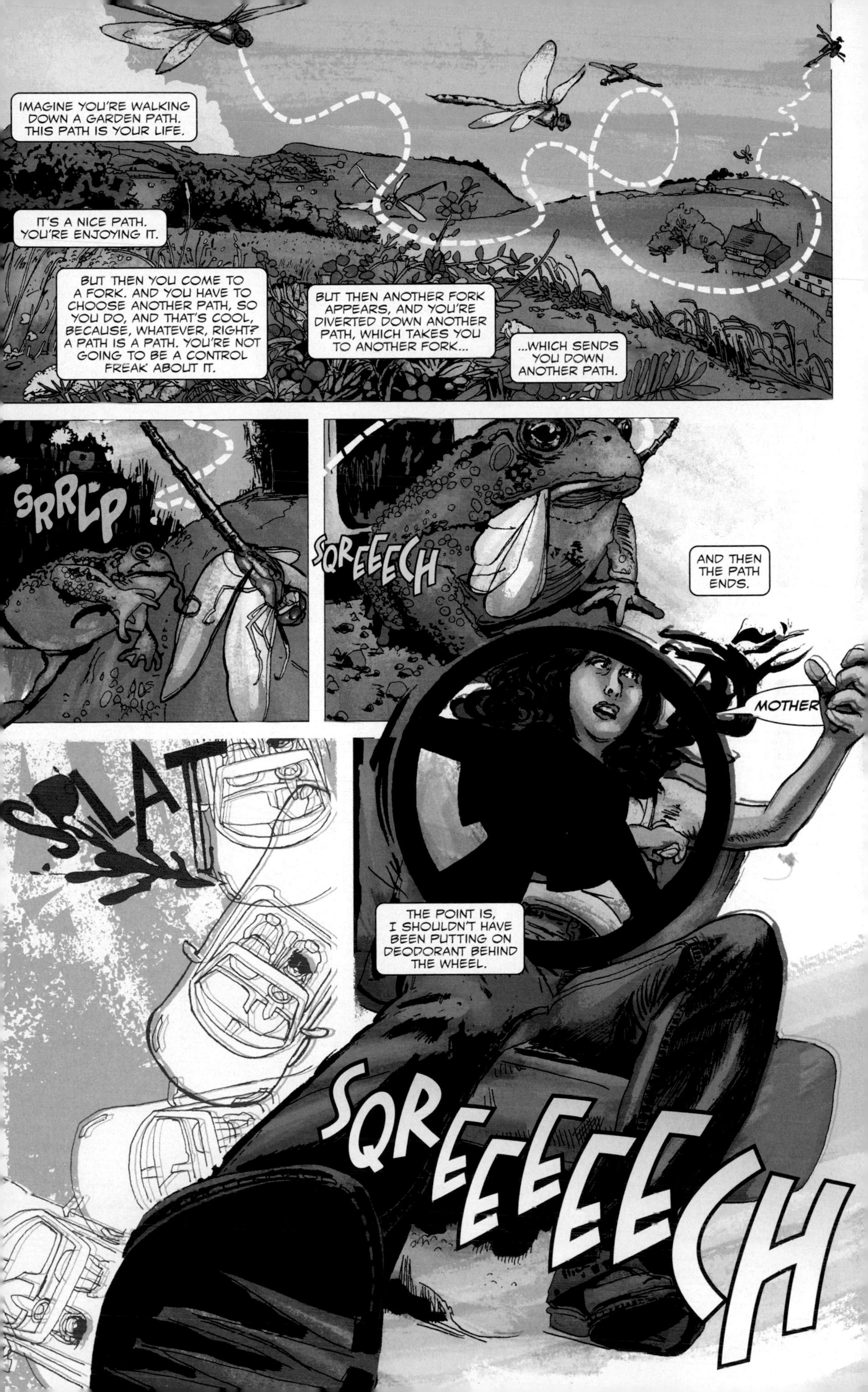
IMAGINE YOU'RE WALKING DOWN A GARDEN PATH. THIS PATH IS YOUR LIFE.
IT'S A NICE PATH. YOU'RE ENJOYING IT.
BUT THEN YOU COME TO A FORK. AND YOU HAVE TO CHOOSE ANOTHER PATH, SO YOU DO, AND THAT'S COOL, BECAUSE, WHATEVER, RIGHT? A PATH IS A PATH. YOU'RE NOT GOING TO BE A CONTROL FREAK ABOUT IT.
BUT THEN ANOTHER FORK APPEARS, AND YOU'RE DIVERTED DOWN ANOTHER PATH, WHICH TAKES YOU TO ANOTHER FORK...
...WHICH SENDS YOU DOWN ANOTHER PATH.
SRRLP
SQREEECH
AND THEN THE PATH ENDS.
MOTHER
SLAT
THE POINT IS, I SHOULDN'T HAVE BEEN PUTTING ON DEODORANT BEHIND THE WHEEL.
SQREEEEECH

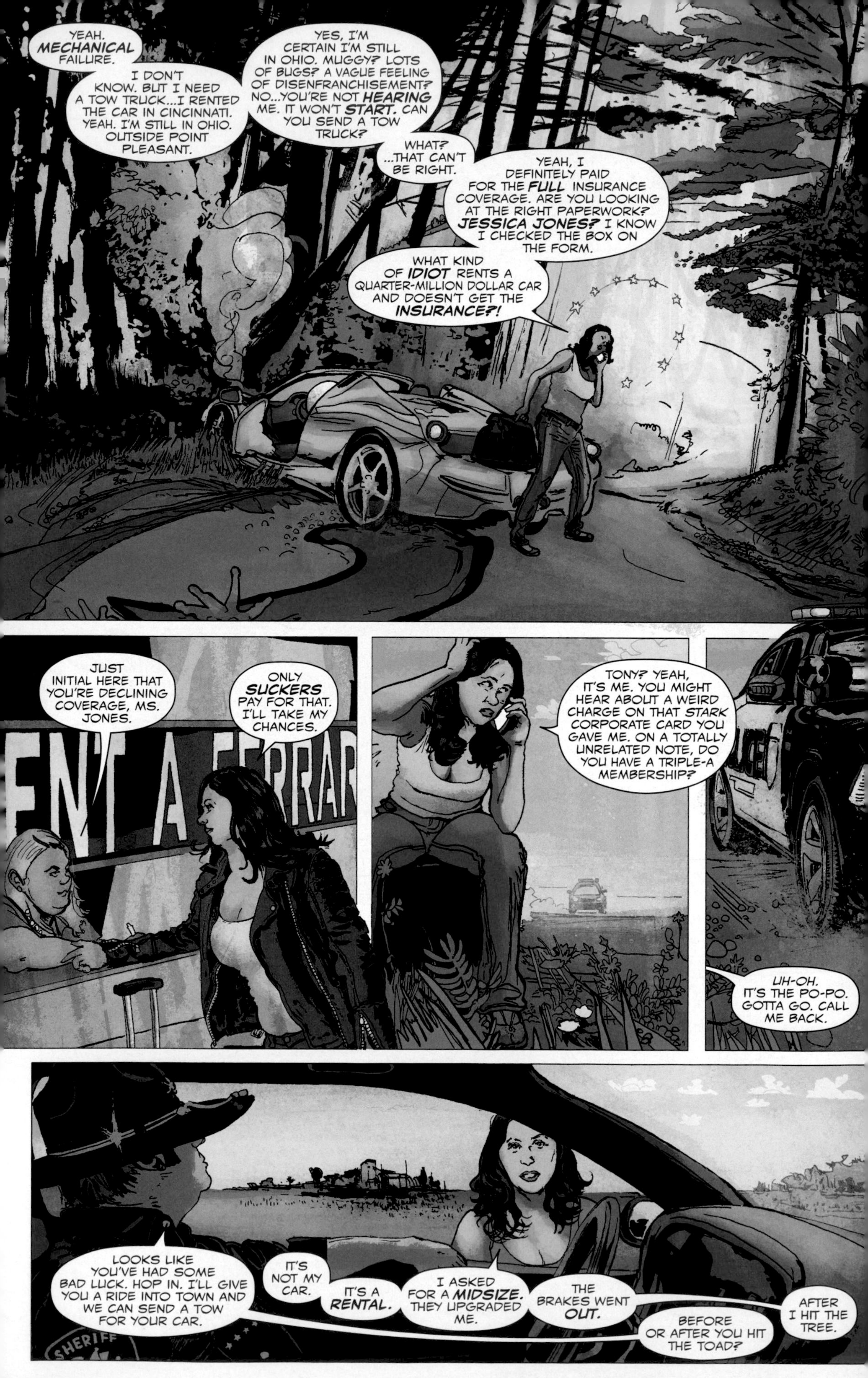
YEAH. MECHANICAL FAILURE.
I DON'T KNOW. BUT I NEED A TOW TRUCK...I RENTED THE CAR IN CINCINNATI. YEAH. I'M STILL IN OHIO. OUTSIDE POINT PLEASANT.
YES, I'M CERTAIN I'M STILL IN OHIO. MUGGY? LOTS OF BUGS? A VAGUE FEELING OF DISENFRANCHISEMENT? NO...YOU'RE NOT HEARING ME. IT WON'T START. CAN YOU SEND A TOW TRUCK?
WHAT? ...THAT CAN'T BE RIGHT.
YEAH, I DEFINITELY PAID FOR THE FULL INSURANCE COVERAGE. ARE YOU LOOKING AT THE RIGHT PAPERWORK? JESSICA JONES? I KNOW I CHECKED THE BOX ON THE FORM.
WHAT KIND OF IDIOT RENTS A QUARTER-MILLION DOLLAR CAR AND DOESN'T GET THE INSURANCE?!
JUST INITIAL HERE THAT YOU'RE DECLINING COVERAGE, MS. JONES.
ONLY SUCKERS PAY FOR THAT. I'LL TAKE MY CHANCES.
TONY? YEAH, IT'S ME. YOU MIGHT HEAR ABOUT A WEIRD CHARGE ON THAT STARK CORPORATE CARD YOU GAVE ME. ON A TOTALLY UNRELATED NOTE, DO YOU HAVE A TRIPLE-A MEMBERSHIP?
UH-OH. IT'S THE PO-PO. GOTTA GO. CALL ME BACK.
LOOKS LIKE YOU'VE HAD SOME BAD LUCK. HOP IN. I'LL GIVE YOU A RIDE INTO TOWN AND WE CAN SEND A TOW FOR YOUR CAR.
IT'S NOT MY CAR.
IT'S A RENTAL.
I ASKED FOR A MIDSIZE. THEY UPGRADED ME.
THE BRAKES WENT OUT.
BEFORE OR AFTER YOU HIT THE TOAD?
AFTER I HIT THE TREE.
SHERIFF

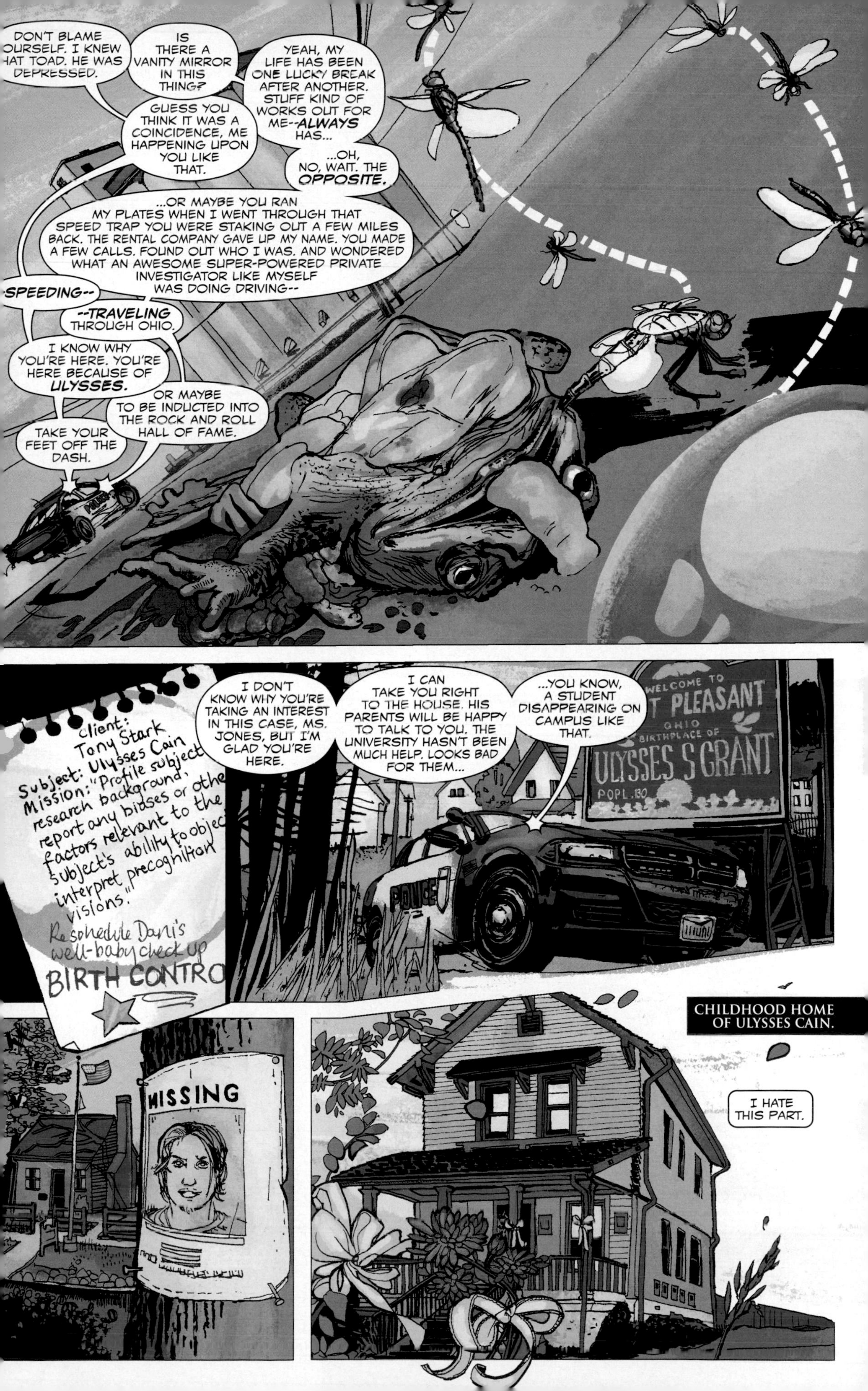

DON'T BLAME OURSELF. I KNEW HAT TOAD. HE WAS DEPRESSED.
IS THERE A VANITY MIRROR IN THIS THING?
YEAH, MY LIFE HAS BEEN ONE LUCKY BREAK AFTER ANOTHER. STUFF KIND OF WORKS OUT FOR ME--ALWAYS HAS...
...OH, NO, WAIT. THE OPPOSITE.
GUESS YOU THINK IT WAS A COINCIDENCE, ME HAPPENING UPON YOU LIKE THAT.
...OR MAYBE YOU RAN MY PLATES WHEN I WENT THROUGH THAT SPEED TRAP YOU WERE STAKING OUT A FEW MILES BACK. THE RENTAL COMPANY GAVE UP MY NAME. YOU MADE A FEW CALLS. FOUND OUT WHO I WAS. AND WONDERED WHAT AN AWESOME SUPER-POWERED PRIVATE INVESTIGATOR LIKE MYSELF WAS DOING DRIVING--
SPEEDING--
--TRAVELING THROUGH OHIO.
I KNOW WHY YOU'RE HERE. YOU'RE HERE BECAUSE OF ULYSSES.
OR MAYBE TO BE INDUCTED INTO THE ROCK AND ROLL HALL OF FAME.
TAKE YOUR FEET OFF THE DASH.
Client: Tony Stark
Subject: Ulysses Cain
Mission: "Profile subject, research background, report any biases or othe factors relevant to the subject's ability to objec interpret precognition visions."
Reschedule Dani's well-baby check up
BIRTH CONTRO
I DON'T KNOW WHY YOU'RE TAKING AN INTEREST IN THIS CASE, MS. JONES, BUT I'M GLAD YOU'RE HERE.
I CAN TAKE YOU RIGHT TO THE HOUSE. HIS PARENTS WILL BE HAPPY TO TALK TO YOU. THE UNIVERSITY HASN'T BEEN MUCH HELP. LOOKS BAD FOR THEM...
...YOU KNOW, A STUDENT DISAPPEARING ON CAMPUS LIKE THAT.
WELCOME TO
T PLEASANT
OHIO
BIRTHPLACE OF
ULYSSES S GRANT
POPL. 130
POLICE
MISSING
CHILDHOOD HOME OF ULYSSES CAIN.
I HATE THIS PART.

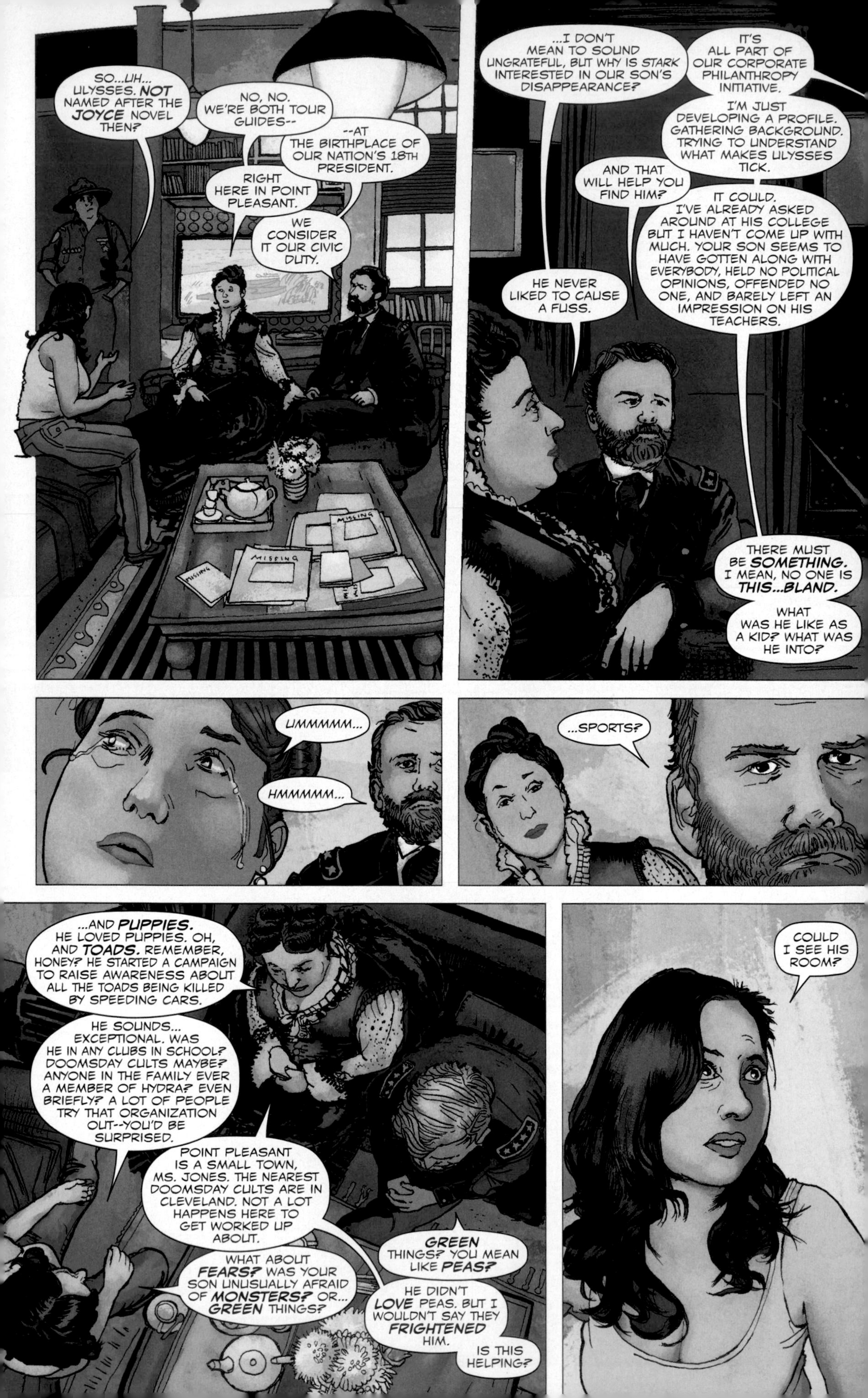
SO...UH... ULYSSES. NOT NAMED AFTER THE JOYCE NOVEL THEN?
NO, NO. WE'RE BOTH TOUR GUIDES--
--AT THE BIRTHPLACE OF OUR NATION'S 18TH PRESIDENT.
RIGHT HERE IN POINT PLEASANT.
WE CONSIDER IT OUR CIVIC DUTY.
...I DON'T MEAN TO SOUND UNGRATEFUL, BUT WHY IS STARK INTERESTED IN OUR SON'S DISAPPEARANCE?
IT'S ALL PART OF OUR CORPORATE PHILANTHROPY INITIATIVE.
I'M JUST DEVELOPING A PROFILE. GATHERING BACKGROUND. TRYING TO UNDERSTAND WHAT MAKES ULYSSES TICK.
AND THAT WILL HELP YOU FIND HIM?
IT COULD. I'VE ALREADY ASKED AROUND AT HIS COLLEGE BUT I HAVEN'T COME UP WITH MUCH. YOUR SON SEEMS TO HAVE GOTTEN ALONG WITH EVERYBODY, HELD NO POLITICAL OPINIONS, OFFENDED NO ONE, AND BARELY LEFT AN IMPRESSION ON HIS TEACHERS.
HE NEVER LIKED TO CAUSE A FUSS.
THERE MUST BE SOMETHING. I MEAN, NO ONE IS THIS...BLAND.
WHAT WAS HE LIKE AS A KID? WHAT WAS HE INTO?
UMMMMMM...
HMMMMM...
...SPORTS?
...AND PUPPIES. HE LOVED PUPPIES. OH, AND TOADS. REMEMBER, HONEY? HE STARTED A CAMPAIGN TO RAISE AWARENESS ABOUT ALL THE TOADS BEING KILLED BY SPEEDING CARS.
HE SOUNDS... EXCEPTIONAL. WAS HE IN ANY CLUBS IN SCHOOL? DOOMSDAY CULTS MAYBE? ANYONE IN THE FAMILY EVER A MEMBER OF HYDRA? EVEN BRIEFLY? A LOT OF PEOPLE TRY THAT ORGANIZATION OUT--YOU'D BE SURPRISED.
POINT PLEASANT IS A SMALL TOWN, MS. JONES. THE NEAREST DOOMSDAY CULTS ARE IN CLEVELAND. NOT A LOT HAPPENS HERE TO GET WORKED UP ABOUT.
WHAT ABOUT FEARS? WAS YOUR SON UNUSUALLY AFRAID OF MONSTERS? OR... GREEN THINGS?
GREEN THINGS? YOU MEAN LIKE PEAS?
HE DIDN'T LOVE PEAS. BUT I WOULDN'T SAY THEY FRIGHTENED HIM.
IS THIS HELPING?
COULD I SEE HIS ROOM?

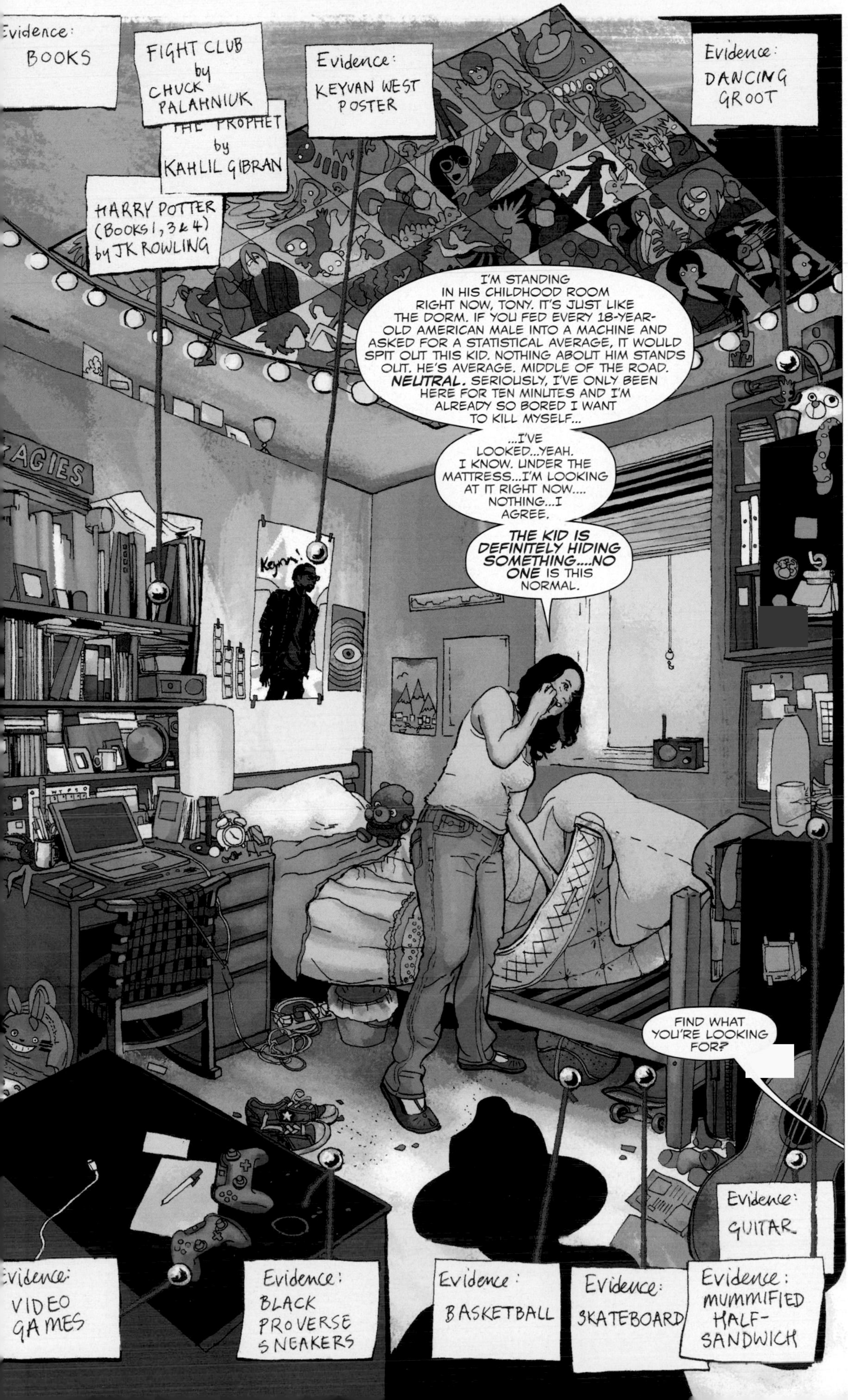

Evidence: BOOKS
FIGHT CLUB by CHUCK PALAHNIUK
THE PROPHET by KAHLIL GIBRAN
HARRY POTTER (BOOKS 1, 3 & 4) by JK ROWLING
Evidence: KEYVAN WEST POSTER
Evidence: DANCING GROOT
I'M STANDING IN HIS CHILDHOOD ROOM RIGHT NOW, TONY. IT'S JUST LIKE THE DORM. IF YOU FED EVERY 18-YEAR-OLD AMERICAN MALE INTO A MACHINE AND ASKED FOR A STATISTICAL AVERAGE, IT WOULD SPIT OUT THIS KID. NOTHING ABOUT HIM STANDS OUT. HE'S AVERAGE. MIDDLE OF THE ROAD. **NEUTRAL.** SERIOUSLY, I'VE ONLY BEEN HERE FOR TEN MINUTES AND I'M ALREADY SO BORED I WANT TO KILL MYSELF...
...I'VE LOOKED...YEAH. I KNOW. UNDER THE MATTRESS...I'M LOOKING AT IT RIGHT NOW.... NOTHING...I AGREE.
***THE KID IS DEFINITELY HIDING SOMETHING....NO ONE*** IS THIS NORMAL.
AGIES
Keyvan!
FIND WHAT YOU'RE LOOKING FOR?
Evidence: GUITAR
Evidence: VIDEO GAMES
Evidence: BLACK PROVERSE SNEAKERS
Evidence: BASKETBALL
Evidence: SKATEBOARD
Evidence: MUMMIFIED HALF-SANDWICH

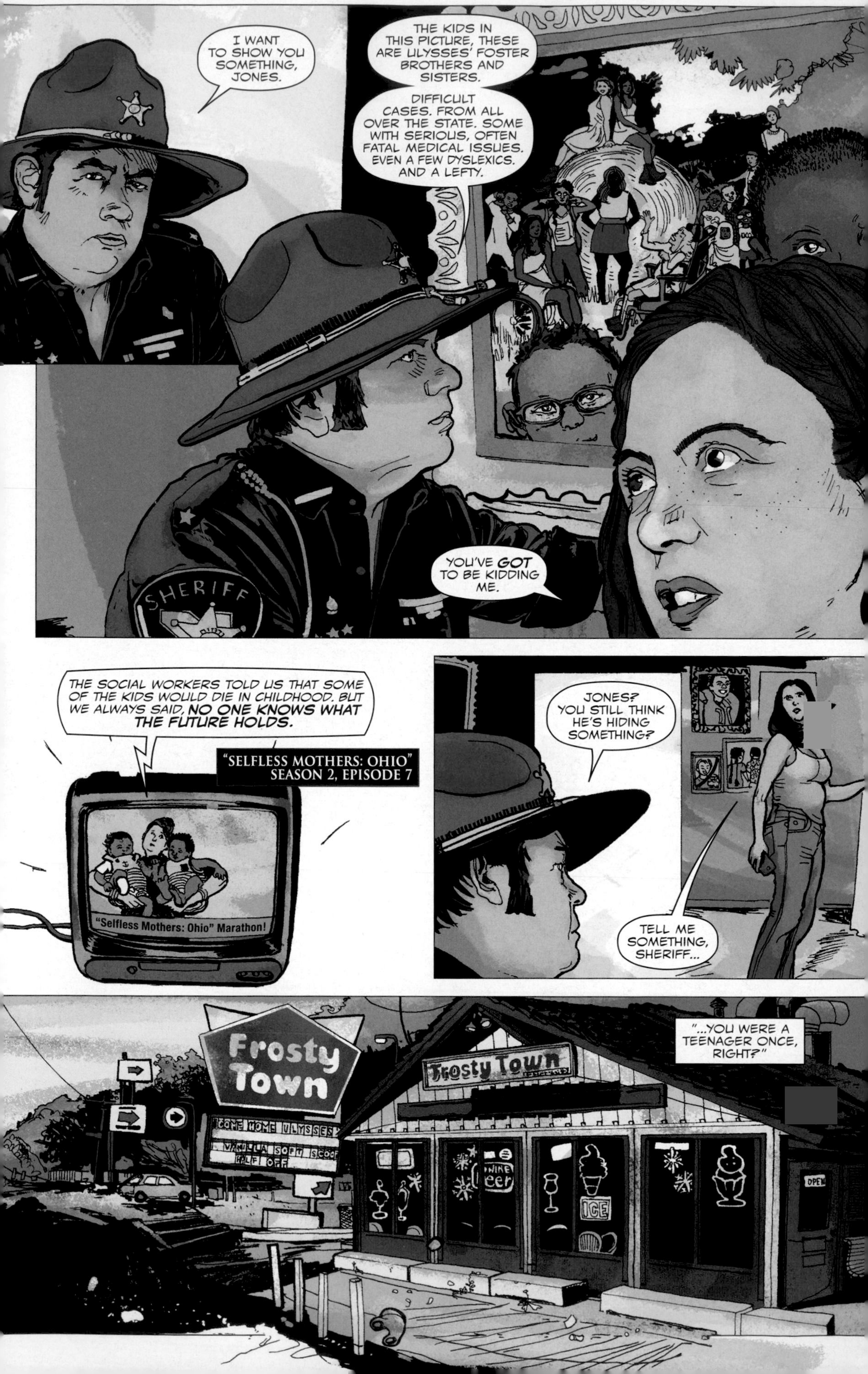
I WANT TO SHOW YOU SOMETHING, JONES.
THE KIDS IN THIS PICTURE, THESE ARE ULYSSES' FOSTER BROTHERS AND SISTERS.
DIFFICULT CASES. FROM ALL OVER THE STATE. SOME WITH SERIOUS, OFTEN FATAL MEDICAL ISSUES. EVEN A FEW DYSLEXICS. AND A LEFTY.
SHERIFF
YOU'VE **GOT** TO BE KIDDING ME.
THE SOCIAL WORKERS TOLD US THAT SOME OF THE KIDS WOULD DIE IN CHILDHOOD. BUT WE ALWAYS SAID, **NO ONE KNOWS WHAT THE FUTURE HOLDS.**
"SELFLESS MOTHERS: OHIO" SEASON 2, EPISODE 7
"Selfless Mothers: Ohio" Marathon!
JONES? YOU STILL THINK HE'S HIDING SOMETHING?
TELL ME SOMETHING, SHERIFF...
Frosty Town
COME HOME ULYSSES
VANILLA SOFT SCOOP
HALF OFF
Frosty Town
BEER
ICE
OPEN
"...YOU WERE A TEENAGER ONCE, RIGHT?"

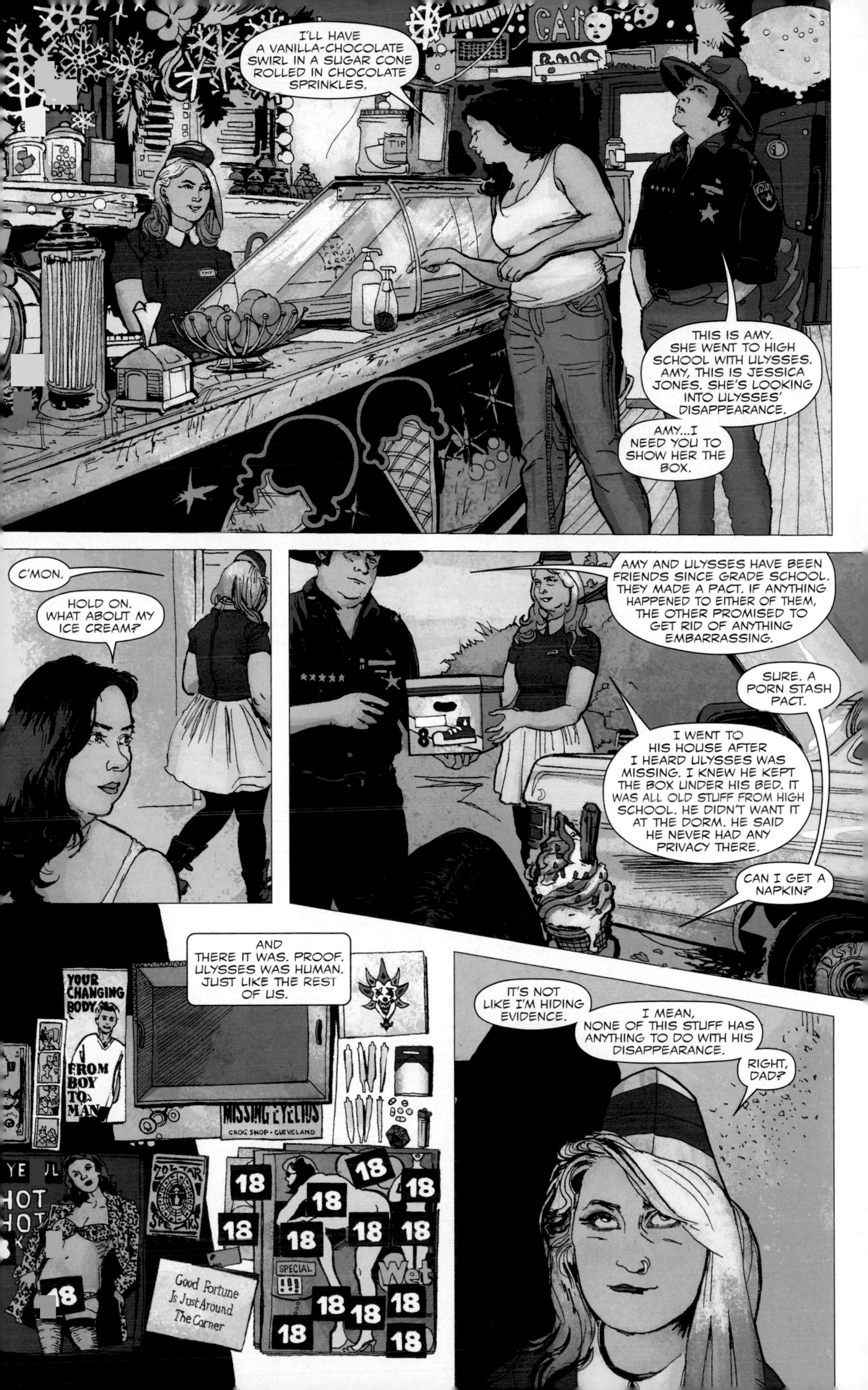
I'LL HAVE A VANILLA-CHOCOLATE SWIRL IN A SUGAR CONE ROLLED IN CHOCOLATE SPRINKLES.
THIS IS AMY. SHE WENT TO HIGH SCHOOL WITH ULYSSES. AMY, THIS IS JESSICA JONES. SHE'S LOOKING INTO ULYSSES' DISAPPEARANCE.
AMY...I NEED YOU TO SHOW HER THE BOX.
C'MON.
HOLD ON. WHAT ABOUT MY ICE CREAM?
AMY AND ULYSSES HAVE BEEN FRIENDS SINCE GRADE SCHOOL. THEY MADE A PACT. IF ANYTHING HAPPENED TO EITHER OF THEM, THE OTHER PROMISED TO GET RID OF ANYTHING EMBARRASSING.
SURE. A PORN STASH PACT.
I WENT TO HIS HOUSE AFTER I HEARD ULYSSES WAS MISSING. I KNEW HE KEPT THE BOX UNDER HIS BED. IT WAS ALL OLD STUFF FROM HIGH SCHOOL. HE DIDN'T WANT IT AT THE DORM. HE SAID HE NEVER HAD ANY PRIVACY THERE.
CAN I GET A NAPKIN?
AND THERE IT WAS. PROOF. ULYSSES WAS HUMAN. JUST LIKE THE REST OF US.
YOUR CHANGING BODY
FROM BOY TO MAN
MISSING EYELIDS
GROG SHOP • CLEVELAND
Good Fortune Is Just Around The Corner
IT'S NOT LIKE I'M HIDING EVIDENCE.
I MEAN, NONE OF THIS STUFF HAS ANYTHING TO DO WITH HIS DISAPPEARANCE.
RIGHT, DAD?

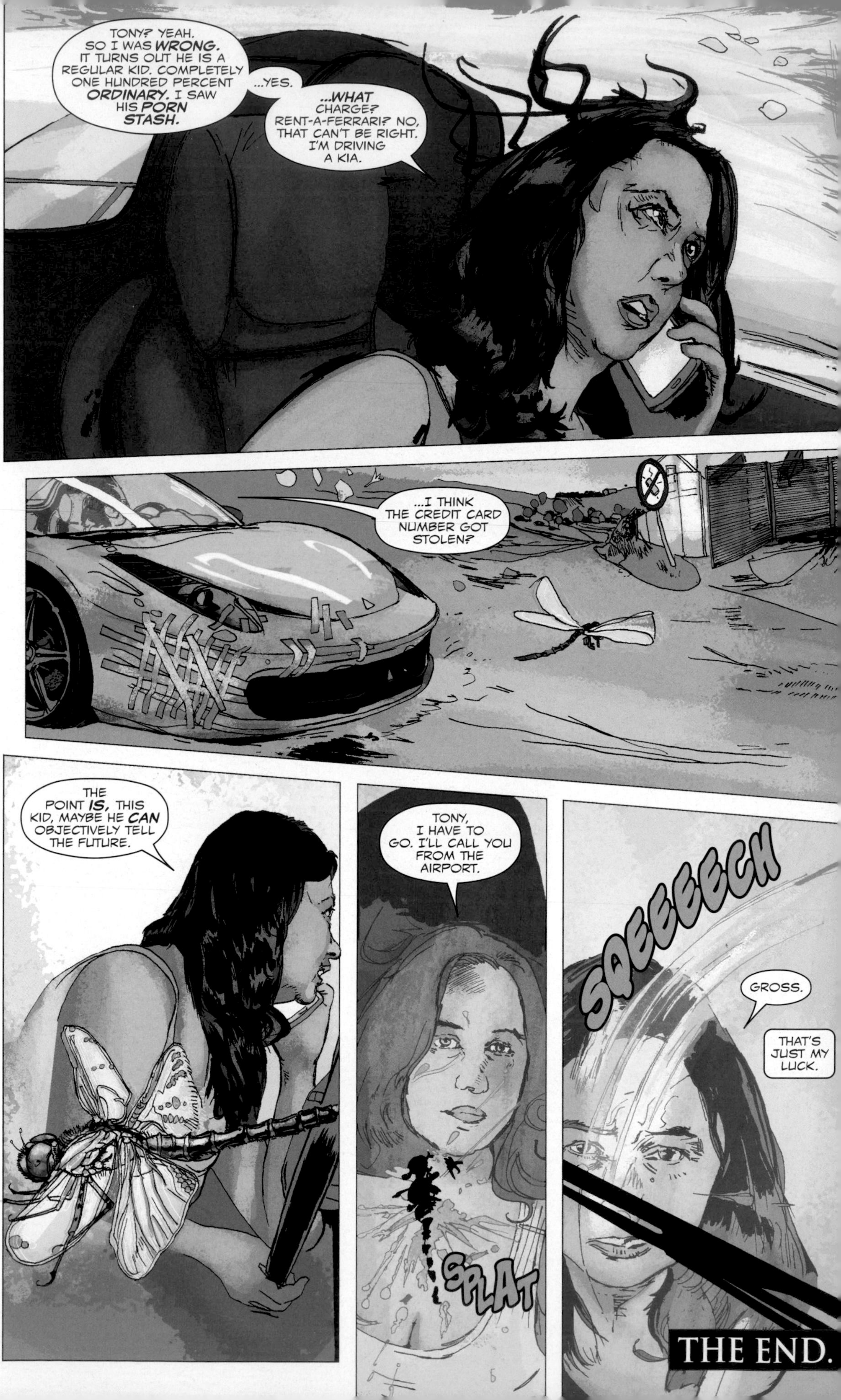
TONY? YEAH. SO I WAS WRONG. IT TURNS OUT HE IS A REGULAR KID. COMPLETELY ONE HUNDRED PERCENT ORDINARY. I SAW HIS PORN STASH.
...YES.
...WHAT CHARGE? RENT-A-FERRARI? NO, THAT CAN'T BE RIGHT. I'M DRIVING A KIA.
...I THINK THE CREDIT CARD NUMBER GOT STOLEN?
THE POINT IS, THIS KID, MAYBE HE CAN OBJECTIVELY TELL THE FUTURE.
TONY, I HAVE TO GO. I'LL CALL YOU FROM THE AIRPORT.
SPLAT
SQEEEECH
GROSS.
THAT'S JUST MY LUCK.
THE END.

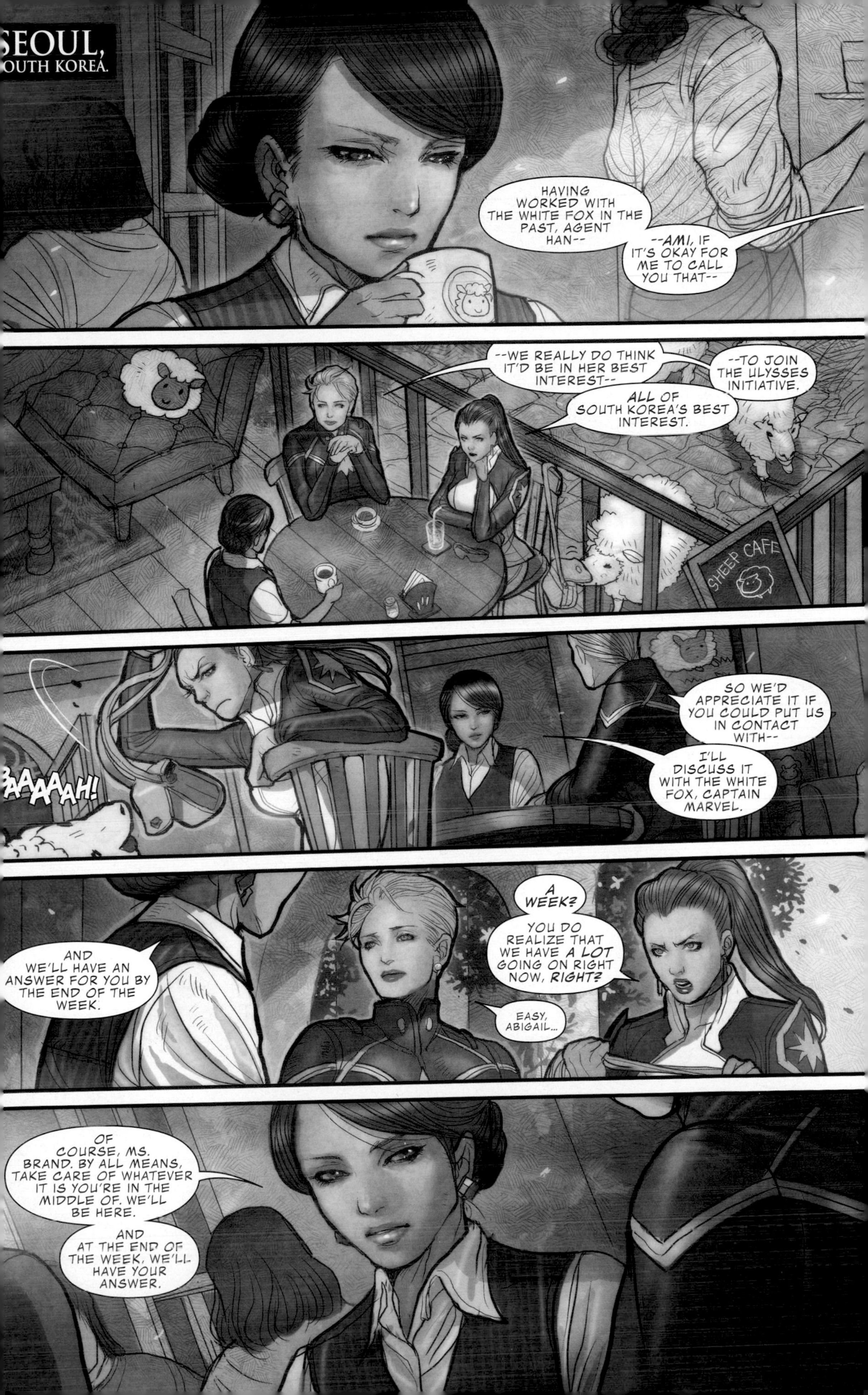
SEOUL, SOUTH KOREA.
HAVING WORKED WITH THE WHITE FOX IN THE PAST, AGENT HAN--
--AMI, IF IT'S OKAY FOR ME TO CALL YOU THAT--
--WE REALLY DO THINK IT'D BE IN HER BEST INTEREST--
--TO JOIN THE ULYSSES INITIATIVE.
ALL OF SOUTH KOREA'S BEST INTEREST.
SHEEP CAFE
BAAAAAH!
SO WE'D APPRECIATE IT IF YOU COULD PUT US IN CONTACT WITH--
I'LL DISCUSS IT WITH THE WHITE FOX, CAPTAIN MARVEL.
AND WE'LL HAVE AN ANSWER FOR YOU BY THE END OF THE WEEK.
A WEEK?
YOU DO REALIZE THAT WE HAVE A LOT GOING ON RIGHT NOW, RIGHT?
EASY, ABIGAIL...
OF COURSE, MS. BRAND. BY ALL MEANS, TAKE CARE OF WHATEVER IT IS YOU'RE IN THE MIDDLE OF. WE'LL BE HERE.
AND AT THE END OF THE WEEK, WE'LL HAVE YOUR ANSWER.

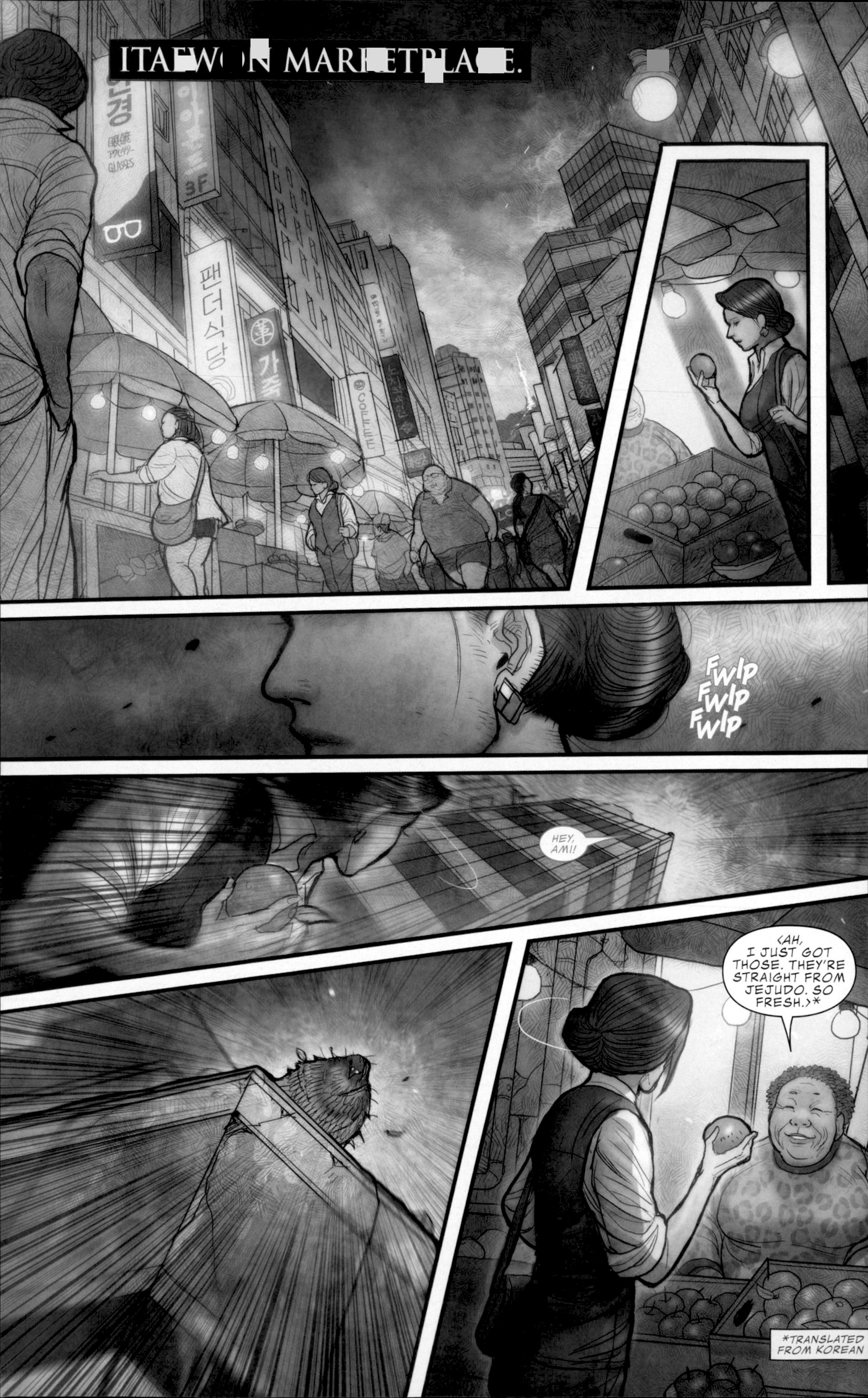
ITAEWON MARKETPLACE.
GLASSES
3F
팬더식당
가죽
COFFEE
FWIP FWIP FWIP
HEY, AMI!
<AH, I JUST GOT THOSE. THEY'RE STRAIGHT FROM JEJUDO. SO FRESH.>*
*TRANSLATED FROM KOREAN

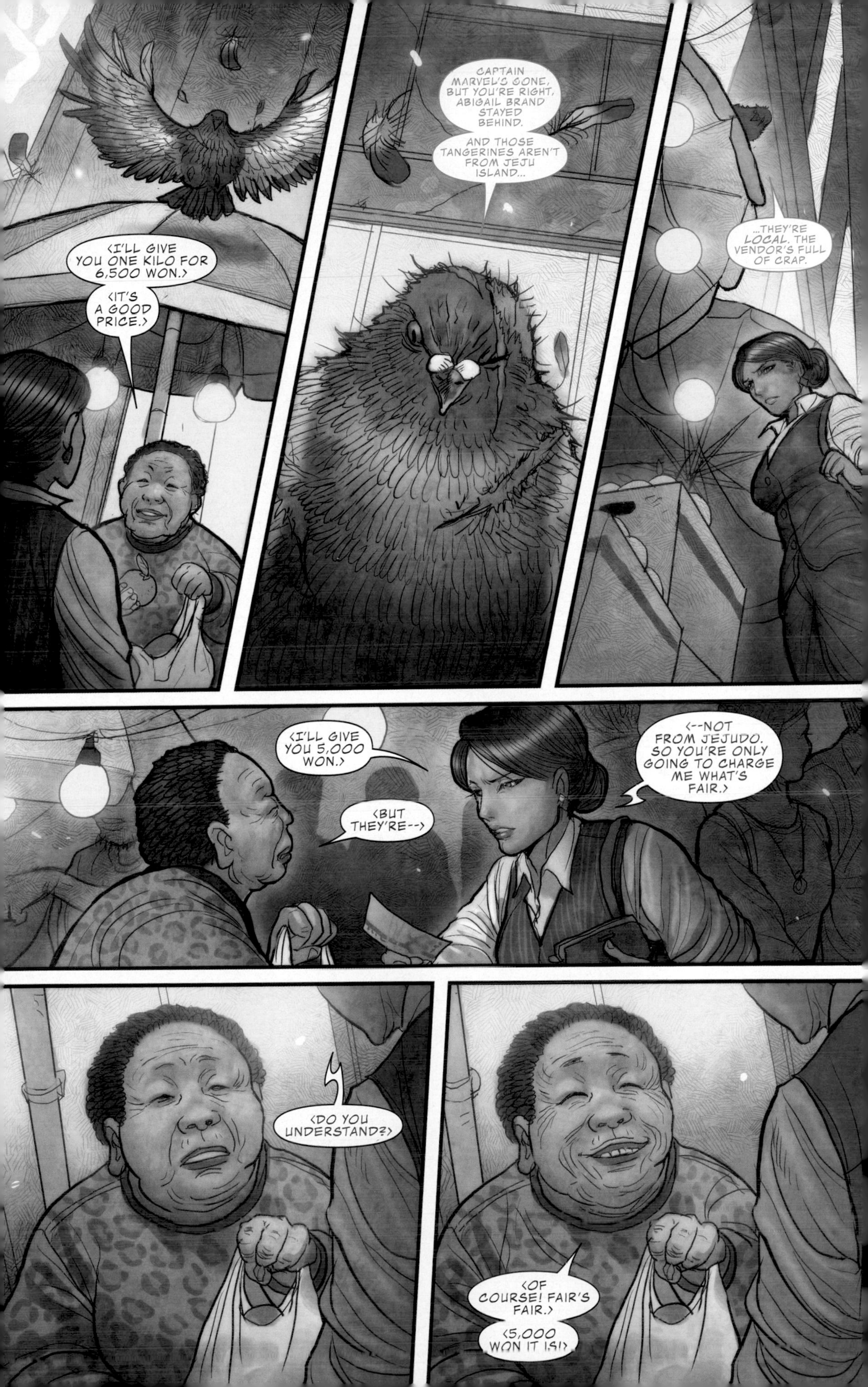

<I'LL GIVE YOU ONE KILO FOR 6,500 WON.>
<IT'S A GOOD PRICE.>
CAPTAIN MARVEL'S GONE, BUT YOU'RE RIGHT, ABIGAIL BRAND STAYED BEHIND.
AND THOSE TANGERINES AREN'T FROM JEJU ISLAND...
...THEY'RE LOCAL. THE VENDOR'S FULL OF CRAP.
<I'LL GIVE YOU 5,000 WON.>
<BUT THEY'RE-->
<--NOT FROM JEJUDO. SO YOU'RE ONLY GOING TO CHARGE ME WHAT'S FAIR.>
<DO YOU UNDERSTAND?>
<OF COURSE! FAIR'S FAIR.>
<5,000 WON IT IS!>

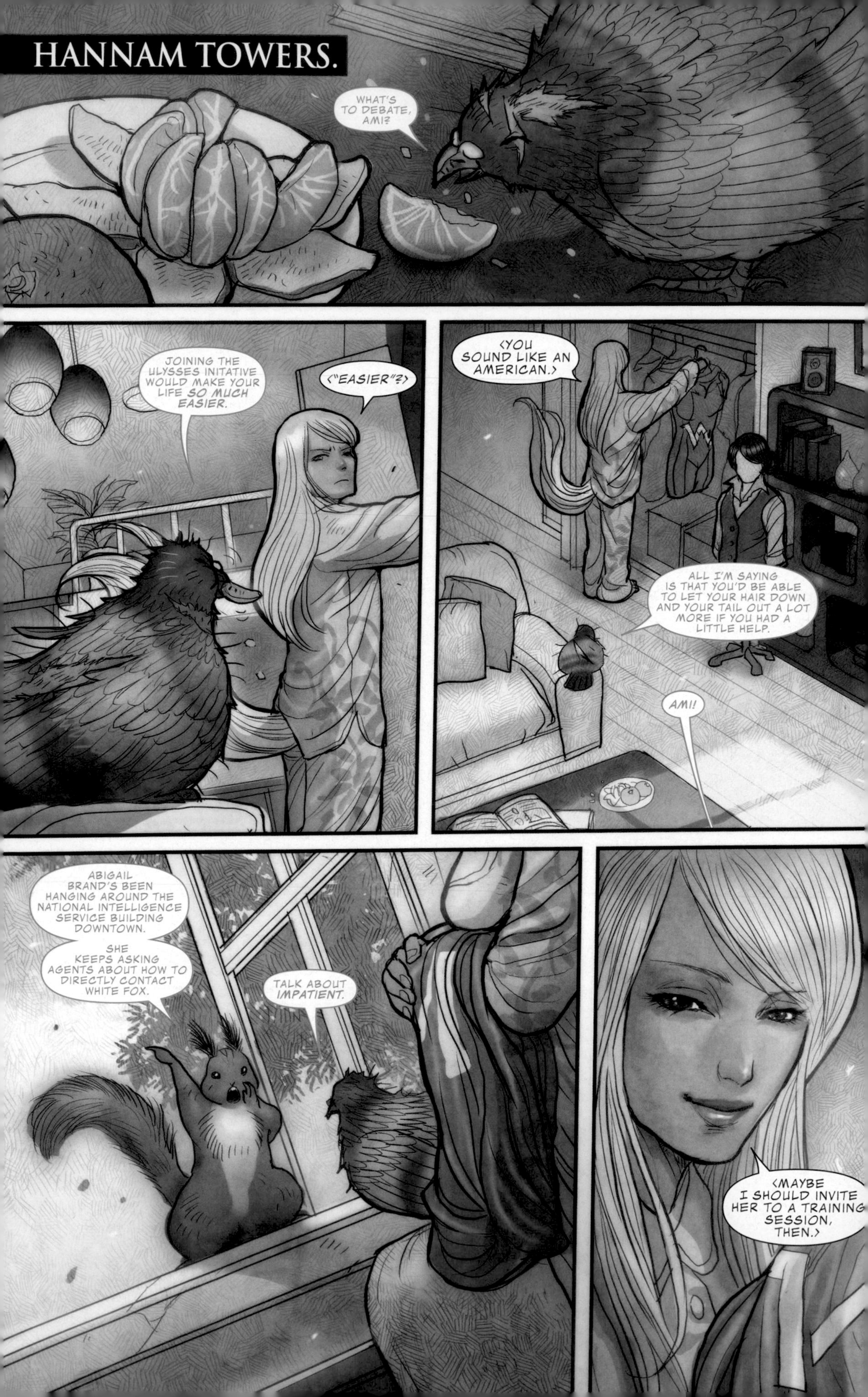
HANNAM TOWERS.
WHAT'S TO DEBATE, AMI?
JOINING THE ULYSSES INITATIVE WOULD MAKE YOUR LIFE SO MUCH EASIER.
<"EASIER"?>
<YOU SOUND LIKE AN AMERICAN.>
ALL I'M SAYING IS THAT YOU'D BE ABLE TO LET YOUR HAIR DOWN AND YOUR TAIL OUT A LOT MORE IF YOU HAD A LITTLE HELP.
AMI!
ABIGAIL BRAND'S BEEN HANGING AROUND THE NATIONAL INTELLIGENCE SERVICE BUILDING DOWNTOWN.
SHE KEEPS ASKING AGENTS ABOUT HOW TO DIRECTLY CONTACT WHITE FOX.
TALK ABOUT IMPATIENT.
<MAYBE I SHOULD INVITE HER TO A TRAINING SESSION, THEN.>

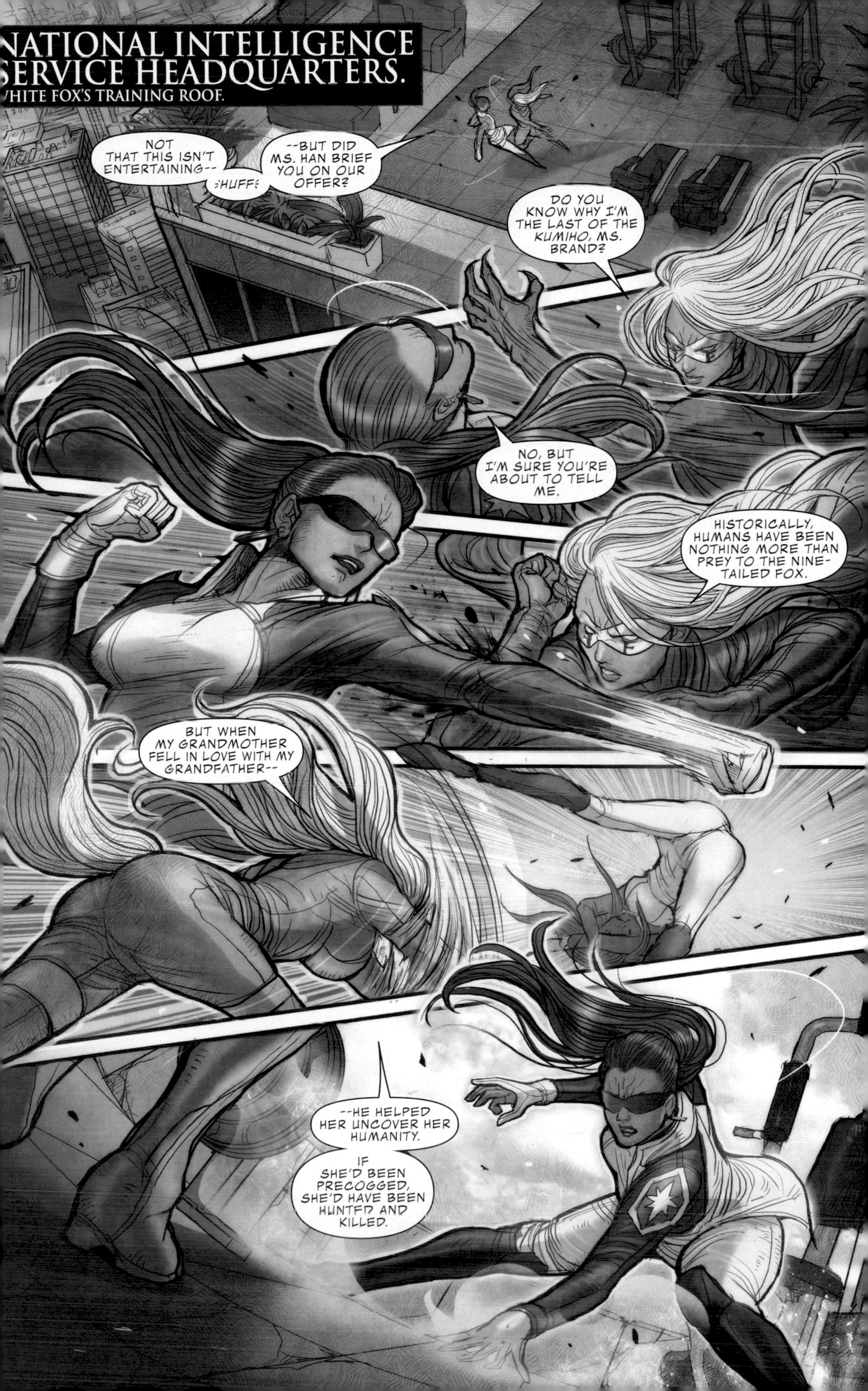
NATIONAL INTELLIGENCE SERVICE HEADQUARTERS.
WHITE FOX'S TRAINING ROOF.
NOT THAT THIS ISN'T ENTERTAINING--
HUFF
--BUT DID MS. HAN BRIEF YOU ON OUR OFFER?
DO YOU KNOW WHY I'M THE LAST OF THE KUMIHO, MS. BRAND?
NO, BUT I'M SURE YOU'RE ABOUT TO TELL ME.
HISTORICALLY, HUMANS HAVE BEEN NOTHING MORE THAN PREY TO THE NINE-TAILED FOX.
BUT WHEN MY GRANDMOTHER FELL IN LOVE WITH MY GRANDFATHER--
--HE HELPED HER UNCOVER HER HUMANITY.
IF SHE'D BEEN PRECOGGED, SHE'D HAVE BEEN HUNTED AND KILLED.

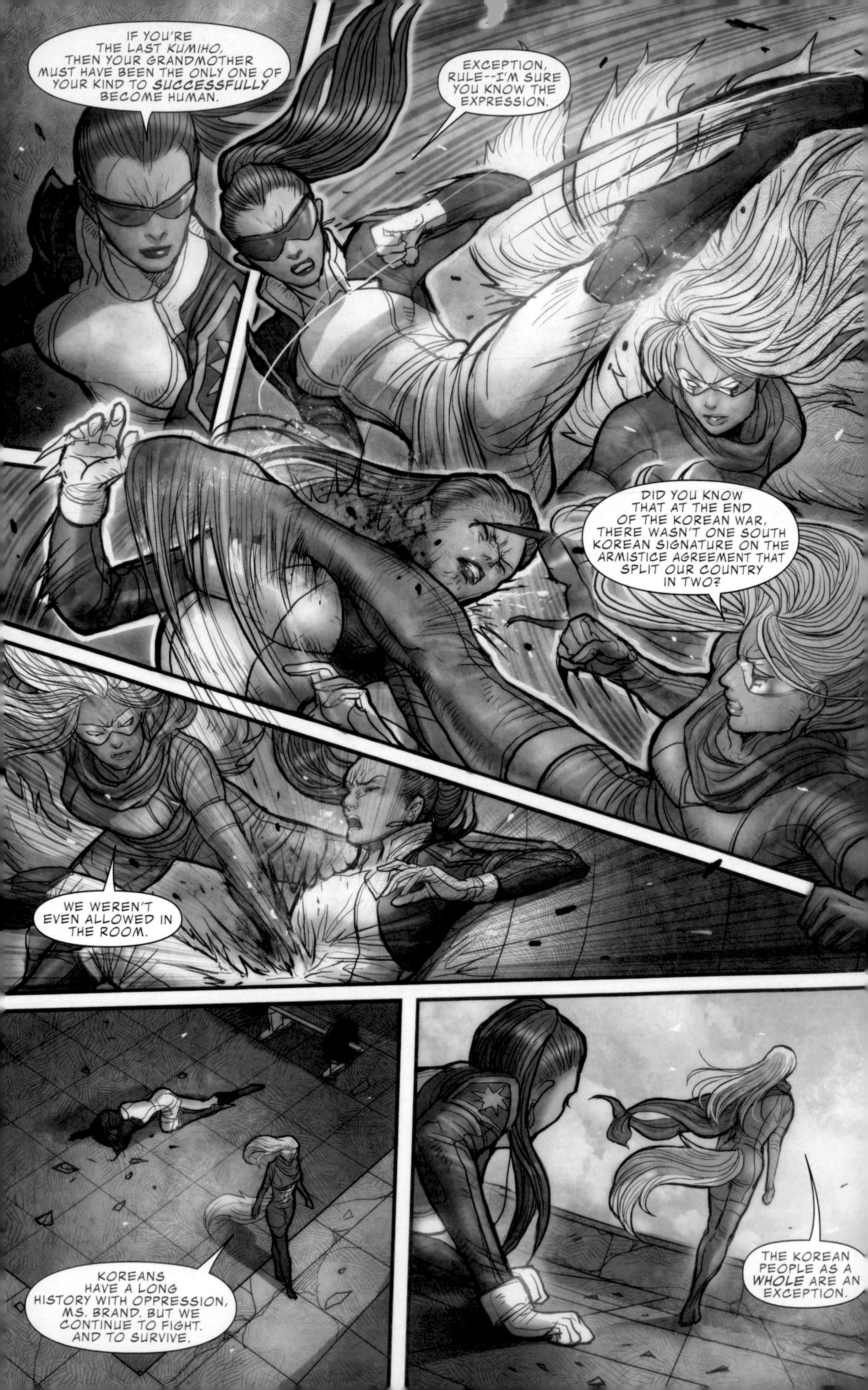
IF YOU'RE THE LAST KUMIHO, THEN YOUR GRANDMOTHER MUST HAVE BEEN THE ONLY ONE OF YOUR KIND TO *SUCCESSFULLY* BECOME HUMAN.
EXCEPTION, RULE--I'M SURE YOU KNOW THE EXPRESSION.
DID YOU KNOW THAT AT THE END OF THE KOREAN WAR, THERE WASN'T ONE SOUTH KOREAN SIGNATURE ON THE ARMISTICE AGREEMENT THAT SPLIT OUR COUNTRY IN TWO?
WE WEREN'T EVEN ALLOWED IN THE ROOM.
KOREANS HAVE A LONG HISTORY WITH OPPRESSION, MS. BRAND. BUT WE CONTINUE TO FIGHT. AND TO SURVIVE.
THE KOREAN PEOPLE AS A *WHOLE* ARE AN EXCEPTION.

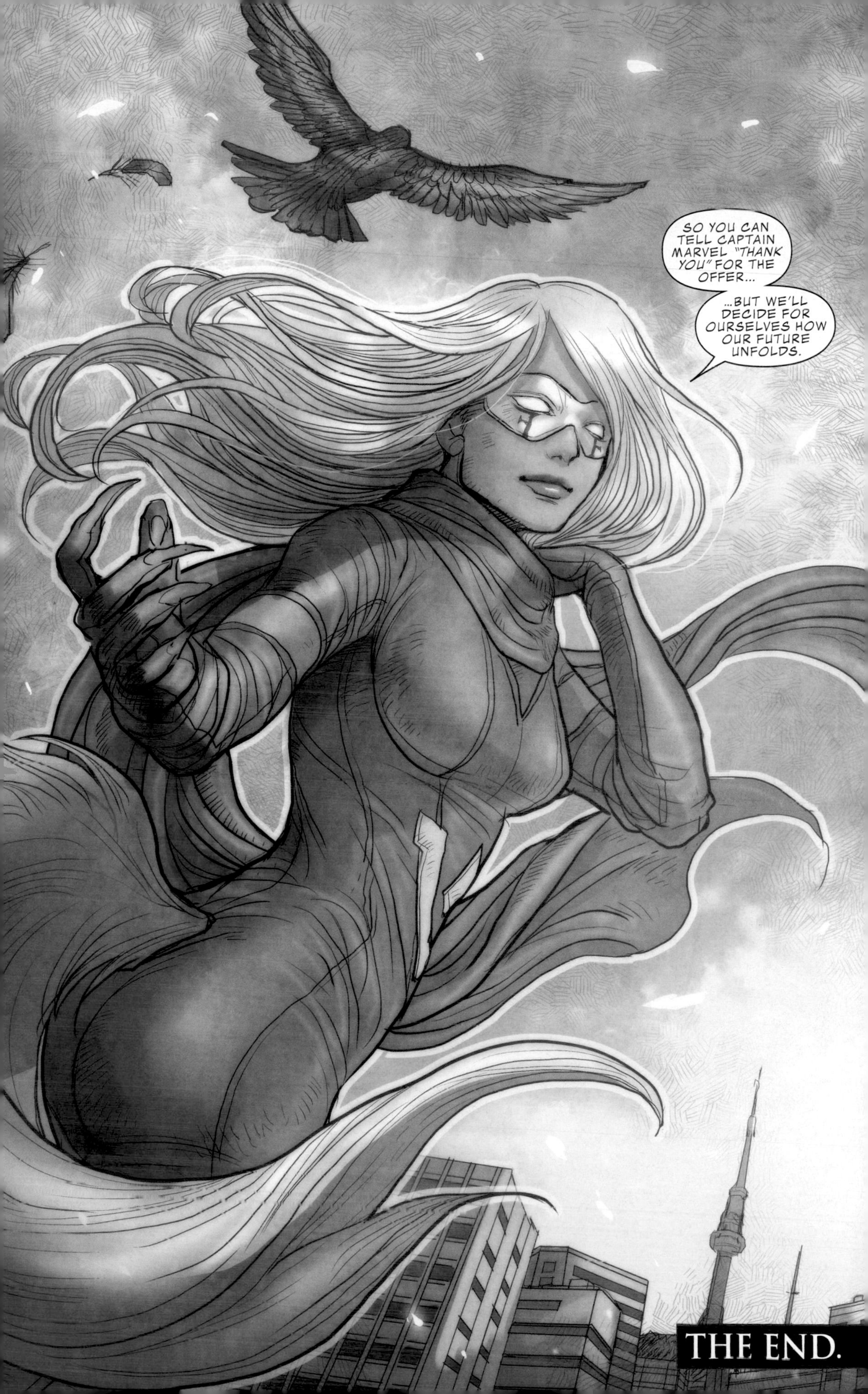
SO YOU CAN TELL CAPTAIN MARVEL "THANK YOU" FOR THE OFFER...
...BUT WE'LL DECIDE FOR OURSELVES HOW OUR FUTURE UNFOLDS.
THE END.

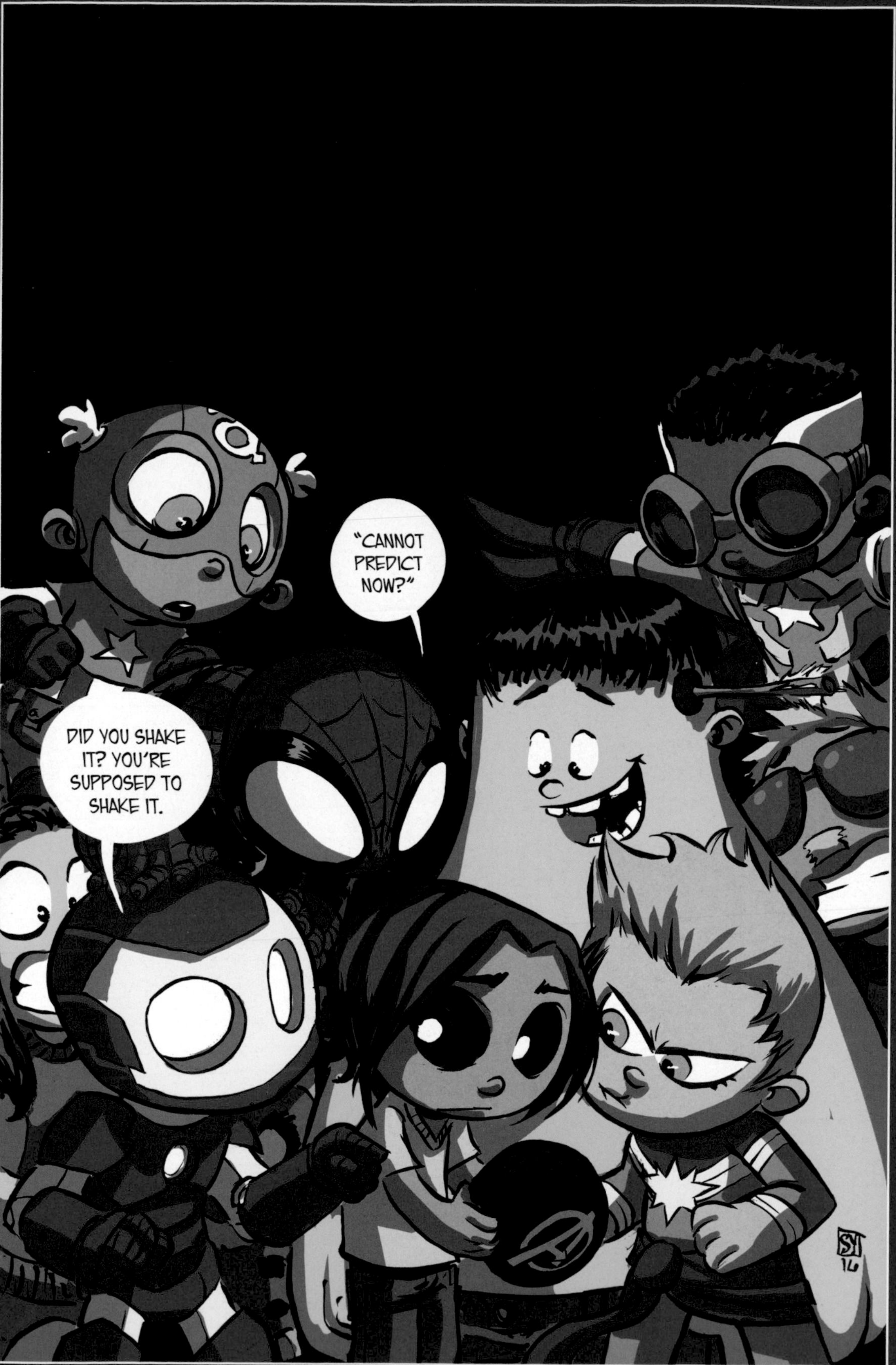
"CANNOT PREDICT NOW?"
DID YOU SHAKE IT? YOU'RE SUPPOSED TO SHAKE IT.

#1 VARIANT BY SKOTTIE YOUNG

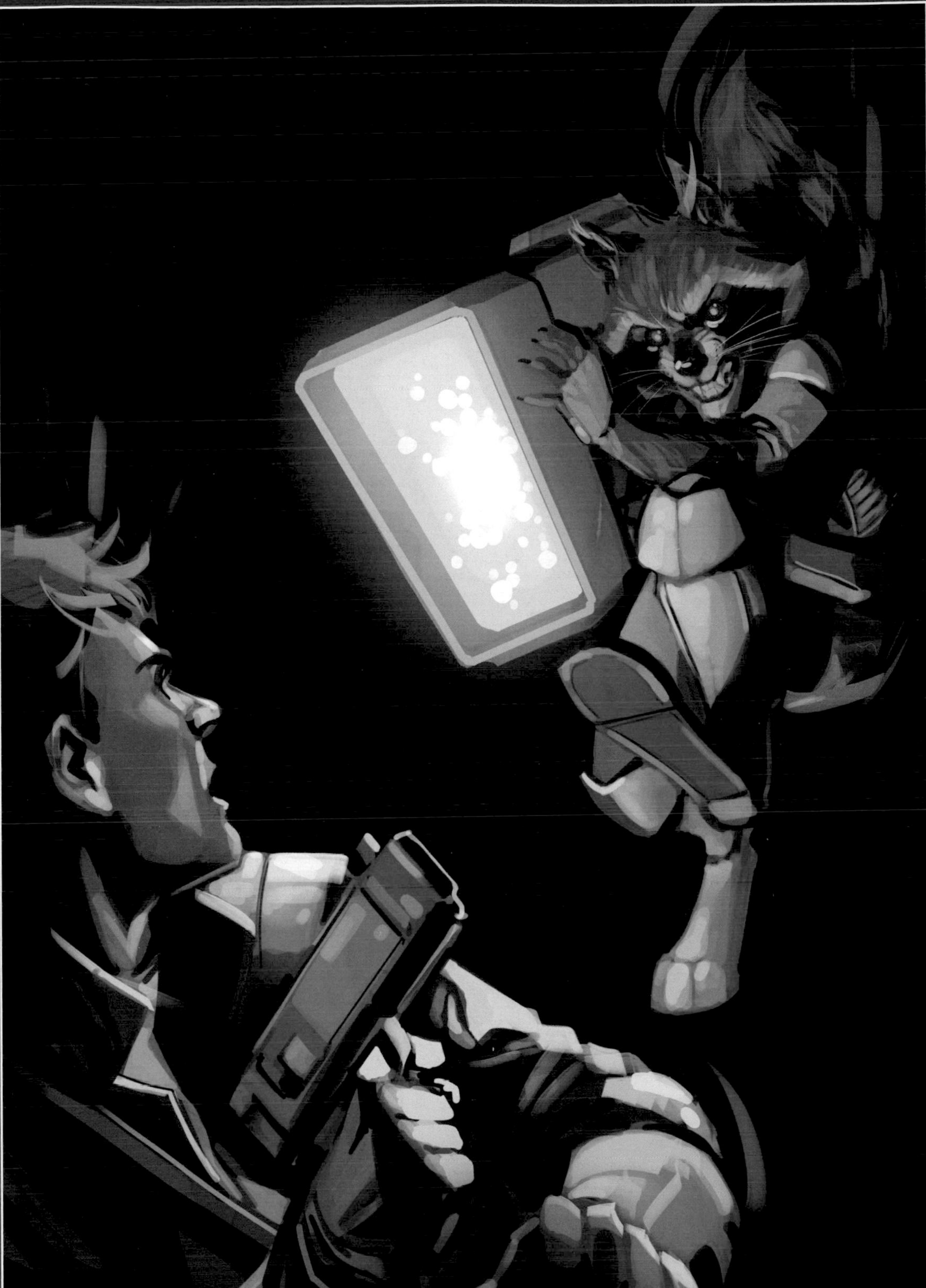
noto

#1 VARIANT BY PHIL NOTO

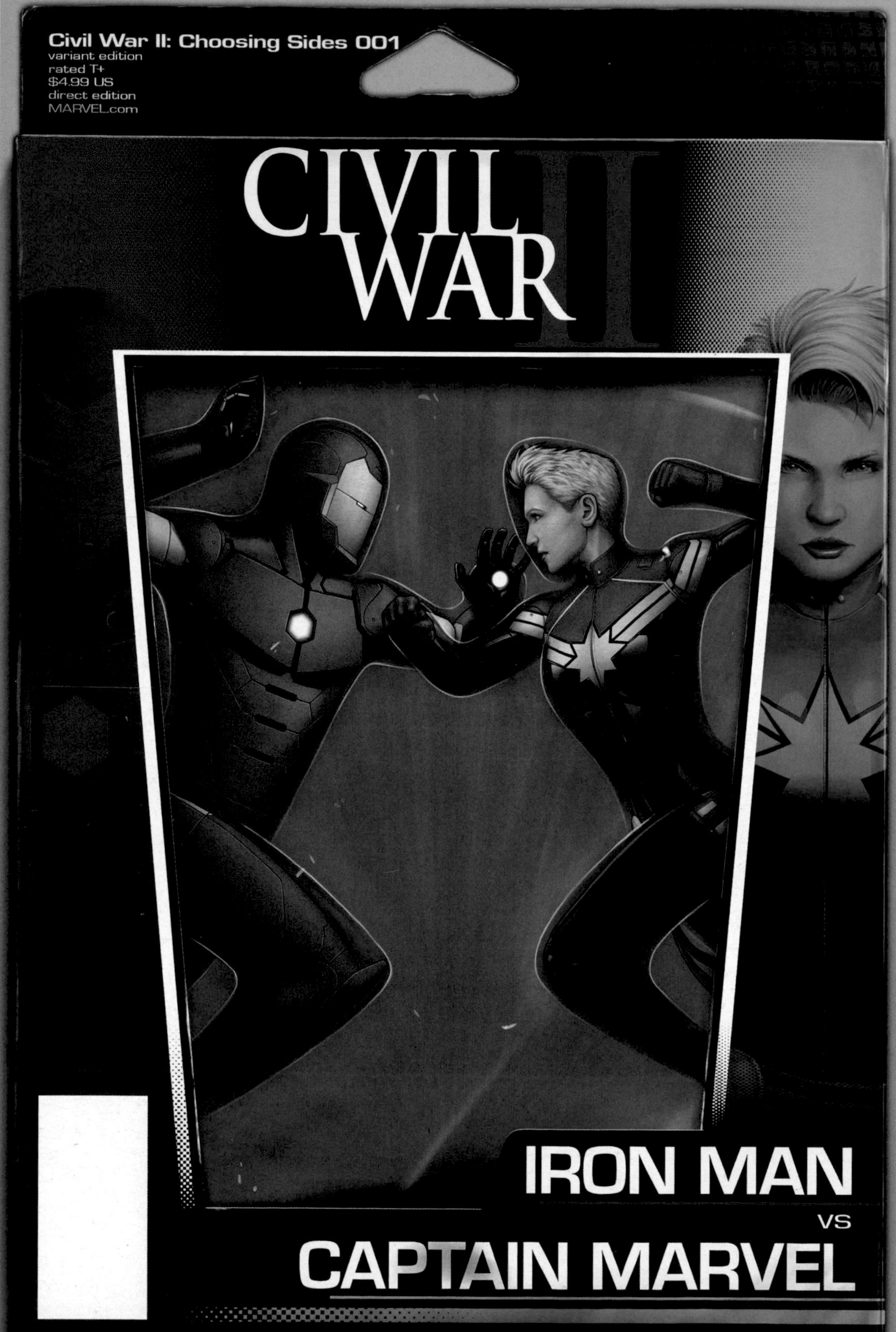
Civil War II: Choosing Sides 001
variant edition
rated T+
$4.99 US
direct edition
MARVEL.com
CIVIL WAR II
IRON MAN
VS
CAPTAIN MARVEL

#1 ACTION FIGURE VARIANT BY JOHN TYLER CHRISTOPHER

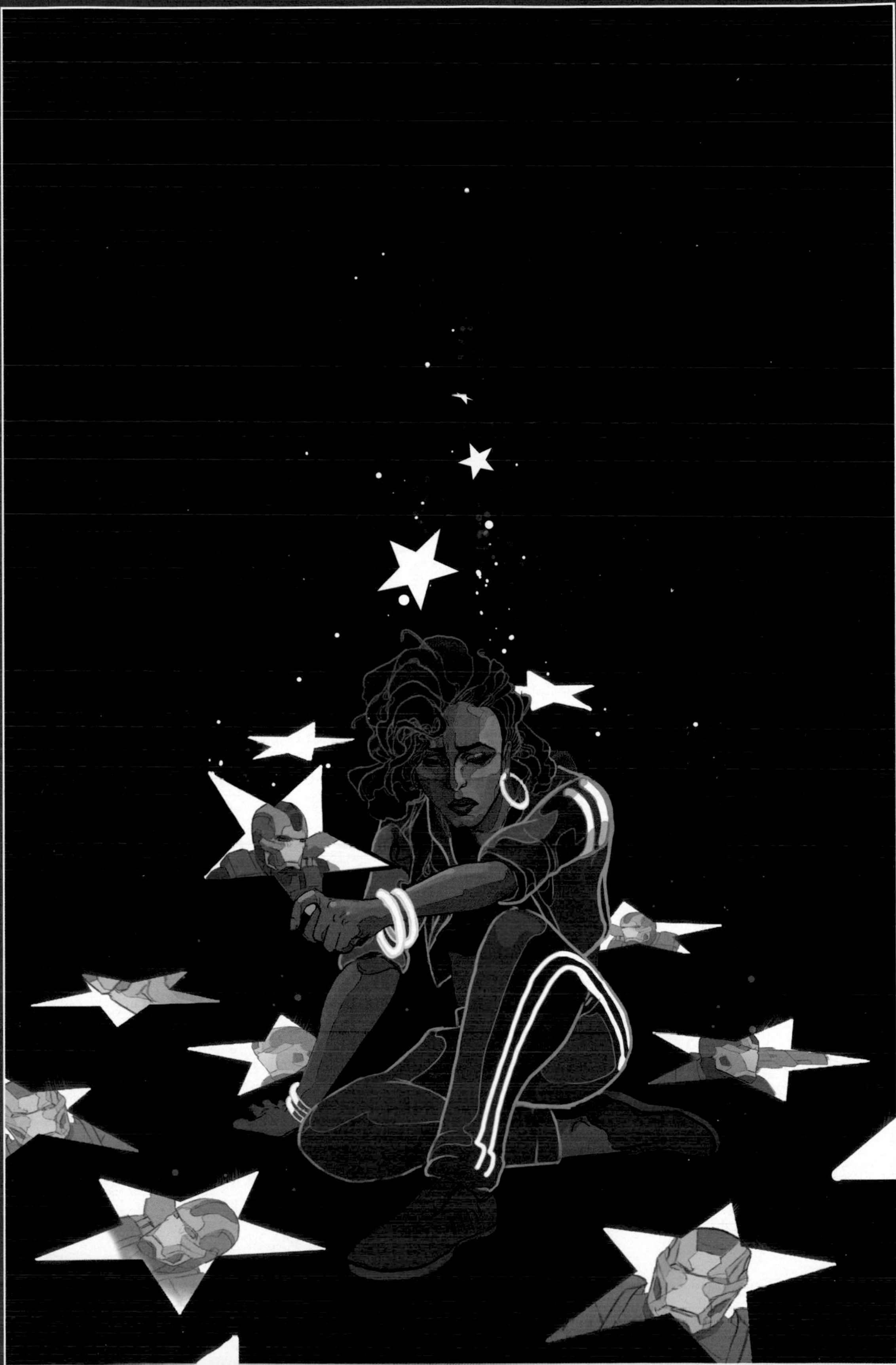

#2 VARIANT BY CHRISTIAN WARD

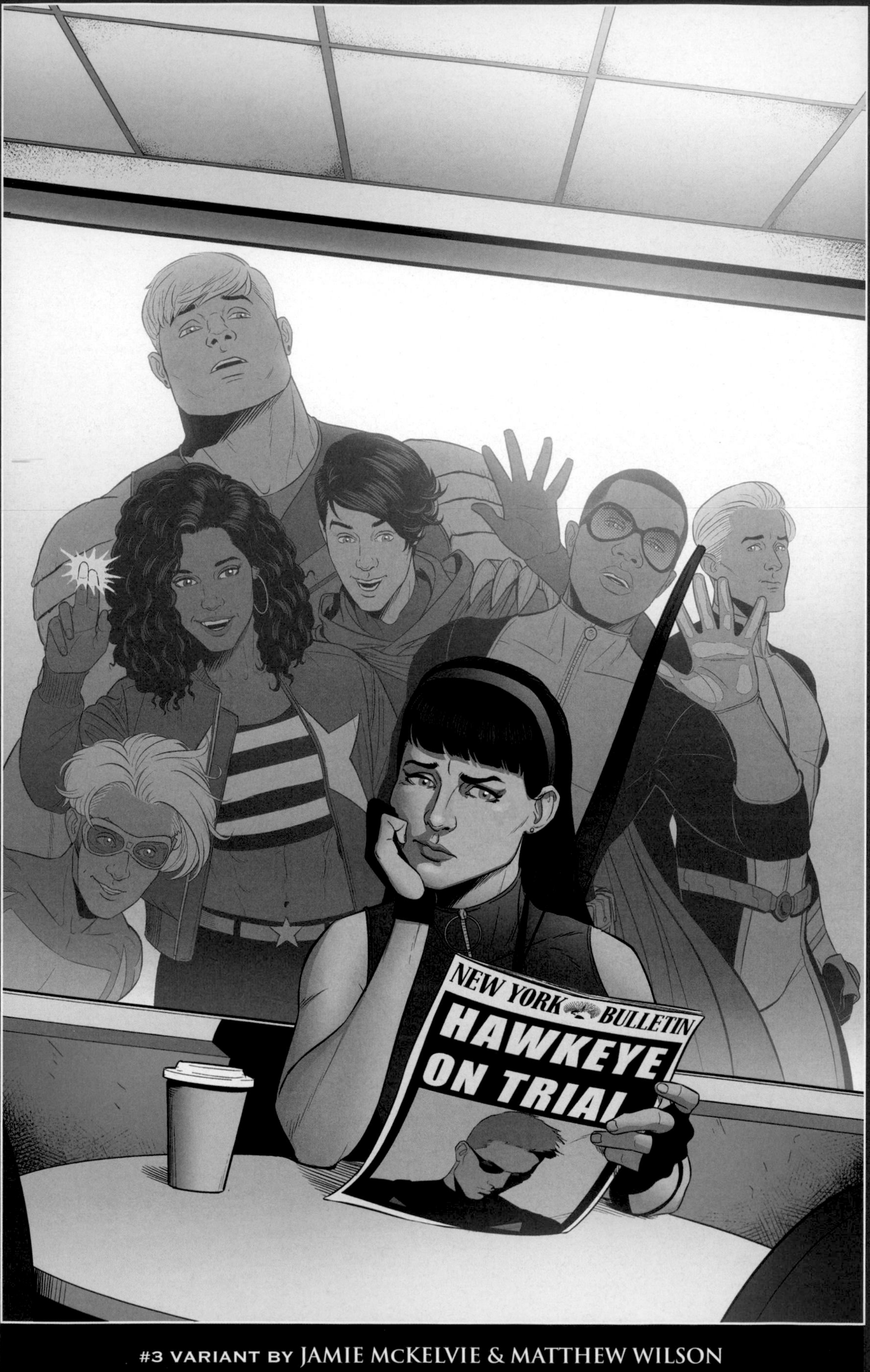
NEW YORK BULLETIN
HAWKEYE ON TRIAL

#3 VARIANT BY JAMIE McKELVIE & MATTHEW WILSON

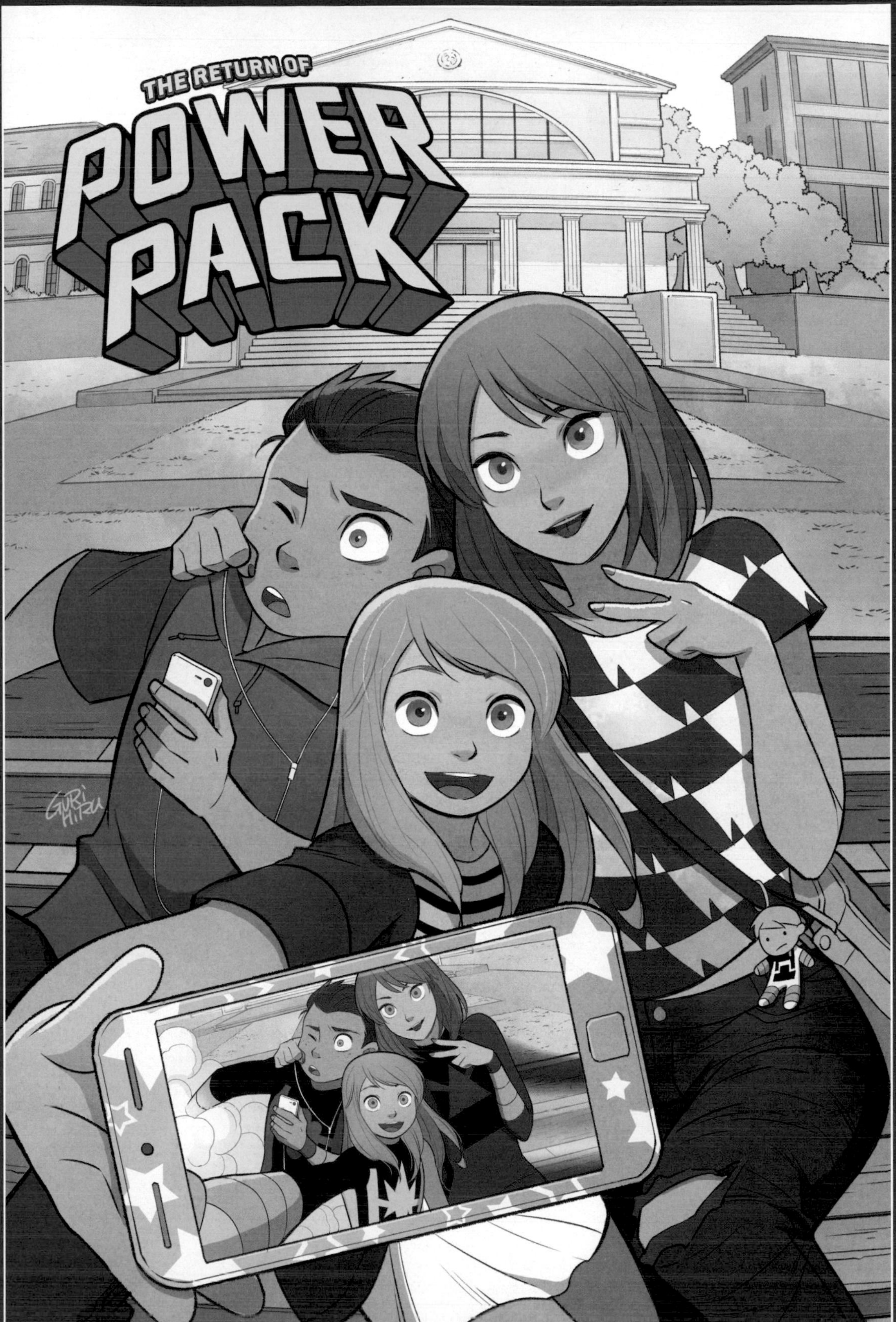
THE RETURN OF
POWER PACK
GURI HIRU

#4 VARIANT BY GURIHIRU

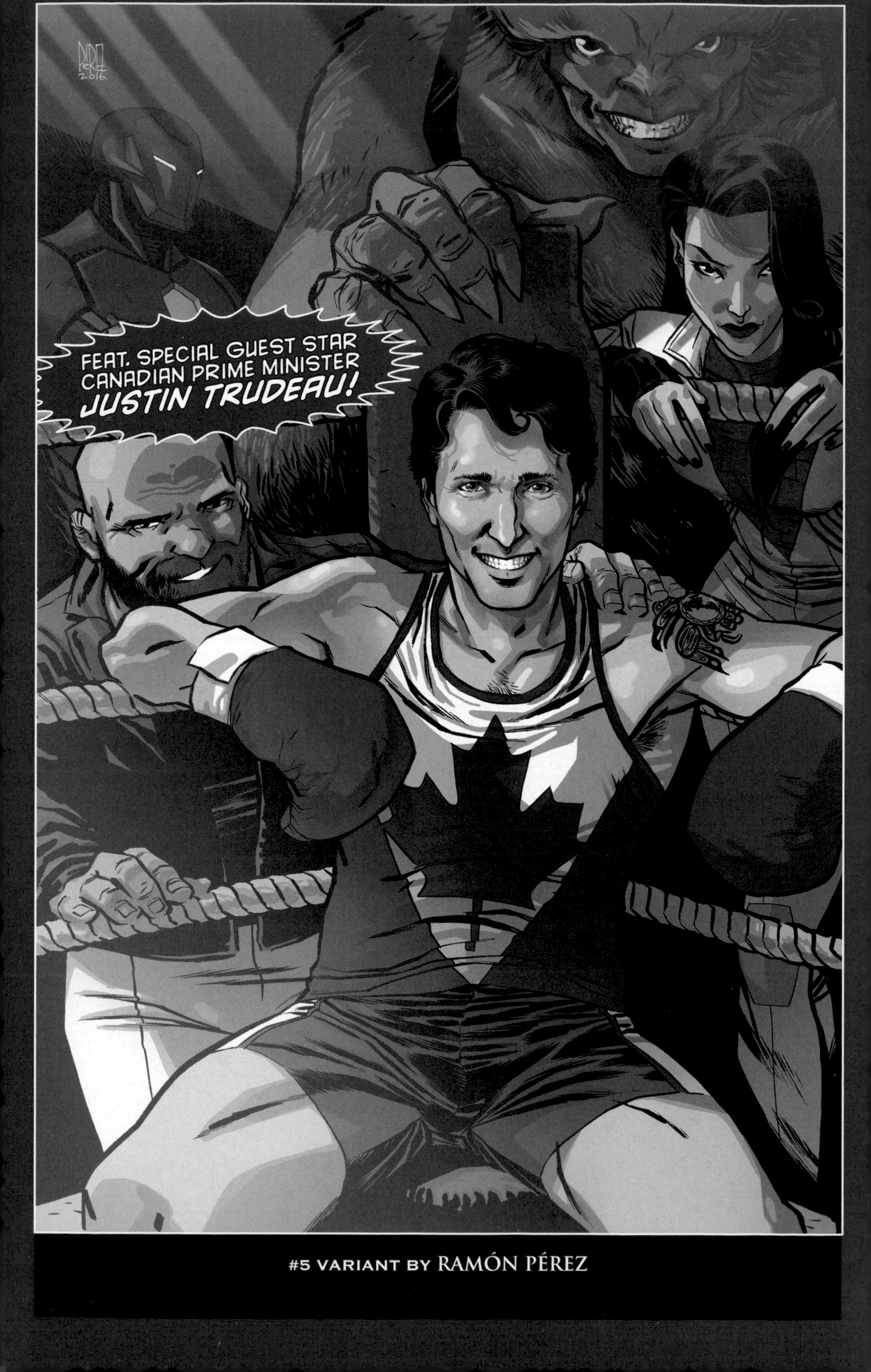
PÉREZ 2016.
FEAT. SPECIAL GUEST STAR CANADIAN PRIME MINISTER JUSTIN TRUDEAU!

#5 VARIANT BY RAMÓN PÉREZ

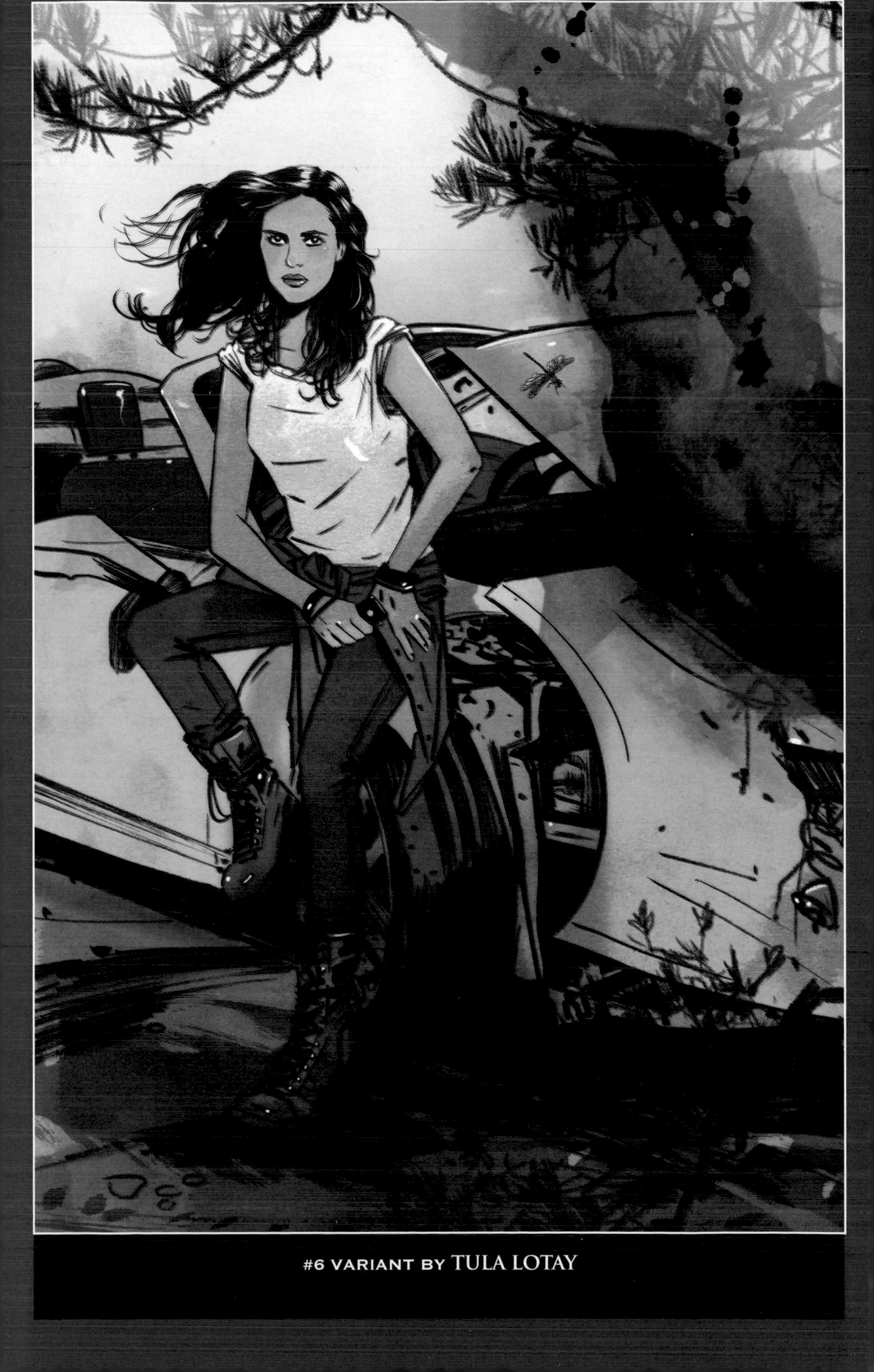

#6 VARIANT BY TULA LOTAY

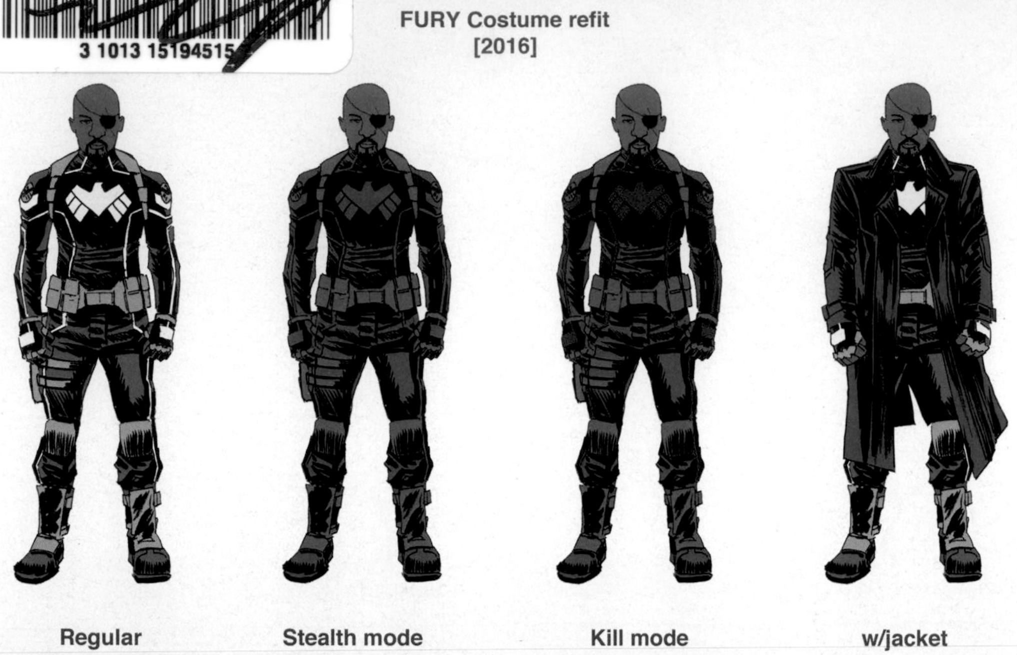
FURY Costume refit
[2016]
Regular
Stealth mode
Kill mode
w/jacket

NICK FURY SKETCHES BY DECLAN SHALVEY

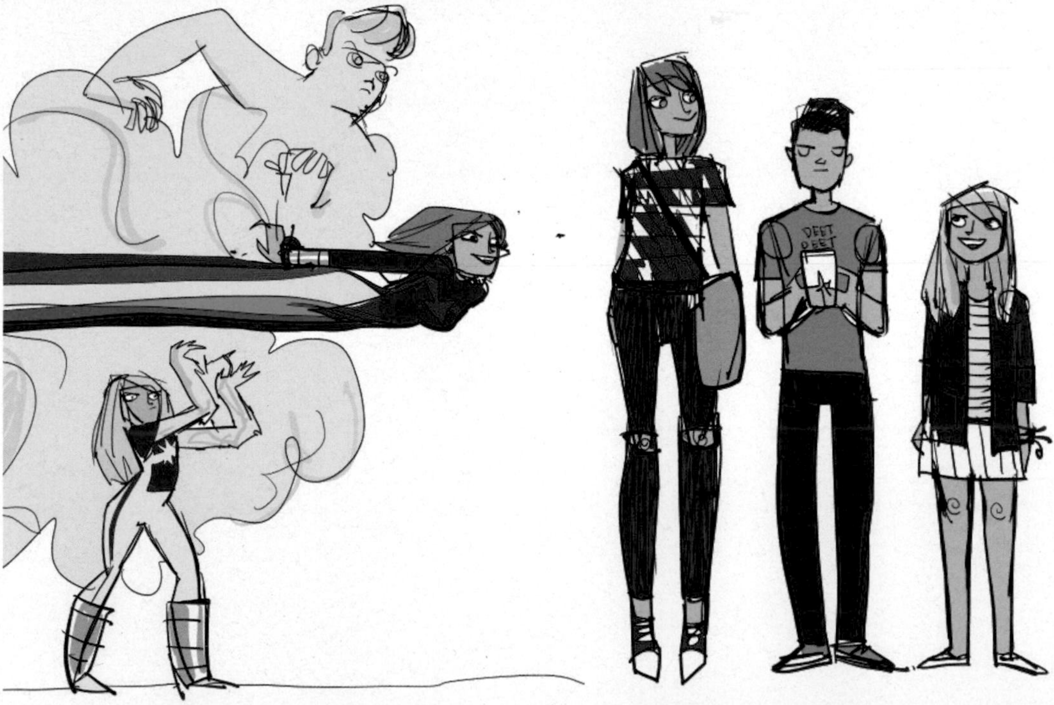
BEEP BEEP

POWER PACK SKETCHES BY JOHN ALLISON